THE SPIRITUAL BACKGROUND TO THE FIRST WORLD WAR

THE SPIRITUAL BACKGROUND TO
THE FIRST WORLD WAR

Sixteen lectures given in Stuttgart between 30 September 1914 and 26 April 1918 and on 21 March 1921

TRANSLATED AND INTRODUCED BY
SIMON BLAXLAND-DE LANGE

RUDOLF STEINER

RUDOLF STEINER PRESS

CW 174b

*The publishers gratefully acknowledge the generous funding of the translation
of these lectures by the Anthroposophical Society in Great Britain*

Rudolf Steiner Press
Hillside House, The Square
Forest Row, RH18 5ES

www.rudolfsteinerpress.com

Published by Rudolf Steiner Press 2024

Originally published in German under the title *Die geistigen Hintergründe des Ersten Welt-
krieges. Kosmische und Menschliche Geschichte Band VII* (volume 174b in the *Rudolf Steiner
Gesamtausgabe* or Collected Works) by Rudolf Steiner Verlag, Dornach. Based on shorthand notes that were not reviewed or revised by the speaker. This authorized translation
is based on the second German edition (1994), edited by Helmut von Wartburg und
Robert Friedenthal

Published by permission of the Rudolf Steiner Nachlassverwaltung, Dornach

A catalogue record for this book is available from the British Library

ISBN 978 1 85584 661 6

Cover by Morgan Creative
Typeset by Symbiosys Technologies, Visakhapatnam, India
Printed and bound by 4Edge Ltd., Essex

CONTENTS

LECTURE 1

STUTTGART, 30 SEPTEMBER 1914

The present as a time of trial. The connection between Germany and Austria and the unnatural connection of France and England with Russia. Understanding the present destiny of peoples through the cycle about Folk-souls. The struggle of the soul-forces in the Mystery Plays as a picture of the struggle between nations. The meaninglessness of the question of blame for the war. Herman Grimm concerning the Germans. The soul of the murdered archduke. Transformation of the forces of fear into courage and enthusiasm. Help of the fallen for those fighting. Development of the capacity for love through spiritual science. War as a teacher of spirituality. Quotation from a person entering the field of battle. Help through the verse 'Spirits watching over your souls...' The Germans' wish for peace. Jagow's pronouncement. This war as a conspiracy against German cultural life. The verse 'Spirit of my earthly habitation!' helps us to gain objectivity towards the Folk-spirit. Hope for the future.

LECTURE 2

STUTTGART, 13 FEBRUARY 1915

Truths concerning hostilities between nations are not universally applicable and are not accessible to human reason. The different mission of the European and Asian races. Great future struggles between them. The distinctive quality of the Germanic peoples. Baldur and Christ. Slavic culture as the precursor of the sixth cultural epoch. The correspondence between Renan and Strauss. The possibility in Central Europe of transcending nationalism. In addition to its outward cultural life, England has theosophy; in Germany, anthroposophy is connected with the rest of cultural life. Words of 1870 about Russia's tendency to advance towards the West. Significance of present thoughts and feelings for the future.

as an example. The lack of any real debate with anthroposophy, and the transferring of this debate to the personal realm. Some examples of the endeavour to combat and exploit anthroposophy for personal motives. Erich Bamler, Max Seiling, Max Heindl. Two measures that have become necessary.

LECTURE 10
STUTTGART, 13 MAY 1917

Materialism as a necessary phase of human evolution. The difficulty of arriving at spiritual knowledge in our time. Examples of this in pronouncements of Ernest Renan, Richard Wahle and Maurice Barrès. The law whereby humanity becomes younger. Present-day human beings adhere to the standpoint of a twenty-seven-year-old. Woodrow Wilson as an example of this. The need to overcome this standpoint through spiritual impulses. Affinity with the beings of higher hierarchies as a natural capacity of former epochs. Some words of Plato in this regard. A book by Kjellén as an example of a thinking that is estranged from reality. An anthroposophical impulse for the future: the journal *Das Reich* by A. Von Bernus. The failure of some members to appreciate it. The two measures.

LECTURE 11
STUTTGART, 15 MAY 1917

Numerical correspondence between the rhythms of the macrocosm, human life and breathing. Perception of the world-spirit as a resounding form of light in the Indian cultural epoch, as light and darkness in the Persian epoch, as an inner soul-experience in the Egyptian epoch. In the Greek epoch: a sense for the belonging together of body and soul. A pronouncement of Aristotle about the life of the soul after death communicated by Franz Brentano. The forcing of initiation by the Roman Caesars and the effect of this in history: Caligula, Nero and Commodus. The tendency of our time towards abstract ideals, and the need to arrive at conceptions that accord with reality. An example: the ideas of brotherhood, freedom and equality as abstractions, and their transformation into realities through spiritual science. The abolition of the spirit by the Council of Constantinople and its effect upon modern materialistic science. The enmity of former students against anthroposophy. Annie Besant, Édouard Schuré.

of Origen. Thoughts about spiritual things as nourishment of the soul for the life after death. Oscar Hertwig's excellent book on refuting Darwin's theory of chance. Eduard Hartmann's spiritual battle against Darwinism. The unsatisfactory nature of Oscar Hertwig's book about social life. Luciferic and ahrimanic impulses in our cultural life: titles and orders and ability-tests. A book-review by Fritz Mauthner as an example of the inadequate sense of reality of our time. Education towards independent judgement through spiritual science.

Pages 269-287

Lecture 15

Stuttgart, 26 April 1918

The difficulty of understanding visible realities as creations of the spirit. A concrete example of this: the accompanying of bodily development by the soul and spirit into the fifties during the ancient Indian epoch, and the ever earlier ceasing of this accompaniment in the ensuing epochs. The present situation: natural development gives impulses for spiritual life only until the end of the twenties. The need to acquire spiritual knowledge from the declining development of bodily forces through one's own effort. Education for a 'life of expectation'. The failure to cultivate a spiritual life in old age, and the atomising of the spirit that results from this. Pictorial instruction as a demand of our time. An example of this: the living grasp of the difference between animal and man. Goethe as a guide towards a living perception of nature. The significance of such a schooling for the further development of souls after death and for the influence of the dead upon earthly life. A question of the theologian Loisy concerning the present world-situation.

Pages 288-307

Lecture 16

Stuttgart, 21 March 1921

Discussion of the question of blame for the war is necessary (opinion of Foreign Minister Simons). The entente considers this question to be resolved. An observation in this connection of Lloyd George. Two guiding principles of leading figures among Anglo-Saxon politicians: 1: The future must lead to the world-domination of the Anglo-Saxon race. 2: The impossibility of Marxism must be tried out in Russia. England's Balkan policy according to these viewpoints. The impractical sense of the 'practical people'. The impossible political and economic circumstances in Austria before the world war. The unnoticed tendency that the problems of the time can be resolved by the idea of threefolding. Conditions in Berlin before the outbreak of the world war.

The solitary decision of General von Moltke under the pressure of these conditions. The publication of Moltke's *Memoirs* planned for 1919 and its prevention by a German general. Regarding attempts to find a way out of catastrophic circumstances through the idea of threefolding and the difficulty of finding any understanding for it.

Publisher's Note

The present volume of the Collected Works or *Gesamtausgabe* (GA) comprises lectures which were given mainly during the First World War in Stuttgart. In the bibliographical survey of 1961 these lectures were originally allocated to various different volumes of the *Gesamtausgabe*, details of which are given in the German edition of GA 174b, which was first published in 1974. The stated intention lying behind the decision to create this new German volume was one of wanting to avoid repetitions. There was also the wish to bring together the lectures given at Stuttgart at this particular time; and the previous volume in the *Gesamtausgabe* series GA 174a (*Between East and West, Central Europe in Cosmic and Human History*) includes the lectures given during the First World War in Munich.

Introduction

Towards the end of Owen Barfield's long novel *English People*, there is a scene where a terminally ill old man, who is evidently a leading member of some unspecified secret society, is giving some last advice before he dies to a person whom he intends to take over his responsibilities. One of his most important pieces of advice is to prevent 'the Three' from uniting, in that any form of threefoldness (as opposed to duality) would, he says, work 'like dynamite!', and, hence, torpedo the carefully laid plans of this society; and it is clear from the whole context of the novel that the society has as its aim the guidance and direction of the affairs of the Western world of 'England' and 'America' (which, he says, for the purposes of the brotherhood should preferably lose their separate identity to become a 'united West'). A further aim specified by this elderly occultist is to defeat the movement led by 'Brockmann' (or Rudolf Steiner), which 'remains a grave threat'.

Apart from the last of these sixteen lectures, which is itself – even more than any of the others – all about the war, all these lectures were given during the unprecedented global conflict of the First World War; and one can sense throughout the lectures – and perhaps all the more because they were given in a place and amidst a group of people where he felt able to speak with a particular degree of intimacy – that Rudolf Steiner was standing fervently for the Third Thing (the 'Tertium Quid' in Barfield's novel) which he could see was under serious threat of destruction through the forces that had brought this war about. The purpose of this introduction is on the one hand briefly to characterize Rudolf Steiner's standpoint in his own terms and from his own perspective and, on the other, to try to assess its significance and validity from the perspective of over a century of determination to assert – *pace* Barfield's elderly occultist – the primacy of duality in the intellectual and social (and, of course, the political) affairs of humanity.

Already in the first of these lectures, which was given in September 1914 and thus shortly after the outbreak of the war, the themes which come to resound throughout are briefly encapsulated. It is also one of those lectures where Rudolf Steiner spoke quite explicitly about the national as opposed to the universally human aspect of the tumultuous events happening around him and his audience. Thus, for example, he states quite clearly that 'the ego of Europe resides in the German spirit', that 'this war is a conspiracy against German spiritual and cultural life' and that 'we [i.e. the German or Central European people] did not want this war'. Both in this and in several of the other lectures there are copious references to what he had said previously in 1910 (thus, as he emphasizes, long before the outbreak of the war) in the lectures on Folk-souls and their mission given in Christiania (Oslo). He recounts his understanding of the way that different European peoples carry particular tasks on behalf of their Folk-souls or Folk-spirits with respect to the development of different attributes of human nature, while always emphasizing on the one hand that this is not a question of attributing value-judgements but, rather, of characterizing particular tasks on behalf of humanity and the spiritual world and, on the other hand, that the individual human being can – and ultimately should – always rise above such groupings even in our own time.

It is especially important to emphasize here what he says about the conflict and perpetual tension between East and West and constructively to understand their respective tasks in our time. Only in the last lecture, which was given on 21 March 1921 and thus well after the end of the war, do we have a full-scale rebuttal of the assertion that was the prevailing view throughout the war and even well into our present twenty-first century, namely that Germany was responsible for bringing about the war. Instead, he makes it very clear – as he also does to a lesser extent elsewhere in these lectures – that the war arose mainly out of the determination of the 'Anglo-Saxon race to exercise world-domination' and to 'resolve the social question' by 'making the Eastern world, and specifically the world of Russia, the field for socialist experiments', a tendency which, he says, was aggravated by the failure of the Central European peoples to 'rise to a broad sense of vision', to 'grow together with a broad visionary outlook' as befitted their particular world-historical task. Not that this prevented Rudolf Steiner from being accused (wholly unjustly, as he makes clear) by the precursors of the Nazi movement (including Adolf Hitler himself) of being responsible for the disastrous terms meted out to Germany by the Versailles Peace Treaty.

Thus throughout these lectures given in Stuttgart during the war, Rudolf Steiner was speaking at least in part as a defender of something utterly precious and essential to the present and future development of Europe and the wider world which was under serious assault, even in the earlier lectures hoping for a military victory and later for a victory of a more spiritual nature. This theme is present in the background even where – for example in the three lectures given in November 1915 – the focus is upon other matters relating to his spiritual-scientific research. Thus in these November 1915 lectures the insights that he gives into the life between death and a new birth are prompted by his reflections about the destiny of the etheric bodies and souls of those who had died prematurely on the battlefields, as evidenced by the meditative verse beginning 'From the courage of the fighters...', which he spoke at the end of the first eight of the present lectures. In some of the later lectures, Rudolf Steiner is, rather, devoting his attention to assaults of other than a military nature upon this precious Central European treasure of the individual human spirit, whether deriving from such as Annie Besant on behalf of the (Anglo-Saxon-oriented) Theosophical Society, from former, disaffected members of the Anthroposophical Society or from present members whose cultivation of anthroposophy he regards as theoretical and abstract, as insufficiently grounded in reality. The penultimate fifteenth lecture translates this understanding again into the broader canvas of outward events; and there is in this lecture an almost apocalyptic tone emanating out of Steiner's awareness of, on the one hand, the abstract spiritual dissipation exemplified by the impulses of the world's 'schoolmaster' President Woodrow Wilson (ever his bête noire) and, on the other, by the sinister nationalism of the blood which was to arise as a tragic distortion of his plea for a renewed visionary quality on the part of the Central European spirit.

How different the understanding that a contemporary English novelist, E. M. Forster, presents of the respective qualities of the German and English soul in his novel *Howards End* (1910), which is at any rate in some ways wholly consistent with that of Rudolf Steiner and has as its motto – in stark contrast to the bellicose hatefulness of wartime – the famous words 'only connect', from the impression that one may have of the situation in our present time! This was starkly exemplified for the present writer by the title of a book published this year (2023) chronicling the recent history of much of that European territory to which Rudolf Steiner assigned the designation Central Europe (*Mitteleuropa*). This book was written by a Polish-American academic Jacob Mikanowski with the title *Goodbye Eastern Europe*. In the course of the book he explicitly states that what he calls Eastern Europe is equivalent to *Mitteleuropa* ('Eastern Europe' in Rudolf Steiner's understanding refers to Russia, including Belarus and Ukraine). The point here is not to dissent from the author's analysis but to draw a very different conclusion, and to understand the significance of the author's analysis in terms of the picture presented by Rudolf Steiner. For it is not difficult to see that 'Central Europe' including of course Germany, Austria and so forth has in our time become largely subsumed within an American-dominated West and that in cultural terms it has more or less lost its identity in a dualistic cultural and political scheme of East and West. Moreover, from this perspective it can be seen that the assumed supremacy of the materialistic Western (Anglo-American) world-view which, according to Rudolf Steiner, was the principal factor in bringing about the First World War, continues to be responsible at least in part for the most divisive conflicts with which our present world is assailed (to say nothing of environmental and ecological issues). There is therefore a need for a dramatic change in the predominant mind-set of modern times. Especially among younger people, there is a growing understanding of this; but here, Rudolf Steiner's insights into national and group identities and characteristics, into the evolution of human consciousness, are badly needed if the tribalism of identity politics, strongly influenced as it is by the deadening anti-thoughts of the post-modernism advocated by such as Michel Foucault, can be transformed into a true commitment to universalism; to not only a respect for but also a deep understanding of the qualities, characteristics and tasks of the multifarious aspects of our universally human world.

May the publication of these lectures serve to promote such an understanding!

Simon Blaxland-de Lange
Advent 2023

My dear friends, we call to mind the guarding spirits of those who are out on the battlefields at this present time:

> Spirits watching over your souls,
> May thy wings bring
> Our petitioning love
> To the human beings on Earth entrusted to thy care,
> That, united with thy power,
> Our plea may radiate help
> To the souls
> Whom we seek lovingly to reach!

And for those who have, because of these events, already passed through the gate of death:

> Spirits watching over your souls,
> May thy wings bring
> Our petitioning love
> To the human beings in the heavenly spheres entrusted to thy care,
> That, united with thy power,
> Our plea may radiate help
> To the souls
> Whom we seek lovingly to reach!

And may the Spirit whom we seek through the knowledge to which we have aspired, the Spirit who gives meaning, significance and content to earthly life, the Spirit who has passed through the Mystery of Golgotha from the divine heights of the Sun, be with thee and thine arduous duties.

On other occasions, the words were formulated as follows:

We address ourselves first to the guarding spirits of those who are out on the battlefields under such difficult circumstances:

> Ye who watch over earthly souls,
> Ye who weave within earthly souls,
> Ye spirits who work lovingly out of cosmic wisdom
> Granting protection to human souls:
> Hear our plea, behold our love,
> Which seek union with thy helping forces' radiance,
> In devotion to the spirit, sending love.

And to the guarding spirits of those who have, because of these events, passed through the gate of death:

> Ye who watch over souls in heavenly spheres,
> Ye who weave within souls in heavenly spheres,
> Ye spirits who work lovingly out of cosmic wisdom
> Granting protection to souls of human beings:
> Hear our plea, behold our love,
> Which seek union with thy helping forces' streaming,
> In sensing of the spirit, sending love.

And may the Spirit whom we seek to approach through our spiritual science, the Spirit who wanted to pass through the Mystery of Golgotha for the salvation of the Earth and for the freedom and advancement of mankind, be with thee and thine arduous duties.*

---

* In the first pair of verses, the word 'your' in the first line refers to the human souls concerned, the word 'thy' denotes the guarding spirits. For the sake of consistency this deliberate archaism is retained in the second pair of verses, even though here there is less ambiguity in the meaning. The reader may prefer to revert here to the more familiar 'you'.—Translator

Lecture 1

STUTTGART, 30 SEPTEMBER 1914[1]

WHAT we have long been able to foresee has rapidly burst upon the world through all manner of events that have occurred recently. We have thereby become witnesses of serious events, the profound significance of which will be appreciated only at a later time; and I would say that there is much even only of the outward appearances of what underlies these grave events that will not be possible to encompass today. However, for us, my dear friends, there is one thing that I need especially to address at this serious time which I should like to express in the following way.

We have been trying for some years to deepen our understanding of spiritual knowledge, we have been trying to make knowledge, feeling and awareness of the spiritual worlds, and also everything associated with this knowledge, feeling and awareness, something that we can call our own. Now, however, we are in a certain sense confronted with a challenge as to whether we are capable, even under the impression of all the grave events that are taking place, of holding on to the great ideals that have been prescribed to us through our knowledge and feeling of the spiritual world. Where friends who are for the most part united in a common feeling are sitting together in our branches, it is certainly easier to stand firmly by what spiritual science may bring to humanity, but we always and in every situation continue to be mindful of what is expressed in our first principle.[2] We are, after all, not a Society that is confined to homogenous national groups; rather do we seek to disseminate a spirit of reconciliation over the whole of the Earth. This means that we are subjected to a certain challenge, for in the time in which we are now living it is truly difficult fully to develop a sense of objectivity towards what is highest, that is, towards justice.

Precisely for the reasons that will emerge from what I shall say today, it is at present easier for those inhabiting Central Europe, and above all the German people, than it is for others to be objectively impartial. But also there it is necessary not merely to give ourselves over to immediate sensations but we must as serious anthroposophists try to penetrate with understanding the language that justice must command today.

It is not because I want to make a personal statement but because it is symptomatic of the matter at hand that I shall mention the following. The first volume of my book *The Riddles of Philosophy* is perhaps already in your possession.[3] The second volume was in the second half of July printed as far as page 204 and it concluded in mid-stream. The passage was noteworthy and symptomatic for me. I had had to characterize the two French philosophers Boutroux and Bergson. I tried to do so as objectively as possible. Then I had to make the transition to Preuß, a little-known, powerful thinker. Once I had characterized present-day French philosophy, I had to go on to speak about the thoughts that had been conceived on this side of the Rhine in Germany. But then the sheet of paper was empty, for in the meantime the war had broken out. I often had to look at the empty areas of the thirteenth sheet.

At that time there then came various voices from beyond the Rhine. These voices are sufficiently well-known to you. People spoke of German barbarism and the like and threw the most hateful accusations and slanders at us. It cannot be denied that it was distressing to experience all this. It was especially respected representatives of French cultural life who stirred up passionate hatred amongst the people. And in this case the personal aspect may probably be regarded as symptomatic. Thus when I had to deal with French philosophy in the course of my book on the history of the development of philosophy, when I had really made an effort to do it full justice, I could feel thoroughly embittered—having tried with all my power to enter with the greatest possible objectivity into the philosophy of the West—that despite all this there is all this screaming about 'the barbarism beyond the Rhine'. It was all the more painful when one of the worst attackers and haters of the German spirit was Maurice Maeterlinck.[4]

It is strange. The first book that appeared by Maeterlinck, one that already brings his being and particular nature fully to expression, is based wholly upon Novalis, and Maurice Maeterlinck would be lost without Novalis. All his later works have fully arisen from this first one, from the foundation established by Novalis. This also sheds some light upon how our age understands the implementation of justice. It is today utterly inadequate to hear words that are spoken in whatever way out of passion, and it is necessary that we are aware of the facts. If these are allowed to speak, this leads us to objectivity; and such objectivity is not the same thing as an indifference towards matters of this nature.

Things are happening on a large, indeed an immense scale; and a future time will find it necessary to refer in connection with what is going on now to significant events in past ages in the sense of how we speak of repetitions. Not one factor but many come together to form a repetition, a repetition that links together significant historical events.

Just as formerly, in the full flowering of Graeco-Latin culture, the Romans had to fight the Punic wars against Carthage,[5] when the memorable battle at Mylae was decisive for the future destiny of the Romans, who had to preserve their blossoming Graeco-Roman culture in the face of an upsurge of declining forces from the outwardly still powerful realm of the Carthaginians, so at the starting-point of the present war do we find something like a repetition of certain events. Something can be said about this at this place where we are gathered today. At that time a remarkable battle took place between the Romans and the Carthaginians. The Carthaginians had a mighty fleet, in comparison to which that of Rome, with its few ships, seemed powerless. Then the Romans had the unusual idea of constructing boarding bridges that led from ship to ship and transformed the sea battle into a land battle, so that the Romans won a great victory on ground that was more familiar to them. Just as something unheard of at that time happened then, so did something that few could have conceived occur in Lüttich[6] which shows a certain relationship to the events described and will be depicted by future times as the very first event of its kind. I mention these things because I should like to draw attention to the significant aspect of the events in which we are involved at present.

These are days when important decisions in both East and West are on a knife-edge. It is heartbreaking when one is aware of what we are being confronted with, and in these days when decisions are veiled with uncertainty our attention may profitably be focussed on something else which is of the greatest significance.

I may speak about these things as I shall because I have, as it were, been prepared to do so through my karma. I was born in that empire of which it is said that it contributed so much to the international war; but as I grew up I see that already from childhood I was destined to have a sense of homelessness. I had no opportunity to experience any real feelings of comradeship in the country or in a national context. Moreover, my childhood coincided with a time when as an Austrian I learnt to hate Germany, when German Austria was still under the influence of the victory of Prussia, when even the Germans in Austria hated the imperial Germans. There was no opportunity for me to engender a bias in favour of Germany. This homelessness that was given to me through my karma entitles me to speak objectively, fully aware that in this respect the anthroposophical world-conception can speak through my words.

It is not fitting today to speak prophetic words. Thus someone who says that it is doubtful where the victory will eventually lie may well remain unanswered. But *a* victory, an important victory, is also associated with a spiritual contemplation that is indelible for all future times and which has already been achieved. What is this victory? It was won before the outbreak of the war. This victory can be characterized in the following way. Was Europe's central region not long connected with the East? We are not speaking of the people inhabiting Eastern Europe. We have been well informed about this people, and anyone who wants to learn the truth about the relationship of this people to the evolution of nations in general should read the lecture-cycle *The Mission of Folk-Souls in Relation to Teutonic Mythology*.[7]

There is a difference between this Eastern people and the trifolium that presently stands there at the head against Germany and its culture: tsarism, Russian militarism, which has suffered a setback, and mendacious Panslavism. There are threads that have gone from Europe's heart towards this trifolium, even though not to its last leaf.

On 31 July this year this thread between the governments of Germany and Austria and tsarism was broken, swept away through the declaration of war. This was a great victory... [The following passage is unclear. The sense seems to be approximately that the event that took place then between Central Europe, the Western powers and Russia has world-historical overtones.]*

In this there are significant features of world history. One does not need to shut one's eyes to the unnatural aspect of the alliance between Western and North-western Europe and Eastern Europe if one stands on the anthroposophical ground of justice. We can but try at this difficult time to cultivate further what we have learnt through spiritual science and also through much that has been thrust upon us.

When we were in dispute with Mrs. Besant,[8] it was even an Indian scholar who said with respect to the way that Mrs. Besant cried out for tolerance that she was behaving like someone shouting to a person whose hand she was about to cut off and who was defending himself against this: Be tolerant, otherwise you'll start an argument! It needs little thought to see that it is an absurdity to demand that the other person should let his hand be cut off without defending himself.

I have often heard in recent weeks that it has been said: If Austria had not started the war with Serbia, this would have been an exhibition of 'tolerance'. Someone intends to cut off your hand, and you are told to be tolerant! We have numerous opportunities to gain objectivity through what is taking place so painfully around us; but for this we must be able to think in the right way. Learning to think is also a task of theosophy. There is that cycle about the Folk-souls. But

---

* The passage in brackets has been inserted by the editors of the German edition.—Translator

if now in this grave time we were not to be able to understand it in its most holy seriousness, all our concern with this cycle at that time would be a theoretical game. These things can only become flesh and blood when we know how to acquire a feeling of the way to gain clarity as to what is now necessary. In the penultimate lecture of the cycle I tried to say that the various Folk-souls relate to one another as I attempted to describe in the last scene of *The Portal of Initiation* with respect to the interplay of the three soul-forces[9]. The content of the speech, the words that each of the three figures speaks there, must be spoken exactly as they are, since each of them represents one of man's three soul-members.

In the penultimate lecture of the cycle on the Folk-souls it is indicated that if we regard the peoples of Italy and Spain as constituting a reverberation of the third post-Atlantean era, the character of these peoples manifests itself as the sentient soul. In France it is the intellectual soul, in England the consciousness soul, and in Central Europe it is the ego.

Do we not know that there can be battles in our own soul, that the individual members can engage in battle with one another? Attention is drawn to this in the second play, *The Soul's Probation*. We can form a picture of what is being enacted in our time if we let everything that comes to expression there work upon us; and we must try to bring this picture to clarity in our soul in such a way that we know that in Central Europe we have the task of seeking the ego. Thus in the days of peace we have in that cycle placed before our souls in quiet spiritual work the foundations of something that fills the world today as a grave destiny. Indeed, much of what is taking place now will become explainable if we take into consideration everything that is expressed in the cycle referred to above. Only then will we achieve the necessary objectivity.

It has been the case in all wars that the one blames the other. My dear friends, it is not fitting for us to think like this. I shall make this clear by means of a comparison.

Suppose that someone has become old, and that he comes to be beside a child all fresh and full of energy. It would not make much sense if the old man were to harbour resentment against the child and say: You, child, in your youthful energy, are responsible for the fact that I bear the afflictions of old age! It is no more intelligent if now, for example, the Germans are blamed for the war. We must make ourselves clear that whatever happens is grounded in the karma of nations. Likewise in the life of nations there is youth and old age; and just as in human life the exuberant energy of children is not to blame for the fact that freshness is absent in old age, so is it also foolish to make such a reproach in the life of nations.

But everything that is being said should not make us blind; we must focus upon the actual facts, upon what is objective. The deeper foundations of the present events still elude discussion (quite apart from the fact that such a discussion today would create much bad blood); but I can call attention to some essential points in a different way.

As anthroposophists we know that the ego of Europe resides in the German spirit. This is an objective occult fact. I should like to call upon a man who was not a theosophist but who lived within the German spirit in order to characterize the way that people have come to think about the ego. I know that this is not merely the view of one individual human being. The words are those of Herman Grimm, who in a spiritual sense still had Goethe's blood in his veins.[10] 'The solidarity of the moral convictions of all human beings is the Church that unites everyone today. We seek a visible expression of this community more passionately than ever. All really serious aspirations of the masses know only this one aim. The division between nations already no longer exists here. We feel that no national difference should prevail over an ethical world-conception. We would all sacrifice ourselves for our fatherland; but to long for or bring about the moment where this could happen through war is something wholly alien to us. The assurance that our holiest wish is to keep peace is no lie. May "peace on Earth and good tidings to all men" be ours.'

Take as an answer to this what anthroposophical teaching brings to us. Our spiritual movement wants to bring about the possibility of satisfying such a longing. And then these further words of Herman Grimm: 'Human beings as a totality recognize themselves as subject to an invisible court of judgement enthroned in the clouds, before which it is *not* permitted to consider them as a misfortune and to whose legal processes they seek to make their inner disputes conform. With anxious efforts they seek their rights here. Just as Frenchmen in our time endeavour to make the war they intend to wage against Germany out to be a moral obligation, whose recognition they demand from other nations including Germany itself!'

One may regard what anthroposophy says about the realms of the hierarchies as an answer to this picture. It is a moving experience to see how the human mind is in its best representatives full of the deepest longing for what spiritual science wants to bring but passes it by, does not find it, and how people then with anxious efforts seek their rights here.

Then a further remarkable fact. Herman Grimm says: 'Just as Frenchmen in our time endeavour to make the war that they intend to wage with Germany out to be a moral obligation, whose recognition they demand from other nations including Germany itself!' This is indeed well to the point. Can one not observe today the effort that comes towards us from the West to represent this war as a moral obligation? I should also like to read you a third quotation from Herman Grimm. Again you will find that it finds fulfilment in what our movement brings: 'The inhabitants of our planet, taken together as a unity, are filled with a universally understood sensitivity that even the coarsest peoples have an inkling of and are wary of injuring. In our time people acknowledge the right of individual self-determination in every individual where intellectual and spiritual things are concerned. Even primitive human creatures let themselves be guided towards these thoughts.' Here Herman Grimm is expressing none other than the first principle of our Society.

So you see that our anthroposophy is an answer to the call that the German spirit has allowed to resound in the voices of the best representatives of its cultural life. The heart of Europe cherishes a deep longing for spirituality. This is also elucidated by the fact that the German, wherever he belongs, adapts to the customs of a country by sacrificing his previous habitual traditions, in this sense sacrificing his nationality but not his spiritual culture.

All this, my dear friends, is on the one hand suitable for letting us be just and impartial, while nonetheless not closing our eyes to what must really be attended to.

There have recently been surprises also for occultists; and I may say that during my course in Norrköping[11] I had to say some things that had their origin in such a surprise. It is true that these events had to happen, one could foresee this for some years, also that they had in a destiny sense to come in this year. But at the beginning of July there was no more to say than that we would gather for the Munich cycle (as could be expected),[12] then we would be facing some significant events. Then came the assassination in Sarajevo.[13] If I have often emphasized how different things are here on the physical plane than on the spiritual plane, how often a contrasting picture manifests itself; so it was also to my surprise when I was able to compare the individuality who underwent this assassination before and after death. Something quite distinctive happened then. This personality became a cosmic power. I mention this in order to draw attention to how things on the physical plane are a symbol of a spiritual reality, and how, to be precise, all events of the physical plane can only be explained when one penetrates to the spiritual plane. Some of you know of my earlier remark. I said that something terrible was hovering in the astral world. It could only sink down to the physical plane, because astral forces had gathered on the physical plane, forces of fear that were exerting a hindering influence upon it.

It was on 20 July when I knew that the forces of fear had now become forces of courage, of boldness. An indescribably wonderful fact; the forces of fear became forces of courage. Then it was no longer impossible to explain what took place on the physical plane as a unique phenomenon: that enthusiasm. This is a fact that was a unique experience for me, and so far as I am aware it was also something of which no occultist had previously had knowledge.

You have all been witnesses of how this enthusiasm has over the course of a few days taken hold of people who were previously truly peace-loving individuals, how a wave of courage passed over them.

The times soon came when it was heard with sadness what immense sacrifices this war demands. When I was in Berlin in the first days of September,[14] my soul was filled with deep sorrow when I became aware what blossoms of German souls had to be sacrificed on the battlefield. I could not help dwelling on my sorrow, and—through no merit of my own—this engenders occult research. When one grieves, occult knowledge is granted to one's soul. I was confronted with the anxious question: If especially the flower of the leaders of the various bodies of troops is carried off, what will happen then?

And then one could see how it was those who had fallen who, after their death on the field of battle, helped those who had to fight after them. This was what was yielded from clairvoyant research. When the dead help the living, this is a source of consolation amidst the grief. My dear friends, what spiritual science represents must intervene in life in moments when all consolation seems impossible, when the right mood of soul cannot be found. Also here, spiritual knowledge is able to give the right mood of soul, it can offer consolation. I know that there will be souls from our community who will derive courage from such knowledge amidst these sorrowful events.

We know from spiritual science that the guides and directors of mankind's development are spiritual beings. In the spiritual world it is prescribed that one thing or another happens at a certain point in time. Let us suppose that by 1950 or 1970 it has been decreed that earthly humanity should have achieved a certain measure of a capacity for love in order to combat egotism. Everything that spiritual science represents wants to engender the capacity for love. It does so in a manner similar to the way that wood generates warmth in a stove. It can be engendered through the word; and within our movement the attempt is made to engender it through the great teachings of anthroposophy. But if human souls were to be insufficiently receptive to the word, if things were to proceed too slowly to the extent that by the time that has been prescribed the capacity for love and sacrifice were to be insufficiently developed, another teacher would need to appear.

In Dornach there is a symbolic demonstration of this. It was actually the intention to have the building ready by the beginning of August. Nothing has become of this; it was not predestined by karma that the whole building should be ready by this time and look down over the region from its eastern and south-eastern elevation as a symbol of the spirit. Nevertheless, the columns together with the cupolas are rising up into the wide landscape as a vantage-point for the spirit. The question of creating a space with good acoustics needs also to be solved within our building. I am convinced that a solution to this has been found. The way that the sound from a certain point has been tested indicates that the acoustics are right for the building. But at first our friends were unable to discern within these acoustics the words of spiritual life; initially they heard the echo of the roar of cannon fire from southern Alsace, and instead of the light from the spiritual world far-off flashes of light radiated from the floodlights of Fort Istein into the building and illuminated it. A strange symbol! A symbol that may perhaps be suggested. Another teacher is sometimes necessary!

Was this not a teacher of immense power? Did it not present a powerful opposition to materialism? What a lot has happened in a week! What an assault has been made upon egotism! So much sacrificiality and human love has been made manifest!

When I recently returned from Vienna,[15] karma chanced to place a journal in my hands. In it there was a description by an Austrian soldier entering the field of battle. He first describes how during the journey to the Front the soldiers are shown kindness from every side, and at the end there is a passage—the soldier had most probably never encountered theosophy—where he says: We who are entering the field of battle try with every ounce of courage and with all that we have to stand up for what is right; but those who stay at home are also able to have an influence. Then come the great words: 'Whom God grants may pray—whoever cannot pray gathers up all his thoughts and will-forces for the ardent wish for victory...', and thus he contributes his own to this! We have spoken for many years of the power of feeling. Thus what we have been cultivating in many years of work is now living in a simple soldier. Whatever may be the immediate result of this or that, there is one thing that the event will yield: spirituality within the human soul, which otherwise would not have been found for a long time to come.

These events have a greatness about them. They can only be compared with great events of the past which are interwoven with one another. So just as the battle of the Romans against the Carthaginians and the wars associated with the great migrations were important and decisive for the cultural development of peoples, the battle in whose midst we stand is of no less significance; and from the many words that I am speaking, one feeling that will continue to dwell within you is that those who have shed their blood in battle offer this blood as a sacrifice for something that must happen. It must happen for the salvation of mankind. And when we contemplate the great sacrifices and grief, there is one thing that, while not striking a cheerful note, can nevertheless fill us inwardly with great satisfaction: that sacred blood is flowing, sanctified by these events; and those who have shed it will be the most important fellow workers for future times. Much will become understandable to us if we can resolve to see in the flowing blood sanctified, sacrificial blood. If we imbue our souls with this truth, the spirit will bear fruit within us. I may put it thus: what that simple soldier has said is something that can fill the souls of our dear anthroposophical friends.

The thoughts that are cherished as a conviction within the anthroposophical soul will sound forth particularly strongly; and this is necessary if the words that have prefaced our deliberations may have an effect. Among those who are fighting there are already those who serve in the right faith.

> Spirits watching over your souls,
> May thy wings bring
> Our petitioning love
> To the human beings on Earth entrusted to thy care,
> That, united with thy power,
> Our plea may radiate help
> To the souls
> Whom we seek lovingly to reach.

My dear friends! It was the purpose of my lecture today that we now apply the significance of the thoughts that we have been considering to the events in order that we can withstand the trial, that we grasp the events and the relations between them with an impartial eye. Spirituality will also come through that great teacher that is now passing through Europe. But man is born for freedom. Much depends on those who are united with us in the spiritual movement. If anthroposophical thoughts will live rightly in your souls in the time of trial, that space that is now filled with interweaving passions will be filled with brightly shining spiritual thoughts, with holy, genuine feelings. Such feelings will live on in a lasting way.

There are many nights when I implore that there may be many anthroposophists who send forth such a light-filled radiant thought; and if we also find the right will we shall have the possibility of lovingly playing our part. We need to be mindful as to where we may also bring love in a practical way into the world. Our karma will bring it about that we are in one or another situation where this or that is demanded of us for which we are required.

It was only with tears in my eyes that I could read the letter written to his mother by a young Austrian who on 26 July heard the words that were spoken in Dornach,[16] how the convictions and strength that anthroposophy can give are living in his heart and enable him to fulfil his duty where destiny has placed him. The same feelings and thoughts came to me from the letter of another young friend who had attended that same meeting in Dornach and had then entered the field of battle. These are the thoughts and feelings that must live today in our souls: to seek to fulfil our duty wherever it manifests itself to us, to hold fast to our power of judgement and to be attentive to where our love is needed. One thing that will then come to fulfilment in the future is that when the peoples of Europe are no longer opposed to one another in battle, the thoughts that we are now sending forth will be the ones that remain and be the strongest; they will represent something eternal. What we now feel will be a healing force if it is connected with the feeling that *one* victory is inevitable: the victory of the spirit.

A statesman in Germany spoke some remarkable words this spring.[17] He said regarding our relationship to Russia that Germany had a friendly agreement with St Petersburg, whereby it had been decided not to pay attention to anything in the press. And regarding England it was said in July that the relaxation of tension was making progress, that negotiations had not been concluded but that they would be carried further in this sense. This is how a notable statesman could still speak in July. One may read these words again and try to realize how human judgement evaluated the situation before events began to take their present course. But one point that clearly emerges from these words is that we did not want the war! Please understand me aright if I make the bizarre statement that one would wish that one were a non-German so that these words might find the attention that befits them, in order to be able to give them the impression that they deserve.

But the human soul needs something that has duration, so that it is not a question of speaking today about things that tomorrow prove to be unsustainable; it needs something that is true today and also true tomorrow. It will only find such truth if it connects itself with the spirit. We may have confidence that the spirit will be victorious. Anyone who connects himself with the spirit will find the right path to that truth which can only arise from the connection with the spirit. In the week before the outbreak of the war I had to read statements in a newspaper such as the following:[18] In spite of Liebknecht's reprimand I consider that one does not need to speak the truth in political life, unless it were to become known or bring harm to oneself. Such a statement arises from the materialism of our time, in which we would be suffocated without this war and the overcoming of which is the task of our movement, which—in contrast to the incredulity prompted by such words—has as a fundamental proposition the words: 'Wisdom lives only in truth'.[19]

This shows us how greatly we need the spirit of truth if we want to understand things in their reality; for what matters is that we penetrate to that objectivity that can only be arrived at through the spirit of truth. Then one will also be able to know what a later time will recognize: that this war is a conspiracy against German spiritual and cultural life.

The verse that addresses the Folk-spirit can help us to discover such an objectivity:

> Spirit of my earthly habitation!
> Reveal the light of thine age
> To the Christ-endowed soul.
> That striving I may find thee
> In the choirs of the spheres of peace,
> Singing the glory and the power
> Of human hearts devoted to the Christ.[20]

Much can become clear for our souls and for finding the right path if we livingly unite with this soul what can come to us from a verse of this kind. Then I know that something will happen, that an important part of what needs to develop will become a reality, something that will live in the anthroposophical soul and which anthroposophy brings into the world, so that hopes that I would want to summarize by means of the following words may be translated into deeds:

> From the courage of the fighters,
> From the blood on fields of battle,
> From the grief of the bereaved,
> From the people's sacrifice:
> There will ripen fruit of spirit,
> If souls will turn in consciousness
> Towards the realm of spirit.
> [Translation by George and Mary Adams]

My dear friends, what really counts is our wish to practise effective love, to be attentively awake to the demands of the day; and then we want to study the circumstances clearly and free from prejudice in order to gain such objectivity as is necessary today and is so difficult for many to attain. Perhaps those of our friends from elsewhere who hear these words can also bring clarity to the situation.

If we achieve such an objectivity and such a readiness for love of a truly active nature, a power may arise from such a striving that can be of use to those spirits who send forth their influences to the destiny of the nations and who are also standing at humanity's side as a source of help and guidance in these grave, difficult times.

Lecture 2

STUTTGART, 13 FEBRUARY 1915

IT must be emphasized again and again that an essential point that we can glean from our spiritual-scientific endeavours is that mere knowledge, insights that reside purely in the form of ideas and concepts, must increasingly be regarded as something of the past; and that we have to seek a knowledge, a sum of ideas and concepts, of feelings and will-impulses, that can become truly alive within us in the fullest sense of the word. It is necessary that from time to time we direct our thoughts and meditative ponderings towards this essential point of our endeavours; for the light that can emanate from this can only fully illumine our souls if we constantly and faithfully keep it in mind. For those of us who want to dedicate ourselves with heart and soul to the aims of spiritual science, it must in this grave time be a heart-felt need to translate the knowledge that we can receive into real life, into the direct life of the soul. We must endeavour gradually to transform mere theoretical, scientific insights into experiences through being enriched from the spiritual world. Otherwise we shall be approaching a time of spiritual aridity; for theories, merely scientific convictions, have the tendency to desiccate the human soul and human life as a whole. But the belief that one must order one's life in accordance with the model of scientific convictions is one that is deeply rooted in our time.

The great events taking place in our time should be a special challenge to souls inclined towards spiritual science to gain real clarity about the difference between life and a knowledge based purely on a scientific model. We must try to come to a kind of self-knowledge, a purely human self-knowledge; we must attempt this in the awareness of how deeply the demon of theoretical conviction is presently living in human hearts. We must inwardly perceive the extent to which this demon of theoretical conviction wants to take root; and we shall not make what anthroposophy can potentially be for us our inner-most experience if we do not direct our attention to facts that can inwardly surprise also anthroposophists, facts which indicate how far one is removed from a direct experience of the spiritual world if one is immersed in modern life and how closely one is related to a theoretical model of research. One must consider such facts in a completely unprejudiced way.

Since these grave events have engulfed Europe and the wider world, I have been able—and what I shall presently be saying is only one instance of several occasions—to speak about experiences asso-ciated with our grave present predicament in many different places in the German-speaking world. I was also able to do so here in Stutt-gart.[21] So I have recounted such experiences in a number of places. What was one of the consequences of my having done so? One of the consequences was that people from other regions came with the request that I should bring what I have been saying in the con-text of the German-speaking world to them as well. This was often requested out of the well-meant assumption that truth is of course the same for all and that an endeavour to bring what is said in one place to another place would readily serve as a means of clarifying the truth in our troubled time. It has, indeed, become the fashion in our spiritual stream to write down everything that is spoken, also what is said out of the direct impulse not only of the time but also of the place and of the people who are being addressed, and to have the belief that this must be of equal service to everyone; because one makes the theoretical assumption that the truth can be formulated only in one single way. Well, my dear friends, the mischief that con-sists in precisely writing down the spoken words and believing that they still have the same content when they are read as a recorded text or delivered again would grow to enormous proportions if one were to believe what has just been indicated.

If those things that the peoples of Europe have to deal with at the present time could be resolved through words, there would be no need for those great streams of blood to flow that have to flow today out of the eternal necessities of earthly evolution. If there was the simple possibility for souls to understand one another out of national aspirations, they would not need to oppose one another with cannon fire. We must attune ourselves to what is given through the character of our experience, we must verify with our knowledge of spiritual science what we encounter as matters of great seriousness. To employ occult truths frivolously for everyday needs of the soul cannot be the task of our spiritual-scientific endeavours. So long as we are not in a position to understand that spiritual powers are indeed active in the world phenomena that we meet with on the physical plane and that we need spiritual science in order to gauge and appreciate the value and inner truth of these spiritual powers, so long as we are unable to do this we do not as yet have the right relationship to our spiritual science.

This must be clear to us. When we stand on the ground of anthroposophy, when we develop for our soul the lofty truths that pertain to man's higher being, we are standing on a ground that is beyond all nationality and is even beyond all racial differences. When we stand fully on the ground of what we learn from spiritual knowledge about the nature of man, the same truths hold good for the whole earthly sphere and within certain bounds for other planets of our solar system. As soon as we stand on this ground, the highest thoughts concerning man's being enter into our consideration. It is a different matter when things are considered from which there speaks, and must speak, something other than this highest being of man. Thus when nations confront one another, we do not have to do with that in the being of man which extends beyond all human differences. When nations confront one another, it is not merely human beings but spiritual worlds that confront one another; beings in spiritual worlds who are active and live within human beings are in mutual opposition. To believe that what must apply to human beings must also apply to that complicated world of demons and spirits that works through them when nations engage in war, to believe that through simple human logic one could reach some conclusion as to what causes demons to oppose one another, means that belief in the existence of an actual spiritual world has not been found.

What do I mean by this? If we now look at what is happening out in the world, we find (and I shall leave aside the actual painful events of the war) that people of different nationalities are in conflict with one another. We find that one nationality sometimes floods the other with its hatred in the most terrible way. Then people try to come to some sort of an understanding, that is, to ask themselves who has the greater right to hate, this nation or that one, or which is more deserving of hatred. They also reflect upon which nation is most to blame for this war. They tend to think about these matters in the way that one rightly does in a court of justice, where one weighs up the different circumstances. But what is one actually doing when one does what has just been characterized and which is the prevailing element in present-day writing, what is one doing? One is denying all spiritual life, even though one would not want to admit this; for one is acknowledging the dogma that, for example, those demons that have brought discord from the East to European life are to be judged in accordance with the model of human reasoning. People do not believe that there is a different reasoning power, a different way of judging things, than is possessed by man. To judge such events as these which are so tumultuous in evolutionary terms from a purely human standpoint constitutes a denial of spiritual science. We only acknowledge the reality of spiritual-scientific life if we clearly understand that spiritual causes come fully to expression in physical events, causes that also demand a different faculty of judgement than that of the physical plane. When people with different opinions engage in mutual hostilities on the physical plane, one can perhaps resort to human judgement. But one cannot do so when nations are at war with one another, because invisible powers come to expression through the lives of nations. It is true that invisible powers are also in evidence within man, but in such a way that they adapt themselves to human judgement. However, they do not do so in the life of nations. It is therefore a question of making ourselves accustomed to acknowledging the reality of spiritual life and realizing that quite different impulses speak in the human soul than those that one can master with the earthly intellect when such great events are enacted.

When one reads what is being said today and what is also spoken by those who want to receive an impulse from spiritual science, one finds that much of this is written or spoken about as if world evolution had only begun approximately on 20 July 1914. Even where people seek the causes of the present complications, they speak as though they had started only in the previous year. One of the practical results that spiritual science must yield is that people come to want to learn something not from the events of the day but that they want to form a judgement from their wider context. This will be a first step; then it will be a case of testing the judgement by what spiritual science is in a position to give. Let us see by means of an example how spiritual science will necessarily become fruitful when it is a question of making sense of an experience and making it our own.

We have consistently emphasized that world or earthly evolution takes its course during the post-Atlantean age in clearly defined different cultural periods. We have enumerated these cultural periods as being the ancient Indian, the Persian, the Egypto-Chaldean, the Graeco-Latin, then the one that can be seen as our present epoch; then we have drawn attention to the fact that a sixth epoch and then a seventh must take over from our own. However, we were not satisfied with simply schematically presenting the succession of these cultural periods but tried to characterize their distinctive qualities. We thereby tried to gain an understanding of our own time, of the transitional impulses living in our own time, in our fifth post-Atlantean age. We also made it clear that nothing rigidly defined is meant by such characterizations, so that for example one cannot say that the distinctive quality of this cultural epoch extends over the entire Earth. It appears in certain places, whereas other parts of the Earth, other territories, remain behind. They do not need to remain behind in an absolute sense, but they remain behind with ancient forces in order subsequently to bring them into connection with advancing evolution in a different cultural epoch. One does not need to think in terms of respective values but only of different characteristics.

One cannot fail to be struck by the profound difference as regards spiritual culture between, say, European and Asiatic peoples.

If we consider the nature of Europeans and Americans, on the one hand, and Asians on the other (quite irrespective of any question of values), we cannot fail to see that the Asiatic peoples have retained certain cultural impulses of past earthly epochs, whereas the European and American peoples have advanced beyond these cultural epochs. Only someone whose soul-life is not entirely healthy will be particularly impressed by the mysticism that Oriental humanity has preserved from ancient times, when it was necessary for human beings to live with lower forces of seership. Such an unhealthy spiritual life has, however, made a strong impression upon Europe; the belief has arisen that the path into the spiritual worlds has to be learnt through Asiatic yoga and similar methods. And yet this tendency is evidence of an unhealthy life of soul. A healthy soul-life must be based upon leading the experiences of the fifth post-Atlantean cultural epoch over into spiritual life, into a path of spiritual knowledge and not upon drawing forth something within humanity which is indeed of interest from, as it were, a scientific point of view but which should not be renewed for European humanity if it is not to fall back into times that are not suitable for it. However, other times will come in earthly evolution; and in these future times ancient forces must again be united with those forces that have advanced further. They must therefore be preserved somewhere on Earth in order later to be able to unite with the forces that have progressed. A sixth age will follow the fifth cultural epoch. Abstract thinking, this dreadful abstract thinking which is the daughter of a purely theoretical, scientific orientation, cannot do otherwise than value the sixth age higher than the fifth, because the sixth is a later development. But we should be clear that there are times of ascent and times of descent or decline; we should be clearly aware that the sixth age which follows the fifth in the post-Atlantean age must necessarily belong to the descent and that what is developed in the fifth post-Atlantean epoch must be the seed for the earthly age that will follow the seventh cultural epoch. One must consider things livingly, not in an abstract, theoretical way, thus letting the sixth age in its greater perfection follow the fifth age as one that is less perfect.

In the age of Atlantis the fourth epoch was the one where the seeds for our present age were sown. In our age it is the fifth cultural epoch wherein lie the seeds for what must follow the post-Atlantean age. And what is the characteristic element that must develop especially in this fifth post-Atlantean cultural epoch? It is what has pre-eminently been inspired by the Mystery of Golgotha: that spiritual impulses have been brought down to the physically human level, that the flesh must be taken hold of by the spirit. This has not yet happened. It will happen only when spiritual science has a greater earthly foundation and far more people bring it to expression in daily life, when the spirit comes to expression in, one might say, every movement of the hand or finger and in the most everyday affairs. But it was in order to bring spiritual impulses down to the Earth that Christ became flesh in a human body; and this process, the impregnating of the flesh with the spirit, is characteristic of the overall mission of European humanity. The task of our fifth cultural epoch, which has been prepared by the other four cultural epochs, is to enable the outward physical body to be a shrine for the spirit; and it must be our task to make ourselves familiar with those cultural impulses that manifest the tendency to ally the spirit with the flesh, with everyday life.

In the sixth cultural epoch of the post-Atlantean age the task will be to come to know the spirit above all as something hovering in the earthly environment, to recognize the spirit in the elemental world; because this sixth cultural epoch has the task of preparing the knowledge of the spirit in the earthly environment. This cannot so easily be achieved if ancient atavistic forces which recognize the spirit in its purely elemental life are not kept back. But these processes do not take their course in the world without the most violent struggles. European humanity is still on the way to receive the spirit ever more deeply into its own being. Asian humanity is on the path of conserving that age when the spirit is kept at a distance from the body, when the spirit is sought purely outside the physical human organism. This makes it inevitable that the transition from the fifth cultural epoch to the sixth will not be able to take place without a violent struggle between European humanity and Asian humanity in all manner of different realms. What precedes these struggles will occupy world history until they are resolved. Future events are reflected in a variety of ways in those that precede them. When we consider what we have become acquainted with through spiritual science, we are in fact standing before something colossal that we can perceive as necessarily taking place in the future.

Thus we have on the one hand a part of humanity with the mission of leading the spirit into physical life in such a way that the spirit pervades every aspect of physical life; and on the other hand we have a part of humanity that must now necessarily identify itself with the descending path of evolution. This can only happen if that which is committed to the pervading of the bodily element with the spiritual brings forth cultural impulses that have a quality of permanence for the Earth, that cannot disappear again from it; for what will then follow as the sixth and seventh cultural epochs must live spiritually from the creations of the fifth, it must take into itself the creations of the fifth cultural epoch. The fifth cultural epoch has the task of deepening the life of outward idealism in the direction of spiritual life; but the spiritual life that is thus won from idealism must subsequently be received, it must continue to live on. The East will not have the forces to bring forth a fruitful spiritual life of its own but only to absorb what has already been brought forth. The course that history must take is that from the humanity of the present which bears within itself the essential cultural impulses a spiritual culture is created which is the historical successor of the fifth culture, and that this culture is developed by what comes after.

One should try to visualize quite objectively and without prejudice the difference between these two streams of humanity. One should try to form a clear idea how since the appearance of that part of humanity which is referred to as the Germanic peoples[*] there has been an endeavour to imbue outward physicality with the spirit and how Christianity in all its depths has been embraced.

------

[*] The word rendered throughout this passage as 'Germanic' (*Germanisch*) refers not only to the German people as such but to all peoples of a broadly Germanic origin.—Translator

The start was made from the outward physical realm, from what in the physical contains the seed for a physical vessel imbued with the spirit. One can hark back to the summer sacrifice, to the solstice sacrifice of the god, Baldur. Its real deeper meaning has long been forgotten, but what is its actual deeper meaning? It can only be understood if one draws one's attention to how spiritual powers rise up in the light and warmth with the ascending Spring Sun, to how the god Lenz* ascends and how with the lighting of the St John's fire man has the inclination to unite with the Lenz forces ruling in nature, to how he kindles fire as a sign that he unites his understanding with the death of the god Lenz at the summer solstice. This is the legend of Baldur: the god Lenz burns in the solstice fire because people received what is fruitful and seed-bearing in nature, in outward physical nature, because they loved the god Lenz and followed him to his death. But because in the outward physical world that had, as it were, a pre-figuration of Christ, who does not die at the summer solstice but is born at the winter solstice (note this contrast between the bodily and the spiritual), because in the god of the summer solstice they had the model for the God of the winter solstice, because for the spiritual aspect they had the reverse of the bodily aspect, they were pervaded with what was related and yet opposite. If Baldur is the god Lenz who perishes at the summer solstice, the Christ God is He who was born at the winter solstice. The one and the other interpenetrate one another as the bodily element of the outwardly physical is pervaded with a spiritual element which is veiled by corporeal darkness, by the darkness of winter. The winter spirit pervades the summer body. And how does this interpenetration take place? In the directly personal struggle of the cultural impulses. For what is the history of Central Europe but a continuous struggle for the dawning of the divine spark in the personal soul, the dawning of the spiritual in the physical? One can disregard everything else, but one must perceive the truth, discern the characteristic aspect of this Central European nature.

---

* '*Lenz*' is an old poetical German word for spring.—Translator

Let us now consider the other part of humanity. How far it stands from this personal impulse of the striving of the spiritual element to assert itself within the physical domain! One could say that as a phenomenon of history it is highly interesting to observe that Chinese culture has retained its Tao and Confucius religion, that Asiatic religions in general have preserved the oldest and most abstract forms. These forms enable the theoretical intellect to feel very comfortable, but they constitute an element of rigidity for personal experience and do not even allow it to reach the level of struggle, because this personal experience is to be protected until the time when what has been won through struggle has so become part of human culture that it can be received. In the fifth cultural epoch a spiritual element must be attained through one's own efforts; in the sixth cultural period human beings will come and receive what has been developed and striven for as their own perception and experience, but as something that they have not achieved for themselves. They are held within the forces that do not struggle and receive the spiritual element as something external which they take for granted. The prelude to that far more distant struggle is what must gradually develop in the form of the struggle between the Germanic and Slavic world. One needs only to be mindful that the Slavic world is in a certain sense an outpost for what the sixth cultural epoch represents, indeed that within it lies the germinal essence of the sixth cultural epoch. This can only rightly be considered in a true, spiritual-scientific sense. It will then become clear that in this Slavic element there must lie something of a receptive nature, something that has nothing to do with this struggle and actually recoils from any struggling of its own. One can see this very clearly. Whereas in Central Europe human souls have inwardly battled to arrive at a conception of God through a personal struggle, the Slavic element preserves religion, the conception of God, the ritual that is already there; it conserves, it does not make the spirit inwardly alive but lets it move over it like a cloud and lives within this cloud, remaining in a personal sense estranged from it.

Central Europe has not been able to remain content with an old form of outward Christianity because it had to struggle. The East stood still and even its cultural forms have become fixed and abstract, because it is to prepare itself for receiving something from without, for the embracing of what the West acquires through personal striving; the East is not in a position to gain these faculties through personal striving. And how, according to the model of theoretical reasoning, will one bring about a mutual understanding between two completely different spiritual impulses? How will one arrive at some sort of judgement between two different spiritual streams, which relate to one another as differentiated things must relate? Do not misunderstand the comparison if I say that it is rather like judging the habits of lions by those of elephants. Events, however, are formed by eternal necessities and take their course in accordance with them. The East had to resist what was necessary for it and becomes increasingly necessary: the connection with the West and its culture; for it could not gain the right understanding before acquiring sufficient maturity. An outward expression of this is the conflict between what one refers to as Germanic culture and what one calls Slavic culture, something which is only now in preparation and will hover over European life as a long period of unrest. Just as a child resists learning of the achievements of the old, so does the East resist the achievements of the West to the point where it hates it, even when it feels itself compelled to accept its achievements. To illuminate these things with the light of truth demands something more than what people love today; although at times they may have a sense of what this means, they are little inclined to direct their attention to such things and understand them from their innermost impulses. For if they were to be affected only to a small degree by these impulses, much of the idle chatter that goes on, which is derived merely from the confusion that is ensnared by the maya of outward appearances, would soon cease.

What will one have to understand by the notion of the sixth cultural epoch? It should be understood as a cultural epoch within which a large part of Eastern human beings will have sacrificed their individual humanity to what has been achieved within the folk culture, in that the East will have let itself be fructified as a feminine entity by the masculine West. What will live in the souls of the sixth cultural period will be the same as what has been achieved by the souls of the fifth cultural period. This means that something that has not yet gained maturity will be flailing about and defending itself against that which must happen. Just as the Graeco-Roman world had to defend itself against the Germanic invasions, so must the Slavic world defend itself against the Germanic world; but whereas the transition from the Graeco-Roman to the Germanic was one of ascending evolution, the transition from the Germanic to the Slavic is one of descending evolution. Inasmuch as the essential task of the fifth cultural epoch has been taken on by the Germanic element, it was this Germanic element that had through inner striving to bring—and will continue to bring—an understanding of Christianity appropriate to this fifth cultural epoch into earthly evolution. It would have been the greatest misfortune in the long run if the Germanic element were to have been conquered by the Roman, for the personal striving represented by the Germanic element that occurred through the fifth cultural epoch would not have been able to happen. And it would be the greatest misfortune if the Slavic element should ever conquer the Germanic.[22] Note the difference. It would be a case of the most hopelessly abstract schematizing if one were to describe something as a misfortune at the transition from the fifth to the sixth cultural epoch which one would have to describe as a misfortune at the transition from the fourth to the fifth cultural epoch. The victory of the Romans would have meant that the mission of the fifth cultural epoch would have been impossible; the victory of the Slavic element would likewise signify a similar impossibility for the sixth cultural epoch. For the significance of the sixth cultural epoch can consist only in the passive acceptance of what the fifth cultural epoch brings forth.

One needs to gain a sense of what follows quite independently of ambitions and national aspirations from these insights when they become a living force; but one must also be clear how difficult it will be for people to understand when the truth is at variance with their passions, or even with their aspirations. If one is wanting to convince, say, someone from Western Europe or England from a Central European standpoint through logical reasoning today, one is doing something that one can see is doomed to failure, in so far as it involves national conflict. We understand one another as human beings on a purely spiritual-scientific foundation; but when one moves away from this foundation and enters into the conflicts between nations, one should be fully aware what difficulties lie in the path of mutual understanding. There is only one way in which understanding will be gained, for example, in the French parts of Western Europe of what is actually going on. It is the path that will arise from the knowledge that it is a travesty of nature that people in the French part of the West are now letting themselves be driven along by the leading-strings of the European East. Only the knowledge of what one has oneself done will bring some understanding, not words coming from others, from those standing on a different national soil. Such things are felt and sensed for a time but then forgotten again; for the most characteristic events that take place are as a rule forgotten.

If only it could have been possible during the last forty years to keep in print the remarkable correspondence[23] between the Frenchman Ernest Renan and David Friedrich Strauß, the German from Württemberg! It would have been useful if people could have been reminded, say, every four weeks of the important letters that were exchanged, since this would have given them some idea of what was inevitable. One needs only to refer to a passage in Renan's letter, where he expresses the longing to collaborate with Central Europe on behalf of West-European culture: this was an impulse that flowed from the forces of eternity. But then Renan immediately goes on to say: but this is inconsistent with my sense of patriotism. For if Alsace-Lorraine is taken away from the French, as a Frenchman I will inevitably be in favour of protecting Western culture from the East. Everything that has happened since is present in seed-form in this statement; it is the seed of what was later to come about. It shows that even an enlightened and inspirational figure openly acknowledged: Yes, I can see where the path lies that is prescribed by eternal necessities, but I do not wish to follow it because I am first and foremost a Frenchman rather than a human being. What I am saying is that people have felt and intuited how things stand in the sense of eternal necessity; but they must gradually learn through spiritual science to follow up their feelings and intuitions with their judgement. They must learn to arrive with their judgement at the true facts. And one does not come to see the true facts without spiritual perception, without having recourse to what the spiritual world reveals of their evolutionary impulse.

We see how what comes from spiritual science can be fruitful for us, how we can shed light on life's most serious events if we embrace in a heart-felt way what derives from true spiritual-scientific knowledge, for example regarding the post-Atlantean cultural epochs. We shall then acquire an objective yardstick, the possibility of extricating ourselves from personal aspirations even on the delicate ground of national experience. And it is the distinctive quality of Central European experience that it really gives people the possibility of transcending a purely national orientation. One should but try to realize that in successive cultural epochs it is Central Europe that— in its wrestling with the soul—within the personal at the same time overcomes the personal, where it does not rest upon the ground of passions and directly instinctive impulses.

Other nations have, to be sure, experienced what beauty is; but the way that Schiller inwardly reflected about beauty and the place of beauty in human experience in his *Aesthetic Letters*[24] is to be found only in Central Europe. Other nations have certainly engaged in battles and will continue to do so; but to be so immersed in a battle that it called forth the deepest philosophical impulses in order to ensoul the battle with these impulses, as Fichte[25] did in his *Address to the German Nation*, that has only been done in Central Europe. Religious wars have been fought elsewhere; but nowhere else in the world have religious wars been so connected with all branches of human experience as they have been in Central Europe.

Consider, moreover, our anthroposophical movement itself as it has developed among us, as we—at any rate a number of us—have struggled, fought and also suffered within it over recent years. We were for a time connected with the English-oriented theosophical movement. What was the deep impulse that no longer permitted this connection with that theosophical movement? Can we be clear, my dear friends, about the nature of this deep impulse? Consider the movement further. What was it that could lead to that absurdity of Krishnamurti[26] and follies of that kind? It was specifically this—that the conviction that they had of the spiritual life was of an external element tacked on to the rest of culture. They are two distinct things: the outward and philosophical life-conception of England, and then—tacked on to it without the two having much to do with one another—a spiritual conviction. There has not even been the need to establish a connection between them. Here we have the sense that we can only come to a spiritual conviction if it grows, in the way that the head grows out of the body, from all that was cultivated by Johannes Tauler,[27] Meister Eckhardt[28] and Angelus Silesius[29] in the mysticism of the Middle Ages and has passed through German philosophy and poetry by way of spiritual preparation, if what we want and must want to achieve grows of necessity out of this as a new member of an organism. We cannot tack spiritual life on to the rest of life; we need a life organism, not a life mechanism. One can be clear about such things without succumbing to arrogance, for one needs clarity as to how the spiritual aspect must relate to other aspects of life and how through it one can encompass and take hold of the rest of life. As devotees of the world-outlook of spiritual science we must be able to become souls whose intentions lie in the direction of the characterization that has been given of the spiritual life of Central Europe. To be sure, a struggle is also involved here; indeed, it has to be said that the truth can only be attained by thrusting errors to both sides of the path. How difficult it sometimes is to recognize how necessary this is! One's experience of recent decades has tragically borne witness to this.

I should like to put something clearly before you. Especially now it has a certain significance by way of indicating how the natural link between the two Central European countries has arisen in our time. In the second half of the nineteenth century there lived in Austria one of the most German of poets, Robert Hamerling.[30] He was also German through the way that he really sought to give birth again to the whole world in his own soul. In his *Ahasuerus* he traces the erring human soul back to Cain, and in his comparison of Ahasuerus with Nero he attempted to solve deep riddles of the human soul. In his *Aspasia* he tried to give birth again to Greek cultural life out of the German soul. That deepening of the religious life that was sought at a certain time he tried to resolve for himself in his Anabaptist epic *The*

King of Sion; while in his play *Danton and Robespierre* he endeavoured to clarify to himself the progressive impulses in the French Revolution. Finally, in his *Homunculus* he sought to give expression to the future trends that cast a shadow over the spiritual aspect of life. But I could say much in order to show the extent to which Robert Hamerling was so thoroughly a Central European and a German spirit.

For a large part of his life Robert Hamerling was bed-ridden; and during his last three decades he was almost always ill. He wrote his greatest works when confined to bed and in pain; but no one would know from these books that they were written by someone who was seriously ill. Everything about them is healthy; one can make whatever judgement about them that one wishes, but they radiate good health. It is true that his works have gone through a number of editions; but in the 1880s I had something like a symbolic perception of what such a spirit could have meant for a part of Central European humanity if his impulses had flowed into their souls. When the theme under discussion in a society was Robert Hamerling's contribution to cultural development, a person came in who was accustomed to hearing himself speak and not paying much attention to what anyone else was saying—there are such people who like hearing their own voice. He declared as though dropping a bombshell that the greatest book in the world is Dostoyevsky's 'Raskolnikov'.[31] Of course, there is no question of denying the greatness of Dostoyevsky's novel, but clinging to materiality, to the soul that is bound to matter and leaves out the spirit, contrasts strongly with the interpenetration of the spiritual and material that Hamerling sought. It may indeed be more interesting and sensational to observe the soul that does not want to leave the material realm and which is magnificently portrayed by Dostoyevsky, but for someone from Central Europe the knowledge of the interpenetration of the spirit and the body signifies knowledge of his whole being and his whole task. This, too, entails a struggle.

In addition to the outer battle there will also be the inner one, that inner battle waged against the opposing powers in their towering might to recognize the spirit. We are in this regard now experiencing the strangest things. From a certain quarter[32] we have been exhorted not to pay too much attention to how the spiritual powers in Europe may be arrayed against one another; for if the purely German was victorious—and this is coming from the German side!—one would have to fear a revival of the kind of ideas that Hegel, Fichte, Schelling and Goethe put forward: one would be in dread of metaphysical dreaming. It is a peculiar fear that is being spoken of; but this fear could become ever greater, and those who have this fear will not be able to accept the spiritual dimension. But the truth is that the idealism of Central Europe must develop towards spirituality as does the child to the man; for this idealism of Central Europe is the child of spirituality, the child that is to gravitate to the spirit. When Fichte spoke, he spoke not merely of idealism but of an idealism that aspires to the spirit. This impulse of spiritualism must not disappear from earthly evolution.

Much of what is meaningful in our time can be expressed with these simple words. There are certain individuals who have sensed and felt these things; but these glimpses of reality pass by without being grasped at a deeper level, without the gravity of the situation being perceived. There is a failure to link what is of secondary importance with what really matters. What really matters is that one does not lose sight of the main lines of direction, that one really sees what is essential in the streams that flow through earthly evolution. And we come to what is most essential when we let ourselves be instructed by what this earthly evolution shows us in the light of the spirit. In particular, if we take really seriously the teaching of the successive post-Atlantean epochs, it must again and again be said that we must get beyond that narrow standpoint that is unable to see the whole picture.

Let me give an example. Among ourselves it is necessary to pay attention to such things. Let us suppose that someone might say the following, and let us try to form some thoughts about it if someone were to say this today[33]: 'As far as I am concerned, I do not doubt for a moment that there exists a conflict between the Germanic and Slavic world, that this is kindled either through the Orient and especially through Turkey or through the conflict between nationalities in Austria or perhaps through both, and that Russia will take a leading role in this conflict on one side. This power is already now preparing itself for this eventuality; the national Russian press is spewing fire and flame against Germany. The German press is already sounding its warning cry. A long time has passed since the Crimean War, and Russia has been gathering its forces; and it appears that in Petersburg a sense of purpose has now been found to take up the Oriental question again. If the Mediterranean should at some point become—to use an expression that is more pompous than real—a "French sea", Russia has the still more active intention of making a "Russian sea" out of the Black Sea and a "Russian pond" out of the Sea of Marmora. It is a firmly established goal of Russian politics that Constantinople should be a Russian city and Greece a vassal state of Russia; and this goal finds a supportive lever in the common religion and in Pan-slavism. The Danube would then be closed at the Iron Gate by the Russian barrier.'

Let us suppose that someone would speak in this way. One could then say: Well, he has been learning from what has just been happening; and yet those who emphatically preach that the war was only wanted by Central Europe and has not necessarily been prepared by the East could nevertheless be right. But this was written in 1870! And indeed, not one year has passed when such things have not been written. How foolish it is to believe that the cause of what is happening today is not to be sought in the forces that have been at work over long periods of time! These words were written in 1870, during the war with France. To believe that present events were not bound to come about, and to think that not all impulses were given by the East, is—to put it mildly—unhistorical, a failure to recognize all the forces that have been most effectively at work. A situation that should not be and which must be prevented by spiritual science is that again and again people, including journalists, express their judgement that the origins of the events that are taking place now were only five or six months ago! When people have been schooled by spiritual science to know that great happenings are prepared by smaller events and that smaller events can be judged only from their broader context will it be possible for something to be gained from spiritual science for ordinary life, something that makes spiritual science an actual experience for us.

I have been wanting, or I should say I have been having, to speak to you in this introductory lecture today again from a certain point of view which is demanded by the experiences of the time. I have been obliged to speak of what spiritual science should become for our judgement of world affairs and for our position in the world. I have been obliged to speak of this. We must indeed again and again take account of this warning to take deeply seriously what spiritual science wishes to give us and not, as it were, to want to live two lives: that life where we explain world-events in the sense of spiritual science and that life where we become absorbed in everyday affairs and imitate what others also do. But it is not so much through words as through the way that I have presented things here in this limited circle that I would wish to evoke within you the feeling that these words desire to be nothing other than eternal truths, in the sense that eternal truths are also the most individual. These words, my dear friends, are addressed to you and to your feelings here in South Germany, with the nuance of feeling that must belong to them here. And if it were enough for these words simply to be transcribed and read aloud everywhere before people in different life's circumstances, it would also be sufficient if I were simply to write my words down and not travel around. In spiritual life it must ultimately be realized that words must be spoken out of particular contexts of feeling and awareness, because where people are gathered together there is a common human aura out of which one must speak.

What matters is that we make everything alive, and that this intention does not remain a mere slogan but becomes a living reality. This means that things need to be considered on an individual basis. They are after all individual phenomena, because they must happen individually. And it would be an abstract belief if one were to suppose that, for example, what I shall say the day after tomorrow in the public lecture[34] in the house that stands opposite the building where there is a memorial tablet to Hegel, that what is expressed in this directly individual situation will apply abstractly to all shades of feeling, as it were for the conversion of the entire world. One must also realize that what one person can grasp, the other is unable to do so. Moreover, if anthroposophical lectures have a certain individual character depending on the situation, this is so to an even greater degree when one confronts such serious matters as we do today. But only when one takes truth seriously, and when one does not believe that what is living can be grasped with words that are lifeless and lacking in vitality and therefore can be universally conveyed, will one understand the general validity of what is most individual. I should like you to reflect upon this aspect of life.

One way to achieve this will be that what I have in my way to bring out of the spiritual world becomes alive in your souls in your own way, so that it is not merely a repetition of what I have been obliged to express. Just as sunlight is reflected differently in every stone or pebble and yet is always the same sunlight because it is part of life, so must spiritual science become something that lives differently in every individual and yet is always and ever the same. Where matters of nationality are concerned, spiritual science cannot live only in *one* way in the Englishman, the Frenchman, the Russian, the German, and the one cannot be swayed by what stirs most strongly in the feelings of the other. Such a desire to persuade or convert arises from the theoretical tendency of our time. The approach adopted by outward, purely materialistic science to lump everything together cannot be the way of spiritual science, because it is something living and because I must speak to you not as an abstract scientific spirit might demand of me but as it becomes alive in me in that I am standing before *you*, for I am doing this not out of *my* heart but out of *your* heart to the extent that I am able. And I would wish to serve the spiritual-scientific impulse which directs the one who has some insight into the spiritual world to eliminate himself and to express what lies in the depths of the souls of those who listen to him.

In a certain sense it may be said that what is expressed in this or that connection springs from the depths of the listeners' souls. Do reflect on this! We must relate to spiritual science as something that is living and not to be known in an abstract sense. Abstract knowledge speaks to our arrogance, to our self-conceit, which so delights in the art of persuasion. What is spiritual wants to be communicated simply; and what I have imparted wanted to be imparted, even if there was not even one person sitting here who believed a single word of what I was saying. If we approach another person with the intention that he should accept our opinion, our experience is not right from the spiritual point of view; whereas what one experiences and comprehends in the direct experiencing of the spiritual world will bring forth the aura that mankind must have in the future.

It must again and again be said that what we are now experiencing amidst streams of blood will only signify for humanity what it ought to signify if something entirely new manifests itself in the cultural life of mankind. But this quality will spring forth if there are people from whose souls spiritual thoughts emanate; these thoughts are forces to be reckoned with. And in the atmosphere that will be engendered when the twilight of war is passed and the Sun of peace shines once more, the thoughts that pour forth into the spiritual horizon must find their place. Then those whose souls look down, those who had to leave their bodies prematurely on the battlefields, will know why they really fell on the fields of battle. And the anthroposophist must say to himself that he will only rightly live through this time if he takes up this characteristic quality of spiritual-scientific endeavour in a living way. If certain souls send their thoughts into the spiritual realm in the consciousness of the spirit, a horizon of light for the future evolution of mankind will indeed rise up from our horizon of blood.

We will continue tomorrow by discussing a particular theme. For today, however, we shall call before our souls the thoughts that unite us with the grave events of our time:

> From the courage of the fighters,
> From the blood on fields of battle,
> From the grief of the bereaved,
> From the people's sacrifice:
> There will ripen fruit of spirit,
> If souls will turn in consciousness
> Towards the realm of spirit.

Lecture 3

STUTTGART, 14 FEBRUARY 1915

I CAN easily imagine that someone may draw the conclusion from what was said yesterday that because those people who belong to the human or national groups which are to receive their special mission only in the sixth cultural period belong to the time when—as was said yesterday—evolution is already on a descending path, they are of less account than those belonging to human groups associated with an ascending trajectory of evolution. I repeat that I can well imagine someone drawing this conclusion. In other words, I can easily imagine that from everything that was said yesterday and from other statements someone may be impelled by all kinds of feelings and emotions to make a value-judgement. Thus what I emphasized yesterday can indeed happen, that something that is said with regard to these matters in *one* place will be misconstrued in *another* place. This is not because it is coloured by the needs of a place or particular people but because it is not comprehended with the necessary objectivity but, rather, with passion and all manner of nationalistic aspirations. Someone might then say that I had merely been using words to say nice things about Central European culture, and those of us who belong to the culture of Eastern Europe feel deeply offended by what was said. Well, if such a judgement is made it only goes to show that what I tried to say yesterday becomes clearly apparent, that such notions must be banished by a spiritual-scientific awareness to the point where a purely theoretical abstract thinking is transformed into direct experience, so that what is otherwise merely a matter of knowledge is imbued with feeling and real experience.

Were someone to form the judgement that has just been indicated, he would be judging purely theoretically and abstractly; for what would be the nature of a judgement based on actual experience in such a case? It would amount to this—that, provided that what was explained yesterday is true, we are approaching a time when those who want to follow the advance of cultural progress should no longer be absorbed in a purely national experience. The fifth cultural epoch has had the distinctive quality that those belonging to it have in a certain sense been absorbed in national feelings and have been engaged in personal struggles on this basis. The sixth and seventh cultural epochs will be of such a nature that those who want to be merely national will lag behind the tasks of humanity. And this is the reason why we pursue the spiritual-scientific view that humanity needs to extricate itself from a purely national sensibility, from a sensibility that is not universally human in nature. Thus what may be concluded from what was said yesterday is something quite else, namely that the national cultures of Central Europe have within them cultural impulses that coincide with the great mission of post-Atlantean culture, but that there will then be cultures that make it necessary for human beings to grow beyond national impulses and that it is not all right if those who are the forerunners of later cultures are wholly absorbed in their national experience and even in an exaggerated way, as is the case with those living in Eastern Europe. In other words, since in their nationalistic feeling they have not yet embraced their mission, the indication to them is that they receive what has emerged in the form of spiritual science in order to grow beyond national feelings. A living understanding is also necessary here.

At this present time which is so beset with passions and prejudices, it will to be sure be difficult to find what is necessary in order that people may stand fully on the ground of spiritual science and its striving for true objectivity, on the ground of the universally human. We pursue spiritual science in order that something may spread throughout the Earth that extends beyond all differences; and those who turn to spiritual science from all nations should be able to gain an objective understanding of what was presented in the lecture-cycle that bears the title *The Mission of Folk Souls*,[35] which should be studied wherever there are anthroposophists. It is, moreover, of significance precisely because it was given some years before this war, so that no one can reproach it for having been engendered out of the mood of the war. What matters is not so much that what was said in one place or another contained generally valid truths but, rather, that one has to recognize that these truths are not universally tolerated. When I spoke here some months ago,[36] I drew attention to the fact that that we in Central Europe find it easier to be objective, easier than it is for others. Why this is so also becomes apparent from that lecture-cycle. Everything that the grave events surrounding us can teach us demonstrates that something must develop from the various subterranean depths of our present world-culture that is utterly consistent with our spiritual-scientific endeavours. In a certain respect one can say that these serious events are something like a powerful indication of the necessity for spiritual science to become a living experience in the world. They constitute a proof that this spiritual-scientific experience must come. What relates to the immediate feelings of a place can therefore, of course, be only of secondary importance for us; our actual task is to embrace within our inner experience what can now be understood everywhere without causing offence, despite the immense prejudice that is evident in so many areas.

What we learn from spiritual science about the universally human aspect of man also prepares us to be able to survey objectively all that is made available to us to experience through earthly evolution; for the circumstances in which we are placed are in a sense the ground from which we grow, what brings about our growth are the impulses that we receive through spiritual science. But we are actually only involved in all the differences extended throughout the Earth with our physical and etheric bodies, which we leave behind on the Earth when we enter the other state of consciousness that we may designate as sleep. When with our ego and astral body we leave our physical and etheric bodies we are in the world that the human individual enters when he goes through the portal of death, the world where all earthly differentiations cease, the world to which the insights of spiritual science are intended to lead us. Anyone who is able to develop initiation knowledge into insights of his own is indeed protected by this initiation knowledge from giving any of the Folk-spirits a special preference. But then, how do we come in contact with the particular Folk-spirit to whom we belong?

When with our ego and astral body we are dwelling in the spiritual world between going to sleep and waking up, we are not in contact with our Folk-spirit, with the Folk-spirit who in a certain sense represents our nationality, but we are in contact with this Folk-spirit during our waking life from awakening until going to sleep. Among the forces into which we dive down when we are immersed in the physical and etheric bodies are also the forces within which the Folk-spirit of the people to which we belong is working. We enter the domain of this Folk-spirit when we wake up; we leave it again when we go to sleep. However, someone who acquires initiation knowledge must, while he is acquiring this knowledge, dwell in the world where his Folk-spirit is not present, for he must enter the world in which we live between going to sleep and waking up. And here something quite particular emerges. Let us suppose that a person belongs to a particular nation. Of course, this applies to everyone, in that each person must be reckoned as belonging to a specific nationality. When as he goes to sleep he leaves the sphere of his Folk-spirit, he is no longer in contact with this Folk-spirit until he wakes up again. Then there may also be someone who is able to acquire initiation knowledge, and during the time between going to sleep he comes to be with the spirits of other peoples living elsewhere on the Earth—but not with his own Folk-spirit. Thus one lives together with the other Folk-spirits in the time between going to sleep and waking up and with one's own Folk-spirit during the time between waking up and going to sleep. However, this living together with the other Folk-spirits is not similar to the way that one lives with each one separately, for one lives with their collectivity, as it were, with their comradeship, with what they accomplish in relation to one another, with the totality of the other Folk-spirits.

So you see that, according to initiation knowledge, human life alternates between an experience with one's Folk-spirit in waking consciousness and an experience with the totality of the other

Folk-spirits during sleep. There is, however, *one* means whereby we may have an abnormal relationship with the other Folk-spirits, when we do not enter into connection with them as a totality in sleep but with one particular Folk-spirit. This is when we have an especially passionate hatred for a nation. The abnormal situation is that when our hatred of a nation is especially strong, we cannot avoid coming into the sphere of its Folk-spirit during sleep; and if someone who acquires initiation knowledge particularly hates a nation for purely personal, nationalistic reasons he would make his way to the sphere of its Folk-spirit directly upon entering the realm of initiation, and he would very soon find it impossible to remain there in an orderly manner. To put it bluntly, I could say that anyone who especially hates another nation out of nationalistic, personal passions is con-demned to sleep with its Folk-spirit. This is a brutal way of putting it, but it should be taken quite literally.

The reality of the spiritual world is such that it endeavours to ensure that the whole human race is a unity, and that separating one-self from it is not possible. But when we consider such a reality, we can learn so much from it. We speak of how the world in which we outwardly live with our senses and our intellectual faculties that are bound to the brain is a great illusion, a maya; but even this truth that the world is a form of maya we take all too abstractly and theoreti-cally. I could say that we content ourselves with grasping this truth intellectually. To understand it in a living way is something that is resisted not only by our intellect but often even our will; for what lies behind the world of illusion is something that we do not want to see. We fight shy of it and fear it, because the truth is uncomfortable. To know that the whole of mankind is actually a unity is not com-fortable; it does not permit us to regard feelings and enthusiasms in the one-sided way that they are generally regarded today and leads us to understand what this signifies in the world of reality. But this is not comfortable. The will often shrinks even more from the truth than does our active discernment, our intellect. We should there-fore not be surprised if the truths of spiritual science are frequently dismissed as folly, for the folly of the age is afraid of the wisdom of the world. Only by looking behind the appearances is there the possibility of understanding what is actually happening. I have already spoken of this yesterday and will explain it further by means of a particular instance.

When we peruse the way that a person passes through the gate of death into the spiritual world, where he prepares for a new earthly life during the time between death and a new birth, we must be clear to what extent he is influenced by his last earthly life in his life between death and a new birth, to what extent he brings the after-effects, the reverberations of his last earthly life into the spiritual world through the gate of death. We know that when someone passes through the gate of death and has given his physical body over to the earthly elements, he initially carries his etheric body, astral body and ego across this threshold. We also know that the etheric body separates very soon from the ego and astral body (with the exception of an extract of it that remains behind), and that the etheric body unites etherically with the overall activity of the cosmos. We have often called this to mind. The fact is, however, that through the knowledge that remains to him after his death a person nevertheless looks back after death at the destiny of his etheric body, which has a significance for him. It means something to him after death to see what happens to his etheric body and to see that the course it follows is in a sense a result of his earthly life.

Now what results from the earthly life differs in accordance with different earthly circumstances, including differing experiences of nationality. The earthly residues that have a significance for someone after death are, for example, completely different for a soul leaving a French body and passing into the spiritual world than for a soul passing today into the spiritual world from a Russian body. Souls coming from French bodies today belong to a culture that has become mature to the point of over-maturity and enables such an etheric body to experience much on the Earth. The distinctive quality of the culture of the French people in general—as opposed to the culture of the individual—consists in that the etheric body is pervaded and imbued with forces and influences and therefore passes through the gate of death and then into the spiritual world in a very sharply formed way. Such etheric bodies do not dissolve for a long time; they remain for a long while as spectres. A person of French origin, in so far as he is representative of the French national character, has a quite definite opinion of himself and of his significance in the world. This is, however, none other than the reflection of the rigidifying forces in the etheric body. The etheric body is rigidly moulded and passes in that condition into the spiritual world. In the case of the etheric body of someone from Russia it is completely different. It is not so rigidly formed, it is more elastic and dissolves more easily in the spiritual world; the souls are therefore less firmly bound by it. Whereas in contemplating the highly cultured etheric body of the Frenchman the French soul is connected for a longer time with the etheric body, the soul of the Russian has only a brief connection with the etheric body. What the etheric body undergoes after death is of less significance for this Eastern soul. This does, however, have a very definite, far-reaching and important influence upon what is happening behind the scenes at the present time. The destiny of the Russian soul is altogether different from that of the French soul in the time between death and a new birth.

We know from various studies that we are in the twentieth century approaching the etheric activity of the Christ Spirit. At a particular point in the Mystery Play *The Portal of Initiation*[37] there is an indication in an exoteric sense of the reappearance of Christ as an etheric bodily vessel. It has also been indicated in several contexts[38] that this appearance of Christ to those people who will be capable of beholding Him has been in preparation since the last third of the nineteenth century, in that the active Time-spirit since this time has been different from before. For several centuries before this, Gabriel had been the active Time-spirit; since the last third of the nineteenth century this role has fallen to Michael. It is Michael who has in a certain sense prepared Christ's appearance as an etheric being. All this has to be prepared, it has to be made possible in terms of evolution and this is what has been happening. It is made possible through Michael leading the battle for the appearance of Christ, through his preparation of souls in their experience between death and a new birth for what has to happen in the Earth's aura. Now where there are sharply moulded etheric bodies around us in the elemental world, they will always be a disturbing influence in the time which must approach when the etheric form that Christ must assume needs to be clearly perceived. Those souls who are less disturbed by their etheric bodies after death are better adapted for a clear perception of this etheric form. Hence the following scenario emerges.

We see that one part of Michael's work consists in contributing to the dissolution of the rigidly formed etheric bodies of highly civilized Western Europeans, and we also see that in this struggle he makes use of East-European souls. Thus we see Michael followed by the hosts of East-European souls battling against the West-European etheric bodies and the impressions that souls have after death. So behind the scenes of present-day existence a lively battle is taking place. This battle in the spiritual world is a present reality. This battle in the heavens is, as it were, taking place in the spiritual world between Russia and France, a living battle between East and West. And this battle is the truth; what is taking place in the physical world is the outward maya, the distortion of the truth. Here too, as so often when one studies the spiritual facts, one receives in this realm the deeply distressing impression that what is taking place here in the sphere of illusion is the exact opposite of what is happening as a true reality in the spiritual world.

Just imagine the terrible shock for anyone who possesses initiation knowledge that an alliance exists between nations which are in the most bitter conflict with one another in the spiritual world! One should, of course, not make generalizations, one should not draw the conclusion that in the spiritual world *everything* is opposite to the physical world. Each individual case must be investigated. But with respect to this case we receive this deeply distressing impression which, I might say, is devastating for what we know. Thus behind the scenes of existence things frequently look very different from the way they appear in the outer world. And yet they become comprehensible in their true context only when we can shed light on what is going on behind the scenes through spiritual science. Then our whole way of looking at things can be imbued with feelings that, as it were, open our hearts to the truth, in contrast to the prejudices in which we are inevitably ensnared when we give ourselves up to the streams enveloping the outer, physical world.

Central Europe is actually wedged today between two opposing powers and must, so to speak, keep them apart. From this, however, derives the connection between what I described yesterday as the struggle of Central Europe and that which oppresses this culture of Central Europe from left and right as though encircling it. This is the karma of Central European culture: to see its development unfolding between a battle that must inevitably take place through a necessity of earthly history. The right feelings with respect to the tragic conflict inherent in the circumstances now affecting Central Europe can only arise from such an awareness. Only if we base our understanding on such a knowledge do we realize that what is truly characteristic of Central Europe is indeed not to participate in the affairs that are actually being fought over, to have an innocent relation to them and an involvement in their common karma. And we have now also seen how this accords precisely with what belongs to evolution: we have seen that Eastern and Western Europe have a participatory role in the coming Christ event. When we consider the endeavour of Central European culture that I characterized yesterday to unite the spiritual and the bodily aspects of life, we also have the specific nature of the Christ impulse, which is after all the bearer of this union between the spirit and the body. Thus in the middle of Europe there is the phenomenon of leading Christianity into earthly events. Here, taking place on the physical plane, something of immense importance, and on the right and the left something that is first being fought out on the higher planes. The physical and spiritual planes come together when we regard them in this way.

This is the addition to what was outlined yesterday. And so it is in fact with all evolution, in so far as it has gradually unfolded under the influence of the Christ impulse; for what is happening now in the twentieth century has been a gradual process of development. The Christ impulse has entered into the earthly evolution of humanity through the Mystery of Golgotha, and it has been active within it. But if the Christ impulse had only been able to work in accordance with people's understanding of it, it would have been largely ineffectual. Only through spiritual science do we begin to have something of an understanding of the nature of the Mystery of Golgotha.

The Christ impulse has been an active force; but it has actually been least active in the quarrels and disputes of theologians. It would have been dreadful if only as much of the Christ impulse had been able to make its mark upon earthly evolution as human beings have understood in the various epochs with their intellect. However, I have indicated how the Christ impulse has been working over the centuries in unconscious soul-forces. I have described to you[39] how on 28 October 312 Constantine confronted Maxentius, and how a battle was fought then which determined the destiny of Europe.[40] The dominant factor in this battle was not the skill of the generals but what was going on in people's subconscious minds. Maxentius consulted the Sibylline books. They seduced him into leading his army out of Rome to confront Constantine's armies instead of letting it remain in safety there. However, Constantine dreamt of having Christ's monogram carried before his army. It was therefore not the skills of the generals that were the source of guidance but dreams, that is, the impulses of the subconscious. From what resulted from this, Europe derived its future form. The actual configuration of the Christ impulse derived not from what the theologians were disputing but from what the living Christ made manifest on the fields where He is able to work. What matters are not human conceptions of Christ but the living Christ, who works through impulses that are His own. When people did not understand Him, He entered into a realm where one does not need to understand, where one apprehends in dreams what is to make the transition to the sphere of the will.

It was again in Europe that the Christ impulse intervened and gave Europe a particular configuration, when in the fifteenth century it was endowed with a different form by a simple country girl, the Maid of Orleans.[41] Had England conquered France at that time (which the Maid of Orleans prevented), the whole course of history would have been different. The shepherd girl of Orleans did not possess human wisdom, but the Christ impulse exerted an influence upon her through its forerunner Michael outwardly in favour of France but actually for the good of England. England would otherwise not have been able to go through the development that it underwent. To anyone who wants to gain spiritual insight into the world, it is transparently clear that the Christ impulse was actively engaged in what was to come about.

I have often pointed out that those legends, those ancient myths and sagas, contain truths that indicate that the period of the thirteen nights between Christmas and the festival of Epiphany (the festival of the Three Kings), the period of the deepest winter darkness, is the time when the Earth forces are especially favourable for clairvoyance. When the physical forces are most withdrawn into inactivity, the spiritual forces are able to work most strongly. An old Norwegian legend[42] relates to us that Olaf Åsteson lay asleep during these thirteen nights from Christmas until 6 January. In this sleep he experienced in imaginations all that we recognize anthroposophically as kamaloka, as the soul-world and the spirit-world. This is a truth. And many a person who, I might say, stands at the gate of initiation can enable this initiation to find fulfilment if he brings it to an especially concentrated point of inner experience at this time, which rightly coincides with the birth of Christ, the spiritual light of the Sun. One might ask: If someone is to experience an unconscious initiation, when would be the best time for this? He would experience it best if he is prepared during these nights, if he is in a state of sleep, a kind of withdrawal from the world, in the time prior to the sixth of January. Might we not suppose that also the shepherd girl, the Maid of Orleans, who was certainly not learned or trained in spiritual science but was inwardly spiritual in nature, could have been best initiated if she had spent these nights in a kind of sleep condition, when she had not been perceiving the outer world with her senses and her intellect? But this is what she did! During the time before one's physical birth, one is certainly not able to perceive the surrounding world through one's senses, for these senses awaken when one is born to physical existence. One is also not capable before birth of using one's reasoning powers, for one's mental faculties are in contact with the surrounding spiritual cosmos.

Now the Maid of Orleans spent the thirteen days before the sixth of January in her mother's body, for she was born on that day. This is a fact that conveys something deeply significant concerning world circumstances. The cosmic spirit guiding evolution needed, in the

Maid of Orleans, a human soul who had spent the last thirteen days of pregnancy up to the sixth of January in the body of her mother and was then born. Here we have a deep insight into those circumstances lying behind the scenes of existence. A soul was born who had been initiated up to the time of her birth by the cosmic spirit itself. It is therefore a question of acquiring a feeling of how the tapestry of outward maya-existence is spread out before us: only if we pierce through it in various places do we gain insight into the mysteries of existence. And this must engender a sense for the transformative quality of spiritual culture. The feeling must arise that in order to behold the mysteries of the world there must be a radical break with the mere observation of outward maya, which did of course have to become a feature of life since the brilliance and glory of natural-scientific research. But this brilliance and glory must for the future be replaced by spiritual science. And what will above all be needed by humanity if spiritual science is really to live within souls is a truly good will for the connection of one's own soul with the spiritual worlds, which necessarily entails a certain self-knowledge. However, self-knowledge is by no means so easy, and one of the greatest illusions that one can fall prey to in ordinary life is to think that self-knowledge, which must be the beginning of all true knowledge, is easy.

It is not even particularly easy where it concerns the most external aspects of life. I have here a book which has whether accidentally or—as I would say—karmically come into my hands again recently. This is the book of a present-day philosopher[43] who was Professor of Philosophy at the University of Vienna, and it is entitled *Analysis of Sensations*. The author of the book makes some confessions which are very interesting. On page 3 he says: As a young man I once caught sight of my face in profile in a shop-window. I thought: What a disagreeable, unpleasant face! Thus you see that even at this level, knowledge of one's purely outward form is not so very widespread. The good man confesses quite openly that a highly unpleasant face with a repugnant character is coming towards him, and then he discovers that it is his own. So little had he known his outward appearance. So you see that not even outward self-knowledge is easily acquired. As this example shows, this does not prevent one from being a university professor. Ernst Mach, which is the name of this professor, also makes a similar confession. He is perfectly honest. He says: I was once returning very tired after a journey and boarded a bus. At the same time someone else also got onto the bus. I thought to myself what a down-at-heel schoolmaster that is, but then I realized it was myself. He had seen himself in the mirror. The good man knew what a down-at-heel schoolmaster looks like and he saw one get onto the bus, but he was not able to identify himself with this person; he did not know that *he* looked like that. He adds: Thus I knew the schoolmaster type better than my own demeanour!

Knowledge of the soul, knowledge of what we actually are in our soul-nature, is much more difficult than knowledge of one's outer form. But without this one will not get anywhere if one really wants to make progress in the realm of initiation. Illusion concerning oneself is one of the commonest human characteristics, and people generally have no idea of what is going on in the depths of the human soul. It is very easy to think: Yes, I know myself, I know what I want! People form certain ideas about themselves; but these are generally of no help when it comes to expressing what we really are. Within the soul itself things often look quite different from how they appear to be in the region where we form these ideas about ourselves. Here are some examples of what not only can but often does happen in human life. Two people are living together. One of them has something against the other, so that he actually takes pleasure in sometimes tormenting and giving pain to the other, sometimes more and sometimes less intensely. The original cause may be an instinctive urge for cruelty. A person may seemingly go about the world as someone who is quite harmless but nevertheless has a cruel side to him and feels a need to torment his fellows. If you speak with this person, he will not forgive you if you consider him to be a cruel rascal who only feels satisfied if he can torment his fellows, but he will say: Oh, I'm very fond of this person, I like him very much, but he does this and that and the other and just because I like him so much I cannot bear it when he does this! This is the person's upper consciousness, but in his subconscious there is cruelty. And the notions living in the upper consciousness are only there in order to cast a veil, to excuse us to ourselves. The way that we form conceptions in our upper consciousness arises out of our wish to give ourselves an excuse. I once knew a man who emphasized at every opportunity that he was pursuing a certain spiritual path out of pure selflessness. I said to him: Your opinion about the things that you do and why you do them is not the point; what matters is why you do them. And you do them because it gives you a kind of sensual pleasure to do just this, because it is particularly flattering to your vanity.

It is not pleasant to admit that one is actually thoroughly vain and that this is why one does something or other. We therefore love our maya, because it tells us something different. The maya that we bear in our consciousness about ourselves is often even more unlike reality than the maya that we have about spiritual science. Love is quite definitely a wonderful thing—and rightly so—in human opinion; but love is often misrepresented in what people say! When we were still connected with the other Theosophical Society, we used to hear again and again that what matters is for people to love one another, and really thoroughly! This love was often only the veil placed over dogmatic wrangling; for love can often be the mask for the most forceful egotism. When one takes a particularly pleasurable pride in doing something or other, one often falsifies what one does and what actually gives one sensual enjoyment by cloaking it in love; and one gives oneself excuses for what one would never admit, which remains in the depths of unconsciousness. Yes, if we immerse ourselves in human nature, we rapidly descend into an abyss. A person can really only come to know himself by becoming acquainted with the great laws of this spiritual existence; for man's being is complicated, and it is the greatest mistake to think that it is in any sense simple. I might say that all the mysteries of the world have been summoned forth to produce the human being; but it is necessary for things to be properly understood.

Playing with self-knowledge very soon ceases when one recognizes something of the spiritual secrets of human existence. Let us suppose that through schooling or in some other way a person arrives at a certain clairvoyance, and that he brings it to the point where wonderful images appear to him that he can convey in some way, so that people come and are quite fascinated by the remarkable connection that this person has with the spiritual world. This connection doubtless exists, but one must come to see what it can actually be in its true reality. You see, the etheric body lies at the foundation of our physical body as its moulder and fashioner, then the astral body, then what we call the bearer of the ego. All this works on the physical body, and every higher element works upon the lower. If you consider the etheric body and examine it clairvoyantly, it is a wonderful structure of interweaving and shimmering colours. What are these colours that flow within the etheric body? They are the forces that work on the physical body, forces which not only build up its organs but are also active within what is accomplished by the organs of the physical body during life. But human organs are of differing significance. Let us take two such organs, the intestines and the brain. Ordinary anatomy investigates the tissues and everything concerned with them on the basis that they are of equal value. But these things are not like that, they are of quite varying nature. If we consider the human brain, as a physical organ it has something complete about it; this is because those streams of colour have been assimilated there. If we look at the etheric body of the human brain, we see that it is relatively pale in colour, for the colours have been used to bring about the structure of the brain. If we look at the intestines, we find that the brightly shimmering colours flow in and out of each other in a wonderful way, for the intestines are actually coarser organs, not so much of the spiritual element needs to be used up in them and the forces still remain in the etheric body, a smaller portion is used purely for the up-building process. Hence the etheric body of the brain is pale, whereas the etheric body of the intestines is beautiful with wonderful flowing colours.

Now suppose that someone attains to clairvoyance in the way that I have described. There are two possibilities: clairvoyance may arise through the loosening of the etheric body of the brain, but it can also occur through the loosening of the etheric body of the intestines. Clairvoyance will often make a person aware of his inner state. Someone who loosens the etheric body of his brain will initially experience a somewhat pale world before him; whereas someone who loosens the etheric body of his intestines can reflect wonderfully flowing colours into the etheric world. In order to bring the paleness of the brain's etheric body in contact with the flowing colours of the cosmos, it is necessary that we draw these flowing colours from the whole sphere of the cosmos. In order to develop the flowing colours of the etheric body of the intestines, we can radiate them forth from ourselves; and a quite wonderful structure can be perceived on the path of clairvoyance. To be sure, it is a genuine clairvoyantly perceived structure, but when one investigates it what is it? It is none other than one's own digestive process, it is what the etheric body does during the process of human digestion; and it is this that is projected into etheric space. From an anatomic point of view this is highly interesting, but one must be clear that it is only when one penetrates into the mysteries of the spiritual world that one really has an inkling of what is actually present in the spiritual world. One is therefore only receiving a suggestion that, from a wonderfully flowing sea of colour of the etheric body there also arises what has to occur within the etheric body in order that the intestines function in the right way. When one perceives this clairvoyantly, this is certainly a clairvoyant process; but it has nothing to do with celestial mysteries, it does not bring us closer to the great cosmic facts of the world and it is, rather, something that draws us closer to our most ordinary lower self.

It is just when we rise clairvoyantly to self-knowledge that we find that the initial wonderful pictures that we experience reflect our lowest aspects. Only when through greater effort we loosen those parts of the etheric body which have to a lesser extent remained within us, because they have for the most part been used for the heart and the brain, do we succeed in radiating forth what is within us and making an impression upon the outward ether through the forces that have been more fully used. And then the following situation arises. When we project the etheric body of the physical organs, we thrust it out into space. When we develop higher clairvoyance we also work outwardly, but we externalize from ourselves what we build up between birth and death so that it may prepare what develops within us between death and a new birth. We inscribe it into space, we bring about an effect in the etheric world; and then we confront what is formed through these activities, the cosmic effects, the cosmic facts.

This is what we unremittingly work towards. The purpose of the book *Knowledge of the Higher Worlds* is primarily to ensure that the right ways are found to fathom the mysteries of the world as opposed to encountering the lower being of man through a beguiling clairvoyance. I have pointed out on several occasions that this clairvoyance is difficult, that it is pale in appearance, that one develops true clairvoyance only through great exertions of the forces that we possess between birth and death and that the mysteries of the world can then be made manifest. One can form some idea of where these forces lie if one studies what was said in the Vienna cycle of 1914.[44] Mention was made there of the forces that a person develops between death and a new birth and which only stammering words can be used to describe, because words are, after all, formulated for the physical world and all that one achieves through verbal formulations is to make it apparent how different the spiritual world is from the physical world of the senses. But people find it comfortable to imagine that the spiritual world is simply a kind of continuation of the physical world, only somewhat more fleeting. It would suit them to see figures going about in the spiritual world as they do in the physical world; but they find it uncongenial that one must accustom oneself to a new form of comprehension if one wants to enter the spiritual world. All this should indicate to you that not only the human intellect but above all the human will resist what spiritual science must now bring into the world in our time. Indeed, it can be said that it is not because large segments of the population do not understand spiritual science today that they reject it but because they do not want it, because they actually find it awful that the world is as spiritual science does and must describe it.

Of particular importance is the conception that one must have of wisdom and consciousness if one wishes to understand the experience between death and a new birth! Indeed, one absolutely cannot say that someone who has passed through the gate of death has no consciousness and must first awaken it. That is not the case; the fact is that he has too strong a consciousness when he has crossed the threshold of death, that he is wholly encompassed by consciousness, that he does not know his way about, that he is completely benumbed by the spiritual sunlight of consciousness and must first begin to orientate himself, as I have described at greater length in the cycle referred to. Here on Earth we must necessarily acquire wisdom; but in the spirit-world we are flooded on every side by wisdom, we have to dampen it down in order to perceive it. The parts that we have toned down to accommodate human weakness are those that we are able to behold. So we must first come to terms with the dimming of our consciousness in order to be able to find our way about. This is something of which one becomes particularly aware when one really observes the phenomena concerned. You see, one then tries gradually to form the words so that they rightly express these phenomena. Not long ago a dear member of our Society[45] died in Zurich. Karma brought it about that, although I had wanted to see this member again in her physical life, I arrived too late and did not see her. But then a few days later we had the cremation in Zurich. I had occasion to speak at this cremation, and I tried to formulate in words what inwardly presented itself to me as the being of this dear member of ours. I tried to capture this being in a few words. Then the cremation took place. And now it could be observed that the first orientating emergence from the excess of consciousness came at the moment when the body passed over into the burning process, when seemingly the flames, in reality the warmth, seized hold of the body. At this moment the scene that we had previously depicted presented itself to the soul of the departed. Formerly, during the funeral address, it had not participated in this, but afterwards, when the process of combustion began, it looked back. And just as in physical life one has space before one, so does a dead person see things in time. What is past is near to the dead, he sees what has been enacted before him. Time indeed becomes space. The past is not past, it rests there, it is beheld. Then the dead person descended again into a general dulling of consciousness, and it takes quite a long time until the soul is able to orient itself. But such moments of light come in preparation for this which are further extended. Then again there is a submergence into the general flood of consciousness until later a total orientation ensues.

And so one must say that it is an important notion to grasp that wisdom, consciousness, is of a different nature after death from what it is before. It is not the case that a degree of consciousness must first awaken for us after death, but consciousness in its immeasurable extent must be dimmed down to a certain level. We must be aware of this. And then we must take seriously the fact that the true nature of things is frequently the opposite of what it outwardly appears to be. I have often illustrated this by means of an example. Someone is walking beside a stream, he falls into it and is drowned. We follow him and find him drowned, and at the place where he fell in we find a stone. We may justly draw the conclusion that he tripped over the stone into the stream and drowned as a result. If we take no further action we can arrive at no other view. But here factual logic may be inconsistent with the physical facts. At the post-mortem we may perhaps discover that the person concerned had had a stroke, and that he fell into the water as a result—that therefore cause and effect are reversed. We supposed that he was dead because he fell into the water; in reality, he fell into the water because he was dead. The logic was incorrect with respect to the outer facts. We cannot at all trust to logic where outward maya is concerned.

Let us take the incident that to our sorrow we experienced in Dornach in the autumn. The little seven-year-old son of a member of the group based in Dornach had gone missing one evening; and once it had become clear that the child might be lying beneath an overturned furniture van it had to be lifted in the middle of the night and little Theo Faiß was taken from under it, dead.[46] What had happened? No furniture van, indeed no van of any kind, had otherwise been in the area. It was highly exceptional that a van was there at all, and for a long time afterwards there was none. Moreover, little Theo had otherwise always fetched what he had to bring a quarter of an hour earlier. That particular evening he had been obliged to wait for a quarter of an hour. Also, whereas he had walked on the left side of the van he would have been able to walk on the right side, but he had had to leave by a different door from the one he normally used. Everything conspired in such a way that it happened to the second that the boy came to be under this van. If one investigates the case spiritually in its karmic context, the soul of the boy had summoned this van in order to meet its death at this moment; everything was arranged, the physical event was a consequence of the spiritual circumstances. One then understands things in a totally different way, and one also understands the connection between what had happened and what further ensued after his death. Little Theo had an etheric body which in normal life would have enabled him to live for a further seventy or eighty years or even longer. All this is not lost, it continues to exist. An etheric body of a dead, seven-year-old child still has the forces that would have been used in life; they are present in the spiritual world. And this is also noticeable to those who have something to do with the etheric aura of our building; for there within this aura is the etheric body of the boy who has died, there are the forces, the strong spiritual forces of this kind, intelligent and good-natured boy. These are forces which help and benefit that which is connected with the aura of the Dornach building.

Thus spiritual and physical influences are connected. The times when people had to look up to the spiritual worlds for what happens in the physical world have not passed, they are still with us. We begin to understand something of this through our spiritual science. But one significant aspect is the extent to which we need forces of help from those who forsake physical life with unspent etheric forces. Think of the thousands and thousands who are passing today through the gate of death on the great fields where the grave events of our time are being enacted, all of them with unspent etheric bodies. These are spiritual forces which could still have been effective for a long time if the individuals concerned had remained in the physical world. In the realm of physics it is recognized that no energy is lost; but this law of the conservation of energy is also wholly applicable to the spiritual world. The forces that an etheric body possesses in order to provide for a life between birth and death until the age of

80 or 90 are not lost when someone passes prematurely through the gate of death. The forces are still there. In addition to what enters the spiritual world with the ego and astral body and has a value for the individuality, the etheric body has a general value for what passes into the universal aura of earthly, human evolution. Thus we can look up to the fresh abundance of the unspent forces of etheric bodies sending down their influences from the spiritual worlds to future times.

Just as we often see today that the dead are fighting together with the living, so on the other hand do we see the etheric sphere, the elemental world, permeated with forces, with strong human forces that have been acquired in high confidence from faith in humanity's aims and ideals and which are left behind by people who have crossed the threshold of death with this faith. Those who will live later must, however, look up to these unspent etheric bodies which will continue to be active. These etheric forces of those who have died prematurely will most certainly demand that they have not passed in vain into the spiritual world from whence they look down. They will demand that they can indeed contribute their share in the re-shaping of the spiritual earthly world as is demanded by mankind. These etheric bodies are there as exhorters who say: We have gone into the spiritual world so that forces may flow to your hearts and souls with which you can work still more strongly for the advancement of earthly evolution in a spiritual-scientific sense.

We need to understand the interaction between the bodily and spiritual aspects not in a vague, nebulous way but as a quite definite spiritual connection between the human beings living here on Earth in the physical body and the souls who have passed into the spiritual world. A true community will emerge if we understand these realities and fill ourselves in the right way with what spiritual science can give. Indeed, insight into the connection between the spiritual and physical can also relate us rightly to the serious problems of our time and enable us to feel that what is happening can only be vindicated by us with respect to the future if it is taken as an opportunity for a great, significant effort and struggle on the part of humanity also on the physical plane. What we already emphasized yesterday must be accomplished out of a right understanding between the spiritual and physical worlds in the sense of what is expressed in these words:

> From the courage of the fighters,
> From the blood on fields of battle,
> From the grief of the bereaved,
> From the people's sacrifice:
> There will ripen fruit of spirit,
> If souls will turn in consciousness
> Towards the realm of spirit.

Lecture 4

STUTTGART, 22 NOVEMBER 1915

MANY of those souls who have united their aspirations with ours have through the great events of the time passed through the gate of death. As I have already been enabled to indicate to you in this very place in the course of these times of war, it is precisely through what has been experienced with these souls that it has been possible to confirm that the souls who have crossed the threshold of death from the battlefields continue to accompany all that the age in its immensity demands of them. They live connected with the spirit of their people, they battle further with spiritual weapons. But especially with respect to these souls, my dear friends, we have an obligation to unite our loving thoughts, our innermost connecting impulses, in love with them. When the storm of present events has passed—in which especially these souls, even though they have already passed through the portal of death, are involved—or when the time is inherently suitable, the possibility will arise to celebrate a memorial festival for these honoured dead people with those thoughts and ideas which must dwell within us on their behalf.

In this storm-tossed time, the power of death has also extended its awakening thrust into our own ranks. On this very day we have committed to the elements of the Earth the mortal remains of our dear friend Sophie Stinde.[47] Many souls from this city will feel deeply connected in the most intimate sense with this person, who was one of the most faithful collaborators in our work. When I shall be in a position to speak in Munich in the coming days,[48] it will form part of my duties—a duty that I shall perform with the deepest love—to commemorate our dear Sophie Stinde further within our spiritual stream.

We are in many respects, my dear friends, therefore reminded of that which stands in the middle of many riddles of existence and encompasses all the other riddles of life, namely death. Death it is that, for those who have an awareness of life's riddles, thrusts itself often so painfully but always so enigmatically into earthly existence, and it is something that, within this context, can never find its elucidation there. There are certainly very sound reasons for bringing together the two thoughts that feature in the title of one of the public lectures, 'The Mystery of Death and the Riddles of Life'[49]; for a study of the theme of death does not, as so many adherents of materialism believe, relate only to something that is remote from earthly life and has nothing to do with earthly human beings. Indeed, a study of death that embraces all its facets evokes from the depths of existence the kind of knowledge that, from the mystery of death itself, endows one's life here on Earth with a strong sense of meaning. Thus in one's search for an explanation of the mysteries of life one should not allow oneself to be prevented by any kind of preconception from approaching the riddle, the mystery, of death.

And so at this time, when death has on the one hand come close to so many also within our ranks in the past year and when it confronts us in so many ways through the historical events in which we are involved, the mystery of death may justly be linked with a number of questions concerning life and the world that we are considering during these days. As we approach the mystery of death, we may begin by considering it at the point where it becomes a direct presence in the midst of life. A person who has died takes leave of this life of the senses, he enters a new sphere; but he continues to be present in the thoughts that live in those in whom thoughts, sensations and feelings were aroused by him while he was dwelling among the living. And not only has it in the past been a beautiful custom arising out of the deepest human needs, wherever the human heart is not cold and barren, to celebrate commemorative festivals for the dead; for these commemorative festivals continue on also into our own time in the Catholic festival of All Souls, in the festivals for the dead of Protestant denominations and many others celebrated on a more or less individual basis. Should we not have the feeling that in the continuance of these commemorative festivals a materialistic age is itself paying tribute to the life of the spirit? Although materialism may have already so corroded human souls that people do such things only unconsciously, even materialistic souls will shrink from doing anything other than approach what is associated with the customary festivals of commemoration with heart-felt devotion. The dead continue to be livingly engaged in what the living are able to feel and think about them. Thus when we consider death in the most intimate sense, we can also begin this study of death in the very midst of life.

We know from all the various studies that we have undertaken over a number of years that we should never say that the physical world of the senses is here and the spiritual world is totally separate from it. The physical world of the senses reaches up into the spiritual world and the spiritual world extends downwards to the physical, sense-perceptible world. And although with our physical senses we perceive the physical world of the senses only as a sensory phenomenon, nevertheless in the same way that air spreads out everywhere the spiritual pervades and interpenetrates everything that we behold in physical life purely with our normal senses. And those who have passed through the gate of death and are in the spiritual world extend their impulses and forces into our sense-perceptible world. Thus we can say: even though the bond that connects those living in a physical body with the dead who live in the spirit lies behind the threshold of normal consciousness, it is nevertheless a real bond; and for someone who studies spiritual science many riddles will arise which must necessarily be solved in order to understand life as it must be understood, not from a theoretical but from a living standpoint that not only thinking but the soul in all its attributes and capacities embraces.

Let us try to envisage what we can clarify to ourselves from ordinary life with respect to death. Someone who has died departs from us. What outwardly changes is that our eyes no longer see him, that we can no longer shake his hand, that our words no longer pass from us to him and from him to us. The warmth that had flowed from his feelings to our heart no longer streams to us in the sensory world. During the time when we were able to live together with him, the image that we could have of him was continually conjured forth anew with the help of his sense-perceptible body with which he was enshrouded. The change that has come about consists in that now, when the soul that was close to us has passed through the gate of death, we no longer have, for our connection with this soul, the help of the image of this person called forth within us by the sense-perceptible impulses emanating from him, together with everything that it aroused in terms of sensations, feelings and will-impulses, of a capacity for love, of sympathy and antipathy. What from now onwards continues to live within us once the soul has departed from us through the gate of death is the image that we carry within ourselves and inwardly pervades us. If we want to call this image forth to a consciousness of physical existence from the imagination wherein it continues to live within our etheric body and especially in our astral body and ego (in a manner that remains outside our normal consciousness), we must cause it to arise from within. We must draw what we have retained from our relationship to the one who has died from the depths of our soul, that is, from our ego and astral body, into that part of our being that engenders consciousness and the power of representation, namely the etheric and physical bodies.

When the soul that has passed through the gate of death was still with us, it still engendered the image; the image radiated to us from without, we needed only to approach it with what our soul had to give. When the dead person has left us, we have to enable what we have preserved of him to flow into our outward human sheaths in order that the concept, the idea, the image of him can appear before our soul. We are then no longer—as we are with the memory of a familiar person who is still alive on the Earth—supported by the knowledge that this memory is not the only one that we can still outwardly have of him. This is the decisive change, that from now on, until we ourselves cross the threshold of death, we shall have to rely on memory.

This memory of unconscious forces within us can never be extinguished in our deep soul-members, in our ego and astral body. When we fall asleep at night, when the impressions of the outside world fade from our ordinary waking consciousness, when all the thoughts that we can have from waking up to going to sleep vanish into oblivion, the imaginations, the radiant images of those individuals with whom we were connected and who have departed from us through the gate of death, light up in what we carry from our body within our ego and astral body. The dead dwell with us in that part of our being that lives within us from falling asleep to waking up, just as those living on the Earth live with us from waking up until going to sleep. We owe our waking consciousness to the circumstance that our physical body, which together with the etheric body is the mediator of our waking consciousness, has passed through four stages of the evolution of our Earth. Night-time consciousness, on the other hand, eludes us because our ego entered into us only during Earth evolution and the astral body only during Moon evolution. What we are at present able to experience when we call forth memories of our dead within our ego and astral body, we will experience as we now share in the life of those living on the Earth, that is, in normal waking consciousness, only in later epochs of our Earth evolution. The ego as the youngest member must first achieve a consciousness which can be as wakeful a consciousness as our present waking consciousness, which has been gained or brought about by the connection that our ego and astral body have with our physical and etheric bodies. The physical body has passed through four stages of earthly evolution, the etheric body through three stages, the astral body through only two; while the ego is now passing through its first stage.

Thus those who have become spirits, disembodied souls, reside in the element that we inhabit during our sleep; but we can bring imaginative pictures of them to our waking consciousness only from our memories. The force that enables a spiritual impulse to live within us is different from the force that makes us conscious of such a spiritual impulse. Our sense-impressions arise through the fact that they are also able to flow from without into our physical and etheric bodies; but for what can only reside within the ego and astral body there is at our present stage of normal development insufficient power to impress it upon the etheric and physical bodies to the extent that it becomes a conscious representation. Nevertheless, a connection of a deeply spiritual kind does exist; for in the most delicate parts of our being we are inseparably linked with the so-called dead. Death does not constitute a break, or even a transformation, of this connection. In these delicate parts of our being such as the ego and astral body are, the dead live as truly as do the living; and the same applies to those who from our ranks have become spirit-beings.

Let us contemplate them with the cognitive means that we have been able to acquire in the course of life. I have often emphasized how different the relationship of a being—thus also of a human being—is to its surroundings if this being does not, as we do in the physical world, have a physical or an etheric body. Someone who has passed through the portal of initiation and has in terms of his perception left his physical and etheric bodies lives in his spiritual surroundings, as does someone who has died. And I have often had to point out that the relationship that the perceiver has to the spiritual world to which he then belongs is totally different depending on whether he is a disembodied human being or a being of the hierarchies or a being of the elemental world. We have had to emphasize that we must choose words differently depending on whether we are referring to the relationship of a spiritual being or to that of a being incarnated in a physical body to its surroundings.

Here in the physical world the things and beings of the outer world make an impression upon us. We are here, other beings are outside us. What they radiate streams through our senses into our soul. In that we have an awareness of this, we say that we are enclosed within the confines of the body; we have a conception of other beings, we perceive them. When we have entered the spiritual world, our words must be differently chosen; we are perceived as spiritual beings by other spiritual beings. In so far as they are sensory embodiments, we perceive animals, we perceive plants, we perceive human beings. As we ourselves enter the spiritual world, we are perceived by the beings of the Angeloi, Archangeloi, Archai and so on. And whereas we say here that we see plants, animals, other human beings, when we enter the spiritual world we have to say that we inwardly experience something which signifies that the spiritual eyes of another being are resting upon us. We are perceived. It is this being perceived, this knowledge that we are being beheld, which distinguishes our life in the spiritual world from life in the physical world.

Since everything is completely different in the spiritual world, words must be transformed if one is to speak in a real sense. To express it figuratively and yet also more than figuratively, when a being from the spiritual world incarnates, it must be prepared gradually to learn—as also a child must learn—to look out into the world through the physical senses, to take in a world from outside, to become an ego that takes in a world from outside. When a being enters the spiritual world from the sense-world through the gate of death or in some other way, it must get accustomed to saying to itself: You are an ego, but an ego that does not live in isolation in the world but continues inwardly to experience something, just as it experienced the memory-pictures emerging from the depths of the soul. But now you know that what now appears are the ideas, thoughts and sensations of the other beings who live with you in the spiritual world. So just as the impressions that we derive from the sense-world, from sensory beings, enter into us from without, so do the ideas and sensations of beings who are in the spiritual world appear within us. But we know that these representations and feelings rising up from what then becomes our inner essence derive from spiritual beings who are with us. We are in the spiritual world, and an image arises within us, the representation of a being whom we must love, a being who gives us the stimulus to accomplish this or that in the spiritual world. Where does this mental image come from; how does it come about that it appears within us as memories do here? Its source is that another being, a being of the spiritual world, has drawn near to us. We do not behold it from without; we know that it is there because it transmits to us what is within it. We are pictured, we are perceived—this is how we would have to speak with respect to what lives in the spiritual world. Thus experience in the spiritual world does not become more abstract or nebulous, it becomes all the more alive. What we experience in the spiritual world becomes as alive as anything that is immediately around us in the physical world. Thus we must familiarize ourselves with the totally different kind of interaction that we have with the beings of the spiritual world.

And now let us consider from this standpoint those who have passed through the gate of death. They enter into a world of which they must say: I am learning increasingly to know that I am being perceived, that discarnate human beings, elemental beings, beings from the hierarchy of the Angeloi and Archangeloi are transmitting to me their ideas, sensations and feelings. All these beings live in me. And as we look up to such a dead person, we have the sense that just as when someone comes towards us in the sense-world we are aware of the blood beneath his skin and the activity of his nerves concealed behind his features, so as we behold a spiritual, discarnate human being are we aware that through what we experience of him the thoughts and sensations of the Angeloi, Archangeloi and Archai are working.

Here in the physical world the physical human being comes towards us. Through his soul and his development he has ennobled the animal, plant and mineral nature; but this animal, plant and mineral nature nevertheless confronts us. When someone appears before us here in physical existence, his soul-spiritual nature is deeply hidden within him and radiates through his bodily frame; and yet what our eyes perceive of his impulses and what is transmitted to us in the world of the senses is pervaded by his animal nature ennobled to human nature—the animal nature has been ennobled but it is nevertheless there. Likewise the plant and mineral worlds appear before us in the human being. We know that the kingdoms of nature live within the human being at a higher level. Moreover, if the mineral kingdom were not present in the human individual, we would never be able to meet with him in that physical realm where contact is inherently possible; for it is only through the mineral part in him that he can make an impression upon us. Just as here we see animality in the physical human being, when as a spirit we confront a spiritual human being in the spiritual world we behold the feelings and thoughts which stream as a force of soul into him from the Angeloi. What the Angeloi experience is directed down to the human body. Just as animality is drawn upwards into man, so in the spiritual world is that which flashes through man's life of soul from the Angeloi directed downwards. And as the plant kingdom is adapted on a higher level to human nature, so is that which the Archangeloi cause to stream into man drawn down to a lower level in his spiritual form. Likewise, just as the mineral kingdom in the sense-perceptible human being lights up within us and thereby enables him to become perceptible in us, so does that which confronts us as a spiritual human being in the spiritual world become an independent imagination because the Archai pour their formative, fashioning power into man. So just as the three kingdoms of nature pervade the physical human being, so do the Angeloi, Archangeloi and Archai pervade his spirit in the spiritual world.

When a human individual has passed through the gate of death, he is—with the exception of the very first period—connected for a long time with his astral body and with his ego. But since, as a human being in the spiritual world, he has brought his ego and astral body with him from the Earth, so is it possible for the Spirits of Form and those spirits whom we have come to know as belonging to the hierarchy of the Archai to exert their influence upon him in such a way as to make him actually perceptible. Just as the mineral kingdom makes a person visible and accessible on this side of the threshold, so does the realm of the Archai and of the Spirits of Form make him a clearly defined being in the spiritual world. And as the plant kingdom is no longer beheld but is only intuitively sensed within man here in the physical world, so in the clearly defined form of man in the spiritual world is that which the hierarchies cause to stream into him perceived in a similar way. Similarly, as the animal in man no longer confronts us in animal form and only spiritual science makes us aware to what extent animality plays a part in him, so in the spiritual world does one likewise not at first discern the somewhat hidden presence of the Angeloi, which is still powerful so long as a person has not laid aside his etheric body. The hidden participation of the Angeloi continues, but it comes less to expression when one perceives a person's spiritual form in the spiritual world. Thus when after some time we enter into connection with someone who has died, we meet him in such a way that we can say that here he is; but what gives him his clearly defined being comes to him from the way that the Spirits of Form exert their influence upon him—and what can be sensed strongly working within him derives from the Spirits of Personality. Thus the hierarchies see to it that the dead person comes to meet us, as it were, from above, just as his physical counterpart comes towards us here facilitated by the mineral world.

When a human soul has departed from us as a result of having passed through the gate of death, we retain a memory-picture of it here within the orbit of our physical consciousness. Everything that is precious to us about the person who has died we retain. It is a different quality of remembering from the memories that we otherwise have in ordinary life. Just think what our other memories are like. What are they? They are thoughts about something that is no longer there, for that is why they are memories. What we remember is not there; it does not happen in the moment when we remember it. The content of our memory-pictures is not a present reality; it is not happening now. When we recall a soul-being who was connected with us and has crossed the threshold of death, we have thoughts about him; but he himself, the dead person, is there, he is in the immediate present, he is a real being of the spiritual world. Thus we do not merely have a memory-picture, we have a mental picture in our soul that is indeed a memory-picture but which corresponds to a real spiritual being. The mental picture lives in us, and out in the spiritual world lives the one who has died. There is the being, and there is the image that we have. So when we reverently recall the dead, when we make what the dead person was to us present within us, the imagination, the picture of this person enters into our waking consciousness. It is there. What does this mean? It means that it is present in our physical and etheric bodies in a living, active process.

In our physical and etheric bodies we form a picture of this for the other part of our life which is not dedicated to the memory of this dead person who is dear to us, we combine it with what is in the physical world. If we call forth within us the picture, the thought- or feeling-image of the dead, with respect to this picture there lives in the immediate present a being through which Angels and Archangels cast their gaze, connecting their picturing faculties with it. Just consider: when we direct our thoughts and feelings to our beloved dead friends, far more is involved than is present in ordinary, normal life as regards connections between the spiritual and physical worlds. Something is present here which, I might say, could also not be so. And one question that arises for the spirit-researcher is: What does it signify for the dead that we are living in the world that they have forsaken, in the realm whose sheaths they have laid aside, what does it signify for these dead people who dwell in the land of spirit that in our waking consciousness, that is, in our physical and etheric bodies, we call upon what connects us with them? This question arises for the spirit-researcher, a question that is of a profoundly intimate nature but which, if the occultist resolves it, will, I believe, shed much light upon the mysteries of life.

We can also pose this question differently from the point of view of a direct experience of life, which is not always available to people but which they nevertheless seek in the way I have previously indicated. Let us put the question in this way: What does it signify for reality as a whole when on some day of remembrance, on All Souls' Day or on some other festival of the dead, people living on Earth in their mortal frames visit graves or unite themselves in thought with friends who have died? What does it mean when we ourselves celebrate days or hours of remembrance for the dead? When we read aloud to them, as is our custom? When we do something in order to join together with them and especially to enliven what lastingly connects us with them? In other words: What does it mean when in waking consciousness we evoke what connects us with the dead? This question can also present itself in such a way to the spirit-researcher.

However, he will have to express it by means of something else which arises for him from spiritual research. The most important facts of the spiritual world can actually be expressed only pictorially. One has to look for comparisons if one wants to describe the phenomena of the spiritual world; for our words are formulated for ordinary life, for the physical world, and if we want to describe the facts of the spiritual world we cannot speak so directly about them with words relating to the physical world. We have to try to evoke such ideas in our souls by means of a comparison which enables us to conceptualize what we want to describe about the spiritual world. Here in the physical world something presents itself to the spirit-researcher by means of which he can form an idea of the question with which we are confronted. We find here in the physical world something that would not affect the natural functioning of the outer world were it not to be there but which those people who endeavour to live their lives to the full would not want to be without. What is it that we find here in the physical world of the senses which does not form part of on-going natural processes but which we would not want to be without? Well, if we create pictures of what is present in our natural surroundings, whether they be artistic representations or are a product of the more modern art of photography, the images that we have thereby made of beings who belong to the physical world of the senses are something that is added to the natural process, which would itself also be able to exist without them. Try just to think how life is enriched by the pictures we make of what is otherwise a feature of a natural process. How greatly we yearn to have art in our world in addition to the processes of nature! How dearly we want to have a picture of something we have experienced! The world could run its course without it. A being remains what it is even if we have no picture of it, but there is a sense in which we need a picture. The spirit-researcher will remember this when he has to form ideas about what it means for the dead that the living call them to life within their souls. The spiritual process corresponding to the processes of nature which the dead, hence spiritual beings, contemplate would be there even if memories of loved ones did not light up in the souls of human beings. But the on-going spiritual process for the dead, for these spiritual beings, would then be barren and empty, just as we would experience a great void if we had only the processes of nature around us and had introduced nothing of a figurative element into human life, into the natural process.

Indeed, one can make the following comparison. When a dear friend from whom you have long been parted but whom you have kept lovingly in your thoughts in his absence sends you a picture of himself, this picture is something that you treasure. It is something that fills your heart with warmth, something that you need. Just as you treasure this picture, so when those dead friends look down upon the world, which would otherwise be for them no more than a series of spiritual processes, experience the thoughts that live in the waking consciousness of human beings, when they feel the on-going spiritual process as being imbued with what is radiated forth from the souls who have remained here, which gives them an awareness of something that might well not be but nevertheless must be there (words that need to be understood in all their implications), this is for them something akin to a picture of a beloved friend. Thus one can say that when one visits a cemetery on Totensonntag* or on All Souls' Day and sees many people there whose thoughts are filled with memory-pictures of those dead people who were dear to them and then looks up to the souls of those who are being remembered, these are then the cathedrals, the works of art for these dead people. Then that which radiates forth to them from the Earth illumines the world for these dead people like a glorious cathedral which lights up the world for us and reveals hidden things, or, like a picture that we cherish and treasure, recalls someone who is dear to us. The world that the dead must forever contemplate would be barren and empty if they were to look down and in the souls of those living here on Earth that which possibly might not be but nevertheless must be was not looking up to them: the thoughts which connect those living on the Earth with those who are spiritually alive, the dead.

A deeply moving polarity reveals itself to us here between earthly life and the life in the spirit. In order to elevate earthly life we must by means of the pictorial element add to earthly life what is not there for those living on the Earth. How barren, how empty would the Earth be were it to be devoid of any pictorial or artistic element, a purely natural Earth! And now let us raise ourselves to the standpoint of the dead. They would perceive the on-going spiritual process, but it would be barren and empty for them, as barren and empty as nature would be for the children of the Earth without art, if memories of the dead were not kept alive, if faithful remembrance were not alert in waking consciousness, if within the unfolding processes of the spirit there were not the thoughts which for the spirit

---

* The Sunday before Advent when the dead are commemorated in the German Protestant Church.—Translator

are like works of art, in so far as they are high-minded thoughts and not entangled with earthly processes but are directed towards those no longer participating in them. What makes a work of art what it is here on Earth, what enhances its beauty, is something that is to a far lesser extent connected with man's innermost being than is the significance of our thoughts of the dead for the spiritual world. For there is in this sense also a beauty in the spiritual world, a real, genuine beauty; but it does not arise to the same degree through outward circumstances, as so often happens in the case of a picture in the physical world. That the paintings of Raphael, Leonardo and Dürer are more beautiful than others is due to the fact that those masters were more capable than other masters. That a dead person feels that a more beautiful work of art (to express it in terms of an analogy) is radiating up to him from the Earth is a reflection of the depth of inwardness, of the holy, spiritual feeling residing in the memory that we constantly cherish for him. The strength of our feeling for the dead makes itself manifest in our soul-life and intensifies it in the sight of the dead themselves. This makes our soul more and more beautiful.

Ponder these thoughts in your own souls, my dear friends, and you will as a result of this meditative reflection be able to understand more about the connection between the spiritual and sense-perceptible world, about that particular region in the spiritual world in which the dead are living and the world in which earthly human beings live. We shall pursue other studies which can lead us into further circles of the spiritual world now that we have completed this first chapter today.

LECTURE 5

STUTTGART, 23 NOVEMBER 1915

I N approaching the mystery of death, one must above all constantly keep in mind something that was also emphasized yesterday, that in order to characterize the spiritual worlds it is necessary to change the meaning that resides in our ordinary words fashioned for the physical world; for someone who has died, a so-called dead person, has entered the spiritual world, and as we have repeatedly indicated things are fundamentally different in the spiritual world from in the physical world.

As is apparent not only to the insights of spiritual science but already to ordinary physical understanding, the first thing that happens for a dead person on entering the spiritual world through the gate of death is the separation of the physical body from that which lies within it. This is of course a purely commonplace truth. Our wish today is to consider the processes that are involved in a description of the portal of death and the further course of the path between death and a new birth, that is, the inner experiences undergone by someone who has died, in the sense in which this can be investigated by spiritual science.

Someone who remains here in physical life has the sense that what was thus contained within the bodily frame has forsaken him, forsaken those who have been left behind, that the deceased person has departed to another world. According to the way that this can be investigated by spiritual science, the first perception that the deceased person has is that he experiences himself as being abandoned by those inhabiting the Earth and also by his physical body, by that which has served as the means of his perception, of his thinking and feeling and capacities of will between birth and death.

So these faculties with which he was endowed and connected distance themselves from him: this is what he initially perceives. This perception is at first linked with the processes that we have often described: that the Earth itself, as it were, goes away, so that it takes away the physical bodily vessel from the one who is crossing the threshold of death. It is as though the dead person were to have the feeling of remaining behind a movement that he has not been aware of here on the Earth, namely behind the movement of the Earth itself; the Earth goes away from him and, with it, everything that has surrounded him on the Earth. And now he is integrated into a completely different world, a world through which he perceives that what was given to him as a bodily vessel is connected with the Earth, also with the movements of the Earth. In a certain sense he has the feeling—although this is a very imprecise way of expressing it—that it has ceased to be possible for him to be part of the path that the Earth and its spirits are pursuing; this is why they are leaving him. He remains behind in a greater situation of repose and becomes part of what can be thought of as a more restful world.

For the deceased person there is much that has its foundation in this perception of being abandoned especially by the physical, bodily vessel, by all that he has experienced of human beings and has experienced together with them between birth and death. The possession of his physical, bodily vessel was something that he took for granted during earthly life. What he is now perceiving is something entirely new; and we shall see how different these perceptions are depending on whether one dies a so-called natural death through illness or old-age or a violent death such as many thousands of people are now having to encounter.

This perception of being abandoned by that which belonged to one as one's natural property is the source of something altogether new that makes itself manifest in the life of soul. It means that something appears in one's soul-life of which one had not been able to have knowledge so long as one was dwelling in the body. The first experience that arises is what I might describe as the inversing of one's feelings towards life. Here on Earth one has the feeling that life is given to one from without, that one lives as a result of the life-forces that are given to one by outward earthly circumstances. Now the Earth, together with what it has given one, has gone away, and through this sense of abandonment there at the same time arises the feeling that henceforth the vitalizing force wells up from within. Thus the first experience is the perception of an internal vitalizing force. It is the transition to a certain state of activity, whereas hitherto one had dwelt in passivity. One enlivens what one now is. One dwells within oneself. What one had previously called the world has gone away; but in that one completely fills out that in which one is now living, this engenders out of itself the vitalizing force, it enlivens itself.

In concrete terms there arises what I have often called the panorama of life, a flowing picture of everything that one has experienced between birth and death. The pictures of this life appear before the soul. The whole of the life between birth and death appears as a mighty, self-generating dream from the point where one is now. But this dream needs strength if it is not to be merely a dream. It would be a fleeting dream if one had not acquired the enlivening power resulting from the awareness that one's mortal frame has separated itself from one's soul and spirit. The dream is enlivened. What would otherwise be only a world of dark, flowing dreams is enlivened from that same point, it becomes a living world, a living panorama of life. One is oneself the source of the enlivening of what thus appears as a dream. This is the experience that one has immediately after death.

All this happens while the person concerned still has hardly any awareness that he has departed from his former state of consciousness; but it is as though something has stirred from the central point of his being which spreads out and which that life to which he had hitherto passively devoted himself evades. What one was not conscious of between birth and death, namely that thoughts, which otherwise surge to and fro like a dream dreamt by the ego, are alive, is something that one now knows; and out of this life from which one was previously estranged, one lives into this life of one's own. One experiences what it means that what was hitherto connected with one more outwardly takes hold of one's innermost being. What was formerly not life but a picture of it takes hold of one's imagination, one's thinking. And as one immerses oneself in this conception, something further arises. This could be described as being immersed in a pervading of the life panorama with sound emanating from the universe. I have already described these things in general terms. However, one needs to examine them ever more precisely in order that one may reach behind the mysteries of the world.

This innermost dream of life is first enlivened, it becomes itself a living universe, a living cosmos. Then, as it were, it fills itself out with what may be called the universal music of the spheres resounding through this dream of life. One experiences that what one was oneself between birth and death as an extract from the cosmos is henceforth received by the cosmos, that it becomes part of what is now not earthly; for one has passed through the earthly realm between birth and death. And then the next thing is that one feels how intimately the cosmos pervades what one was thus as an extract. One has the feeling that it is as though an inner light were to arise and illumine what one was. All this, however, streams and, as it were, resounds into the panorama of life. Then the etheric body is cast off—for these processes all take place while the human individual is connected with the etheric body; and there occurs what one refers to as the loosening of, the separation from, the etheric body.

What one now experiences, this perceiving of the panorama of life and its permeation with the resounding and radiating substances of the cosmos, is similar to the incorporation of the physical body into the human organization when one enters into existence through birth. Just as the human substance which is given to one by the Earth becomes an integral part of human soul-nature, so after passing through the portal of death are the universal forces of the cosmos likewise incorporated. This experience which has been described is necessary. And if one investigates life between death and a new birth in a truly spiritual-scientific way, one notices what significance this first experience after crossing the threshold of death has for the whole life between death and a new birth.

As I have frequently emphasized, we must be quite clear about the fact that here in physical, earthly life we have our ego-consciousness by virtue of living in a physical body. I say expressly that I am speaking of ego-consciousness, not the ego. Our ego is something that we receive from the Spirits of Form, and this is a different matter; but we owe our ego-consciousness to our being immersed in a physical body. We must be clearly aware of this ego-consciousness that we have in our waking state on Earth. You can best do this by imagining that you are walking through a particular space. At first you feel nothing, but now you come up against something. The outer world comes in contact with you, but you become aware of *yourself*. You become aware within yourself of the encounter that you have had with the outer world, you become aware of yourself through the outer world, you feel yourself through having come up against the outer world.

Indeed, we have our ego-consciousness in the physical world because we are always coming in contact with the outer world. Of course, we have such encounters not only through our sense of touch but also when we open our eyes, that is, we encounter the light outside of us; when sounds are heard by our ears, we become aware of ourselves through our hearing coming in contact with these sounds.

But we also become aware of ourselves in this way when we come from the spiritual world every morning and immerse ourselves in the physical world. This diving down into our physical body, that is, this encounter of our ego and astral body with the physical and etheric bodies, brings about our ego-consciousness. Thus the reason why ego-consciousness is as a rule absent in the world of dreams is that for ego-consciousness we need this very encounter with the physical and etheric bodies.

We need this direct encounter for a clear, wide-awake ego-consciousness. Now someone who has passed through the gate of death is bereft of the outward garment of the physical body. In the same way, he cannot engender ego-consciousness as he can between birth and death. He would have to tread the path between death and a new birth without consciousness of his ego if this ego-consciousness were not now engendered in a different way. This other path is that whereby all that we now experience directly in the etheric body continues in existence the whole time between death and a new birth once we have crossed the threshold of death.

A person's experience in the spiritual world between death and a new birth is also in this respect opposite to the physical experience that he has here between birth and death. Here in the physical world, no one can in normal consciousness recall the moment of his birth; memory begins only later. He does not remember the process of his birth, it lies, so to speak, at a greater temporal distance than the path of memory can reach. But what someone now inwardly experiences from the other side of death remains present for the soul throughout the life between death and a new birth. The experience of death continues in existence just as surely as the experience of birth vanishes away when a person enters the physical world. The physical human being does not see back to his birth in the physical world, whereas in the whole time between death and a new birth he looks back upon his death. This looking back, this encounter with the experience of death, is what gives rise to ego-consciousness between death and a new birth; it is to this that we owe it.

The contemplation of death is, if at all, something terrible when viewed from the side of physical existence. Only when one views it from this side does it hold horrors and terrors. Someone who has died, however, sees it from the other side; and when seen from that side there is indeed nothing terrible about the knowledge that the moment of death is, as it were, a permanent feature of his whole life between death and a new birth. For although it is also a destructive power when viewed from this physical side of life, it is the most glorious, the greatest, the most beautiful, the most sublime of events which can constantly be perceived from the other side of life. It is a continual testimony to the victory of the spirit over matter, the individually creative life-force of the spirit. In the spiritual worlds, ego-consciousness is marked by this feeling of the individually creative life-force of the spirit.

Thus one has this ego-consciousness in the spiritual worlds because one is inwardly engaged in a continual process of self-engendering, because one never appeals to an existing being but is forever summoning oneself into existence; and the retrospective progression after the moment when death occurred has its basis in this self-engendering process. We can therefore also explain how ego-consciousness, the self-consciousness that we have in the time between death and a new birth, is evoked. This experience of the birth of ego-consciousness in the first period after death has great significance. Of course, this first experience is of a different nature depending on whether the person concerned has, shall we say, reached old age and is passing naturally through the gate of death or has perhaps been carried off in early childhood or in the flower of youth. And with respect to the difference in this sense, the age of around thirty-five is of particular significance. It is currently happening on an enormous scale that young people in the prime of life are passing through the gate of death; and we shall see tomorrow how this is further modified through the fact that death approaches them from outside. But when someone crosses the threshold of death at a young age, the perspective of the life tableau together with its enlivening processes (as already discussed) differs in nature from that of someone who crosses it after his thirty-fifth year.

Although it is, of course, difficult to find the right words for circumstances of this kind, one may say that someone who dies at a young age will have the feeling: The dream-picture of your life appears, you engender it from the midpoint of your life. But as you are pouring your own enlivening forces over this life tableau, something like a residue from the world from which you came by virtue of having been born lies behind this tableau of your life.

When a child dies, the life tableau is extremely short. When, for example, a six-year-old child dies, the life tableau still has little by way of content. But, as it were, behind this tableau and casting its shadow upon it, there is still much of what was experienced in the spiritual world before birth or, as it used to be said in the German language (Goethe used this expression[50]), before one 'became young'. A beautiful expression, which has now been lost. And when a child dies who has as yet no memories to draw from, a child who has not yet reached the age to which one can remember back, it does not have such a life tableau where it feels directly identified with it, as a person who dies later would do; what appears through the whole tableau of life is, with some slight modification, that which it had around it before birth. One can therefore say that this beholding of certain residual elements of the spiritual world that can be experienced before birth is lost to one's retrospective survey after death only if one has lived beyond one's thirty-fifth year.

One should never—I say this in parenthesis—fall into the temptation of yielding to the thought which, I must say emphatically, is not without danger as to whether it might be better for a person to die before his thirty-fifth year or to die after it and to experience what we shall go on to describe. One should not pursue or cherish this idea but should bear in mind that *when* one passes through the gate of death is something that should in the strictest sense of the word be left solely to karma.

It is important to understand these things. If one dies after one's thirty-fifth year, one does not have the possibility of beholding something of the residual element of spiritual life that preceded one's birth. This is obscured. But the life tableau nevertheless appears. And one has a strong feeling that one engenders it from within, that one, as it were, spins these threads oneself; but this web is imbued with life. With respect to the life tableau there is a significant difference between dying before one's thirty-fifth year and dying after it. The tableau of a life ending before the age of thirty-five still has far more the character of coming to one from outside as from a spiritual world, one merely transmits to it one's own experiences. The life tableau of someone over that age is at first characterized more by an emptiness, something dark coming towards one from without, and one brings towards this darkness what one has acquired during life. The inner experience is, however, modified through the fact that in the one case it resembles the approach of a Fata Morgana that one goes towards, whereas in the other case one brings one's individual world to the world of the cosmos. All this has great significance for life, as we shall see tomorrow. This karmic process whereby at a certain age of physical life our physical body is torn away from us has a great significance for the nature of life after death, and it is intimately connected with the whole of our karma.

Then comes the time when we have the feeling: Now you have really departed from the earthly sphere! To put it in plain terms, one could say that immediately after crossing the threshold of death one has the feeling that one's earthly body is going away. The friends, the human beings with whom one has been, are going away, as are the experiences that one shared with them. One is for a while on one's own, alone with what one has experienced. Of course, all that one has experienced with others is in the dream of life; one perceives it as what people have inscribed within one, but in such a way that one experiences these times within one and makes the life-dream inwardly alive. One then has the impression that the Earth, too, is going away but that one is still living wholly in the sphere where the Earth is, in the sphere that still belongs to the Earth. One also experiences the laying aside of the etheric body in such a way as to have the feeling: Now you are not only away from the Earth and the substances of which it is composed but also from the most immediate environment of the Earth, from light; you are also away from the dense substantiality of the Earth which makes the music of the spheres inaudible. And perhaps the last impression, which is very significant and produces a lasting effect, is that the habit of letting yourself and your surroundings be illumined by an external source of light is broken. In parenthesis, I should point out that those who believe that one would be constantly flying through light if one were to fly from the Earth to the Sun have the stupidest conception of reality. This fantastic notion is one that is currently cherished by materialistic physicists. The belief that the Sun spreads light in the way described in physics, that light passes through space and falls upon the Earth, is a superstition of the worst kind. One realizes this after death when, upon becoming aware that one is free from the etheric body, one has the experience that the sunlight that we have here in physical life exists only in the realm that belongs to the Earth. One perceives that one is now no longer disturbed by this light. Now it is the inwardly generated light that is diffused in what is for the first time pervaded with sound. The inner light can only be effective because the outer light no longer disturbs the inner light.

With the laying aside of the etheric body there now begins the entry into that world which is so often called the world of kamaloka. We wish to call it the soul-world, for after the initial inner enlivening force has manifested itself one then experiences something like an inner pervading of one's being with sound in the solitary situation in which one now finds oneself. And after the pervading of one's being with inner light something occurs that is like an inner engendering of warmth. Here on the Earth one has the experience of being warmed, in that one receives warmth from outside and accordingly feels at home in one's physical body. And now this process of inner warming manifests itself, and it leads one to feel: In the element in which you are living you are now able to call forth within yourself the feeling that you had previously, but in the form where warmth was having an effect upon you. This pervades the life tableau with warmth and one enters thereby into a completely new element. One has the feeling that the etheric body is now leaving one. This is the entry into the world which was quite deliberately called the Region of Burning Desires in my *Theosophy*, because the warmth that comes from within is at the same time desire, flowing, self-generating desire, a sensation of the element of will. And mingled with it is something that now remains for a fairly long time: the experiencing of the soul-world, which I have frequently described (we can only gradually delineate these things more precisely) as a retrospective experience of life. One journeys from the experience of death back towards one's birth. Everything that one has experienced here in the physical world is now experienced from the other side. But one does not experience it as one did here in the physical world; rather does one experience it in a moral way. If, shall we say, one inflicted an injury to someone at a certain point between birth and death, one will at the time have had an inner sense of what one did but not the pain that the other person felt. One now experiences the same incident again, but not the anger or antipathy that lived in oneself but in such a way as the other person experienced it. If I may put it thus, one extends one's own experience to the effects of one's deeds as they were between birth and death. One penetrates all the effects of what one has done.

This is in a certain sense the basic theme of life between death and a new birth, that during one's experience in the soul-world one gradually lives through the effects of what one has done between birth and death, that one gradually dives down in it. It is indeed the case that just as from childhood one entered little by little into the world of nature, learning to perceive and understand it, so in the time after death does one live into the effects of one's own deeds, into the effects of one's own thoughts and words, in short into the whole world of effects; one flows out into the world of effects. Spiritual beings will surely also gradually appear from this foundation: the beings of the higher hierarchies, the beings of the elemental world. So just as here we do not merely experience nature but animals, plants and minerals appear in the context of nature, so in the course of this retrospective experience when we enter into the effects of our deeds—for this is then actually the foundation of our world— do the spiritual beings of the spiritual world appear. Then as do physical beings in the physical world, among the spiritual beings of the elemental realms and the higher hierarchies there also appear to us the souls who have had a connection with us, souls who have died previously and are in the spiritual world or souls who are still incorporated in a physical body with whom we have been associated here on Earth. All this enlivens this foundation of existence after death, this giving oneself up into the world of one's own deeds.

It should in a certain sense be observed that there is a difference between perceiving a soul that is dwelling on Earth and a soul that has already passed through the portal of death. The deceased person does of course know whether he has to do with a soul of one or the other kind. If he has to do with a soul that is still dwelling in an earthly body, he has the feeling that this soul approaches him, as it were, more from without, that the image, the imagination, forms itself of its own accord. In the case of a soul that is already disembodied, a far more active experience is involved. One then has the feeling that the soul approaches one but that one has to form the image for this soul. The deceased friend approaches one with his being, one must oneself form his image; someone who is still living brings his image towards one when one looks down upon him.

And now one experiences with a certain moral emphasis what one can call one's deeds, that is, the effects of that which one has done, thought and willed. One immerses oneself in this, one penetrates into it—and one does so in a quite particular way, namely that one has, for example, the experience of having hurt someone and one now experiences what the other person has experienced through having been hurt. This is now one's own actual experience, what the other person experienced here in the physical world. This experience is undergone. And in this process, a power appears within one through some inner elemental necessity: You must compensate for this, you must make amends! You can use the following comparison: a mosquito flies towards you, you shut your eyes. You carry out an action under a certain impression. After death you experience the effect of whatever you have done; you then inwardly respond by giving rise to the power to compensate for this, thus to balance out what the other person suffered through the injury. That is to say, by experiencing this in a reverse direction in the soul-world, you take into yourself the power living in this person who suffered it through you to annul it. This gives rise to a desire to be with him in earthly life in order to make amends for what one has done to him. Thus during this retrospective experience all the forces leading to the producing and balancing out of karma are engendered.

Thus already in these first years or decades after the passage through the gate of death, one gives rise to the fulfilment of karma. And just as it is true that in the seed there is a growing power which only comes to fulfilment in the blossom, so is it true that already now, in the time after the passage through the gate of death, there exists in the one who has died the germinal power which then lives as a potential throughout the life between death and a new birth, and which in the new earthly life or in subsequent earthly lives comes to fulfilment as a karmic compensation for what he has done. Thus the will arises which then as unconscious will becomes karma.

Now we can consider more closely something else which is important for the knowledge of this picture of life between death and a new birth. We can observe this if we cast our eye once more upon the interaction between the circumstances of earthly life, which are well familiar to us in their outward manifestation and to whose inner mysteries we have devoted much study, if we consider the interaction between this waking day-consciousness and the night consciousness of sleep.

We shall today consider waking and sleeping from a particular aspect. Viewed outwardly, sleep consists in that we are with our ego and astral body outside the physical and etheric bodies. Unless it is pervaded in a certain way by dream-life, sleep remains, to begin with, unconscious, but this does not mean that it is without activity. On the contrary, in terms of soul-life this life of sleep is—even if during normal earthly life it is initially unconscious—inwardly far more active than is the waking state. Waking soul-life is only as intense as it is because the activity of the ego and astral body encounters some resistance from the etheric and physical bodies, and in these mutual collisions between the ego and astral body on the one hand and the physical and etheric bodies on the other there develop continual thrusts and counter-thrusts. It is this that appears to us as waking life, whereas in normal earthly life we are not yet able to bring the continual, but intense activity during the night to consciousness. This activity does not clash with the physical and etheric bodies and therefore does not become conscious. But in itself, waking life is weaker; it becomes conscious only because it continually comes up against the etheric and physical bodies. One is aware of this opposition, whereas the more intense activity of sleep life takes on an indefinite form; it cannot come up against anything and therefore remains unconscious.

But what is a person concerned with during sleep life? When dreams occur in normal life, these dreams are not the real activity that takes place during sleep life; they are actually a picturing of the activity through memories of ordinary life. The images of dream life arise through life spreading its carpet over the real inner activity; this is why many things can be perceived in dream life. The ego and astral body are engaged in living activity; when this comes in contact with the etheric body and the human individual forms a direct connection with it, the dream arises. But the dream makes use of the physical memories from the etheric body in order to make the consistently invisible activity of the ego and astral body visible. Thus one reaches behind the dream only if one views these images in relation to the development of their character, if, therefore, one learns to understand these images. Dreams must first be read in the right way; they must be approached with the right form of interpretation. Then they will give an indication of this deeply meaningful reality in which the ego and astral body are engaged in sleep. This activity that a person carries out in sleep is revealed to a serious and worthy form of spiritual research.

In what does this activity from going to sleep to waking up consist? It consists in that one inwardly experiences the day's events again far more intensely, that one becomes in a certain sense the self-evaluator of the day's experiences. It seems a simplistic way of putting it, but it is nevertheless inwardly true to say that one lives during the day in normal consciousness, one lets the events taking place around one flow by. During the night, however, one takes the events of the day far more seriously and meaningfully through one's ego and astral body, through one's soul. One weighs them up and examines them with respect to their cosmic value. One considers what kind of significance they have in the whole context of the world. An immense, inner thoroughness in the way life is observed is expended over the activity taking place from going to sleep until waking up; but it remains unconscious in normal life. All this that a person experiences every night in living once more through the events of the day has a great significance as a preparation for the life after passing through the portal of death.

Just consider this ongoing life between birth and death with the means of ordinary physical observation. One may of course say that one remembers back to a certain point in this life. In truth one does not recall the whole of one's life, but one remembers in the evening what took place until the morning of that day. Then there is a break in one's recollections. Then comes the previous day, and then again the night, which one does not remember. Thus one remembers back, but our recollections are like links in a chain, a white and then a black link. One does not remember the night in the life between birth and death. Now what is distinctive about this time when one is living in the soul-land is that one remembers the way that one lived through the experiences of the day during the nights, tracing them back night by night. Here in physical life one remembers one's days; in the land of soul one also remembers this, but one recalls how one has worked and lived through the days during the nights. One journeys back through one's nights. This gives us an insight into the whole nature of our experience in the soul-land.

In order to make this absolutely clear, let us look at a specific case. You have met someone on a particular day of your life, you experienced this or that with him. You experience it with him not only during the day but also again during the night, and also during the following nights; it is a kind of reminiscence. You experience this inwardly in your ego and astral body. Everything that you have experienced here in waking consciousness you experience again in night consciousness. And the way that we have experienced it in night consciousness gives you the foundation for the way you need to deal with it in the soul-world. You experience your nights again. This is a very important truth of spiritual research, and one can through such a matter be mindful of the fact that research of a spiritual nature is not as many people think it to be.

Many believe that when he has entered the spiritual world the spirit-researcher immediately knows the whole of the spiritual world and everything about it. This belief is just as naive as it would be to think that someone who has explored a part of the Earth knows the whole of it. He may know some parts of the Earth very well, but he knows nothing about other parts of it. To no less a degree does someone who knows one particular aspect of the spiritual world know everything about it. This is the object of lengthy research. It is therefore so difficult to speak about spiritual science, because one constantly encounters this prejudice. When spiritual-scientific lectures are held, people demand through their questions that an answer will be given to everything. Such questions need to be judged as if someone had, for example, become familiar with a certain number of minerals or plants and he was then asked to explain the mysteries of the animal world on the grounds that he knows the one and he must therefore also know the other!

It is indeed the case that every detail about the spiritual world must first be worked out through careful study. Above all, one must be able to wait until insight into one or another matter is granted. You have been able to see that in my books *Occult Science: An Outline* and *Theosophy*[51] I have spoken about the approximate duration of the so-called life in kamaloka, the life in the soul-world. From a certain point of view one can undoubtedly speak of it in this way. But the spirit-researcher now enters a situation which can be compared with journeying through different countries. One comes from one place to another, and so one comes in this situation from one region to another. Thus the spirit-researcher can arrive at a different standpoint; and to the question, 'With what is the activity of the ego and astral body during the night concerned?' this standpoint yields the answer: 'The experiences of the night can be regarded in such a way that they are a further assimilation of the day's experiences.' I have indicated that life in the soul-world lasts for approximately a third of the duration of the last earthly life. If we sleep through our nights, how long will life in the soul-world last? Well, we are asleep for approximately a third of our lives here on the Earth; some people more, others less, but as a rule we are asleep for approximately a third of our earthly lives.

These are some immensely significant impressions that one can have in relation to the verification of spiritual science. For in spiritual science something is presented to one from a certain standpoint from which one gains insight into the spiritual world, and a truth results from this. Someone may question the validity of this truth. Then one proceeds from a different standpoint and arrives at the same truth, as is now the case with the retrospective journey through the nights. This makes verification possible. Such an inner agreement is an important criterion. You will find this everywhere in spiritual science wherever it is seriously and worthily pursued: that the same phenomenon is viewed from these different standpoints. When people acquire a feeling for the value that this manner of approaching spiritual truths and then finding this spiritual truth has for the pursuit of truth, they will also sense that what can be investigated in this realm is immensely more true than everything that can be investigated in the physical world.

The essential and most important point is that here in physical, earthly life we have a memory of what we have experienced in waking consciousness, and that during the time that we spend in the soul-world we have the ability to remember what is developed further during the nights on the basis of what our waking consciousness experiences.

In order that we can most fruitfully approach the important truths that we shall be addressing tomorrow, we shall call to mind something that I have already mentioned in another context with respect to the great events of our time. When someone passes through the gate of death such that his life is, as it were, snatched away from outside or has in whatever way died at a young age, the separation from the etheric body also takes place shortly after he has crossed the threshold of death. But this etheric body would have had the power to sustain the rest of the person's life with external life-forces. Generally speaking, a human being receives sufficient forces in his etheric body for sustaining him with life-forces into old age. If his life is broken off, these forces nevertheless remain; they are also present in the etheric body which has been laid aside. And just as no forces in the physical world are lost but are merely transformed, so these forces, too, are not lost but remain in existence. If you translate this into concrete terms, you will say that when someone dies in the flower of his youth he bequeaths to the world the life-forces that he still has in his etheric body, forces which he could have used himself. To put it even more specifically, take a young man, say a twenty-five-year-old, who has been mortally wounded by a bullet: he makes available to the world etheric forces which he could have used from the age of twenty-six for the remainder of a long life. This remains; it is a gift that the dead person bequeaths to the spiritual atmosphere of life in which we dwell. We continue to be surrounded by these forces. And in these forces there reside the sacrificial convictions with which the person who has died in this way has imbued his etheric forces. This remains. And those who come after do not realize how they actually live within the forces left behind in this way by their predecessors, how they are surrounded by these forces and how our spiritual breath of life is permeated by them. They pay no attention to what is thus left behind by the departed at such a time, when in a relatively short span of time so many etheric bodies with unspent forces are being given over to the Earth's atmosphere. We shall speak further about this theme tomorrow.

We shall in conclusion direct our attention to what is revealed to us by such deep connections through which we are able to gain insight into the spiritual world, and to behold the spirit no longer in an abstract and simplistic way as befits the sense-world or as a nebulous conundrum but by discovering in it something concretely and intrinsically spiritual. Alongside the destinies unfolding in human individuals who have crossed the threshold of death, we behold beings of the higher hierarchies, beings of the elemental world. But we also perceive what continues to be inwardly connected with the Earth: that which has remained behind in etheric bodies. The unspent etheric forces that are left behind by those who find death on the great battlefields of our present time will have a quite definite influence. This will be united with the understanding that is offered up to these seeds for the future on the part of the children of the Earth. And with this in mind we say, as we have often said at the end of our contemplative studies:

> From the courage of the fighters,
> From the blood on fields of battle,
> From the grief of the bereaved,
> From the people's sacrifice:
> There will ripen fruit of spirit,
> If souls will turn in consciousness
> Towards the realm of spirit.

LECTURE 6

STUTTGART, 24 NOVEMBER 1915

WE shall devote this evening to giving consideration to the interplay between the spiritual and physical worlds. This has already been the subject of our studies during these days. Our chief purpose will be to develop further the theme that we have broached; but I should like to proceed from a more general viewpoint that will show us how it is possible to think in a more abstract, general way about the interplay between the spiritual and physical worlds or the super-earthly and earthly domains, how this can be encompassed by a simple thought. From this more general viewpoint we shall then proceed to what really concerns us: the relationship of someone who is disembodied through having passed through the portal of death to those who are embodied in this earthly life.

Let us first consider our Earth as the scene of what presents itself to our senses. I shall begin purely hypothetically with some thoughts and ideas which may at first appear to be somewhat contrived. Suppose that all the forces related to our Earth are, as it were, concentrated or compressed in a small image of them which has somehow been formed. Thus we would envisage that we had a small, tiny body which nevertheless contained in miniature certain forces that the Earth has within it on a large scale. We want to represent this schematically. We want to imagine that we had a little Earth, that is, a little, tiny body, which contained the same relationship of forces as may be found in the greater context of the Earth's body. Let us imagine that this little earthly body is in some way connected with the Earth.

Now if we are to have a right conception of the Earth, we must not think of it as some kind of lifeless being as, for instance, a geologist or mineralogist who imagines it to be purely lifeless would conceive it to be; for if the Earth were only mineral in nature as the geologist thinks, it would never be able to engender plants, animals and human beings. Of course, the geologist is right to delineate what is dead, but he would have to be aware that he is dealing with only one part of earthly existence. If, however, we conceive of this Earth as a living organism, we should also think of it as being so imbued with life that the living course of time belongs to the being of the Earth. Thus as we have frequently pointed out, the Earth in winter is in an entirely different state than in summer, just as a human being who is asleep is in a different condition from when he is awake. We should not think that winter and summer simply extend over the Earth but that they are phenomena that take hold of the Earth's condition as a living being in the same way that the states of waking and sleeping take hold of us. Hence this temporal succession forms part of earthly existence if we regard earthly existence as something living. But at the same time this means that every being that is connected with the Earth (and hence also the little Earth of which we are speaking here) shares in these changing conditions of the Earth and is an integral part of them.

What is the significance of these changing states for our Earth? Let us say, for example, that spring has arrived. The coming of spring means that, as regards its influence upon the Earth, the Sun enters into a quite different relationship than exists during the winter. We could also say that when the spring arrives the Earth is gripped by the influences of the Sun. Whereas during the winter our little Earth was, together with the greater Earth, as it were, reliant upon itself and the Sun did not concern itself with our little Earth, our little Earth is now encompassed by the Sun's influences, by what is outside our Earth. The sum of forces residing in the little Earth is torn away from the Earth. Our little Earth is, so to speak, no longer dependent solely upon the Earth; it is claimed by the Sun, it is torn away from the Earth. Indeed, when our little Earth is thus torn away from the Earth, other forces than the pure earthly forces influence our little Earth, forces from without are imparted to it.

We must now think of this little Earth as clothed in material substances. The nature of this material substance is of no present concern. Thus from autumn to spring this little Earth is left to itself and can unfold within itself its own forces. Then, however, comes the Sun which draws these forces forth, so that under the Sun's influence what was initially confined within our little Earth now enters into a sphere of influences external to the Earth. It is torn out and is subject to outer-earthly influences. That which was pressed together can spread out and acquires a relationship also to the surrounding spatial world and to the influence of the Sun.

After a certain time as autumn approaches, the Sun's influence now begins to cease and this development cannot take place. The forces emanating from the Sun's influence then withdraw from those of the Earth, that is, this latter complex of forces is restored. It gathers the material substances together: the Earth again takes hold of what it had for a time to leave to the Sun. The influences of the Sun are now absent for a while and winter comes. If they remained available to the Earth, the Sun would lay claim to a little Earth within the greater Earth. The system of Earth-forces must be active during the whole of winter. The Sun would otherwise gather up this little Earth wholly for itself. In return, provision must be made that when the Sun reappears it may again take hold of this little Earth; otherwise, it would simply become a little spherical ball which would be swallowed up by the big Earth. A power must assert itself whereby the Sun can, when it reappears, again approach this little Earth. But provision must be made for this.

If the forces of the Earth are now contained within this point [a drawing was made on the blackboard], this will be a little Earth. The Sun has withdrawn, and now this little Earth is left to itself together with the big Earth. If the Sun were to return, what should it do with what has become only Earth? The Sun must be able to take hold of the Earth again (and it makes no difference whether the Sun goes round the Earth or the Earth around the Sun); it must be able to exercise its influence when it thus enters into a new relationship to the Earth. You can envisage it in the following way. Think of someone who takes up a firm position and summons all his strength in order to remain where he is. You approach him from the side and try to push him away. If his determination to remain where he is has intensified, you will not be able to move him. But if he himself begins to move, you will be able to influence the direction of his movements. Let us suppose that there would here be a power such as the rotational movement of the Sun exerts upon the Earth as a kind of centrifugal force; let us suppose that this centrifugal force of the Sun is imparted to the little Earth: the Sun could then again influence this movement which it has initiated. It could in this way again tear the little Earth away from the Earth, and the process could take its course as described. In other words, with the approach of spring we would have a little Earth influenced by the Sun through impulses of movement which it imparted to it during the previous autumn. The Sun intervenes, tears the little Earth away from the pure Earth-forces and, in proportion to the Sun's influence, develops on a larger scale what is confined to the little Earth. The forces must draw themselves together, and the little earthly sphere must be endowed with the Sun's centrifugal force. You will already have an idea of what this is about: I have been describing in outline what happens during the growth of plants in leaves, blossoms and fruit. I have described to you the influence of the Sun's momentum: this is when fructification takes place; the seed is fertilized and remains in this state until the following year when it is again subject to the Sun's influence. The little grain of corn that brings about fructification in the plant is that to which the Sun's ripening process entrusts the possibility of imparting this centrifugal force to the earthly part.

You see, we have here a living interaction between the earthly realm and what is spatially outside the Earth. We cannot imagine that the plant's growth will continue unless the Sun leaves it with a reflection of its centrifugal force which it can again connect with the following year. In other words: if we study the plant, we actually do not merely observe something that is connected with earthly activity but we see in the whole cycle of plant development an interaction between Sun and Earth. Other planetary conditions should also be taken into account; however, we shall not enter these now, we want to understand the significance of the whole process. We want to imagine that what we see on the Earth is not merely the product of earthly forces but that it is also a product of the Sun. The circumstance that human knowledge is usually limited to what happens on the Earth in an inner and an outer sense prevents one from arriving at a real conception, a real knowledge of things; for only our minerals are formed from purely earthly forces. The moment when we go beyond the purely mineral realm into that of the plant, we must say that the forces that form things can no longer be found in the earthly realm itself.

Materialists always hope that one day they will be able to produce a plant seed in the laboratory as if it were just another chemical compound. The opposition to materialism does not have to do with this but arises through the reality that, as one passes from the mineral to the plant, from a chemical substance to something living, this can be brought about only through a super-terrestrial process. And before this ideal of materialism to manufacture plant seeds as one would mineral products or chemical substances can be successful, the materialists will—though this would be pushing the bounds of possibility—have to learn to believe in astrology, to believe that they must subject a process that they will want to be effectual to the influence of the workings of the stars. There will have to be laboratories which function in such a way that they work with the course of the year and likewise take account of the position of the stars, just as the starry constellations are taken into account in nature. One must raise oneself from the Earth when one rises from the dead to the living; for the etheric bodily nature must collaborate in the engendering of living substance. This etheric element is, however, never purely dependent on what belongs only to the earthly realm but on what is disseminated in the world as a whole. When we survey our earthly world, our field of vision embraces what is purely physical; in that we survey the earthly world, we perceive the physical from the earthly standpoint. But that which is of an etheric nature for our Earth is always subjected to the whole universe.

If we go still further as far as the astral world, we come to an element which is no longer part of the visible world. Were I to develop a diagram for the animal world as I have drawn for the plants, it would be more complicated; but you would see that not only the extraterrestrial element and all that is visible in the starry world enter into consideration but the supersensible element as a whole, which is not confined to the world of the stars. One must go beyond the sphere of the visible world.

I wanted to place these thoughts before you in order that you might gain an insight into the deeply mysterious nature of what is going on even in ordinary life, in the daily growth of plants, so that you might gain an insight into how what needs especially to be borne in mind when considering the fructifying grains of the plant's blossom, which are arranged in a circular or in some other form around the pistil, is that they contain extraterrestrial influences, and how what is important about the seed itself is that it is essentially a reflection of the entire activity of the Earth, that it is a little Earth. The interaction that takes place in the plant's blossom through fertilization is a reflection of the process occurring between the Earth and the entire starry world of the surrounding cosmic spaces.

We are indeed surrounded on all sides by mysteries, and knowledge and the striving after knowledge is always a spur to the deepest modesty. Just think how far one has to go from having a general conception of such things to an actual perception of the details concerning everything that makes up the plant-covering of the Earth. The field of knowledge then reveals itself as infinite. We confront infinity, as it were, at every point of our existence; and it forms part of the right mood that a person should develop towards the world to have a sense that one is actually gazing everywhere into an infinitude of existence. One thereby also feels a certain bond between the finite individual life of a human being and the infinity of the world as a whole. This is a mood that one should pour forth over every detail that spiritual science can bring to us, for without this feeling of reverence towards the infinite nothing in spiritual science can be grasped with the frame of mind that is appropriate to it. One must from time to time renew such a mood within one so that one ceases to regard knowledge as something that is ancillary to the real concerns of life; it should, rather, belong to the holiest and most spiritual aspects of our lives.

If one devotes attention to such moods, one will also receive with the right attitude what will from now onwards into the future need increasingly to be communicated in our present time out of the sources of spiritual science for the progress that the world needs. And if we have developed such an attitude, this is a frame of mind which becomes an active force within our soul. It is not merely something abstract but it takes hold of our soul, it pervades our soul with warmth and light. And the right thing will emerge from spiritual science only if our soul is transformed through feelings that have embraced what has resulted from spiritual research. Only if we fill our soul with such feelings will we be able rightly to solve the riddles concerning aspects of life that otherwise pass us by without our being able to confront them in the right way.

There really is an inner soul-connection between these general observations that I have just been presenting and what I now want to go on to say with regard to human life. If one directs one's attention to a plant and sees it sprouting from the earth, one can attune one's soul in such a way that it has the feeling: the green shoot that is springing forth has its origin in a little entity, the seed, which is so complicated that this little entity is—from a certain point of view—a reflection of the whole Earth and that the whole universe collaborates in what I see there shooting up and developing from leaf to blossom, from the blossom to the fruit. When I contemplate the green leaf of a plant on its stem, I am aware that in the way that this leaf is attached to the stem and flourishes, what was first enclosed within the little Earth, what was torn away from the Earth until the influences of the Sun took hold of it, is being embraced by the Sun's influence. But then the Sun withdraws its radiating influences once they have made it impossible for what was within the little Earth to spread out, when it is again necessary for it to draw itself together. In the sprouting, developing plant we see, so to speak, a picture of certain influences of the whole, vast cosmos. We must in this way regard what presents itself to our senses as something that at every point reveals to us mysteries which waft and weave through the entire cosmos.

But human life is also connected with the whole cosmos and also with that which confronts us from the bodies and processes that are visible in extraterrestrial spaces. A particularly significant aspect of what appears to us in earthly processes is, however, evident if we take into consideration deviations from what we are accustomed to regard as normal earthly life, normal human life. Indeed, we are constantly aware of far more deviations or anomalies than normalities in life, but ordinary cognitive faculties—limited as they are to the world of the senses—do not engage with these deviations from the norm, they do not enter into their meaning. We are living at a time when a whole collection of such anomalies are manifesting themselves which are at the same time true riddles. Do we not see, at this time of great trials for humanity, many of our human brothers passing prematurely through the portal of death? We see them passing through the gate of death in such a way that they are doing so not through some kind of illness, thus through something residing in their own organism, but as the result of a violent death. For it is a different matter whether a human soul passes through the gate of death as a result of dying through illness at a young age or if its bodily organism has been struck by a bullet or in some other way forcibly severed from its soul-spiritual nature. But I have already explained yesterday that everything that takes place here between birth and death is of significance in the whole context of life; we must view it in terms of karmic connections, we must acknowledge karma in the way that it is given to us. And yet everything that happens has its significance.

Let us now consider the case where the physical organism is taken away from the soul-spiritual nature by a bullet at a relatively young age. In comparison to what we are accustomed to—that a person himself uses up what resides in his organism—this is an abnormal situation. A twofold riddle is therefore involved here. Whereas death itself is for immediate perception a riddle that spiritual science can solve, a further riddle arises where the course of life is not of such a nature that the organism is severed from the soul and spirit through inner organic processes but if this is brought about by a bullet.

An inner mood is engendered within the soul by such simple reflections which fills us with an inner, intensified awareness of the mysteries of the universe and of our place within it. And when the soul is gripped by such feelings, we shall also approach the event which I have just mentioned, that the physical body is severed by violent means from the soul and spirit, with the necessary reverence and dignity. This question then appears before us as a riddle. For the *way* in which such a question arises determines whether or not one can contribute something to its solution. If someone has taken part in a festive meal and then after having a rest sets about his spiritual work, he will not solve this deep riddle; for he will not be able to awaken the necessary mood. If, however, he approaches the riddle by filling his soul with the right feelings towards the universe, he will find the answer to it.

If, then, the spirit-researcher approaches with such a mood the riddle of death that presents itself to us where the physical body has through violent means been torn away from the soul-spiritual nature, all manner of things arise in the soul which can contribute to the solution of the riddle. The right impressions that one needs to bring clarity to such a matter will then emerge. They cannot arise from any mood of soul but only one that is appropriate. I have adopted the course that I have chosen today in order that you may have an inner perception of the task facing the spirit-researcher. Thus when the spirit-researcher has developed the appropriate mood, the riddle in question rises up before him. But something quite different then also arises. Just as otherwise one thought can follow another at random, so in response to the question an impression then presents itself as if in obedience to a law. And then if one has experienced something of this riddle of death, one may come to feel that another question that belongs to it also arises, namely: How do human beings relate to life in their individual ways? And then all kinds of thoughts begin to develop, thoughts that I should like to place before you now.

In our present cycle of development, people only really accept as a reality what is not a 'mere thought'. A thought for them has nothing real about it. And from their point of view they may be right, but this gives rise to a certain mood of soul. What is real, they say, should approach one more solidly than a mere thought, it should be far more robust. A mere thought is, after all, merely a thought! But what one designates as having real existence should not on any account be merely a thought for people today; for a mere thought has no real existence. Something that has real existence must be a solid presence in the world, it should not appeal to thought alone. Out of this mood people only believe that they are dwelling in reality when they can speak of this reality as something which actually exists, as a being, when they are forced to recognize this reality through something that has existence.

Now when we ascend from the world in which we are now living to the spiritual world that a person inhabits when he has passed through the gate of death, the most uncomfortable thought is, one might say, the thought of the existence that has taken shape here in the physical world. The form of existence that one has in the physical world disturbs the disembodied person in the spiritual world. Precisely that which one characterizes here—in contrast to real existence—as something unreal is the true reality. If in the spiritual world we would encounter things that have real existence to us here, we would reject them, they would fill us with horror, they would be something that that does not belong in the spiritual world. This is a thought of immense significance. If one were to speak in the spiritual world as superficially as one does here, one could as a spirit say on encountering something in the way things are here: What am I supposed to do with this? There is absolutely no reality in any of it! For in the spiritual world I must have the possibility of being able to participate in everything that confronts me as an imagination (in the spiritual world this occurs at the lowest stage of knowledge), that is, of being able to convert it into a perception through my own activity. Whereas in our time people only acknowledge the reality of what they have done nothing to bring about, one cannot do this in the spiritual world; for the situation in the spiritual world is that one must do something, one must play one's part, in order that what is to appear to one as a reality may arise.

The fact is that someone who is disembodied in the spiritual world beholds the spiritual world around him to the extent that he is active within it; and what he sees without being active is the world beyond the threshold, that is, our world that is on this side of it. When a disembodied person beholds the Earth he sees what is there without taking part in it. Just as here on Earth we designate our visible world, our real existence, as being on this side, and what we do not see as being on yonder side, the opposite situation pertains from the standpoint of the spiritual world. In the spiritual world there is nothing other than what we create out of nothing in the present by collaborating in placing it there; and this then constitutes 'this side'. Otherwise, 'this side' in the spiritual world is dark, inert and desolate if we are not active within it in a soul-spiritual sense; it is a 'yonder' world if it exists without our collaboration. Whereas here on Earth we look up to the unknown, from the spiritual world we look down upon what is familiar to us here—but this is 'the beyond' which has no reality, because it exists without our having done anything towards its existence. We must make ourselves familiar with such notions.

Now there is something within our physical existence, our physical reality, which not all but nevertheless certain people regard as significant, even though it does not actually exist. It is something that particular people introduce into this otherwise existing reality and to which those who have an understanding for such things relate in such a way that they attribute validity to it, even though it lacks the solidity of ordinary reality. These are the ideals which people cherish. Idealists bring something into our sense-perceptible reality which has a value: the ideals governing people's lives which are bereft of solid, material reality and which only the coarsest of materialists reject. These ideals are at the same time something of immense value in that they govern people's lives. With ideals, something unreal from a materialistic point of view must be introduced into our sense-perceptible reality in order to prevent a situation arising which we may perhaps characterize by saying that life would be desolate if there were no ideals, if people were unable to find them anywhere. Those who have no ideals have to associate with idealists who, as it were, develop something in our reality that is a reflection of that yonder reality which is not an existent reality, which has no claim to actuality but is nevertheless something of value, indeed, of absolute value.

When the spirit-researcher has developed the impression that he is able to form, his research leads him back to the riddle concerning someone who has been hit by a bullet when he is still young. He now has to ask himself: Is there something which, for that yonder world in which disembodied people and beings of soul and spirit live, corresponds to the idealism that is a feature of earthly life? Is there for the beings dwelling beyond the threshold something similar to ideals here on the Earth? When faced with such a question, the following picture emerges. Take the case of a person who has been hit by a bullet in his youth: his etheric body separates from the physical body, the physical body has been wrenched away from him. Of course, this violence must come from without. What I have said can never apply where a personal decision is involved. The process *has* to come from without. Thus as I have already emphasized, the etheric body has forces within itself which could perhaps have supported life here on the Earth for several decades. These forces do not fade away, they continue in existence. Someone who discards his etheric body in this way imparts the forces of his etheric body to the universe. He has entered the spiritual world in the manner indicated, and by the same token his body has been taken away from him; and thus he now ascends into the spiritual world as a disembodied spirit. Something of him remains behind in the physical world which he would have been able to use but has not done so. Just consider the situation! The human being in question ascends into the spiritual world without having used up something that he could have used.

Let us now turn our attention to the individuality of such a person. The human being in question enters the spiritual world without have used something that he could have used. He thereby comes into the spiritual world with something that could have had a reality down in the physical world but has not become a reality in the outward sense. Such people who have entered here into the physical world, who have come to the Earth, with the predisposition for using their etheric body for a longer time but have not had this degree of use enter into the spiritual world differently from those who have used this etheric body until their declining years. In entering the spiritual world they embody within this Earth what has the potential to be but has not actually come into existence. This evokes within them a mood through which they become something similar for the spiritual world to what idealists are here for the physical world. Thus someone who passes in this way through the portal of death brings something into the spiritual world that constitutes idealism for it, something similar to the ideals that are brought by idealists into the physical world. A significant and meaningful connection!

Thus at such times of martyrdom as the present, souls enter the spiritual world whose span of life has been shorter than normal. They have lived on the Earth in such a way that something that could have existed did not become a reality for them, and the manner of their entering the spiritual world is that the connection which they manifest there with the earthly world is of a kind that idealists here manifest for the Earth with the spiritual world in their ideals. In other words, these human beings who have thus passed through the gate of death have the task of proclaiming in the spiritual world that not everything on the Earth is so solidly real as that which under normal circumstances one here calls reality, that the Earth also contains something that is indeed predisposed to existence but does not express this existence in a coarsely substantial way. That such an inner soul-mood is also borne up into the spiritual world gives rise in the time between death and a new birth to something similar to idealism here on the Earth. And if we consider such a period of time as our present one from the standpoint of the wisdom of the world, then—provided that we have engendered the right mood as we contemplate the deaths that arise in this way—our perception of the world will be such that we say to ourselves: Within the whole, wisdom-filled course of the world, let us also accept this in such a way that we reverentially develop an understanding of it. We will then recognize that at such a time of martyrdom as ours something is given in a great, all-encompassing sense to the spiritual worlds which must live in them as idealism lives among us here on Earth, in order that the human beings who enter the spiritual world and experience the life between death and a new birth find something similar in this world to the idealism that we find here on Earth. These periods of time must therefore arise. Whether they will continue to have to arise in the future is a question that does not need to be discussed today, for it is dependent on what way, not only on whether but in what way, the cognitive life of humanity on the Earth is spiritualized. No one should draw the conclusion from what has been said that such periods should always be defended; but if one penetrates into their true meaning, what I have explained can be seen as applying to the present situation of humanity.

Then we will contemplate the wisdom inherent in the world and say to ourselves: What is the real connection between the fear and terror, the pain and sorrow, and what those who pass through the portal of death must necessarily find? We see how pain, sorrow, blood and sacrificial deaths that manifest themselves here from the one side are seen from the other side. One may well think that there are people who want to be more clever than the Gods and therefore pose the question: Could the Gods not have brought about in the spiritual world something corresponding to idealism on the Earth without inflicting such a period of martyrdom as the Earth has had to endure? Only those who want to be more clever than the Gods ask such questions. People who wish to gain a right insight into this period of mankind's evolution want to understand the world because they are convinced that it is as it is because it has to be, and that everything that may be fancifully elaborated about something that might be better for this world would only make everything worse.

We look upon idealists, perhaps the most idealistic person in the world; if we have a sense for ideals we may perhaps have tried to say: Look at this person, he is bringing heaven to the Earth, for he brings as something that has value for existence and is a guiding impulse for human beings what does not exist in any substantial sense! The souls who have passed normally through the gate of death and are experiencing the life between death and a new birth can also perceive souls in this life who have in some way undergone a sacrificial death and whose physical bodies have been externally taken away from them through some earthly necessity. They look upon these souls as upon those whose task it is to tell them that down on the Earth there is not merely existence in the solid sense but that with the Earth are also connected human predispositions which could potentially be existing and yet do not come into full existence and, instead of using their existence to the full, pass into the spiritual world at an earlier point of their lives between birth and death.

The significant question that surely arises here concerns the difference between such a violent death and a death which is the result of an illness early in life; for what I have just said is nothing other than a statement of facts. It is those whose physical lives have ended in the way that I have described who are, so to speak, the idealists of the spiritual world; and they are idealists because—as further contemplation shows—their physical body has been taken away from them through earthly events, through events that belong to earthly life.

When someone suffers an illness, his body is taken away from him by forces that are different from earthly forces. After all, even in the process of plant growth not only earthly forces are involved but also extraterrestrial forces. This is, of course, also the case with animals and even more so with human beings. Our illnesses do not derive only from the Earth. The only way that we will encounter death purely from the Earth is if we suffer a violent death. However death may occur, it is never the result of earthly circumstances unless it has, as indicated, been brought about through violent means. Even though death may be caused by illness or by suicide (which is not an earthly event since it is the result of a decision of the soul), there is no death which is brought about by earthly forces other than that which through sacrificial death, through forces belonging to the Earth, severs the body from the soul and spirit. Thus here there is a reciprocal relationship between earthly forces and connections and something of a spiritual nature. Death is otherwise always something that fully extends beyond the Earth; it is never simply an interplay of forces between the Earth and the spiritual world. An etheric body which has been prematurely withdrawn from its activity is given over to purely earthly conditions, to something that belongs to events of a purely earthly nature; this is the source of what one can call the idealism of the spiritual world. For death—and what I have to say now needs to be seen in the context of many thoughts that have been expressed during these days—when viewed from the physical aspect appears quite differently than when it is viewed from the spiritual aspect. I have indicated this in various ways.[52]

But when death does not occur in the way that I have now been indicating, it is always something that, when viewed from the other side, can be understood from this other side. If one enters the other world as a result of an illness, because of old age or even suicide, one has in this spiritual world what one needs to understand such a death. But if death is brought about by a bullet on the field of battle, one must look to purely earthly circumstances in order to understand it. It is similar with accidents. As one looks down from the spiritual world, one sees that one belonged to the earthly world; death has to be explained through earthly circumstances. This means that one must look down from the 'this side' of the spiritual world to the 'yonder side' of the physical world in order to understand such a death.

Just as here on Earth ideals connect us with heaven, so do heavenly ideals connect these dead people with the Earth. Thus a person who in this way crosses the threshold of death is someone who in the life between death and a new birth weaves into all that takes place among the human souls who are approaching a further incarnation that which gives our Earth a leaven of something spiritual, that which enables the Earth itself to consist also of our thoughts and feelings and not merely of earthly things.

It has to be admitted that it is difficult to characterize these things of which I have been speaking. However, it is understandable that it must be difficult, because one is speaking with words that are appropriate for physical circumstances about what extends far and away beyond these circumstances. It is in any case a different matter whether one, so to speak, looks blankly and with incomprehension at the puzzling nature of such events which arise in human life from out of the womb of history, such as our present time of trials for humanity, or whether one regards them in such a way that one says to oneself: What gives meaning to such an event has significance not only for our Earth but for the whole of life! And one will in this feeling also be led to the deep significance and the wisdom-filled course of the totality of life. One gradually learns to have an inkling of all that must work together in order that man is placed into the world in the entirety of his life's course.

This is what I wanted to indicate in my second Mystery Play[53] from the mouth of Capesius, when he says that the thoughts and collaboration of many Gods are needed in order to enable man to appear as their goal from out of all worlds. What comes to expression in this play from the soul of Capesius as a cosmic feeling can perhaps become an objective fact if one tries to identify oneself with the kind of thoughts as we are wanting also today to instil within our souls. In such personalities as Capesius, such moods acquire a tragic quality because they can also arise without there being any possibility of fully finding a solution to the riddle. This is one thing that needs to be pointed out; and the other is that we must always bear in mind the extent to which such studies call upon our modesty and humility, not our pride and delusions of grandeur.

Rightly acquiring human self-consciousness entails inwardly and constantly making it a present reality. And when we begin to sense the full extent of what our consciousness can encompass and how far the horizon of the world-riddle extends, we will be preserved from succumbing to such a thought as this: 'O man, you are indeed an epitome of the entire cosmos!' I believe that this is just the kind of thought that we will have to avoid. On the other hand, this other thought may well suggest itself to us: 'How little we consciously know of what it is possible to know!' An infinity of things is needed to make a human being; but we have never managed to know more than a very small part of it. Modesty and humility are the qualities that will emerge from this knowledge and fill our soul once its scope has been extended. One can never learn more than one already knows about the spiritual world without at the same time coming to realize that the things that can be known are infinite. And the sense that one has of this infinity becomes more alive the more one knows. And one learns to understand that an intrinsic part of life consists in thus letting oneself be gripped by the great, mighty riddles and mysteries that penetrate existence to its core.

Much of what humanity must now struggle to achieve was known by human beings in ancient times as part of an ancient wisdom that belonged to them as an inheritance. What human beings possess today has been gained only because this inheritance has been lost to human souls. It had to disappear so that human souls might be able to regain this wisdom; it had to disappear so that it can become wisdom that people develop for themselves. We must again set to work in order to rediscover for ourselves in a distant earthly life, in the future course of earthly existence, the inherited wisdom that has disappeared from human souls. This is how we must view the perspective of the future of mankind; and we shall then understand the necessity that spiritual science finds its place in the world. It is this endeavour to discover a living relationship with the infinite that has been characterized which gives us the possibility of taking hold of that aspect of science which is veiled in secrecy as something inwardly alive, something that is also an active force within us which can enable us to become true collaborators in forming and fashioning the Earth, which indeed we must become if the Earth is to develop further.

In order to add further weight to this, I should like to mention something else. There are people to whom we are supposed to listen because they say the right thing from the standpoint of the present. They say that in former times there was no knowledge of criminals or of why someone becomes a criminal. But today we know all about this. If one dissects the head of a criminal, one finds that it has a particular quality: the posterior lobes of the brain do not fully cover the cerebellum as they do in the case of a normal person. This was a great, significant discovery that Moritz Benedikt,[54] the famous criminologist, made which shows how a simple physiological characteristic of the back of the head causes someone to be a criminal. Just consider: one becomes a criminal if the posterior lobes of one's brain do not cover what should be covered! No objection can be made to this truth. It is a fact, and one would be naive to take issue with it since it is an objective fact. But think for a moment. If one is a materialist, what should one say? Well, some people are born with little brain-lobes, so they are predestined to become criminals. I do not need to say anything further about the infinite hopelessness of such a view of the world! Just think of how every human feeling would have to change if one had no alternative but to say, in answer to the question of why people become criminals, that they cannot do otherwise because this is how they were made by nature.

But if one has some inkling of the fact that one has an etheric body, one can give a different explanation, there is something else that one knows. One knows that this etheric body encompasses all parts of the body, and that where a person's posterior lobes are too short, the corresponding etheric parts can still attain their full development. Whatever the situation may be with the physical body, a corrective can be achieved with the etheric body. If, then, we succeed in developing a pedagogy whereby we call upon the help not only of physical but also of spiritual science, we shall be able to see from the way that a child behaves what is necessary for its education and what precautions we must take so that the etheric body develops in such a way that it paralyses the influence of the stunted posterior lobes. Then if the etheric body is normally developed at the back of the brain, a person can nevertheless become a good man even if he was physically predestined to become a criminal. Here you see how spiritual science can and must influence life in a practical way; for a purely physical science has no option but to allow a criminal brain to be a criminal brain, because it is only a science of physical things. But if we take spiritual science into consideration, we paralyse the physical deficiencies. From this it becomes clear to you how things must develop in the future.

And now consider how it would be if spiritual science did not exist! There would then never be any possibility of developing the etheric body in such a way as I have just described. This means that someone who was born with a stunted brain would have to live out his life in accordance with this brain. There would be no possibility of making amends for this through pedagogical means. The consequence would be that human beings would have to become what their physical organization dictated. And this would continue further, so that people would arrive at the Jupiter condition and what materialists dream up today would have become a reality. If that which derives from the purely material organization is not overcome through spiritual science, human beings will gradually develop in such a way that this material organization will be the decisive factor; they would then be merely a result of their material development. Through spiritual science intervening in life, this will not happen on Jupiter; for the etheric body will exert a transforming influence on the physical body. If the etheric body is rightly developed in a life in which former karmic antecedents have led to a stunting of the physical brain, in the next incarnation the physical brain will develop properly. This affects everything. Thus spiritual science indeed becomes a reality in that it is able to exert a transforming influence upon mankind.

If you bring all these thoughts into a single focus, you will be able to see that what materialists today think of man is not as yet a reality, for man is still able to gain access to the spiritual world. But it could turn out to be as materialists think if things were to take their course in accordance with their ideas, if spiritual science were to be eradicated by the materialists. Thus human beings would live on Jupiter purely as a consequence of their material organization if the dreams of materialists were to be fulfilled.

But what, in reality, is it to be a materialist? Materialists have a conception of the world which does not at present correspond to reality but which could one day become a reality as far as human beings are concerned. These materialists are prophets, but they are false prophets! They dream of a world that, were it to develop in their way, could come into being. Materialists are dreamers, but one must counteract their fantasies. If one sees that materialists are dreamers, then one must say to them: You are part of the world, but you do not perceive its reality; you dream of an existence that could only arise in the world through your lack of insight; you are false prophets and you dream up all manner of fantasies!—one will have a right assessment of them. Thus we will have to have the opposite judgement of what materialists dream up for themselves. Then the time will have arrived when spiritual science can really be understood. In a certain sense spiritual science will transform the world already out of this insight.

In the course of these days I have tried to give some indications of the connection of the physical world with the spiritual world. I have spoken out of impulses arising from the significant events of our time. At a time when death confronts us daily in a thousand-fold different ways, such considerations—if they are presented as possibilities—may indeed speak to our situation. For how could one refrain from searching for the meaning and purpose of existence at such a difficult time of trial as the present! It has given me deep satisfaction that at this difficult time I have been able to be with you again to speak about such questions. I wish only to add the thought that at this present time there is much that must be viewed in accordance with the nature of what is going on now. It is currently not so simple to travel about everywhere as in times of peace. Thus our members, too, must be conscious of something that indeed all people need to be aware of, namely that times of war are different from normal times and that we cannot expect everything to be as it is in normal times. I say this quite especially because it is often quite notably overlooked by our members, whereas it is precisely our members who should have a deep understanding of what is going on at present and, moreover, a living connection with it. It frequently becomes apparent that our members are unable to see how necessary it is to be aware that we are living in difficult times, and that not everything can continue to happen with the same regularity as normal. But we must keep firm faith in our cause. What each of us can do at this time towards enabling the various branches or groups of our Society to achieve much with respect to the aims that we serve will indeed be done not only for the sake of our cause but will bring healing on a much wider scale.

It is natural that the community must now become looser; and the work in our branches must be all the more intense, especially as regards matters of the soul. This is what I particularly wanted to place before your souls and hearts. Let each of us try especially at this time to remain faithful to our ideals, to stand by the convictions that we have been able to form in the course of time through spiritual science. Spiritual science must be safeguarded not only when times are easy but also in times of difficulty. A quality that may admittedly seem banal but is nevertheless a fundamental aspect of all our strivings needs now to form an especially deep part of our inner lives: the endeavour to comprehend life in a many-sided way. In contrast to so much that is now put forward in the outer world with its inclination towards materialism (and often in an utterly one-sided way), we want to aspire to the manifoldness of life. We want to be sure that, because we face eternity at every moment, we must constantly be on our guard against any comfortable one-sided opinions.

Some of you may perhaps have heard that in one place where our spiritual science is cultivated it was necessary to speak about all sorts of shortcomings which have presented themselves here and there. If one or another person has been hurt by certain things that were said, such people should not have recourse to one-sidedness of a different kind. I say this not to discuss such things at length but merely as an example. If, for instance, people who have spoken about all kinds of occult events and experiences did not do so in the right way, one should not from this draw the conclusion that occult experiences are not of the greatest importance in our Society. They are indeed of primal importance, for our endeavour is to proceed from externalities to inner depths. There was also no need to raise an objection to occult experiences as such. Whatever may be the level at which these experiences manifest themselves, this is what anyone within our movement needs to see that must be taken into account. For it is by no means the same thing to speak in a certain jocular way about occult experiences as to say that one does not wish to hear any more about them. We have been speaking for three days about occult experiences of the most intimate kind. It cannot be that a purely abstract science of thinking is what is being created in our circles. This is not what our Society is for. We should not go from one kind of one-sidedness to another.

I should like especially to draw attention to the intimate nature of our Society, to that part of it which is connected with the innermost aspect of our soul experience. What matters is that we transform our soul into something else when we involve ourselves with spiritual science; and this must also happen when times are difficult. For this reason I wanted to present some thoughts that may perhaps be suitable for inculcating within us that mood of reverence for the spiritual life which is appropriate for a true spiritual scientist; for it is the case that the greatest and most insignificant events of life, indeed everything in life, are things that fill us with deep reverence only if we are able to penetrate from these particular situations sufficiently deeply into their spiritual backgrounds. Also the painful events of life, whether they be great or more minor in scale, can through spiritual science be placed in such a light that contemplating them helps us to bring our soul into a right relationship to the wisdom that works and weaves through the world.

It has been our endeavour to consider from the standpoint of cosmic wisdom certain events in life which are connected with what is taking place around us today on so great but also so testing a scale. If we can cherish such feelings with respect to our time, we shall have the appropriate feeling for what we have sought to indicate with these words:

> From the courage of the fighters,
> From the blood on fields of battle,
> From the grief of the bereaved,
> From the people's sacrifice:
> There will ripen fruit of spirit,
> If souls will turn in consciousness
> Towards the realm of spirit.

May we be souls who in this way turn their minds and hearts towards the realm of spirit! Then we shall be able to contribute to the fruits which must ripen as a healing, sun-like power for mankind from the seeds that are scattered over the Earth in the blood-drenched battle-fields of our destiny-laden time.

LECTURE 7

STUTTGART, 12 MARCH 1916

TODAY I should like to offer a spiritual-scientific, historical study which can be of importance for us with respect to the weighty events that surround us and which involve the whole of European humanity, and on the following Wednesday I shall touch upon a more intimate matter concerning the spiritual life of man. If perhaps to many of us what will be considered today may appear somewhat remote, this is nevertheless only seemingly so and should not be far from our minds, for it is the task of spiritual science to fill our souls with the deepest attentiveness to what can contribute to an understanding of our time. As said, on Wednesday we shall return to a matter of a purely human, spiritual-scientific nature.

I shall begin with a question. But if I place this question at the forefront of our considerations, do not trouble yourselves with thinking that I am wanting even in the least degree to rake up old issues concerning our movement. As you will see, in spite of the fact that I shall proceed from the outset from questions that may initially be easily misunderstood my concern is with something totally different. The question that I should like to ask is this: Why precisely during this time of war does Mrs Besant[55] slander our German movement in her English journals? Why did she find it necessary in the first months of the war to allege that our German movement had the sole intention of being a kind of agent for political manoeuvres hostile to England on behalf of Germany? Why did she find it necessary to say that this German movement of ours had the intention to bring about her own—Mrs Besant's—removal from her office as president of the theosophical movement in order to establish itself in India and from there to organize a kind of pan-Germanic movement against England? Why does Mrs Besant now continue to make these slanderous accusations that she has issued in so hateful a way during this war against our German movement and will no doubt also go on doing so?

Nothing is more necessary for us within our spiritual-scientific movement than to have a clear, insightful eye upon what is going on in the world. What I may be permitted to refer to as a certain obsessive tendency to sleep through the events of the world, which so easily befalls someone who feels fully at ease within our movement, is a great, great disadvantage to such a spiritual movement. It must be our aim to have the clearest insight into the concerns of outward existence; for nothing is easier than to ascribe all manner of charlatanism and mendacious aspirations within the context of human evolution to such a movement. And since, within the limits that we have often emphasized, a certain trust is necessary in the admittedly small number of those who want to understand certain things here, it also arises that, seduced by a certain excessive trustfulness, people belonging to our movement are so to speak befogged by those who do not want to impart anything right to them but wish to cram all sorts of things into their souls in order to cultivate by way of a theosophical or some other spiritual belief a kind of spiritual reinforcement for all kinds of endeavours which are in fact not truly the spiritual aspirations of mankind.

We have often drawn attention to the position of the Russian people within the evolution of the fifth post-Atlantean cultural period, and—as I have often discussed this matter in this Stuttgart branch during this time of war[56]—I do not want to return today to what you can read about in various lecture-cycles.[57] I would much rather speak about certain fundamental qualities of the Russian people which render it especially suited to contributing to the evolutionary course of the fifth or also the sixth post-Atlantean phase of cultural development.

Thus to begin with there is a quality of the Russian people which one might call a quite particularly far-reaching adaptability to, or willingness to conform with, anything of a spiritual nature that a Russian person encounters in whatever way, a certain adaptability of soul.

The fact is that Russians are less productive, less creative in their own soul than their Central European or West-European counterparts; that they are, as it were, dependent on receiving and experiencing what they have received with a considerable level of intensity, while not developing it further independently out of themselves. Thus you can see the way that Russians took up the religion of Byzantium and allowed it to remain at the standpoint that it had when they embraced it. And today one can still see from the ceremonies of the Russian Church how something of an ancient Oriental nature shines through these ceremonies. One can, I might say, perceive through the form of the Russian Church an ancient, holy Oriental quality and also experience this ancient, holy quality of the Orient.

Compare this with what has become manifest in the West, where in what has, as you know, been a much-disputed development of dogmas and ceremonies a constant transformation has taken place, thus a creative intervention into what that community which then became the Roman Catholic Church, Protestantism and so on originally adopted. This adaptability, this faculty of receiving, is what one might call the first basic quality of the Russian national character.

A second fundamental quality is a certain aversion that the Russian has towards what we may call the pervading of life with intellectuality. He does not like to be hemmed in socially by lots of precisely defined laws. He asks to be able to live out his life with a degree of arbitrariness. He does not, at any rate in practice, understand that the intellect should spread out a net of legalities and that the individual should adhere to such intellectual forms in social life, even though he may from time to time accept them theoretically. He asks, rather, for what the ego wants out of the inspiration of the moment.

A third element in the Russian character is one that Herder especially referred to at some length;[58] the Slavophils took up this conception of Herder's, which was of course a German view, and developed it into a kind of megalomania. This is that Russians have preserved something that one finds in the whole Oriental nature, namely peaceableness. However strange it sounds it is part of the Russian nature, for Russians as such did not want this war: their rulers fomented it. Russians naturally have a peace-loving attitude. They have the deep belief that quarrels and squabbles have developed through the way in which the religion of Western Europe has evolved. It does not lie in the character of people from the Orient to wage war on their fellow men on account of religious dogmas. However strange it may be to say so, it is nevertheless true that this is even something that strikes people so infinitely strongly about the Turks (who also have this Oriental quality), that they do not become aggressive with regard to the religious life itself. As said, this lies in the belief, in the consciousness of Russians.

These three qualities are, on the other hand, quite particularly suited to being exploited by those who want to take advantage of them. It is very easy to abuse the quality of adaptability or willingness to conform that is possessed by Russians, as the Slavophils have done and now the pan-Slavists are again doing, in order to tell the Russian people that they have the calling to get rid of the old and weary, terminally declining culture of Europe and to replace it with Russian life.

Moreover, if one exploits the second quality that I have mentioned one can tell Russian people that the whole of Western and Central European culture has become decrepit because of its particular fondness for intellectualism, for a kind of rationality, that this West-European culture is devoid of any really true mystical feature.

And thirdly, if one wants to take advantage of the third quality of the Russian people that has been mentioned, one can pervert the most peace-loving of qualities by organizing the otherwise peaceful population and summoning it to the bloodiest of battles; for indeed, one meets with opposites in the world, and especially such opposites as are in question here. But what the Russian people has to signify in the evolutionary course of European culture is not connected with what Russian rulers are now doing supposedly on behalf of the Russian people but with the three qualities referred to.

These three qualities therefore determine that the essential nature of Russia enters into a certain connection with the essential nature of Central and Western Europe. Because the Russian character is adaptable, it has the task of bringing about what we have spoken of in the sixth post-Atlantean cultural period, not initially through a creative deed but through its experience, by receiving what comes to it from the West. I have often called it—years, I may say decades before the outbreak of this war—a kind of spiritual marriage, a kind of marriage that is necessary between Central Europe and Russia with respect to soul development.

Through the fact that the Russian people have a certain aversion to intellectualism, certain social institutions can be created with the Russian people which will only be possible if the marriage just referred to takes place.

And similarly, the Russian national character will have to react to what can be given from within Central Europe. Tomorrow in the public lecture[59] we shall speak of such things that have to follow from Central Europe and which must be incorporated as something great, mighty and immortal in the whole evolutionary course of mankind. But the Russian people will have to take on what is achieved by Central Europe. It does not initially have the capacity of individual creativity within this post-Atlantean time.

But now, in contrast to what one can thus characterize as the essential nature of the Russian national character, there exists the national characters of Central Europe and of Western Europe, that West-European national character which since the reign of Queen Elizabeth of England[60] has become in all essentials a British, an Anglo-Saxon national character. And among the many results of these present significant events, which of course it cannot be my job to describe, one will quite definitely be that the other Western European states become vassals, dependent peoples of England. The French, in particular, will have to experience the bitterest disappointments. But it is not this that primarily concerns us today but, rather, to emphasize the great contrast that exists between the essential nature of Central Europe and that of Western Europe and specifically Britain and the Anglo-Saxon world.*

---

* It should be noted here and elsewhere in this lecture that the terms used to refer to aspects of Britain or the Anglo-Saxon element are direct translations of the terms used by Rudolf Steiner.—Translator

Even though this is not noticed today by those who do not want to think and especially do not want to observe, there has never been a greater contrast in world history than this contrast between the nature of Central Europe and the Anglo-Saxon nature. Not that the individual, the individual personality cannot rise above this. There is no question of this; but I am speaking of matters of national character. Certainly, when such things are being characterized there can never be any question that an individual Englishman can of course rise above what is presently being characterized. One also does not need to think that one has to succumb to the errors of our military opponents by hurling abuse at England because it is different, but it is, rather, a matter of sharply characterizing the contrast. It would, admittedly, take much work if I were to try to gather together all possible building stones that would be necessary for a full understanding of the contrast between the two. But this contrast can become clear to us from the standpoint of, on the one hand, observing the essential nature of Central Europe, with Germany at its focal point, in relation to that of the eastern entity of Russia, and on the other hand contemplating the essence of Britain and France in its relation to the Russian East. Herein lies one of the greatest contrasts in human evolution. I can only refer you to much today that I shall explain here in tomorrow's public lecture. But I would wish that the small number of those who belong to the spiritual-scientific movement will understand what I shall say in more detail tomorrow more deeply than it can be understood if one has not entered at a deeper level into spiritual science.

You see, this Central European nature is one that is national in a completely different way than any other national character in human evolution. Consider all West-European peoples: they are national by virtue of the blood. The German's nationality derives from his soul. The German is national in that he unremittingly aspires to raise certain aspects of his soul-life above the general soul-life and implant them into his own soul. This is why we experience something within the German nature as great as the artistic works of Goethe, Herder's studies of history and the world-conceptions of Hegel, Schelling and Fichte.[61]

Although these things are not so widely known today, they will become more familiar; for contrary to all the opinions that are expressed about them, I must affirm that they can become popular, they can be presented in such a way that—whatever anyone may think—every child can understand them. This will indeed happen. Everything pertaining to the true German world-outlook grows out of the deepest soul-nature of the German national character. And a spiritual-scientific movement that is to be fruitful would never be able to arise within the essence of the German nature which had a similar character as the spiritual-scientific aspirations of the West. We should not sleep through this difference; we must keep it clearly in mind. Within the context of the German national character, every-thing pertaining to the content of spiritual science must be in har-monious connection with that which the people as such bring forth. Thus when I was last here in Stuttgart,[62] I said that when one con-templates the world-outlook of Schelling, Fichte and Hegel, it is as though the whole people were meditating. One always feels a sense of belonging to the national character, but to its soul-aspect, when one speaks of the German national character. One cannot speak of the German national character other than by taking account of its soul-qualities, of what is to be striven for. And it is impossible in the German context to do what is possible in England, that science on the one hand exists and on the other hand this science totally ignores faith. For the German national character this is in the long run not possible. The German wants to have oneness. He wants to have a spirituality that can stand fully on the ground of scientific rigour, and he wants to have a science which knows how to justify itself to spiritual life.

This contrast appears most openly in the colour theories of Goethe and Newton. I have been trying for more than thirty years[63] to assert the validity of Goethe's colour theory as against that of Newton. Whereas Goethe's theory of colour has its origin in the soul's deep sense of oneness with the world, that of Newton pro-ceeds from a mechanical observation of the world and has no fur-ther aim. And physics today is so anglicized that it takes it for granted that anyone who takes Goethe's colour theory seriously is a fool.

There is within the German national character a striving for spirituality. Hence one is as an integral part of the German national character also obliged to see in that which emanates as an ardent aspiration of soul from the best of this people, from those whom we have already mentioned and from those whom we shall name again tomorrow, a quest for a path to spiritual science. But this German national character cannot do otherwise than to strive in a down-to-earth way, to devote itself to the matter at hand. This is what the English and the French are unable to understand. The Frenchman wants to have everything formulated in a beautiful slogan, and he is then content. The Englishman wants to see where the profit from some aspect of knowledge or insight may lie. But that knowledge that is striven for is something that must grow out of the soul like the blossom from the plant if a person is to feel himself to be a whole human being is that neither the French—of course as Frenchmen, I am not speaking of the individual—nor the Anglo-Saxons understand.

The task of the German spirit is to develop soul-experience into a world of ideas in succession to the high-point that the world of ancient Greece achieved for the fourth post-Atlantean cultural period. And one really does not need to be a nationalist in a petty way but a completely objective observer of the evolutionary course of humanity if one emphasizes this. Moreover, you should also be aware that I am not using the war as an occasion to start emphasizing this, but these observations have been evident in what I have been saying in our circles for years, indeed for one and a half decades. But because this belongs to the German spirit, there are very solid reasons why it is called upon to enter into the soul-marriage with the Russian East that has been indicated. And the cultural task of the future will never be able to be fulfilled other than by Russia, with its quality of adaptability, receiving what can come from the German national character. Moreover, all cultural development of the future is a question of this bond between Central and Eastern Europe.

It is different with Western Europe. Western Europe has taken over what the fourth post-Atlantean cultural period has bequeathed and developed it independently, but in a way that I have often described, namely, only through the three soul-forces of sentient soul, intellectual soul and consciousness soul. What this fourth post-Atlantean cultural period essentially sends forth is seen as not productive, and especially the British Folk-soul, the Anglo-Saxon Folk-soul has the task of developing the consciousness soul, of developing that which is above all else organized for profitability on the physical plane.

This explains all the phenomena that we see appearing within Western Europe, especially within the Anglo-Saxon world. But now especially those belonging to the Anglo-Saxon world feel instinctively that what lives in Central Europe, and essentially the German element of Central Europe, is what is really fruitful [for the future]. And those who lead the so-called occult movements of Western Europe, and of the Anglo-Saxon people in particular, know the implications of this. Those who lead these occult movements are filled with two trains of thought: the one is that they say to themselves that Roman Catholicism has had its day, it belongs essentially to the fourth post-Atlantean age; and the Anglo-Saxon impulse must take the place of this Roman culture. Every occultist of a certain kind, that is, every occultist who has an affinity with his national character, knows—that is, he imagines that he has a right knowledge—that the 'Anglo-Saxon race', as he calls it, must replace Rome. This is taught in all occult schools. This is a firm dogma.

These people also instinctively know that Russian people are, as it were, the recruits for introducing into life everything that culture must bring, the recruits who must passively receive it through their adaptability.

The Anglo-Saxon occultists know these two things very well, that is, they see things in this way, this is their conviction. Their conviction is, on the one hand, that the Anglo-Saxons must take over from Rome; everything else, Protestantism, Calvinism and so on, is merely a secondary matter. The Anglo-Saxons have to engender something in the world—as said, I am speaking now of the occultists—which represents for the fifth post-Atlantean culture what Roman Catholicism has manifested in the second half of the fourth post-Atlantean culture extending even into the fourteenth, fifteenth and sixteenth centuries.

And every occultist is convinced in this respect that before all else the bridge must be created between that which the Anglo-Saxon persuasion ascribes to itself and the essential nature of Russia. The ideal that emerges for every Anglo-Saxon occultist from the second of these two trains of thought is to pour into the Russian soul that which Anglo-Saxon occultism wants to teach: to use the Russian soul as a kind of wax in which is engraved what is wanted by Anglo-Saxon occultism. In the circles of which I am now speaking, this ideal grows far beyond everything that we are mainly concerned with here.

The main thing for us is real knowledge, a real penetration of the truth, and it is our honest conviction that when we find the truth, this truth will give human beings what they need, and that if we rightly aspire to it and seek it this truth will fructify future cultural epochs, that what must happen with the peoples of Europe will happen if the truth is rightly and honestly sought. One does not need anything other than to seek truth; this is the true principle of spiritual science.

But in opposition to this is a principle such as I have just characterized, namely to bring a particular race to a leading position, to make a particular race powerful, above all with regard to the life of soul. We are not now speaking of political matters, we are speaking of occult intentions that are rooted in the depths: to make the Anglo-Saxon soul-world powerful and to make use of the adaptability and receptivity of the East-European nature and to pour into it what is wanted in order that a marriage can take place between the Anglo-Saxon world and Russia.

Consider these things very clearly; they are of extraordinary importance. I have spoken of them as they are increasingly taught in all kinds of occult factions of the West, especially in Anglo-Saxon occult schools. But what is, rather, concerned only with cultivating the consciousness soul cannot arrive at any real content. True occultism, which does not give rise to a craving for power, stands fully in an organic, living connection with German development and has its roots in this same soil.

But what has occurred, my dear friends? If evolution since the Middle Ages until our time had not been disturbed by ahrimanic forces, what has happened in Europe with respect to spiritual science—we shall have to speak tomorrow about a very recent event—would have developed organically and without ahrimanic influences, and one would see more easily today that everything that the West has achieved in terms of spiritual science has arisen from the German spirit. But, imbued with an Anglo-Saxon element, German spiritual science was conveyed in a mask to the Anglo-Saxon world and also to France, with only the terminology, the names given to particular facts, adapted to the French or English language. If, however, one looks to the fundamentals, everything that is contained in French and English occultism is only masked German spiritual-scientific research, Central European spiritual-scientific research.

In a way that I have just explained, also that which has called itself the Theosophical Society has contained none other than facts upon which Indian or other names have been imposed that are found within German spiritual science. And the Theosophical Society did its best to hide this fact from the Germans; for the intention of the Anglo-Saxon world is everywhere to efface Central European development with respect to spiritual science and to put itself in its place. This is a craving for power of the highest order which has its source in occultism. And it was a simple necessity that that peeling away took place[64] which has now indeed been accomplished since the turn of the century, that what was originally German and which our Germans have unfortunately only all too willingly received from English sources has again returned, that it has again been restored in its original purity. A truth has been established. It had to be established. That this truth has been established is something the English Theosophical Society will never forgive our German aspirations as they have been from the beginning. This can only be veiled with a mist through slander.

But all those who want to wield power within occult endeavours proceed very systematically, in a very goal-oriented way. Hence it is so necessary that one is not asleep to these endeavours but develops a certain clarity. Clarity is primarily necessary when it comes to significant phenomena; and it is, for example, quite especially necessary with regard to a personality who is of such decisive importance for the Theosophical Society, Helena Petrovna Blavatsky.[65]

Reference may be made to two facts that can lead to clarity in this realm. The first fact is that Helena Petrovna Blavatsky was a Russian and grew up in a Russian environment. The second fact is this, that she left behind in an English garment a kind of occult science that she gradually developed to perfection, albeit with deviations of various kinds, into what Anglo-Saxon occultism aspires to, to some extent with deviations which were determined by the considerable gifts of this woman. Helena Petrovna Blavatsky was, one could say, a mediumistic personality who could with such adaptability also develop occult soul-qualities only out of her Russian nationality. What Russians universally have as human qualities, Helena Petrovna Blavatsky had specifically with regard to occult qualities. It therefore happened that in Western Europe she was found suitable first by French occultism and then by British occultism of a certain kind for her soul to be flooded with occultism of an Anglo-Saxon nature. It was thought that something might be given to the world which represents a kind of anticipation of Anglo-Saxon occultism while manifesting itself from the Russian soul. In place of what should and must come about, the connection of the essential nature of Central Europe with that of Russia, there was a conscious, deliberate plan to imbue the Russian nature—through Helena Petrovna Blavatsky as a representative of the Russian national character—with Anglo-Saxon occultism in its power-political form. Those people who, so to speak, want to have hold of the threads of life as it develops outwardly towards the physical plane were not uninvolved in this. Around the poor figure of Helena Petrovna Blavatsky much of a tragic nature was enacted which I cannot enter into now. Precisely because of her deeply rooted and wide-ranging mediumistic faculties, which were receptive to all manner of influences, much, much took place. And it was a long path from the starting-point when there was an initial attempt to impart a Central European impulse directly to the unfortunate Blavatsky, which then came to the light of day in a kaleidoscopic, virtually unusable form in *Isis Unveiled*. But very soon she came under quite other influences of personalities who took possession of her; and in the place, and behind the mask, of the one who was originally her guide, who wanted to lead her to the essence of a Central European orientation, there later appeared the so-called Kut Humi individuality, who was, however—according to occultists with a real knowledge of such things—a person who was in the pay of the Russians and in a certain sense wanted to forge what could emerge from Blavatsky's soul-capacities together with Anglo-Saxon occultism. One is dealing here with the direct opposition between an original individuality—many would call him a master; one can refer to him as one wishes—and a later rascal, a swindler, who had taken on the mask of the former and had received from the side of Eastern Europe the task to which I have referred.

Then began the time when Blavatsky was to connect herself with the occult stream of France, where she quickly wanted to achieve certain aims; she therefore placed conditions upon a lodge of occultists in Paris which could not be fulfilled so that she had to be excluded, because under the influence of the individualities standing behind her she always confused occult intentions with impulses of political power. There followed the American episode, which again had a political background. All these things proceeded from the basis of placing something before Europe which might convince it that out of the connection between the soul-qualities of Russia and the Anglo-Saxon desire for occult power a new world religion for Europe could emerge. This was to be presented to Europe; and what has arisen from Germany was to be overridden.

O my dear friends, I well remember—and it could be unpleasant for many how clearly such things appear before me—how Mrs Besant held her very first assembly within Germany in Hamburg,[66] and how I interrogated her at the time within a small circle regarding the way she thought about the development of occultism in the nineteenth century. The answer that she gave then in Hamburg was to the effect that, whereas at the turn of the eighteenth–nineteenth centuries something of the nature of an occult aspiration had asserted itself in Germany, the Germans are currently stuck in pure abstractions, and that it has become apparent that the great—the way she expressed herself was always on a grand scale—that the great wave of spiritual life had been assigned to the British people. Of course, she said this in English; but it had even more grandeur in English!

For Blavatsky the time then came when it became necessary that all those who had serious intentions with regard to spiritual science and could not become involved with Anglo-Saxon cravings for power did something. What happened as a result was that Blavatsky was placed in what was later referred to in occult circles as 'occult imprisonment'. The decision to impose this 'occult imprisonment' upon Blavatsky was taken by a gathering of genuine occultists, or at any rate the greater number of genuine occultists, in the last third of the nineteenth century.

Occult imprisonment consists in that a person's aspirations are—and this is possible through certain processes—as it were, confined to a sphere from which he cannot penetrate, so that his endeavours are thrown back on themselves and he is unable to cause certain harm that he would otherwise inflict.

The process which I am now relating, this imposition of occult imprisonment, is not without its drawbacks; but as said, there is no other way that people can deal with such a situation. Blavatsky was a very powerful psychical personality and could exert a strong influence. She therefore also had this energy which was on the one hand overpowering, and on the other hand had the capacity to impose itself on others, in her writings.

One can describe what then happened by saying that certain Indian occultists who wanted to avenge themselves against being held within England's grip took possession of the personality of Blavatsky, and from this derived the Indian intervention. I have explained this in more detail elsewhere,[67] and I wish only to indicate it here.

The Indian element therefore entered in at this point, and through this arose that dubious occult science which was cultivated in the Theosophical Society and had to be purified by the spiritual science that was to appear in Central Europe; for what is to appear in the form of spiritual science in Central Europe must be thoroughly honest in the sense that I have indicated, that is, it must aspire to the truth as such and be convinced that the truth, in that it flows through our souls and through the evolution of mankind, will bring about what is right in the lives both of peoples and also of human individuals: a pure, honest quest for truth!

And this pure, honest quest for truth is the main task that initially stands before us.

I wanted this to be understood here more precisely within our spiritual-scientific movement; for I would then also be forgiven if I have to place certain additional conditions, and it would be seen that these conditions must be taken for what they are. How often I tell our friends that in order that what is to be brought to the world in the form of spiritual science can remain pure, in order that it is not adapted or adjusted in any way, one should not come to me with all sorts of other things that one so easily combines with spiritual-scientific endeavours. Of course, people like to do everything that human wishes may demand, and much can happen in a friendly way; but it must in any case be understood why, for example, I say again and again that it should not be thought that I am even only in the remotest degree—no more than into other, not directly spiritual-scientific regions—involving myself in medical affairs.[68] It is indeed necessary that our members should get used to taking it seriously when I say that one should not come to me with medical concerns. It is significant that one understands these things because it is necessary at any rate for today to keep spiritual-scientific striving in so far as I have presented it far away from other things. There are enough medical experts within our movement in whom our members can have confidence. As I emphasize again and again, one should in principle take it really seriously when I say that I do not want in any way to be drawn into curing [anyone]; for through this the world will only misjudge what the spiritual-scientific movement is intended to bring about through me, and this should not fail to be recognized.

How little right understanding there has actually been in the Anglo-Saxon world for the pure, objective striving for truth is something that will be known by those who heard a noteworthy lecture by Mrs Besant about 'Theosophy and Imperialism'.[69] One could through this lecture feel much of what I was obliged to say today from the facts: no one should associate spiritual science in its reality with a desire for power of any kind, with any sort of directly political aspiration, although of course someone who is a good spiritual scientist can be the best possible politician. But it is not this that is the issue but rather that spiritual science should not become as the occultism that I have tried to characterize is in the Anglo-Saxon world; spiritual science should not become something of the kind that Blavatsky and then also in many respects Mrs Besant sought to make of it, although with less talent and with lesser gifts than by Helena Petrovna Blavatsky. The aim was to establish from the side of the Anglo-Saxon world, in a dazzling fashion through the soul-experiences of the kind of personality that Blavatsky was, the kind of occult religion which the Anglo-Saxons bring directly to Russia by excluding Germany. In the schools where the things that I have already indicated are now taught no longer in the manner of Blavatsky but in accordance with Anglo-Saxon occultism, this war in which we are now engaged is spoken of as something that is necessary. And the outcome of this war is again and again spoken of highly suggestively in such a way that it is said: This or that must happen as a result of this war. They say this not initially out of a wish to make prophecies but because this is what they want, because they want to gain as much influence as possible, because they want to prepare people through all available channels. For if one inflicts all manner of occultism on people behind a mask, one is wanting to prepare them in accordance with a certain school of thought. I therefore have to ask—I must speak about these things because they are already being spoken about in public, and because someone such as myself whose task it is to represent spiritual science must make his relationship to these matters clear: Why has a person from Paris with occult knowledge who is well-known to occultists[70] been travelling again and again to Rome since the outbreak of the war between Germany, Russia, England and France and was still doing so in October 1914? Why did she play a role in Rome that subsequently had an influence upon the circumstances of Italy, a similar role as has been played by certain people belonging to the 'Grand Orient de France' or connected with the Anglo-Saxon Freemasons, who had a profound influence upon the whole form of present events, far more than one thinks?

There is something else that I must ask: Why does it say in the annual publication[71] which the same personality, who is made use of by certain streams, one could also say exploited for all sorts of dubious purposes (as I say, because this is already in the public domain it is necessary that I show where I stand as regards these matters), why does it say in this year-book of 1913 which this personality edited and which appeared already in 1912: The one who thinks he rules Austria will not reign but another, younger person will reign who is not at present identified for this? Why does it state this in 1913 in an annual publication of a medium who stands within a certain occult stream? Why is the same thing repeated in the same publication for 1914—thus published before 1914 already in 1913: The tragedy of the House of Habsburg will be enacted more quickly than one might have thought? Moreover, why is the wish that the successor to the throne of Austria, Franz Ferdinand, must be murdered stated in a Paris newspaper which one could call the *Paris-Mittag* in German[72] already in 1913? This newspaper corresponds roughly with the Berlin newspaper *B. Z am Mittag*: *Paris midi* is much read. Why does it say in the almanac on the one hand what I have indicated: The one who thinks he rules will not reign but a younger person will reign, and on the other hand the wish is expressed that this arch-duke is murdered? Why does it state in this same newspaper, precisely when the debate was taking place in France about the three-year period of military service, with cynical words: If it should come to mobilization in France, the first to be murdered will be Jaurès?[73] Do you think, my dear friends, that this was a mere prophecy? I should like to show you that I am not on the side of those who regard this as a prophecy but that everything points towards the deepest and most horrible subterranean regions in the abuse of an occultism of charlatans who are at the same time a danger to humanity.

I wanted to say something to you today that is not exactly elevating but it is all the more serious. I wanted to ask you in your souls whether a person should not develop for himself really clear insight if he wants to stand within an occult stream, and whether it might not turn out for the worse if one were content to sleep through things of the greatest importance. My dear friends, anyone who also wants to study the connection of the Theosophical Society—as it has increasingly become—with such things needs only to cast a sharp eye upon the activity of such personalities as, for example, Mrs Catherine

Tingley.[74] And this, too, is instructive, that when something was to be introduced from a more Christian perspective, and, moreover, on a strongly mediumistic path, into what was intended to be a purely Anglo-Saxon affair in the form of the little book by Mabel Collins, *Light on the Path*,[75] the slander began. For much of what was advanced against the medium through whom *Light on the Path* was given to mankind is slander.

I wanted to speak to you today with a degree of seriousness in order that from this seriousness many of us may acquire a conception of how necessary it is to become conscious of the mission of Central Europe with respect to spiritual science, and that it is utterly necessary that this Central European mission becomes a world mission. This Central European mission must above all things be a pure, honest striving for truth. But this pure, honest striving for truth was comprehended in a strange way, and the misrepresentations of the truth were also bizarrely conceived. You know that relationships between the German spiritual movement to which we belong and the Theosophical Society were broken off long before the war. All this that I have indicated was comprehended in a strange way. Just consider that, for example, Mrs Besant caused it to be said that I had tried to become president of the Theosophical Society in India in order to force her out of her position as president and from there to give effect by way of India to pan-German streams hostile to England in favour of the German Empire. You are bound to believe that this is not true, that this is an objective falsehood!

The following is evidence of the opposite. It was 1909 when a society was founded to counteract Mr Leadbeater's reign of terror and subsequently also the humbug of Alcyone, a society that was to encompass all countries of the Earth and to be, so to speak a counterweight to those led astray by Mrs Besant. At that time I was called upon by India to become the chairman or president of this international society, and I not only declined but in 1909 told Mrs Besant in Budapest before witnesses that within the context of the spiritual movement of modern times I never want anything other than to be the one who leads this movement within the context of the German people. I said this to Mrs Besant before witnesses in 1909. Now she gives her version of the truth by writing in her English journal that my aim had been to go to India and so on in order to supplant her from there! Here one is no longer speaking of objective falsehood but, rather, of a conscious, deliberate lie. But it is necessary that such means are employed where what is at stake is that one has to battle against the course of truth itself; and this is indeed what has befallen Anglo-Saxon occultism! For the truth is that what has to penetrate human culture in the form of spiritual science has a fundamental connection with the essential nature of Central Europe. But this must be obscured, veiled, masked in one way or another by England. And in the twentieth century Mrs Besant has also increasingly become the instrument of this endeavour to obscure the truth.

The need to reflect upon what should flow within our movement is everywhere apparent. The spiritual and earthly task is indeed evident. It is true that we have no particular inducement for it, unless we check that the one or the other person adopts an attitude of blind allegiance. But then it is not exactly something that can be very enticing today to want nothing other than honest devotion to the development of truth. You know that from all sides within and outside our Society the attacks and also the mockery and scorn rain down upon us. But something else also belongs to this, namely that from out of our spiritual-scientific movement this increasingly flows into one or another soul—anyone who has an eye for this already feels what is flowing to such an extent into human souls from our books or our public lectures. However, if these people who really appreciate what they receive in this way were unreservedly to ponder upon what is to find its place in the spiritual course of human development, some remarkable phenomena will come to light. It is sometimes indeed the case that people gladly find much truth in what is engendered within our movement, but that they conceive of every honest, wholehearted attempt to stand by us as though they would get their fingers burnt, for example, through a real contact with me personally. It is a very common phenomenon, more common than one might suppose! Among those who associate what they recognize as an honest spiritual-scientific striving for truth not with any particular personality but with my own, it is only to be expected that they confess to this in so absolute a way. For seriousness, my dear friends, is something of great, even immense importance.

What I have said should not be expressed out of any sort of nationalistic feeling. I have actually been telling you only of facts; they are intended to characterize the occult counterforces present in Europe and, for one who is willing to perceive it, also much of what lives as counterforces on the physical plane.

I should like once more to emphasize that we need seriousness, seriousness in order to find the right orientation in a serious time, so that what resides in these words that I have already spoken here may become a reality:

> From the courage of the fighters,
> From the blood on fields of battle,
> From the grief of the bereaved,
> From the people's sacrifice:
> There will ripen fruit of spirit,
> If souls will turn in consciousness
> Towards the realm of spirit.

LECTURE 8

STUTTGART, 15 MARCH 1916

WHEN we spoke together here during my previous visit,[76] we considered some spiritual facts which relate to the life of the human soul after a person has crossed the threshold of death. Our intention today is to consider some facts of the spiritual world associated with this event which can cast further light upon it, facts which are, however, not only capable of throwing light upon the event of death but are at the same time able to illumine what takes place in the life between birth and death, what occurs in the physical life in which we are now involved. I must again emphasize that spiritual science must make the attempt not merely to remain trapped within outward schematic conceptions of man's being but to penetrate ever more deeply into the various members of human nature.

We shall first devote our attention to what we have often referred to as the human etheric body. In the public lecture the day before yesterday,[77] I indicated that one should not conceive of this etheric body as merely a kind of rarefied physical body—this would be a materialistic conception—but that one should imagine it as something that manifests itself through an inner experience. We also came to see that what, strictly speaking, we call thinking or imagining in the way that one lives here on the physical plane is actually a function of the etheric body. But the physical body is necessary in order that thoughts may form through this thinking, through this conceptual activity; for the physical body has to receive its impressions if thoughts are to be inscribed as memories here in physical life.

The process is, therefore, this. When we think, the thinking does of course originate from the ego and passes through the astral body, but it takes place mainly in the movements of the etheric body.

Whatever we think, whatever we imagine, is enacted in the movements of the etheric body. These movements of the etheric body exert a formative impression upon the physical body. This is only a rough way of putting it, for the processes involved are actually far more delicate and do not constitute a single major impression, but one can refer to them approximately in this way. And through these movements of the etheric body being thus impressed upon the physical body, thoughts manifest themselves within our consciousness; and these thoughts are also retained within the memory. Thus when we have a thought and later draw it forth from our memory our etheric body comes into movement in the course of this work of calling forth a memory, and its movements are adapted to the physical body; and by entering into those impressions which this etheric body has made upon the physical body through the thought in question, the thought is again brought to consciousness. Thus memory is associated with the possibility of the movements of the etheric body being impressed upon the physical body. Of course, memory is linked to the etheric body, but the etheric body has to have some kind of guardianship of its movements in order that memory can arise in physical life. Thus we live our lives between birth and death, we have our experiences and remember our experiences, our thought life is enacted within us. In our waking state, we more or less constantly have this life of thoughts unfolding its development within us.

As a human being in a physical body, one therefore has the feeling that what takes place in our thinking, in our imaginative life, is an inner experience, something that is taking place within us, that is our property. And for physical life this is also initially perfectly correct, for the thought experience which is being inwardly enacted is not outwardly visible to other people. It is therefore our property. But with respect to the spiritual world, what takes place within our life of thoughts is certainly not our property.

Indeed, our thought life has a significance of quite a different order than we often suppose when we speak of it as our property; and we want to ponder a little about the world-significance of our life of thought. In order that I can make myself clearly understood, I must start with a comparison. We human beings work here in the physical world. Let us suppose that our work consisted in making machines. It could also consist in something different, but we shall suppose that our work is to make machines. In order to make machines that can be put to the service of human life, we need wood or iron or whatever else of which the machines are made. We need the appropriate materials, and we must develop these materials. As physical human beings, we cannot make iron or make wood; these materials have to be available. We take these materials, we form, develop and incorporate them in our machines. We human beings thereby exercise a certain activity. We bring about the existence of a realm of machines, but we create this realm of machines upon the foundation of the materials that we derive from the Earth.

Let us now imagine that we did not have to do with human beings, who manufacture machines out of earthly materials such as iron or wood, but with beings of the next highest hierarchy to whom we give the names Angeloi, Archangeloi and Archai. One might now ask: What is actually the task of these beings? Do they also have something to do which can be compared with the activity that has just been spoken of and which leads to the creation of a world of machines? Yes, these Angeloi, Archangeloi and Archai also have their activity; but this activity takes place only in the spiritual world. And just as we human beings have to take our iron and our wood from subordinate regions, thus in the first place from the mineral kingdom and from the plant kingdom, in order to assemble our machines, so do the Angeloi, Archangeloi and Archai also need materials in order, shall we say, to build—although this is rather an indelicate word to use—what they are to build. And what are their materials? For much of what the Angeloi, Archangeloi and Archai have to accomplish in the spiritual world, the materials are the thoughts that human beings regard as their property. And it is indeed the case that whereas we pursue our path through the world and cherish our thoughts, contemplate our thought life, as it were, from within and regard it as our property, the Angeloi, Archangeloi and Archai are without our knowledge working on our thoughts. The very least that is living in our thoughts comes to consciousness within us, for these thoughts signify something that is quite different to what comes to consciousness within us and lives within our souls. Whereas we think and remember our thoughts, the beings of the next highest hierarchy referred to are working, as it were, from outside in accordance with the way that they are able to make use of our thoughts. Thus with every human being you may imagine that what is enacted within his consciousness is only one side of his life of thought. While he thinks, the hierarchic beings referred to are constantly hovering around him and are working with the help of his thoughts; and what they develop in this way through their work belongs to what is needed in order that Jupiter, Venus and Vulcan may come into being from the Earth. This forms part of what brings about progress in the evolution of the universe. And these beings of the higher hierarchy work from without on our thoughts throughout our lives until our death, in so far as they are, as it were, encompassed within our being.

And when we go through the gate of death, our etheric body will—as already indicated during my previous visit here—be taken away from us and be incorporated in the universal world-ether. Not only will that which we see by looking upon the one side of our fabric of thoughts be thus incorporated in the universal world-ether but also what the beings referred to have developed. Whereas they are, as it were, working upon the fabric of our individual thoughts during our life, they then combine together the individual thought-structures of one, another and a third person in accordance with the way that they need them in order that something new may arise in the further evolution of the world. What they are able to acquire by combining these individual etheric bodies which they have developed during the time of physical life must be incorporated in the universal world-ether.

You see from this what serious matters are involved with the inner life of our thoughts. We are indeed dealing with something of the utmost seriousness. After we think, we are found to be useful to the course of world evolution. Someone who has devoted his whole life to merely thinking of stupid things or has been preoccupied with thinking of things that are reflections of the physical world will not provide very good building material for what is to be incorporated in the universal world-ether from his etheric body. The inner life, the inner life of thoughts that appears to us to be our own property between birth and death, is a matter of a serious nature. It actually belongs in the manner described to the whole world. And just as little as we human beings could make machines work without wood and iron, so could the higher beings equally little work on world progress if they were not to find their building materials through the thoughts that we are able to give them in the course of our physical life. We are for them the foundation out of which they take their wood, their iron and so on, that is, the fabric of our thoughts. They exercise their sublime activity with these materials out of their wisdom which extends beyond man's being; but the materials must be provided by what resides within us.

What we are in this way able to give to these beings, the Angeloi, Archangeloi and Archai, forms something that we have to look upon and contemplate for the whole time that we spend between death and a new birth. We know that we have to spend a few days after we have crossed the threshold of death. But as we continue to live between death and a new birth, the eye of our soul is ceaselessly turned towards what we have in this way been able to devote to the universal fabric of the world-ether. And just as we ourselves now have again to collaborate in the forming of what will subsequently be connected with physical matter in order to furnish us with a new incarnation, so does the perspective of what we have given to the great world exert its influence upon this work of ours. In short, much with respect to the nature of our capacity to prepare for our new incarnation will depend upon whether or not we have something to contemplate from which we can derive new impulses for a forthcoming incarnation in this fabric of thoughts that has been incorporated in the world-ether.

Thus our thoughts are bound to our bodily nature before we pass through the gate of death. They are then in a certain way taken away from us, and they are incorporated in what the beings referred to have made out of them in the universal world-ether, in order now to have an existence not within us but an existence outside of us. Thus in spiritual science one can—in order to keep it constantly in mind and accessible to meditation—designate this process as one where the inner becomes something outside of us. For just as with our physical eyes we look upon mountains, rivers, clouds and stars, so after death do we look upon what has been woven out of our thinking in the form of an outer world that has been taken from us and incorporated in the universal world-ether. It is now an outer world, an outer world that uplifts us or makes us feel dejected, that strengthens or weakens us. The inner world has become an outer world.

Then we know that our retrospective experiencing of what we underwent in earthly life will last a further, indeed a very long time, though it will be different in nature from our experience in earthly life. As we know, we live through the life that has run its course at three times the speed between death and a new birth in a reverse sequence, thus firstly what we have experienced in the last year, then that from the previous year and so on. Thus after death we retrace our life in imaginations, but differently from the way we lived it here in the physical body. After our etheric body has been separated from us, we retrace our life but in such a way that we experience not what we have experienced in our feeling and in our will-impulses during our physical existence. To take the extreme case that we had injured or offended someone during our physical existence, we will have felt something when we offended him. But he also felt something. What we felt is that which impelled us out of our feeling to offend him, and there may also have been the feeling of a certain satisfaction about the deed. In short, you can picture to yourself what a person feels in both a good and a bad sense when he is the cause of something on the physical plane. But the other person to whom what we did was directed feels something different. The one who has been hurt or offended feels something different from the one who is the source of the offence. After death, in the course of this backward review that is now being characterized, we feel the effects that we inflicted upon other people, and also upon other beings, with our deeds, with our will-impulses and, indeed, also with our thoughts. Thus we now feel not what we felt while we were in the physical body but what we inflicted upon other souls, other beings. That which remained outside of us during our physical life now becomes an inner experience. Just as through the separation of the etheric body the inner becomes our outer world, so through this process of retracing our lives does the outer become an inner experience. Our soul is filled with the effects that we have brought about in the course of our physical existence. This now becomes our inner life: what was outer becomes something inner. Thus the inner becomes an outer and the outer becomes an inner. Everything therefore changes for a person once he has crossed the threshold of death.

Just as you previously had to picture the Angeloi, Archangeloi and Archai as having a certain relationship to the world of human thoughts, now picture to yourselves the spirits of the higher hierarchies: the Spirits of Form, the Spirits of Movement, the Spirits of Wisdom and even the Spirits of Will, the Thrones, as similarly having the kind of relationship that I am now characterizing to how a human individual acquires a new inner content which is now welded together from the outer world. With their spiritual eye—if I may employ this picture—the Spirits of Form, the Spirits of Movement, the Spirits of Wisdom and the Spirits of Will look down upon that remarkable, deeply meaningful spectacle which is enacted after a person has between birth and death inwardly experienced this or that through his deeds, through his will-impulses; namely, what he now experiences after he has crossed the threshold of death, when he, as it were, gathers up the effects in order to make them into a new inner world, into that inner world which can then come to expression in karma through the building up of a subsequent incarnation. From their spiritual heights the spirits referred to behold how everything that is disseminated in the world as the effects of our deeds becomes an inner experience. And what they behold in this way is now for them the material for incorporating something other than the aforesaid lower spirits are able to do into the further evolution of the world above all to provide help in order that karma can be fulfilled, in order that what is in this way thrust inwards from without forms the foundation for a slow upbuilding process which between death and a new birth unites those threads that then descend to the physical substance of heredity, so that it may as spiritual content join with what the human individual inherits from father and mother. Much is necessary in order that what in this way descends from spiritual heights and must join together with the substance of heredity deriving from one's ancestors may come into being. After a person has crossed the threshold of death and has laid aside his etheric body, after he has completed that backward journey through the soul-world, there already begins the work that must be accomplished between death and a new birth in order that the new birth, the new incarnation may come about.

What is it that is accomplished there? It is very difficult to characterize the manner in which we are worked upon out there in the spiritual cosmos. If I were to characterize it, I could perhaps do so in the following way through a somewhat schematic impression. Let us suppose that a person crosses the threshold of death. His etheric body is then laid aside. What he himself still surveys continues for a relatively long time to be in a certain sense in the proximity of the Earth. I have characterized such things to you over the course of time. But what the Angeloi, Archangeloi and Archai have woven extends so widely—in that it is incorporated in the universal world-ether—that it develops in the form of an extensive sphere with the Earth at its centre. Thus the world-ether encompasses the Earth like a spiritual atmosphere; and in the world-ether is incorporated what we have woven from our thoughts. Do not be apprehensive as to where there could be room for all this fabric of thoughts: the spiritual dimension pervades everything, and all these thoughts are contained within this sphere.

As his journey progresses further the person concerned now perceives this fabric of thoughts not from within but from without; and his further life is a kind of expansion, an ascent into the cosmos. And during the whole time that the life between death and a new birth runs its course, he sees constantly from an outward perspective: this is what you are—like a still mighty, extended sphere; and on this sphere you imagine something like an immense map. All this is, of course, expressed pictorially and in broad outline, but it approximates to the actual state of affairs. Thus on this map, on this globe is engraved—in that everything is marked as it is spiritually incorporated: firstly, that which has been developed by the person himself in his etheric body and which he is able to behold, then also what has now become an inner human reality in the way that I have described. All this is incorporated, in that Spirits of Form, Spirits of Movement, Spirits of Wisdom and Spirits of Will are working on him between death and a new birth. And when the time has come when the new incarnation is to arise, this fabric is ready. It is, therefore, a mighty sphere that can then be beheld. You again do not need to fear that there would be no place for all these spheres; they can all be within one another. It is of course a picture for a spiritual phenomenon. Then this sphere begins to become smaller and smaller, and it is inverted in the way that one turns a glove inside out, so that the inner becomes outer and the outer becomes inner. That which is, as it were, the outer aspect becomes wholly internalized, it is completely inverted and becomes so small that it can unite with the human germinal essence that forms in the body of the mother. This is also a picture.

One can of course also picture these things in a different way. This has also already happened here. But the picture that we want to present today is that, according to the measure of what a person has given to the beings of the higher hierarchies during his life between birth and death, these spirits of the higher hierarchies work both upon the world and also upon forming the spiritual foundations for this human individual's new incarnation. This, I think, is a mighty thought if it becomes firmly established in our feelings, if we become aware of what our life—if thus regarded—signifies for the universe as a whole and of how we stand within this same universe. And it is necessary that from the present time onwards ever more and more people develop an awareness of living throughout their lives in connection with a spiritual world.

The very clever people of today, the opponents of spiritual science, will say: Human life will surely continue even if the knowledge that is disseminated among human beings is not of such a nature but is far simpler than this; for matters of this kind can only burden one's thinking, but one does need to weary one's life with such thoughts. There are bound to be very clever people who say this. And they will then perhaps also add that people were formerly ignorant of such unnecessary wisdom and have also been able to make progress.

Those who say such things have absolutely no idea of how stupid what they are saying is, because such an assertion is made under the presupposition that it really is true that people have always been as lacking in knowledge of the spiritual mysteries of existence as they are now. But it is not so long since their knowledge has been so limited. This can everywhere be demonstrated even in matters of a most outward kind.

I shall give you such an instance. I have never had the opportunity here to visit a picture gallery in order to see whether there are similar pieces of art here in Stuttgart. But we recently visited a picture gallery in Hamburg, and the following emerged from this. You see, if painters come today with the intention of painting what we know as a great, powerful picture but a picture representing what we know to be a truth, the Fall at the beginning of the Old Testament, if painters are to paint the Fall of man on the basis of what they consider today to be right, they will paint a tree with Eve on the one side and Adam on the other. They will paint these human figures more or less depending on whether they are expressionists, impressionists or '-ists' of whatever kind; but they will in any case paint a snake beside or on the tree. This is naturalistic, is it not, a realistic approach? But for someone who can think and considers the matter more closely, it is certainly not realistic; for I should like to know the woman—even if she were an epitome of Eve—who would let herself be tempted by an ordinary snake with the kind of head that a snake possesses to do the deed that Eve was tempted to perform. I do not think that such a woman exists. No Eve will let herself be tempted by such a snake. We know, of course, that we are dealing here with a temptation by Lucifer. But can Lucifer be portrayed by means of an ordinary snake? This is the best that can be expected of the picture. But we know of Lucifer that he actually owes his existence to the fact that he remained behind at the Moon stage, when there were no such snakes as there have been during Earth evolution. It is therefore totally unrealistic to paint a true snake with an enormous snake's head. How should one actually paint Lucifer if one wanted to paint him properly and realistically in the sense of our spiritual science? One would have to paint him in such a way that one expressed how Lucifer was during the Moon period for an evolution still expressive of the imaginative element, as I have described in *Cosmic Memory*. That is, if one enters into it more closely, one will find that what has now become the physical earthly head in man together with the thick, and sometimes very thick, bony skull was at that time still thin. It could be seen imaginatively. But what is attached to it—you can see from the skeleton that man actually consists of two parts, the brain and the spine—is only like a very thin sliver. The rest of the skeleton is really the result of earthly forces. Thus the part of man that is associated with the skull derives from the Moon, and the spinal cord is a later appendage. This other part has all been added through the development of our earthly nature. So what will Lucifer have looked like to an imaginative perception? He will have had a human skull, and appended to it something like a snake's body representing the spinal cord in mobile form. This is what he will have looked like. If one wanted to paint realistically, one would therefore have to paint the tree beside which is the human head with a snake's body attached to it representing the spine. One would then be painting according to the truth. But one would have to have had some knowledge of the mystery of existence, of the spiritual worlds with which man is connected.

In the art gallery in Hamburg you can find a picture from the thirteenth or fourteenth centuries by the so-called Master Bertram.[78] Here the Fall is painted exactly as I have been describing to you now. The artist has not simply painted a snake, but what is by the tree is directly equivalent to the way that I have just described it. What does this mean? It means that it is at most a few centuries since human beings have ceased to know how they stand in relation to the spiritual world and that there is altogether a spiritual world in a sense that can be recognized. Thus people have become so foolish that they think that the way that they now behold the world merely with their physical senses and with an intellect that is purely bound to the brain is how people have always perceived it; it is only that they were more childlike and thought up all kind of myths. This is how people think today in universities. But it is all nonsense, for it has only been a few centuries since humanity has lost the living perception of the spiritual world. When compared with the great tasks of knowledge, the materialistic science of the present is none other than a dull-witted approach to the spiritual world. And this utter tediousness is what struts around today claiming authority and is wondered at as representing great progress. It had to come to this. We know why it had to come: so that human beings are protected through their purely physical development and are able to gain freedom. This must be perceived. And even from such evidence as I have presented to you, people could—if they had just a little nous in their heads—see how little time it has been that spiritual perception has been lost to human beings. But it does not occur to them to have any real insight into these things. They prefer to choose external means of power because this is easy, because they do not need to learn anything particular but need only to stand before some laboratory table and mechanically apply certain methods; and they then explain through external pronouncements of power that all talk of a spiritual world is erroneous nonsense and pure fantasy. This is what is at present being given to human beings in place of a real inclination towards the spiritual world.

But, my dear friends, it is at present still the case that everything belonging to the gift of invention is still the remnant of an inheritance from those ancient times when there was insight into the spiritual world. When this too has gone, people will no longer invent anything. And if spiritual science were not to reignite the flame of human thinking, it would take not even a further fifty years before everything that works in this way out of pure materialism would be confined to lecturing about outward matter, and nothing would any longer occur to anyone that could enrich art or ideology or, in whatever way, outer life. Thus it is the most urgent demand of the time and not a mere preference for some sort of spiritual fantasy that an awareness of mankind's connection with the spiritual world becomes established, that people are again able to look upwards. And they can do so once the old atavistic clairvoyance has faded away by exploring what spiritual science has to offer.

It is in this sense necessary that people learn how fruitful it is not only for a knowledge of the spiritual world but for a right thinking about the whole of life to make the approach to spiritual science.

Again and again one learns how disinclined people are at the present time to involve themselves with that somewhat complicated inner life of soul which must be cultivated if one wants to find a relationship with the spiritual world. Just think for a moment and consider an average sort of professor today (of course, there can be exceptions; no one should feel offended, and all the more praise should be given if there is one such person in this circle), a respectable modern university professor who gives lectures will as a rule have absolutely no wish to listen to such things; all this is far too uncongenial for him. If one wants to speak today of spiritual things, one must speak in empty, vague generalizations which say as little as possible and which also convey the least possible meaning for real life.

When I recently gave the same lecture in Leipzig[79] that I gave here the day before yesterday concerning an aspect of German cultural life that has virtually disappeared, two gentlemen came up to me after the lecture (they were of course the clever sort of people to whom I have been referring). One of them said that he had been surprised that I had spoken as I had, for he had expected that when someone gives a talk from a theosophical viewpoint it would be more in tune with his way of thinking; he was, you see, a pacifist, and his way of regarding the war was strongly coloured by his views as a pacifist.

Pacifism is this view that has been cultivated for some time under the aegis of various people: of Bertha von Suttner[80] and also of that individual who is regarded in Petersburg as both Caesar and pope.[81] I have already said many years ago in my Berlin lectures[82] that it is characteristic of aspirations for peace that, since we have had them, the biggest and bloodiest wars in world history have been fought. But this movement is one of those that live by evoking the vaguest possible slogans to be found anywhere but which inveigle themselves into people's feeling life because one cannot but spread them, and one is indeed disseminating pure love and pure goodness. I permitted myself to say to the gentlemen: You see, we are now living amidst the most terrible of the wars that have hitherto occurred in world history; we have had the experience that in June or July 1915 more ammunition was discharged in a single day than in the whole of the Franco-Prussian War! We have already reached the point that now in this war as much ammunition has been used as in all wars that have been conducted with such ammunition in the whole history of humanity. I said: Is it not possible to see that the culture that has now prevailed for centuries has now continued ad absurdam, that it has been shown where it is leading? Well, his rejoinder was: I see this war as a sickness, and it must be healed; it is merely a sickness which can occur.

Such a statement as this is profoundly illuminating because it is so understandable and because from a certain aspect it is quite obviously correct. But the point is not whether something is correct but, rather, to what extent it is superficial. It is obviously correct to say that it is a sickness. But I said to him: If you were to study an illness more deeply, you may ask why it is afflicting the person concerned. And the answer is that something was previously the matter with him! The illness is actually the reaction to something that was not right. Thus if you were but to think further from your standpoint, you would come to see that it is a sickness, but that it has occurred because things were previously out of joint. It is because there is a state of disorder that the sickness has manifested itself—that makes perfect sense. But such people even manage to muddle up all manner of correct things, because they think only on the surface and because they are unable to enter into things at a deeper level. This is the serious issue that one has to recognize at the present time.

If you consider such a phenomenon as that which I presented the day before yesterday in connection with Karl Christian Planck,[83] whose spiritual capacity is evident simply from the fact that in 1880 he precisely foresaw what is taking place today, you will see from the way that he is valued and recognized that this culture that has been developing is fit for making the sovereignty of the inept, with their ability to suppress all true striving, into a world power. There should be no lack of clarity about this. It is something that one has to discern at the deepest level.

I shall tell you a little story. Someone once heard that Goethe had written a version of *Faust*, and he said that he wanted to know what is contained in Goethe's *Faust*. The person whom he therefore consulted found that he had to discover the easiest and most convenient method of enabling the other to learn what this *Faust* actually consisted of, and he pondered deeply over the question: How can I impart to this individual who has not the slightest idea of the meaning of Goethe's *Faust* what it contains? Then he had an inspiration. It occurred to him that a new edition of *Faust* was about to be published by a particular press, so he thought: I shall tell this fellow about this. And he said to him: Look, in three weeks' time *Faust* is going to be brought out by this publisher. In all the hundreds of type-cases there lie the different letters, and if you pay attention you will see that the typesetter takes out this or that letter and forms the individual letters into words. You will see precisely how one page after another is set, and then how at the end *Faust* emerges out of the different letters. Thus the other person spent several weeks seeing how the whole of *Faust* was brought together by the letters through the agency of human hands!

Yes, you see, I can also relate this in a somewhat different way. The modern age was approaching. Then people wanted to know what is actually going on in the life of the soul and spirit, and they had a need to gain insight into the way that ideas, thoughts, will-impulses and feelings are bound up with the human soul and what they signify for the world as a whole. They asked—human beings. Well, along came modern science, this purely naturalistic science, and it claimed to be able to provide the answers. Then, to the extent that this is now possible, we examine the various pathways of the brain, the nerve fibres, the ganglia and the rest, as all this is interconnected. And there we have the life of soul. One has exactly the same relationship as one has to Goethe's *Faust* if one comes to know it like the person referred to above who sat for three weeks in the printing-house; it is exactly the same! If you take all the testimonies that are fabricated today from so-called psycho-physiologists, you have with regard to the spiritual knowledge of the world something similar to what you know about the whole of *Faust* if you have watched how *Faust* is manufactured out of type-cases. It is only necessary to see this and the shattering feeling will overwhelm the soul that is necessary in order to progress further in the evolutionary course of mankind.

You are fine opponents, the adherents of naturalism will now say, in that you so discredit our science, the true science which operates in accordance with strictly natural principles! But it does not occur to us to blacken its name. If *Faust* is to come into existence, the typesetting work does of course have to be done for the published edition of *Faust*; but it must be recognized in its right world-situation.

All this that I can indicate in this way belongs, in the sense that I also indicated the day before yesterday, to the serious, significant tasks which will await their fulfilment in Central Europe. All this relates to these serious tasks. And it is, moreover, urgently necessary to call these things to mind at this present serious time in which we are living; for it is utterly necessary that a deeper sense for real truth infiltrates the world than can be sustained under the influence of a materialistic or strictly scientific world-conception. One does not need to oppose the fact that people learn typesetting in order that editions of *Faust* can be prepared, any more than one creates opposition to people studying the brain and the nervous system; but one must be a decisive opponent of that presumptuous arrogance that manifests itself today in materialistic science, of the fact that the feeling that the spiritualization of culture is something that must be achieved, which emerges seriously and worthily from Central Europe (for Western Europe has lost all sense for these things), engenders such a terrible degree of suffering. I say this not merely in order to express something paradoxical or forceful, but I say it out of the necessity that causes one to speak about such things in our time. A time will come when people will have to consider various things on the basis of their true reality; but there is today not as yet much receptivity for such a survey. I could give you thousands of examples of the inner untruthfulness of present-day trends in science and literature. Allow me to cite at least one that I would gladly have mentioned the day before yesterday in the public lecture, but there is never enough time—lectures must, unfortunately, be kept so very short.

You can, for example, again and again find in many books about Ernst Haeckel[84]—you know that I greatly appreciate Ernst Haeckel in the realm where he can be valued—that he refers to Karl Ernst von Baer,[85] the exemplary naturalist whom he calls his teacher. People today, of course, take hold of Haeckel's books, study them and regard them as a kind of new Bible or at least comparable to writings by a modern Church Father. For the difference is not that people today believe in their own judgement whereas at the time of the Church Fathers they relied on the Church Fathers; the difference is of quite another nature. At the time of Tertullian and Gregory Nazianzus,[86] these were the Church Fathers, and people swore allegiance to them. Today especially those who found monistic associations or associations for a eugenic conception of the world or fine things of a similar kind swear allegiance to Saint Darwin, Saint Haeckel or Saint Helmholtz.[87] It is—albeit on a somewhat different level—exactly the same! There are no connotations of sainthood, but that makes no difference whatsoever. Thus people read Haeckel, and when he refers to Karl Ernst von Baer in this way they venture the opinion: Well, one can see that this great naturalist Karl Ernst von Baer was in full agreement with Haeckel as regards the rejection of any spiritual world. I should like to advise anyone who has got some taste of Haeckel's or Darwin's books today to consider very carefully before establishing a monistic association. Thus, for example, when Haeckel cites Ernst von Baer, one should oneself first find something that Karl Ernst von Baer has written and read it. I shall read you a passage from Karl Ernst von Baer, where he speaks about the way that the spiritual world is related to the earthly world. Baer says: 'The body of the Earth is only the seedbed on which man's spiritual inheritance proliferates, and the history of nature is only the history of the continuing victory of the spiritual over matter. This is the fundamental idea of creation, for the favour or, rather, the enrichment of which individuals and a whole series of procreation processes are allowed to disappear and the present rises up on the framework of an immeasurable past.'

So what is Baer saying? The body of the Earth is the seedbed and into it spiritual seeds are planted in order that they may unfold. This man Baer has expressed the exact truth at the beginning of the nineteenth century! Ernst Haeckel searches for those statements from Baer that he finds acceptable. Those who do nothing other than—at best—found monistic associations in order to further the wisdom of the world know nothing of this other than what Haeckel says about Baer, and they continue to live in the lie without having the slightest inclination to set about seeing for themselves what underlies it. Our literature today is full of such tapestries of lies; and especially in our popular scientific literature, Europe is everywhere deluged with the striving for what one might describe as the greatest possible deforming and fanciful perverting of spiritual endeavours and an extreme reluctance to perceive and evaluate these things with clear, sure human judgements.

In order to give you some actual instances, there are for example in the West among the French, among the British and among the Italians all kinds of Freemasonic Orders with high grades, some with thirty-three grades but there are also those with ninety grades. Much fishing in troubled waters has been going on especially in such Orders in the course of recent centuries. And if one investigates with a sober, healthy judgement the influence of every kind of unhealthy, foolish prank (though most probably consciously undertaken in accordance with personal and political aims), if one studies the influences and streams of the Freemasonry that exists in the West of Europe upon the participation of Italy in this war, one will get an inkling of many dubious elements and much fishing in troubled waters in our so-called culture! What has taken place especially in such Freemasonic Orders since the outbreak of the war will one day form the basis for a curious chapter. The German Freemasons will come away from this relatively well, for the only thing that will be said of them is that they have been the losers in the whole game. After all, in so far as they have lived in a state of brotherhood with others, they have not noticed anything. And that is after all something that still—indeed!—can be said in their favour. But one should not think that what is asserted from such sides is without influence upon what is living and working around us in the so-called cultural environment and which can only work and live for as long as other people do not want their judgement clarified and strengthened through insight into the spiritual world.

In my book *Thoughts during the Time of the War*[88] I have—to the extent that this is possible in public literature—sought to promote some understanding of something that is little understood, namely, certain streams prevailing everywhere in the East and the West. These streams, for example the Eastern stream of the Slavophiles to which I have referred in this booklet, have, however, a much deeper origin. Already at the end of the eighteenth century and especially at the end of the nineteenth century but also several decades earlier, in particular the Western Freemasonic Orders had considerable influence upon the spiritual and cultural life of Russia; they transplanted, infected and injected that which was to appear there. In many respects, Slavophilism and Pan-slavism are really the sprouted seed of what has been implanted from these Freemasonic Orders. Under the mask, under the mantle of ceremony, people were, so to speak, befogged; all manner of frippery was presented to them so that they could then be imbued with an inclination for certain plans. And when other events come in place of military battles, humanity will finally be convinced of all the things that are being enacted in Eastern Europe from this Western side.

If these places where we are assembled in our branches are the only places where one can speak even today, it is essential that what I am saying is discussed here.

I wanted today to take up the question of the great, sublime nature of man's connection with entire hierarchies which can come before our souls when we recall that the life of thought and feeling that we bear within us is already within our physical frames between birth and death, and then also between death and a new birth, enshrined in a fabric of thoughts, a cosmic work, on which whole hierarchies work in the whole context of the world. What matters is not that we have great knowledge about a particular thing but that we are able to imbue ourselves with such a feeling for the world and that you, my dear friends, go away from such a study as this with the feeling for what man actually is within the world, and for what he should know about this connection that he has with the world. That is what is important. That all this flows together in your souls, in your hearts into a cosmic feeling, and that in this way something lights up within you of the power that can be engendered by what may be incorporated in our culture to the extent that each person is able to do this according to the place that he occupies in the world. Official scholars in our time have not worked on these things; and they will not do so. It is therefore necessary for people to open their eyes to the position that official scholars occupy in the world: that they, in so far that they engage in laboratory work, are to be compared with typesetters, and many who are not involved in such work merely with people who describe the typesetting process. Most of these today are the philosophers who preach at the universities.

That this is so is something of which individual souls should be aware. For it is not a criticism of the age but merely a characterization. The only way that the forces have been found to bring evolution further on its way is that in the various ages people have known how things stand—this has indeed been the only way.

This is what I wanted to place before your souls at this difficult time, when one cannot always say that one will see one another again: some aspect of knowledge which, if we have a right feeling for it, can be transmuted into a holy inner duty of the human soul towards the world as a whole. Innumerable deaths surround us today in the events which are on the one hand the fruit of previous developments but which should mark the significance of much that needs to happen if mankind is to move forward not in the way that the describers of the type-case want but in accordance with the necessity of world evolution.

It is true that I made mention the day before yesterday of the father of materialism, Lamettrie,[89] who had said—of course, there is also some truth in this—that it would only have been necessary for a little cog in Erasmus's nervous system to have been different and he would not have been Erasmus but a fool. I have said that one does not need to refute such a statement; but now that we have perhaps been a little more prepared, our knowledge of such things has a somewhat different colouring.

If we gather together everything that we have been considering today and allow it to impregnate our feelings, we will then say to ourselves how true it is that the many sacrificial deaths that are presently being suffered are related to earthly existence in such a way that the etheric bodies which are taken away from human beings at an early age remain connected for a long, long time with earthly existence, and that there must now be people who are able to become conscious of what lives in these unspent etheric bodies, which still contained everything that these human individuals might still have been able to make use of if they had lived for several decades longer. But there will need to be people who are conscious of this in the time to come, so that earthly culture and not Ahriman receives the fruits of what is contained in these etheric bodies. Let us therefore, in view of what we have prepared in our souls for what will happen, imbue ourselves with the words that have often been spoken here:

> From the courage of the fighters,
> From the blood on fields of battle,
> From the grief of the bereaved,
> From the people's sacrifice:
> There will ripen fruit of spirit,
> If souls will turn in consciousness
> Towards the realm of spirit.

Lecture 9

STUTTGART, 11 MAY 1917

IT is my intention today[90] to speak to you during my presence here of things that make the events of the present a little more understandable to anyone with a searching mind. These things will not be discussed superficially but with the object of giving some indication as to how one can gain some broader spiritual understanding of this present time of ours. This intention, which I have long cherished for this visit to Stuttgart, is one that we shall also carry out; and the lecture next Sunday is also available for this purpose.

Taking into consideration much that, I might say, is playing into our movement from without as—and I say this in a carefully considered way—waves breaking on to our modern shores, it seems to me to be necessary to begin with to lay down some principles today by way of an introduction which may serve to dissipate many misunderstandings concerning anthroposophy that can arise only too easily at a time where there is a hatred of any depth of thought and feeling and which, on the other hand, can help us to gain for ourselves a right relationship to what anthroposophy can be for us.

Let us try to address the question: What are we looking for when we choose the path leading to the anthroposophical movement? We are looking on this path for the possibility of gaining a relationship to the spiritual world which corresponds to the need for this spiritual world that is born within us out of the forces, out of the life-circumstances of the present. After all, no one who is not by nature superficial will approach us who can readily acquire a relationship to the spiritual world other than with us. No one comes to us who is able to acquire a relationship to the spiritual world on those paths that have been outwardly fully recognized for centuries and which owe their continuing use to the circumstance that people have forgotten to reflect about the legitimacy of what is brought to bear upon the general necessities of life. There is, in contrast, much discussion about legitimacy when something must, as it were, appear in the world for the first time. We cannot sufficiently often keep in mind what anthroposophy needs and wants to be out of the spirit of our time and bring it into connection with that in us which can progress towards anthroposophy, which seeks to bring us to anthroposophy.

You see, my dear friends, anthroposophy would not be there if there were not one or another person who finds it congenial to— well, let us use the official expression—agitate for the kind of ideas that live in anthroposophy. Anthroposophy derives in absolute terms from the knowledge that there are in our time seeking souls who are able to find what they are seeking only on the path of anthroposophy. It is not because someone wants to have anthroposophy that it is pursued but because souls long for it. This is not inconsistent with the fact that many people deny this, for in the soul there lives much that is subconscious and unconscious which, if rightly interpreted, represents none other than the longing for anthroposophy: the longing above all—if we take something from anthroposophy itself—to come on this path to know the Christ impulse that meets the need of the present, to find the path to the Christ impulse in the way that the heart must yearn if it really seeks to understand itself within the life-circumstances of the present. Such general, abstract statements as I have now expressed them may surely be enlightening for someone who has for some years been working upon the foundations of anthroposophy. But what matters is that our souls should be so pervaded with the spirit of these words that they do not remain within us as something purely abstract and theoretical but that they become the content of our entire life and above all the content of our way of thinking.

I have also here already related an example which is particularly characteristic. I once gave a lecture in a South German town on the theme 'Bible and Wisdom',[91] where by describing how anthroposophy can through its presuppositions enter more deeply into the great, inexhaustible mysteries of the primal book of humanity, the Bible, I tried to explain how also someone with a positive relationship to Christianity can, if he rightly understands his inner questions, find the path to anthroposophy. After the lecture, two Catholic priests who had listened to the lecture came up to me. It was apparent from what they said that from their Catholic doctrine as they understood it, as they knew it as theologians (perhaps not so much as priests entrusted with certain obligations but specifically as theologians), they were unable to raise any particular objections. So they approached the matter indirectly and said: Yes, you see, there is nothing particular to say from our standpoint against what you have presented today other than this. When *we* speak, we speak in such a way that everyone can understand what we are saying. You do indeed also speak of Christianity, but only for those who have reached a certain level of education or have specially prepared themselves for this manner of speaking. My reply was on these lines: Yes, you see, Reverend Fathers, it does not so much matter what you or I think about the question as to what should be spoken to all people, for this leads the whole subject into the error of personal opinion. It is by no means surprising that each person thinks that what he pursues is of universally human validity. Why should one wonder at this, since what would be the point of pursuing it otherwise? But the point is not what you or I think is right. Our way of engaging in research about the spirit has its beginning in that we raise ourselves above this personal opinion and consider the reality of the situation, the true reality. In our case this reality is very obvious. It lies simply in the answer to the question: Do all the people today for whom you speak—and you believe that you are speaking for all people—still come to church to listen to you? The question as to whether you think that you speak for all people is answered by a fact. That this should be valid for all people is only a matter of your opinion; the alternative is simply a fact. Tell me whether everyone goes to church! All that they could say in reply was that a number of people do not go to church. This proves you wrong, I said, for you are then not speaking for those to whom *I* have to speak and who also have the right to find the path to Christ at this present time.

This means not to direct one's judgement towards what one personally considers to be true or false but to subject it to the demands and tasks of reality. It is to be sure much more comfortable to spin theories about what is right or wrong than to study reality concretely in all its details, to listen constantly with an attentive ear to what reality is demanding of us. Anthroposophy does not want to be anything other than a means of giving answers to questions that it does not itself pose but which hearts and souls pose in the present when they rightly understand themselves. And I am conscious that the questions that are posed in my very numerous writings have not been posed by me. The answers have mostly been given by me but the questions are not mine. The questions are posed by that which the culture of the age brings forth, by what, for example, natural science brings forth; they are questions that everyone must ask who has an interest in the demands of the time and for whom the most important needs of the present are a matter of serious concern.

If one calls these prerequisites to mind in a certain way, we can see the truth of the fact that there is an underlying intention in the whole of the anthroposophical literature that is available to you, a basic view, a basic tendency and a basic orientation. As one peruses all these writings, not with the inherently favourable outlook that we may perhaps have acquired within our circle but with the critical eye that one can gain from present-day culture, there is one thing that one will find as the central point of the whole of this anthroposophical literature. This is that everything has its origin in the aim to bring to the human soul that for which it must above all long in the present: independence, a power of judgement that emanates from one's own inner being. I have frequently had to resist the urge which has been impressed upon me from one or another side to write in a popular way. I have always resisted this urge for the simple reason that it can never be a question within anthroposophical literature of giving people an article of belief which, if they want, they receive with limited understanding, and that in this literature it is of paramount importance to call forth one's own faculty of judgement, one's own inner quest. As everyone who wishes to do so knows to be the case, this is the dominant theme throughout this anthroposophical literature.

There has never been the intention to call forth blind belief. It is true that things are related that cannot readily be verified, but they are related as facts of the spiritual world which everyone can receive as information and to which they can apply their critical standards on an on-going basis if they so wish. And we have indeed seen that friends endowed with a good understanding of the content have recently managed to tackle to a high level the subtlest things with the instrument of unprejudiced criticism. That which is contained in the anthroposophical literature referred to here has nothing to fear from this unprejudiced criticism. It will withstand this unprejudiced criticism; it will withstand it all the better the more unprejudiced this criticism is. No one will ever hear anything from me where this question is concerned other than this: continue testing and testing but do not be content with this but seek above all to arrive at some verification by trying to enter ever more deeply into the phenomena in question with the means of modern thinking. Because this is striven for, anthroposophical literature is able to make people independent.

Now it is true that one can have many different experiences when one surveys the manner in which anthroposophy is received. I have again and again encountered people who have heard one or another lecture or have read something that I have written and I never see them again. That is of course entirely their right; no one should be reproached for this. And when they have been asked by someone they know why they are no longer appearing (in all friendship, of course, not with any kind of reproach), they reply: Yes, if we become more closely involved, we have a fear of being convinced. These are indeed significant words, but they are also an indication of significant facts. What is being attempted here is precisely to get away from the besetting evil of our time—putting forward personal opinions, personal theories—and to direct souls to what the spiritual substance of the world itself imparts, if we find the possibility of devoting ourselves with our whole soul to this spiritual substance and of speaking of the methods and means through which the soul succeeds in a certain sense to apprehend it.

A world-conception that arises out of the deepest needs of the time but which is so thoroughly at variance with what people in our time believe will only slowly and gradually be embraced by them. The souls of human beings depend on what they are used to; they are happiest when they hear their own lucid thoughts from the pulpit and are able to say to themselves regarding what they hear: This is what I have long already thought. The anthroposophical teachings that appear at present are, to be sure, not the kind of truths which have been 'long already thought'. But in the eyes of many people this is precisely the main problem, that they are not able to say to themselves: This is what I have long already thought; and that they do not want to say to themselves: If I dig down deeply into my inner being, nothing is being expressed here that is a personal opinion but what I hear is connected with factors concerning human evolution. We shall return in manifold ways to such factors concerning human evolution during my present stay in Stuttgart. Thus it is understandable that many hindrances and impediments arise when people try to approach anthroposophy or spiritual science.

My book *Knowledge of the Higher Worlds* has been much read over the years, not only among those who belong to the various circles of the Anthroposophical Society but it has also been read elsewhere at the present time. When people read this book they often have an experience that is remarkably characteristic. Someone who reads the book *Knowledge of the Higher Worlds* may write me a letter—and, of course, I am always pleased when someone writes me an intelligent letter about any book but especially about this particular one. But what usually happens is that the person in question has not understood the book and has transformed the most important things in the book into the materialistic orientation of the present. For what people mostly assimilate when they begin studying this book is the following. But there is something that we should say first: Anyone who reads *Knowledge of the Higher Worlds* may be struck by a whole number of doubts, and there will be many people who can testify that I am always prepared to discuss these doubts with people; and therefore I would most certainly not want what I am now saying to appear as though anyone should be deterred from writing the letter of which I have just spoken. No one should be deterred from writing such a letter, but letters are very often written whereby people take hold of a particular aspect and change it into its materialistic opposite. Much is said in the book *Knowledge of the Higher Worlds* that when rightly considered leads a person out from himself to find the path into the spiritual world. Especially this book is accordingly intended to make a person as independent as possible, not in any sense to compel him to follow a particular subjective path but to clear away the hindrances so that he can himself find the truth. The best means of approaching this book would be to make its content one's own through an inner deed. But then people clutch hold of the statement that anyone who has reached the necessary maturity will, if he seeks rightly, find his spiritual teacher.[92] So there we have it! I shall therefore write a letter to the one who has written the book, he will be my spiritual teacher; that is the simplest thing to do! Here we have the translation into the materialistic opposite. That this passage might be the holiest incentive for someone seeking independence to search further in order to find the path which could well consist in something quite different from writing a letter to someone saying: I ask you to give me instructions, is highly uncomfortable for very many readers of this book! They do not look sufficiently in the book. And so this book, *Knowledge of the Higher Worlds*, despite being perhaps the most read book of its kind today in the German-speaking world and translated into many foreign languages, is one of the books that have been most misunderstood. And it is, after all, child's play to understand if one has an open, unprejudiced attitude to it and does not translate it into something that is materialistically comfortable.

In this respect, too, people do, as it were, seek what they are accustomed to seek in other areas. Thus people today are strongly imbued with the habit of not helping themselves, that is, not learning ways in which one can find help in one or another situation and failing to attend to the principles according to which they can be helped. Why should one pay much attention to the way in which one may best live healthily? People let someone whose job this is to prescribe something for them and then they do not need to examine the principles in accordance with which he prescribes; they surrender their destiny to someone who is regarded as an authority. Why should one not also have the urge to surrender one's destiny to someone else on the spiritual path, on what is humanly the path of the greatest importance? After all, the most that can be expected of the work that one is stimulated to do is the task of making the human soul independent!

One can say that natural-scientific research has today reached a certain position, and this position of natural-scientific research would be accessible to those who are called today to represent the various scientific disciplines, although most of them simply spin a cocoon around their own subjects and would not venture beyond its limits. But if, say, a dozen of these official representatives—and only these are heard today—were to devote themselves with innermost honesty to what is written in my *Occult Science* and *Theosophy* and were then to examine them from this natural-scientific standpoint, they would find that the truth of everything is proved in terms of looking at life to see whether life confirms what can be learnt through spiritual science, what is being sought here from the spiritual world. Anyone who really understands natural science comes to be able to certify what is given through anthroposophically oriented spiritual science. This is an absolute truth. But we stand before the strange fact that those who would be able to undertake such an examination pay absolutely no attention to it and until now have not done so, that no one has even raised these questions (I leave aside those from our circles who have been stimulated to do this), that no one has set about the task of properly examining the spiritual-scientific results of anthroposophy by means of a fully understood natural-scientific path of research! Spiritual-scientific research truly does not need to have the least to fear from such an examination; it will withstand it. It should simply be done and the test will be successfully passed. But at a time when people do not even have the inclination to explore the most primitive truths, this examination may still have to wait for a long time.

The urge not only to be logical but to be in tune with reality, that is, to form one's judgement not only according to abstract logic but through being immersed in reality, is one that few have in our present time. Many do indeed strive to be logical, but only a certain capacity to go behind logic makes it possible to gain an insight also into the consequences of logic itself; and one otherwise does not notice what confusion can be wrought by such wholly matching judgements. You see, it is certainly logical to be always in agreement with one's own judgement or to be in agreement with the judgement of someone else, but it can lead to really strange collisions. Charles V, the Austrian, and the French king, Francis I,[93] arrived at the same thought. They were, so to speak, in full agreement with respect to a certain thought which they wanted to transform into a reality. Francis said: My dear brother wants exactly the same as I do. We both want the same. They both wanted to conquer Milan! Yes, you see, one sees the point when one adds the final remark. But few people at present have the inclination even only to think that such judgements fly around on an enormous scale and govern the thinking of the present to its detriment.

It is remarkable that—forgive the prosaic image—enlightened individuals do at times try to bridle the faculty of judgement today by the tail, just as if someone were to bridle a horse by the tail instead of by the head. But such a way of bridling immediately becomes applicable if the person in question is officially authorized. Anyone with a sense for the living aspect of thinking, feeling and will has for many years had to endure real torment through the nature and form of much of present-day thinking. I can still now recall the first lecture that I heard in Vienna about elliptical function theory—please forgive the term, but I use it in the spirit of what I want to express and not in order that what I am referring to may be understood. I was listening to lectures by the famous professor, Leo Königsberger.[94] He was so famous that when he was made a professor he could immediately write to the government saying that he wanted to be appointed a Hofrat[*] and not merely a professor. So when I heard his first lecture, he came to consider the question: How can one understand numbers? People recognize positive and negative numbers. Positive numbers correspond to money that I have, negative numbers to money that I do not have, that I owe. But there are also other numbers.

---

[*] An honorary title conferred in Austria on senior civil servants.—Translator

Mathematicians designate positive and negative numbers by means of a line in the middle of which they write a 0: plus 1, plus 2; minus 1, minus 2. And then the famous Gauß added a further line of new numbers, so that one can fill the plane with different kinds of numbers. However, I do not want to speak about the validity of this plane of numbers. It is, rather, that Leo Königsberger began his lecture about elliptical functions by saying: It could be that someone would say today that one could also equally well consider numbers that are perpendicular to this plane. When as a young whipper-snapper of sixteen or seventeen I came to know about the plane of numbers, I made the objection already at that time that one could also think of space as being filled with numbers. The teacher reassured me in a friendly way by saying that this could be left to future centuries, which of course made a strong impression on me at the time! Then I heard Leo Königsberger speak in Vienna about the same question. He said: Let us suppose that there are these three kinds of numbers, not only the numbers that lie in the plane of both lines but numbers that lie in the third dimension. We shall hypothetically accept that there are such numbers, and that I would multiply such a number by another number. Now I shall show you that if one multiplies it, the product can under certain circumstances be zero. Since this can never be so, there can be no such number. Now you see, it is a torment to hear something like this. I do not wish now to speak of whether the whole of this is right or not, but if one accepts the one not in order to accept the other but to put forward the assertion that because the product is zero such a number cannot exist—to listen to something like this is a torment, because of course the correct thing to say is that if one has two numbers that make zero, one must suppose that zero can indeed arise through multiplication and not the opposite; this is the most obvious solution. But whether these judgements live now in mathematics, whether these judgements live in political memoranda, for example in the memoranda of Mr Wilson,[95] they always lead back to the same thought-forms. But when these forms of judgement live in those judgements that seek to exert influence upon human destiny, an error in judgement is an entirely different matter from an error in a narrowly confined scientific speculation, as in many respects the doctrine of Leo Königsberger is.

It needs to be pointed out that it is a characteristic of our present time that people do not want their judgement to comport with reality. They do not want to live in reality, because they do not want this in the simplest of things. As regards the simplest things they want to presuppose what they like, not what arises from reality. That one must in many respects learn to think differently in order to extricate ourselves from the disastrous situation of the present, that one must learn to not merely think about everything but to think differently, is the key to so much in our time. If people with their old habits of thought could in this way rightly take hold of anthroposophically oriented spiritual science, they would be far more readily able to embrace anthroposophical truths. But they cannot be grasped with old thinking habits but must be understood with the new thinking; and people find it inordinately difficult to engage with it.

This forms part of the reason why it is so difficult at present to get anywhere with anthroposophically oriented spiritual science, simply because it has to come up against the most obvious prejudices. But precisely because this is so, spiritual science is not actually opposed; for the opposition to spiritual science is, it has to be admitted, based on very weak foundations. Look for those scientific discussions where there is an attempt seriously and in a focussed way to consider spiritual science as it has been presented, look out for treatises or similar things of this calibre! Anyone who has even endeavoured to do this will see how little there is that goes in this direction. But it may perhaps also be not very comfortable to proceed in this way. Thus, for instance, some years ago a student who was just about to embark on his doctorate as a philosopher at a very well-known university told me that he wanted to write a dissertation[96] which he had been advised to undertake by a famous professor. This dissertation was to be about the great Russian thinker Solovyov. At that time, Solovyov's work in German translation was limited to a few examples which Nina Hoffmann had made available; later much more of it appeared. I asked the student: Why does the professor give you the advice to write a dissertation about Solovyov? Yes, said the student, the professor knows absolutely nothing about this philosopher and would like to learn something about him. That is the best way: one lets one's pupil write a doctoral dissertation about Solovyov, if he knows Russian; and then one can learn something about him. This is how the doctoral thesis about Solovyov arose. But a large number of doctoral theses arise approximately from the same idea. This is commonly a maxim for how themes for such dissertations are given. In this way, however, a certain scholarly attitude is invoked and cultivated, one could say. The professor in question would naturally have only had a way of really getting to know Solovyov if he had had the intention not only to be a professor of philosophy but also to become acquainted with the philosophy of the present in one of its most outstanding representatives. He would have had to study Solovyov himself as well as possible, even if the smallest part of his work has been translated and he is not himself familiar with Russian. It is an irksome path, it has to be said; but for many who wanted to arrive at their own judgement about spiritual science, the path leading to a real understanding of it today is far more challenging. For there is still a difference whether a professor has a dissertation done about Solovyov or whether he has one done about spiritual science. Regarding Solovyov it is partially successful as a means of forming a judgement once the dissertation is finished, for the pupil had doubtlessly been well trained to make this judgement in the sense that philosophy is taught. But what is the use to a modern professor of, for example, a dissertation about spiritual science? It is no use to him at all. He would not know what on earth to do with it. And of course the path to getting to know it not by way of someone's dissertation but by studying it intensively oneself is even more problematic.

But for someone who is honestly seeking and endeavouring to find the truth of the present, these things are no impediment; such a person may perhaps have a longing for spiritual science. But they are an impediment for most people who are attuned to the habits of modern life to recognize this spiritual science and to do anything other than drill holes in it. It does not originate from them, and since this is so it must be exposed to remorseless analysis. This cannot be done in an objective way; this is shown today by the facts. For those who have tried to approach spiritual science have by and large not become opponents; while they have certainly not become blind adherents, they have also not become opponents. There are such people. But many of our contemporaries simply have the personal interest to eradicate this spiritual science, to make life in the present impossible for it. If they try to do this on the path that anyone who stands firmly on the ground of spiritual science* can fully recognize, if on the path of an honest literary battle they bring up something to counter what someone else has said, there is of course nothing objectionable about this. But this is not what they want to do; it is too awkward. It is far more congenial for them to divert the whole matter into the personal realm, to speak not about what is said in spiritual science but about all manner of other things. And this, you see, is precisely what is being attempted today in our immediate presence and will increasingly be attempted in times to come; and it is to this that I should like to draw your attention. For this will lead to a situation where many discontented people who forever become discontent within our Society for personal reasons can become tools for those who want to rid the world of anthroposophy but do not make the effort to do so honestly (and they would not achieve their goal by honest means), those who do not want to have open-minded discussions but avoid the honest path and aim instead to associate the anthroposophical movement with some kind of scandal and translate everything into the personal realm.

Since my time for speaking about practical concerns has run its course,[97] so that no one can say that I am taking up their time for what has to do with the Society and its interests instead of speaking about practical issues, I shall now add the following. There are increasingly more of those people who are proving to be suitable for being used by those persons whom I have been characterizing, and if one has an honourable intention towards anthroposophically

---

* The German word '*Geisteswissenschaft*' is being used here by Rudolf Steiner to refer not only to his science of the spirit but also to its more academic meaning of 'the Humanities'.

oriented spiritual science one is obliged to speak more precisely about these things.

There was someone whose name first came to our attention many years ago. He came from a small town, and one day Frau Dr Steiner[98] received the kind of letter that appears so frequently: I am unhappy in my situation, and I should like to improve it. And one of the letters which had this tone posed the question concerning some advice that the person concerned wanted to be given: whether it would be better for him to marry into a family or into a business, or else to seek his further path in the world in some other way. Yes, one has to state the unvarnished truth if one wants to tackle things at their foundation and if one does not want to be blind to what will shortly occur. Now this person was made to understand that we cannot concern ourselves with the question as to whether or not he should get married, but since he did not desist much was also placed at his disposal which was suitable for meeting his needs following spiritual instruction which he claimed to have. In that he devoted himself to such spiritual things as he conceived of them, he very soon came to realize that it would be pointless for so great a spirit to pursue a business in a small town. He longed for broader circles. He had evidently saved up something and came to Berlin. He found that it was absolutely fine to pursue spiritual science, but he also felt that he had a special artistic talent; and he now demanded of the Society that it help to promote this. It is good to help people, is it not? The samples that the person in question provided of his art spoke against his having any talent, but many people even without talent learn so much that meagre attributes are sometimes sufficient. And so it happened that this person was recommended for support to various members who were able to sort something out for him. But it always turned out that these efforts came to nothing, since while wanting to pursue an artistic career he did not want to learn anything; this was because he was of the view that he was more capable than the teachers who wanted to provide him with support. And the consequence was that, because he ran away from every teacher, there was in the end nothing more that anyone could do. Many allowances were made for him, but all to no avail; nothing could please this person. For of course it was in his eyes scandalous that the world failed to recognize his genius! That no one else could honestly share this view was truly not our fault. That is the essential point, everything else is of secondary importance. And so it went with this person as it does with many others. They first seek support within our Society, and when this support is in their view not granted they become opponents. And then they come out with all sorts of things. Of course, they never speak about what lies behind what they say. The best way of refuting these things is that one sets forth the underlying reasons. In this case it was of course a matter of the purest vanity and incapacity; and all the hoo-ha that had its foundation in this was the stupidest fabrication, the stupidest fantasy. But today one does of course find the journals that take up these things; for the person to whom I am referring is called Erich Bamler.[99] And when through such investigations one really penetrates such things to their foundations one does not need to get hold of such an article, which for the most part means nothing whatsoever; for what is being said on the surface has its source in something altogether different. It is actually foolish to take serious issue with something that is without reality; for what matters is not this but what lies behind it.

Let us take another case. A man who is not exactly lacking in vanity[100] met with anthroposophy after he had first raised all manner of objections to it. I would have been the last to have sought out this particular individual. He found his own way. It became apparent through a number of inconsistencies that this person was behaving in a very detached way in our Society. This is not an area where one can make demands, and therefore there should not be any criticism if sometimes there are instances of purposes pursued to a certain extent for personal interests. One also at times sympathizes with such personal purposes because one can by this means lead people to the right path. And so it was that the person concerned was thoroughly satisfied with us, and it turned out that he wrote something.[101] I even brought myself to write a postscript for it, and it was also published by our press. He was on good terms with us; we were people with whom he felt able to speak. Then he had something else published,[102] and after the destiny to which this publication was subjected (which does not concern us now) he offered it again to the Philosophisch-Anthroposophischer Verlag. However, it was impossible to publish it there. On the first page of this book it says that I had merely hinted at certain matters concerning the problem of Christ and that the gentleman concerned would like to develop these indications more fully. I say this truly not out of a wounded vanity, although in this case I am being reproached for this; but the statement accusing me of vanity is a downright untruth, for the affair that is mentioned there did not take place.[103] Irrespective of the fact that I did perhaps have grounds for not pursuing things further, there were additional developments of the kind that are reminiscent of another sequence of events that occurred and of which this story is a kind of miniature version. I must also return to this other story and will shortly do so. In this book of the person in question, all kinds of things that I have only said in lectures were simply shared as information. Frau Dr Steiner rightly objected to this and withdrew the book on behalf of the press; and because his book had been returned to him, the gentleman developed into an opponent. Now it is not all right to say, if one writes an article for a journal: The Anthroposophical Society is a load of rubbish because my book has been returned to me by the Philosophisch-Anthroposophischer Verlag. That will not do! But this was alleged to be the truth! Thus in spite of the fact that the person in question has been fully informed of this on innumerable occasions, a fairy story is invented based on contradictions. He knows very well that it is all a mass of contradictions, but he writes a newspaper article about it! What is written in these newspaper articles has no significance, for the person concerned did not become an opponent on account of this. He would have been aware of the real issue a long time ago when he joined. He became an opponent for the reason stated. Many people doubt that one can so readily put forward the hypothesis that what comes afterwards is also causally determined by what preceded it; but at any rate it remains striking that Herr Max Seiling's opposition directly followed the rejection of his book by our publishing house.

One can of course easily deny something of this kind, one can make all sorts of objections, but it does not really matter what one or the other may object but, rather, what the facts are.

This is thoroughly reminiscent of a case on a somewhat higher level; this is only a small-scale version of it. This more striking case is that a gentleman who was formerly in America[104] but is a good European was some years ago asked by a long-standing member to spend some time here in Germany and heard a number of lectures; he also sought with great industriousness to obtain the lectures that had been given over the years and demanded them of one or another person. After he had faithfully packed everything up, he returned to America. He said there that he had been here, that he had become acquainted with my teaching, that he was not satisfied with it but would have to go much deeper; one would therefore find much through him that cannot be found in my books. For when he had extracted everything that he could glean from my research, he was, he said, summoned to a master who lives somewhere in the Transylvanian Alps; he had imparted much to him that he now incorporated in his book. However, everything that he included in his book was what he had listened to in the lectures and which he had written down! And the book was then called *The Rosicrucian Cosmo-Conception or Christian Occult Science*.[105] It appeared in America and made a great impression there; this was, therefore, the book which was put together from what he had heard from me and from what the master in the Transylvanian Alps was to have said to him. People who read it did not need to verify what was from me, nor were they able to do so, since some of it had been said in our more esoteric lectures. But it was not enough that this now appeared as a book written in English or American; for a German bookshop was found that translated the book and published it as *Weltanschauung der Rosenkreuzer*. The publisher was Dr Vollrath.[106]

These are some samples of practice as one can observe it, my dear friends! Such things can well be perceived and they must be perceived, for these are the means with which on the one hand people make use of what is growing on our soil and, on the other, how they oppose it. It should be said that it is possibly the case that worse means have never been used to oppose something as have now been initiated against us, and specifically against anthroposophically oriented spiritual science! You will therefore find it understandable if, as it were, following an iron law of necessity, we avail ourselves of the only means that, while not averting the problem, can perhaps bring some improvement, although everything is combined to create the greatest conceivable difficulties for the personalities associated with the affairs in question. There is, however, one thing that should be borne in mind: too much has been said about this matter but always mainly for deaf ears. There is therefore nothing for it other than—in order to serve in the appropriate way the cause to which we should all be devoted—to submit to a certain iron law of necessity. This iron law of necessity can be described very simply. If it were the case that spiritual science should appear as literature, it would exist as literature. It would then be completely impossible—it is possible in theory, but in actual practice it is completely impossible—for all these things to be included in spiritual science that have been included, and which have been endorsed in truly the worst and most unworthy way. What we must distinguish from the spiritual-scientific movement, which wants to be a movement on behalf of a knowledge and a world-outlook for the present, is the Anthroposophical Society. In theory the Anthroposophical Society is very good, but in practice it is in many respects developing—not as it seems to *me* but as the facts proclaim—in such a way that on a daily basis phenomena present themselves to us which show (and this is no exaggeration) that within this Anthroposophical Society cliques are developing very readily on a considerable scale circumscribed by specifically personal interests. It is difficult to separate personal interests from those of a more objective nature on the basis of a Society. But just think that precisely through the affairs of the Society the door is opened to those people who do not want to approach spiritual science through honest discussion but, rather, want to bring about the downfall of spiritual science through personal slanders couched in terms of personal smears. For one can indeed say that they want to bring about the demise of spiritual science.

Some years ago I decided to comply with the wishes of several members for personal discussions, embracing the youngest and oldest members in the most far-reaching way. Only in recent years, when matters developed in the manner indicated, did it sometimes sporadically become necessary to depart from the old custom; but only occasionally, in exceptional circumstances. Although it has often been emphasized that in what is in the literature and in what is said here in the lectures that which the individual needs for his independent development is richly available, so that personal consultations could only be a matter of a person-to-person talk, it will happen again and again that in relation to personal conversations of the members with me the most fantastic fibbing—please excuse the expression—becomes woven into the fabric of the Society, and ways are sought by outsiders to disseminate all kinds of denigrations and slanders. What I mean by fibbing is that only too often people within the orbit of the Society are strongly inclined to use a well-sounding snippet of a word that they have made their own for their own deep satisfaction. How nice it is for many people if they can say: I have become an esoteric pupil. And how much pleasure it gives to them if they can say: Well, you know, that is something very secret which I cannot tell you; I am unable to say anything about it to you. Putting oneself in the position of giving a certain impression is what is hidden behind many an expression that is used and which is then exploited in a thoroughly malicious way by people outside the movement. All these things that are now often being used for malicious intent would never have been able to gain traction if that which corresponds to justified wishes and perhaps to an equally justified willingness to comply with these wishes had not been placed in a false light and, in view of what the outside world has made of it, can no longer be sustained, however difficult this is also for me, my dear friends. Of course, friendly associations can exist in the Society, but an iron law of necessity compels me to put a stop to private audiences. I am particularly sorry because many will say: Why should the innocent suffer with the guilty? But when one is in a Society it is of course a question of the karma of the Society, and things cannot be otherwise. Everything that has taken place in private discussions that have been sought is something that, in view of those malicious slanders, must simply cease.

Do not think that I am any less sorry than you, but I know that, just as everything that I have said about such things has been in vain, so would what I am saying today also be in vain if measures were not taken that simply make it unavoidable that the seriousness of the situation is brought to consciousness.

It is easy to correct slanders with what has been said in private conversation with individual members when these slanders reach the level where, for example, it is said somewhere or other that a certain member has been hypnotized. Now, my dear friends, I shall with respect to such eventualities have to adopt quite different measures, from which you will see—and I am indeed speaking out of a simple feeling of duty towards our Society—that the most deadly serious aspect of this matter to me concerns the sacred nature of spiritual science. If the principle underlying a movement such as this is simply not to invade anyone's sphere of freedom, and if this is strictly adhered to, if everything that invades a person's sphere of freedom is strictly rejected, and rumours of this nature then begin to stir, it will then be necessary for everything that seeks to flourish on the ground that we have created to enter fully into the public eye. When everything develops in the full light of day, the ground will be taken away from the slanderers. But another method will no longer exist in the future. I shall therefore, to the extent that I am able, endeavour that anthroposophically oriented spiritual science increasingly unfolds fully in the public eye. It must not shun publicity. And I shall today expressly say to you that with regard to those private conversations that have for years taken place with the members, I release everyone from the promise not to speak about the content of the conversation. Everyone can to the extent that he wishes speak about what has at any time figured in a private conversation with a member. Nothing will be found that might fear the light of publicity. There will then no longer be difficulties with the kind of things that stand upon the following ground. I shall give you an example of how these things can be used with the crassest ignorance and with a will for the crassest ignorance.

Not only Erich Bamler but also others who fight their battles just as 'honestly' as he does have expressed and believe in the argument that in addition to many other principles regarded as esoteric there is also this one that has been given to them: 'Look at everything that surrounds you in the light of necessity as if it were needed as an inevitable stroke of destiny'. It does someone good for as long as one believes one's prospects to be furthered within the Society through such a rule to say: 'Look at everything that surrounds you in the light of necessity'. But why has this rule been given, been rec-ommended specifically to these people? For the simple reason that they needed it on account of their soul-constitution! It was by no means a piece of advice that interfered with their freedom but advice whose consequences and esoteric nature you may judge if I give the following indication. In his prize-essay concerning the freedom of the will, Schopenhauer says contrary to the conclusion of his essay in relation to our attitude towards the course of the world and des-tiny:[107] 'Everything that happens, from the greatest to the least, hap-pens by virtue of necessity'; and he speaks of the reassuring effect of the knowledge of the inevitable and the necessary. Thus there is nothing that has been recommended to these people other than what Schopenhauer regards as a tried and tested means of extricating one-self from certain depressions of the soul.

Now in the course of speculation based upon the crassest igno-rance and upon the will for the crassest ignorance, all kinds of lovely fairy tales can of course be told to people: that one has become green and blue, especially in the legs, by following such basic prin-ciples. And in the case of those who in everything want to suck something esoteric from their fingers, these things can of course take the form of slander. But precisely when we know that the things that are cultivated in anthroposophically oriented spiritual science are actually demanded by needs of a particular urgency, we shall be able to find it understandable that such a measure as was previously mentioned has to be adopted simply for the reason that one sees that the matters with which it is concerned are seriously meant. Do not direct your complaints to me, who experience it as harshly as you do; complain to those to whom I have been referring and who make it impossible for such a measure to be avoided. It is today very difficult for me to have to refuse for these reasons of principle private conversations which numerous members want. Of course I also know that this, too, will be used as a means of slandering me, but I cannot allow myself to be governed by personal considerations and must be directed by what is necessary for our movement. This means that I must adhere to the principle to be serious about what on the one hand gives cause for fibbing and, on the other, is the cause of the denigrations and slanders on the part of those who do not want honestly to oppose spiritual science but want to eradicate it from the world in another way.

Examine much of what has occurred, and you will find that the causes always originate from the Society. The Society itself is very seldom attacked; I am myself—or my immediate colleagues—usually the point of attack. But when I am attacked, it is already the case that people are wanting to encounter spiritual science in me. For it is a matter of the greatest indifference to them whether a foolish piece of advice is given somewhere or other; there is plenty of that in the world. But what is not a matter of indifference to people is that spiritual science in its anthroposophical orientation is a cultural factor of our time, that it wants to address them. This is not a matter of indifference to people. Obscure esotericists are of little interest to them; but not an esotericist whose destiny it is not to remain in obscurity. They would not want to meet an obscure esotericist sitting in Berlin in front of fifty people and giving them advice. The attacks began only when the books circulated among a certain number. It would be a sin against the spirit of anthroposophically oriented spiritual science to let it be destroyed if this may perhaps be prevented by having to do something perhaps only for a time, because the morality of people today turns out to be the way that it has now.

One often has the experience that things are misrepresented; but the way that this is done with respect to the affairs of anthroposophically oriented spiritual science, the way that things are invented that do not exist and where something is related that is totally different from what actually happened, is virtually without parallel even in the history of humanity. And one must have the inclination to see not merely the avalanche that buries the villages down below but also the snowball that falls from above, for this becomes the avalanche. I have, to be sure, long watched this going on and have repeatedly drawn attention to it, but these warnings have not been heeded or at any rate little has been done in response. People outside the Society reproach me by saying that one of my greatest errors—today they list even greater ones, but this was the case a year ago—is that I turn people into blind followers, that I have blind adherents who believe in my authority. I might say that when it is a question of people showing trust in me on the part of the members of the Society and then doing something or other on the basis of this trust, I do by and large have very few followers. This is how it has been for years. What has happened has always been the opposite of my own opinion. But this is not noticed, because in many circles a particular method has been followed: they do not ask for my opinion but follow their own and then say to people: This is what he said. I was very far from having said such a thing, but the person concerned would have wished that I had said it and so he told everyone that I had. The fact is that when it is related in the outer world that I have blind followers, the practice of the Society shows that the actual reality is the complete opposite, at any rate with regard to circumstances where I would have to be approached with a certain trust, since I have sometimes worked for years to arrive at a judgement and the other person has not.

All this has not been said in order—as one says in Austria—to grumble and grizzle or in a certain sense to moan; rather is it said because there are now on a daily basis symptoms which show that there is an intention to do away with our movement in the manner indicated, and because there needs to be an inclination to look up to see the snowball and not only the avalanche once it has come crashing down. Just a few hours before I arrived here I was made acquainted with the contents of a letter which stated that two people have come together; I do not want to name names, so one has to mention such a case simply as a case. The one is accused of hypnotizing the other, of even sitting behind the other and meditating on the back of his neck so that all sorts of harmful things arise in his soul. And the matter is then being followed up. It is only a case, the last—no, not the last, yet another came after it; but it is the one I read about three hours ago. This is today a harmless affair, in a few years it may well not be: that one person sits behind the other in order to meditate on the back of his neck and thereby influence him with all manner of harmful thoughts. That the affair in question is relatively harmless there is no doubt. But today, my dear friends, this is happening between two members; in a few years it will be made into a 'Steiner case' which will again supply a very nice instance for such 'studies'. Perhaps things will proceed more quickly and will not need as much as a few years.

So please understand that I am being confronted with an incredibly harsh necessity if for the foreseeable future I have to accept that on the one hand I say that efforts must be made that spiritual science is enacted fully in the public eye. No one will lose out in any way because of this; no one will be unable to find what he must seek because everything takes place in the full light of day. But all the tittle-tattle about secret mystical matters that cannot be spoken about and so on will no longer be able to provide a reason for all sorts of slanders. Our relations can still be as friendly as ever, but for the present they can only be of the kind that takes place from friend to friend; for private conversations must in principle cease for the time being. However uncomfortable it may be, our dear members may perhaps find it necessary to enter into things somewhat more fully and pay attention to matters that have hitherto been attended to very little indeed.

As said, please forgive me for mentioning these things here today; I have made mention of them in the time when the lecture itself was already over, but I have had to bring them because they are connected with the life-questions of the Anthroposophical Society and the anthroposophical movement. It is this and not a wish to be unfriendly if with the utmost regret I am unable for the foreseeable future to hold the private conversations with the dear members that I have always been willing to maintain. Then that which is so dearly sought by ill-intentioned enemies will not be able to arise, will in actual outward terms not be possible.

For, my dear friends, you could of course make an objection; and each person will make one that is wholly understandable in that from his perspective he can say: But surely, he could speak with *me*. Each one of those who are now launching their attacks in the most unbridled way has said the same; and many of those who are now the instruments of their protectors were introduced to the Society by very, very respected members of the Society. In a certain respect things must become different, but they can only become different through the members.

LECTURE 10

STUTTGART, 13 MAY 1917

IT is perhaps only too understandable if the need to comprehend the distinctive quality of the time appears more strikingly in the souls of people today than is perhaps otherwise the case. We are, after all, living in these years in the midst of events which not only demand the most enormous sacrifices on the part of many people but which truly present complex riddles to human thinking, riddles of the most diverse kind. Why did these things have to manifest themselves in our time in so terrible a catastrophe as now passes through the evolution of mankind? This is certainly a question that concerns the souls of people today. We are thoroughly aware of the outer events; but we must try to make ourselves increasingly prepared not merely to seek the most immediate causes of such momentous events but to direct our eyes to the deepest forces of the time and, hence, to the foundations of these deeper forces in human evolution as a whole. We can then perhaps for our feeling understand much that otherwise remains incomprehensible to us and which we can, as it were, only stare at in bewilderment.

Let us ask ourselves: What is in the deepest sense a serious way of characterizing our time? Now, from discussions that have frequently been conducted here we can certainly not deny the fact that what in the broadest sense of the word we call materialism has thrust itself to prominence in recent times. Materialism! Let us conceive of it today not so much in the way that we relate our feelings, our sympathy and antipathy, to what we mean by this word; let us, rather, try to sense that a time had to come when materialism is, so to speak, the predominant element in human evolution. Humanity needed materialism, the passage through materialism. But it should not lose itself in materialism; it should not give itself up so strongly to this materialism that it loses the connection with the spiritual world not only from the eyes but also from the soul. That this does not happen, to ensure that the connection with the spiritual world remains intact, is the task of spiritual science. Today I should like to try to draw your attention to some aspects of the evolutionary laws of the human race which, if we understand them aright, can contribute to a comprehension of what is going on around us.

That we live in the age of materialism we do not in any sense merely owe to the wickedness and shamefulness of the human soul in general but to certain laws of evolution. To be sure, the countenance of materialism in our age has nothing beautiful about it, especially if one can compare this materialistic countenance with the cultural face of older periods of time. Nevertheless, no one should therefore succumb to the reactionary idea of cherishing the belief that the old cultural forms should be restored. Indeed, a quality of the materialism of our time that is fully significant for us is that even outstanding personalities of the greatest spiritual significance are completely unable to extend their soul-impulses to an understanding of the spiritual world. They simply cannot do this. One has to admit this completely without prejudice. Let us take a characteristic figure from the nineteenth century of whom much was spoken in the international intellectual life of Europe in the second half of the nineteenth century, Ernest Renan,[108] who tried to understand the Christ impulse as this was possible at his time. Ernest Renan's *The Life of Jesus* made a great impression in the widest circles and had a considerable influence. But Ernest Renan is on the one hand someone who had a serious view of spiritual matters but who, on the other, was completely unable to conceive of the idea that it might be possible for people to find a path to a perception of spiritual worlds. Let us take a remark that Ernest Renan made when he was fairly young. What he said was this: Modern man is aware that he will never know anything about the ultimate causes of the universe and about his own destiny.[109] This is a leading cultural figure of the present who says that he regards it as an important point to be aware of that man can never know anything about the ultimate causes of the universe and about his destiny. And this Ernest Renan was not a superficial man. He lived a life devoted to knowledge. And it is characteristic that when Renan became an old man he made another characteristic remark. This man, who lived his entire life in the belief that man cannot find the path into the spiritual world and must conceive of this as a higher form of knowledge, said at the end of his life: I wished I knew for certain that there is a hell, for it is better to have the hypothesis of hell than the hypothesis of nothing.[110] Here you see something spoken from the oppressed heart of the present. Nothingness confronts a person when he has the longing, the desire to gain access to a spiritual world, a spiritual world that he could enter when he passes through the portal of death. And someone who believes that he has risen to the idea that man is above such things, that he renounces such a knowledge, says at the end of his life that it would be better to know that there is a hell than to gaze upon nothingness. One has to gain a feeling for such things if one wants to have a sense for what is characteristic of our time.

One thing that we must all agree about is that humanity needs guiding spirits in every age. Whereas in olden times they were the priests of the mysteries, in our age this function is performed by certain philosophers who increasingly acquire a natural-scientific character. A philosopher whom I still knew very well personally made the following remarks in his most recent work, *The Tragicomedy of Wisdom*.[111] He says: We have no more philosophy than an animal, and we are distinguished from animals only through the frantic attempts we make in our wish to arrive at knowledge and through the ultimate resignation in not knowing. The person in question, who from his excavations in the intellectual domain therefore came to the conclusion that man can have no more philosophy than an animal, has become a Professor of Philosophy and a university professor. So it should come as no surprise that more deeply inclined natures want to seek a path of some kind into the spiritual world and that, because they cannot bring themselves to do this from the impulses that the age offers them out of materialism, they, as it were, throw themselves into the arms of whatever is nearest to them. We can see this from many such examples in our present time, as for instance the Frenchman, Maurice Barrès,[112] who during the time of war has attained a certain fame among those who have developed a terrible hatred of Germans. Before the war he was, characteristically, the leader of those young Frenchmen who, to the extent that this is possible, were trying to seek a path to the spirit. Maurice Barrès sought for a long time, and after he had spent a long time searching he threw himself into the arms of the commonly accepted brand of Catholicism, the Catholic Church, as so many young Frenchmen have done. This is ultimately only a particular example of a general characteristic living in our time which has come to expression in his espousing of Catholicism.

But let us now try to gain some insight into souls such as that of Maurice Barrès, into how he orients himself to the search for the spiritual life. The following statement by Maurice Barrès is, I have to say, characteristic of him. Thus the following words slip out from a present-day seeker of the spirit: 'It is a vain endeavour to seek the beyond. Perhaps it does not even exist!' And then he goes on to say: 'And however we take hold of it, we cannot learn anything about it. Let us leave any kind of occultism to the enlightened and the charlatans. Whatever form mysticism may take, it contradicts all reason. But let us go nevertheless to the Church, firstly because it is inseparably linked with French tradition and then because, with the authority of centuries and great practical experience, it formulates the will of that ethic that the peoples and the Church must be taught, and finally because—far from delivering us up to mysticism—it directly defends us against it, silences the voice of the secret groves [by 'secret groves' he means everything that has come from the mysteries], interprets the Gospels and offers up the magnanimous anarchism of the Saviour to the needs of modern society.'

Why should one submit to the Catholic Church? Because, he says, it has understood how to sacrifice the magnanimous world-outlook of the Saviour to the lukewarm need of modern humanity, that is: thoroughly to adapt Christianity to those whose idea of Christianity is, one might say, what an average Christian today experiences as Christianity. Were not one to understand that such a view is predicated by a certain necessity, one would have to call a view of this kind frivolous in the most extreme sense, cynical and frivolous. But that precisely the more profound minds come to such a view is something that one should feel, and it is necessary that one should do so. However, we may ask ourselves: What is the deeper cause? What is the deeper reason that it is so difficult for people today to find the path into the spiritual world? Here we must again direct our attention to the evolution of mankind, at any rate to that time which has elapsed since the great Atlantean catastrophe and in whose fifth period we are now living.

We have hitherto divided this evolution of mankind into the first period, which we have called the ancient Indian, the second, which we have called the ancient Persian, the third, which we have called the Egypto-Chaldaean-Babylonian, the fourth, which we have called the Graeco-Latin, and finally we have our fifth period; it is in this that we are living. In this fifth period those things have emerged regarding which we have made indications from a certain point of view. I have tried at various times to characterize to you the evolution of mankind in order to place the present within its context. Today I want to do this from a different point of view. This different point of view will, when one considers it for the first time, seem thoroughly paradoxical, but let us understand it initially without preconceptions. Let us try to equip ourselves with that way of regarding things that we are able to have after having developed anthroposophy for so many years.

From what we have hitherto received into our souls, we can know that not only does an individual human being undergo a development between birth and death but mankind also undergoes an evolution. Today we are considering that portion of this evolution which in the manner that has been characterized follows the Atlantean catastrophe and in whose fifth period we are now living. The paradox will want to appear if we ask ourselves: Can we speak with respect to humanity, with respect to a portion of human evolution, more precisely of a development in time in the way that we speak of such a development in time in the case of an individual human being? We say that a person will, to begin with, develop by passing through the first seven years from the first to the seventh year. Then he lives through the period from the seventh until the fourteenth year (as you know, the divisions in the sequence are only approximate), then from the fourteenth until the twenty-first year and so on. A human individual develops, as it were, in stages, in that between birth and death he always adds a year when a year has gone by.

How, then, can we think if we want to consider the portion of human evolution that has been indicated? It will be helpful if we also ask ourselves: How old is humanity, if we want to compare its age with our individual human age? What is the age of present-day humanity? It will not be uninteresting to consider this spiritual-scientifically; and such a consideration will be highly fruitful. I characterized a similar question some years ago. Spiritual science has the quality that one can know much and yet can formulate it or re-formulate it only several years later. It is such a re-formulation of the riddle that has been indicated that I should like to present to you today.

Let us first consider the evolution in question schematically:

first period, the ancient Indian evolution;
second period, the ancient Persian evolution;
third period, the Egypto-Chaldaean-Babylonian evolution;
fourth period, the Graeco-Latin evolution;
the fifth period is ours; then comes the sixth.

If we now compare the age of humanity with the ages of an individual human being, essentially how old was humanity in the first period after the Atlantean catastrophe? How old was it then? You see, if we know how old the whole of humanity was, we could evaluate how we must regard ourselves, how we may view the evolution of humanity in conjunction with the ages of our own life. It was not so easy to investigate this question spiritual-scientifically. It was first necessary to see the purely spiritual-scientific reality, to associate some significance with this purely spiritual-scientific reality of the first period. And when a view of the particular spiritual configuration of humanity as it was then had been arrived at, one had to ask: With what personal, individual age of life might this configuration of that time be compared? And one discovers that humanity as humanity—not the human individual, of which we shall speak later—that in this first post-Atlantean period humanity had an age of between forty-eight and fifty-six. Thus if one considers the spiritual configuration of cultural life at that time, one sees that humanity at that time was of an age that one can compare with the age of a present-day man, and of course also of a present-day woman, of between forty-eight and fifty-six. It was not easy to arrive at this; but it was possible in the end; and so this is an actual result of spiritual-scientific research.

Now the question is: How is it with the second, the ancient Persian period? It was again necessary to give the same consideration to this question. What emerges if one considers the spiritual content of the culture of that time is that one can only compare it with the age of life of someone today between forty-two and forty-eight. And if one now continues further to the Egypto-Chaldaean-Babylonian period, this corresponds to the age of someone between thirty-five and forty-two. If one now comes to the Graeco-Latin period, this corresponds to the age of someone between twenty-eight and thirty-five. And if one comes to our fifth post-Atlantean period, this corresponds to the age of a human individual between twenty-one and twenty-eight. And one can foresee that the sixth period will correspond to the age of life between the fourteenth and the twenty-first year; while in the last period, before a new great catastrophe, there will be a correspondence with the age of life between the seventh and the fourteenth year.

I may well admit, my dear friends, that the result that emerged when it was formulated was one of the most surprising that I have arrived at, indeed the most surprising. For as you see, what is so remarkable is that whereas the human individual ascends in numbers, the evolution of humanity goes in a reverse direction. Humanity is, remarkably, becoming ever younger! So it is: humanity is becoming younger.

Now one naturally has to ask: What does all this mean in a wider context? After all, very many riddles of evolution are associated with this. I first asked myself: What does it signify for the first cultural period that humanity was between forty-eight and fifty-six years old? The following thoughts arise. Of course, the human beings who were born and lived at that time began by being one, two and three years old. That is clear. But then they also became forty-eight years old. For each person the point of time came when he was living between the forty-eighth and fifty-sixth years of his personal, individual development. And then these people could say to themselves: Now we are entering personally into a time of life when we have the personal age-qualities that are contained around us in the group-spirit of humanity as a whole. We are growing into that which is present in our surroundings. Formerly, before the forty-eighth year, we had, so to speak, concluded a development that belonged to us, which was for us; but with the forty-eighth year we are growing into what is in our surroundings. If one became older than fifty-six, then one went on developing, one lived on and, so to speak, grew back into what was before the Atlantean catastrophe. One experienced something that went beyond what was manifested around one in the group-soul of mankind. With the forty-eighth year one therefore found the connection to the group-soul nature of mankind.

In the next, in the second cultural period, one found this connection already earlier. As one became forty-two years old one grew into that which was in one's surroundings, one grew into what was in the whole aura of humanity.

And then with one's thirty-fifth year one grew to the point where between one's thirty-fifth and forty-second year of life one could say: What is now within me corresponds with what is around me. After the forty-second year what was around one could no longer give one anything, so one had, as it were, to continue living out of oneself, for the age of humanity had become so much younger. In the time of one's forty-second year one was no longer in one's surroundings; one grew beyond them, one was thrown back upon one's own resources.

Thus the ancient Greek, the ancient Roman, was thrown back upon his own resources when he had reached the age of thirty-five. Between his twenty-eighth and thirty-fifth years he lived with his surroundings; then humanity had nothing more to give from its age, for this life had passed away; humanity could no longer become forty-eight years old when in its retrospective course it had come to the age of thirty-five.

And in our fifth period, just think, we live into the group-spirit of mankind, into what constitutes our surroundings, between our twenty-first and twenty-eighth years. From this point our surroundings no longer give us anything. What comes thereafter we have to attain through our own development, we have to draw forth from our inner being; for it no longer flows to us from without. Humanity has attained the age of twenty-eight, and when we have become twenty-eight years old we need to have a foundation, something within ourselves that we can carry forward; otherwise we will never become older than twenty-eight. And now so much of the fifth period has elapsed that humanity has returned to its twenty-seventh year. So that if nothing is done by way of active inner development, human beings will only become twenty-seven years old. This means much, my dear friends! It means that if everything is left as it is, present-day humanity will not have an intellectual or any other kind of inner development other than what belongs until one's twenty-seventh year. And if something that they develop further is not poured into their souls, they will remain at the age of twenty-seven for the rest of their lives.

They remain at the age of twenty-seven for the rest of their lives: this is a great mystery of the present evolution of mankind. In the sixth post-Atlantean period human beings will not become older than twenty-one. If nothing is done to expand their inner being and to strengthen their intellect, initiative and will, a general dementia would prematurely set in. People would in their living development be confined to their twenty-first year. Anything later would merely be a meaningless token.

Let us understand this in connection with the individual aspect of human nature. Just think that as regards one's individual-personal attributes one becomes more and more mature. A child is always a materialist; a young person then becomes an idealist, but his ideals are abstract, they venture into unreality. Only in later years of life does one develop to the point of forming ideals that dive down into reality, that live with reality, that are truly in accordance with it. Let us suppose that a human individual today is wholly a child of his time. What kind of quality will he be able to manifest if the possibility has not been offered to him to receive something spiritual? This alone brings the soul forward. If he continues to be left to what constitutes the modern spirit of the time, it will be the destiny of such a person not to progress beyond a development of twenty-eight years. What is later remains stuck at the age of twenty-eight. It is possible for someone who is inwardly stirred to go beyond the twenty-eighth year, but the other situation is the general rule; what I have described is what follows from the law of evolution. A person who does not get beyond the twenty-eighth year, who remains twenty-eight years old (even though he may be fifty, fifty-six or sixty years old), will under certain circumstances be able to develop great abstract ideals but he will have only lived through what may be described as life's years of apprenticeship, not the years of testing, which make those who have such ideas as can be realized—which do not only dazzle people through the power of youth but can become actual realities—into practical people in a spiritual sense.

This naturally raises the question: Could an example be cited of a real child of our time who has become old and yet has not come beyond the twenty-eighth year? Of course, if one cites such an example today in a world which wants to know nothing of spiritual laws that are also actively involved in evolution, one will be laughed at as a fool. But among us here, where we have developed so much spiritual-scientifically, it may perhaps be possible to speak quite concretely about such things in order to gain a better understanding of our time. Why should the spiritual scientist not be allowed to speak in specific terms to those who are his friends and who would like to hear something about the mysteries of the time?

I have after really mature investigations of our time been struck by a thoroughly characteristic example of a personality who, however old he may become, is condemned to be unable to become older than twenty-eight years old, and that is the President of the United States, Woodrow Wilson.[113] Yes, you laugh, my dear friends; for me this has been a very significant insight which so far as I am concerned solves an immense number of riddles of our time. Why do the ideals of this person, which he has transmitted to humanity in various diplomatic notes, have so dazzling an effect, and why are they turned into the exact opposite of what is stated in words? Because they are youthful ideals which remain stuck in this form, in spite of the fact that the person who expresses them becomes older. Because they are abstract youthful ideals that do not want to venture into reality, which do not want to be satisfied with reality and which therefore cannot be applied to real, practical life, where not only material but also spiritual realities are at work, especially when it concerns the ordering of the social structure of human society. To the extent that one can think today without what can only be established inwardly, so is he, Woodrow Wilson unable to think.

A Wilson of the sixth period would only be able to become twenty-one, even if he became a hundred years old. But you see, the fact is that if we consider the fourth period, the individual, personal age of someone in the mid-point of the thirty-fifth year coincides, as it were, with the age of humanity as it descends to the age of thirty-five. They come together in the middle. Hence also the remarkably harmonious life of the Greeks, hence this accordance of the individual life of the Greek with the life of Greek humanity. But now humanity has regressed and no longer experiences the years from the age of twenty-eight onwards; and a human being has to live through them individually, wholly individually.

You see, this is all connected with things that stand behind the physical, sense-perceptible world. You can deduce some aspects of these things from my booklet *The Spiritual Guidance of the Individual and Humanity*. Today I want to address this from a different viewpoint.

When a person was in his forty-eighth year in the first post-Atlantean period, he succeeded through his individual development in finding the connection with the age of mankind. This was, however, associated with the fact that in this first period there was at that time still an inner contact between certain beings of the higher hierarchies with humanity here on Earth. The beings of the higher hierarchies whom we think of as belonging to the hierarchy of the Archai or Spirits of Personality still, as it were, descended to the Earth and united themselves with human evolution; they inspired, or actually intuited, mankind. It was because mankind here on Earth was in a particular connection with the Archai that it could develop so far, that the age of the life of humanity continued to so late an individual age. In the second post-Atlantean period there was a similar connection with the Archangeloi; in the third with the Angeloi. In the fourth post-Atlantean period, however, in the Graeco-Latin, man had to rely on his own resources. In the third period it was still the case that the Angels, the Angeloi, descended and inspired or intuited human beings, endowed them with imaginations. Then came the Graeco-Latin period, when the spirits of the higher hierarchies no longer descended in the same ready manner; and man had, as it were, to begin to swing to and fro, up into the realm of spirit and down again into the earthly realm. In other words, man had to find himself. But now, in the fifth period, we have entered an epoch when the opposite must take place. We must now make ourselves so strong inwardly that during this fifth period we gradually return through our own strength to the vicinity of the Angeloi, that we meet them again but through our own strength, and that the Angelos implants the evolutionary impulse within us; that we are able to find through ourselves that which humanity can no longer give us through the higher hierarchies.

So you see why we have materialism in our time. You see that there have been times when through the fact that humanity was older, that it was not so young as now, it reached further into the spiritual worlds, when in its origins it was closer to the spiritual worlds than human beings are now when they approach death. You see where the deeper ground of materialism lies, but where also lies the necessary impulse truly to seek something that can stimulate people individually in an inward, spiritual way, that can lead them forth from what one can receive from one's surroundings.

It is also impossible for education, which flows to a person only, as it were, out of its own momentum, to bring to him today anything beyond a life-age of twenty-eight. Intellectual conditions must therefore be spiritualized. If things were to continue as they are, thus if spiritual science were to be buried deeply in the ground, if things were to carry on along the accustomed lines, there would be a general coming to a standstill in the twenty-eighth year. If one were to research only in natural-scientific laboratories and clinics and find what can be given from external sources, if nothing were to be inwardly stimulated within human souls and no science of the spirit were to be implanted into them but only what has produced the greatness of the modern age, the greatness of materialism, progress would eventually amount to human beings remaining forever young. This would, however, be something of significance only if they did not merely remain youthful inwardly but also in their bodies. But in their bodies they are already old. It is therefore the case that what lives within them no longer corresponds with their outward bodily nature.

What still happens today is that, in many respects precisely out of the inappropriateness of what we experience with humanity, certain forces are awakened in our inner being. We can through mankind only become twenty-eight years old, but we nevertheless have to live longer in the world in our various incarnations. Thus the situation is that, where humanity is only twenty-seven years old, there are for the time being still forces which are then further developed for the Angelos in the life between death and a new birth. Today this is still the case. However, when the sixth period will begin, a person will on the Earth only be able to become twenty-one years old through what is around him. What is it that develops by the time of the twenty-first year? The physical body is in development until the seventh year, the body of formative forces until the fourteenth year, the sentient body until the twenty-first year: only the bodily nature is developed. If a person does not develop the soul-nature—the sentient soul, intellectual or mind soul and consciousness soul—from within, they will not be developed at all. The bodily nature is developed until the twenty-first year. Then the human individual would have lost too much out of his own forces to be able after death, between death and a new birth, himself to make up for what he has missed out on if he has received no spiritual stimulation.

You can see from this that the position that humanity arrives at corresponds not to an accident but that it is a deep necessity, that it corresponds to a surprising evolutionary law of mankind. Indeed, there has never been a time in human evolution when human beings have been so disinclined to acknowledge that life gives us something that matters. Everyone today wants to be clever as early as possible. Why? Because they are secretly aware that they must be fully mature by the age of twenty-eight. To receive something of whatever kind after twenty-eight is for many people an absurd idea, a wholly absurd eventuality. This is how people conduct their lives, but they want to receive only until their twenty-eighth year, or even precisely—and this accords with the facts—until their twenty-seventh year.

But if one considers such a mystery of human evolution, one will also find it understandable that it is not regarded as something arbitrary if the need is expressed for a spiritual development, but one understands this in such a way that this need is one that is indeed present, that a person remains, as it were, incomplete in our modern age if he does not receive a spiritual impulse. One feels this wherever life is not viewed today by looking upon its reality. There is specifically the remarkable fact that so many people are incapable of entering into certain paths of thought; this rests on the fact that they do not reach their thirty-fifth year, that there are so few who are able to say something that is associated with the mature experience of later life.

These things must be considered completely without prejudice, thus embracing the impulse to receive a degree of spiritual consciousness. If one does not do this, one aligns oneself with those who want to condemn humanity to an immature youthfulness.

Yes, certain thoughts, certain insights that come to us from spiritual science are of such a nature that, if we are full human beings, they appear to us as profoundly radical; but we must develop the inclination at every moment to feel this radical aspect. Because spiritual science grows out of a radical source, we do not need to be surprised if it meets with resistance. It meets with it not merely because people are stubborn but also because of the very nature of human evolution.

I have perhaps been saying much to you now that is paradoxical. It is in any case already paradoxical for people today that if one goes back to the second, third, fourth cultural periods one can say that at that time the people who have really found a connection with humanity were, to use a somewhat trite expression, on familiar terms with the Angels, Archangels and Archai, that they had a relationship with them. Indeed, for someone who in our time becomes no older than twenty-eight, this is of course a crazy idea to maintain: human beings formerly did not only make arrangements amongst themselves but reached agreements with Angeloi, with Archangeloi and with Archai as we today reach agreements with others on the physical plane. That this latter perspective holds sway and the other seems to be utter nonsense is only because people have forgotten the ancient knowledge. You can find a remarkable, very important passage in Plato, thus still during the period when humanity offered a human individual between twenty-eight and thirty-five years. Plato said:[114] Before intellectual man became immersed in the sense-perceptible world and lost his wings, he lived among the Gods in the rational spiritual world, where everything is true and pure. Plato means by this not only the life before birth but life in ancient times, when human beings still derived their knowledge from a relationship with the Gods themselves. I have also referred to this in the one Mystery Play[115] where an old initiate speaks of the old teachers who drew their knowledge from a relationship with the Gods, that is, with the spirits of the higher hierarchies.

But certain things are connected with human evolution which, because this is how things are, are no longer understood. People have strange experiences in this regard.

Allow me to make reference to a pleasantly pleasant experience. Yes, a curious expression, but that is what it is. Pleasant for the reason that I must mention the name of a man who displayed a very friendly attitude to my essay *Thoughts during the Time of War*, someone who comes from the northern lands and who, so far as he can, finds his way in the world, Kjellén,[116] the political scientist, who is now in Uppsala. I do not want to attack or criticize the man; on the contrary, I am choosing this example because Kjellén is one of our friends. He has recently written an interesting book, *The State as Living Form*. In this book he describes how one might have a certain deeper conception of the state. Yes, Kjellén tries to arrive at some kind of view of the state as an organism. For someone who has insight into these things and knows from spiritual-scientific research how political science, if there were to be such a thing, would have to be set forth in order that it might be fruitful in the political life of the state, for such a person Kjellén's book, for all one's great liking for the author, is simply a torment, a real torment. Why? You see, Kjellén does not get any further than ask: If one conceives of the state as one whole organism, then man lives as part of it. But what is man? Obviously, he is a cell! So for Kjellén man is a cell of the state organism. In the book *The State as Living Form* Kjellén builds much upon this idea. Man is a cell, just as we have cells within us; and the state is the whole organism which is organized through its various cells.

You see, if one is simply aiming to make comparisons (and it is not more than that), one can actually compare everything with everything. One can indeed logically advocate any thought, for if one does not think consequentially one can also compare an organism with a penknife. What always matters, however, is that one has a sense for penetrating into reality. But one ventures into very strange cul-de-sacs if one considers Kjellén's book, into very strange cul-de-sacs. In an organism there are cells which are next to one another, one borders upon another, and through the fact that they adjoin one another and have the effect that ensues the organism is an organism. This is no longer applicable to the interaction of human beings in the so-called organism of the state. In short, if one wants to continue to be abstractly logical, one comes with every clever thought to the point of being able to write a pretty thick book about it, and then to countenance the idea that this is also of some use. But if one has a sense for reality, the thought has to be developed further. It must be properly immersed in reality, only then can it be called knowledge. I recommend that you read the book; it is a representative book of the modern age. Buy it and read it and experience this torment of which I have spoken. The thought that will then occur to one is this: What can one compare to the organism, if one wants to apply the idea of the organism to the social life of humanity? Only the life of humanity on the whole of the Earth. And it is only the individual states that one can compare with cells.

The life of humanity on the whole of the Earth may be regarded as an organism, and the individual states may be thought of as cells, but not the state as an organism and the individual human being as a cell. If one considers the life of the state as a whole, one can compare it only with a plant. Never with something other than a plant organism. And if one wants to hold on to the concept of an organism, one would have to picture the organism with man protruding out of it. For man develops beyond all aspects of the life of the state; he cannot be absorbed in this life of the state like a cell in the individual organism but must be outside it. That is, there must be aspects of human evolution which cannot be subsumed within the state. One will see that man has to extend into a spiritual realm, that he can reach down into the life of the state only in his lower embodiment but also up into the spiritual world. It is interesting in this respect how it has been spelled out to many researchers that in olden times, when the mysteries were still a living reality, people knew something of this. And Kjellén himself refers to an interesting book, a book that was written fifty years ago by Fustel de Coulanges, *La cité antique*.[117] And he arrives at the remarkable awareness, which neither the author Fustel de Coulanges nor Kjellén can understand: What was the state in olden times? Of what nature was it? Coulanges comes to the conclusion that states in former times were all based on the cultus. Why? The state was a religious service, because one felt that man had to reach up into the spiritual world. A person could achieve predominance in the state only if he was initiated into the mysteries and had received guidance from the mysteries concerning the social structure. This was still the case in the third and in the fourth periods. People come to see this through outward research, but it doesn't mean anything to them despite what they read about in history.

It is hugely tragic to experience the effect of the last page of Kjellén's book *The State as Living Form*, where one sees that he is wanting to construct something of the nature of a science of the state but is nevertheless faced despondently by the awareness: What is the significance of the cell in all this? One could, if one wanted to bring Kjellén's idea to realization, actually only decapitate human beings; for with their heads they cannot belong to the kind of state that is envisaged in Kjellén's scientific picture of it, since with their spiritual part they must extend beyond what the state represents.

You see, one arrives at quite remarkable conclusions when one considers life more deeply. And it is therefore the case that what one calls political science today still does not know what it wants to become. There has never been a real science of the state for present-day circumstances. It is all still talk. For a real political science will only be able to arise when there is some understanding of the way that man is connected with the spiritual world, when people again come to know how much one can organize in the earthly life that we share and how much must extend freely beyond organization. These things must be drawn forth from certain depths. In the present case you can sense, my dear friends, how there is a tragic component. Humanity must carry within itself its laws of evolution, it must feel something of these evolutionary laws.

In specific cases—forgive me if I conclude by referring to an individual case—one causes considerable offence if one feels it to be a necessity of life to think in a real way. To think in a real way also means to think spiritually; for someone who does not think in accordance with the spirit does not think realistically but he thinks in meaningless abstractions. If one has developed the habit of thinking realistically, one inevitably causes offence today. Forgive me if I choose a seemingly very obvious example.

Incidentally, I can say that nothing impresses me less than when someone today enters the realm of the German language and writes so-called beautiful poetry, perfectly beautiful poetry of the kind that pleases people. Something that has behind it a development such as the German language has, together with such possibilities for development, is able to form so-called beautiful poetry as though out of itself, especially in the time of youthful immaturity until the twenty-eighth year. If one is artistically solving poetic problems, one does not go to what people today consider to be beautiful poetry, for it actually belongs to what someone enjoys when he steps back to earlier times. Thus very many people manage quite well to compose beautiful poetry, but what matters is to advance further in evolution.

It must often happen that someone may perhaps write less beautiful poetry but is trying from an elementary standpoint to establish a new artistic form. Many will naturally come along and find it terrible that someone is making the attempt to arrive at a new artistic form, which may still be very imperfect as regards what it seeks to become. You see, I should now like to say something of a personal nature. I do not want to speak about my judgement of the verses in which Herr von Bernus[118] has presented anthroposophical thoughts in *Reich*. But you can all be quite sure, even though the verses—which have the potential to give pleasure—may not have been to everyone's taste, that Herr von Bernus would have been able to shake them out of his sleeve whenever he felt the inclination. Nevertheless, things are not so simple. And today, when so much exists that malevolently denigrates and slanders what we are trying to achieve, this journal *Das Reich* has appeared with the best will, and precisely because of this very best of will it should have been supported irrespective of how one relates to any particular part of it. Thus it was difficult for me to hear that Herr von Bernus has received mountains of letters from the circle of our members which reviled what appeared in the journal. One might far rather have taken the opportunity to contemplate what is directly setting out to destroy our movement. Thus one experiences that someone who has made it his business to utter untruths about all that we undertake[119] can assert : '*Das Reich*, which stands in the sign of Steiner'. Now I have no other connection with this journal than I might also eventually have with any other; I did not found it, it is the project of Herr von Bernus; it has no connection with any other personality. I write articles for this journal but carry no responsibility for it. This can also be known to the individual who on one page after another used the injurious, slanderous expression—in such a case it is always slanderous—'this journal serves Steinerian purposes'. One should, on the other hand, also be able to take some pleasure if something manifests itself *for* us from a totally external standpoint. Hitherto our experience has, however, generally been that it is precisely at those who wanted to support our cause that stones have been thrown by our members, that in contrast they have been advised against supporting our cause with good will and in a bold manner, whereas no attention has been paid to all the defamatory things that have been happening on a broad scale.

Much could still be said. I wanted to mention this because I should really like to emphasize that it had not occurred to me to speak about this or that in *Reich* other than discursively, that is, to see whether perhaps behind the seeming imperfections there is a struggle for a development, and it was really not my concern to look at what many people have seen who have felt themselves called to send their judgement in letters to the writer in question concerning what is in any case a lot of nonsense, even though not without taste. This is the most tasteless and most damaging path; for there is no need personally to approach with a defamatory letter someone who has made the effort to compose something. Even if the letter were justified, he would not be able to understand it; he is fully involved in what he has written. One can express one's opinion to anyone else, but one should not send it to the poet on his own doorstep.

Well, my dear friends, all the things that have been said in this way do of course always apply only to the one side, the side of the few. But it is the case that through the Society the innocent is ensnared with the guilty and now has to suffer for them. This is what is more painful to me than to those who suffer under the present measures.

But one thing I should still like to add. Someone who in the circle of the Society merely communicates the one regulation, that I shall in future no longer discuss personal matters in private conversations, would be expressing only one side of the picture. Something further belongs to the whole picture, which is that I expressly release every-one from the promise—in so far as the person concerned wishes this—to keep secret what has been said in private conversations. This belongs to it, and it is important. In every smear campaign, believe me, these regulations are so necessary that exceptions cannot be made. But no one should lose anything. What can be achieved esoterically will also be able to be achieved if it has to be in complete openness. And although I cannot and shall not make any exceptions as regards private conversations, I shall find ways and means whereby each person will be able to satisfy the esoteric needs that he wants to satisfy also in the future. Just have patience for a short while.

Even without private conversations there will be ways and means so that everything that may be justly demanded for the esoteric life will be satisfied without the damage that has indeed arisen through the slanderous effect of the nature of private conversations in our Society.

And I still want to say that I should like to present something that is deeply connected with what can lead us to an understanding of the difficult time that we are now experiencing, that I have indeed not finished what I have wished to say to you during this present stay. For those who want to come, I shall therefore be speaking here again on Tuesday evening.

Lecture 11

T HE purpose of today's amplification of what I have been able to present in the course of this visit to Stuttgart is to add something to what I have already said and in a certain sense to round it off.

It will to begin with be best if I make a connection with what formed one part of the theme of yesterday's public lecture.[120] We saw then that the soul-nature of man has, in its threefold structure, connections with the bodily and the spiritual aspects of man's being; and we particularly emphasized the fact that the feeling element of the soul has as regards the body a connection with the breathing life, that what lives in the overall sense in the body as the element of breathing, with all its branches and other ramifications, is the instrument for the feeling life. On the other hand we have been able to indicate that the life of feeling has a particular relationship to everything that is accessible in the spiritual world to Inspiration. But what is accessible in the spiritual world to Inspiration is also at the same time everything that is contained in the world to which we belong with the part of our being that passes through births and deaths, thus the world that we live through between death and a new birth, the world in which of course we also live between birth and death. This world is, however, veiled through sense-perceptions and our ordinary intellectual faculties, hence also through the life of the body. Thus what corresponds to breathing and feeling actually extends in its implications into the great, all-embracing world to which we ascend when we pass through the portal of death, the world to which we belong when we no longer make use of the instrument of our bodily life. The instrument of our bodily life in a certain sense binds us to earthly existence. From various lectures that have been given in the course of many years and have been set down in the cycles, you know that when the soul has passed through the gate of death it is not bound to earthly life but ascends into the cosmos in order to live in the spiritual worlds of this cosmos, in what can simply be called the spiritual world. Is it not therefore to be expected that the life of feeling, which corresponds in a bodily sense to breathing and in a spiritual sense to the world of Inspiration, has a much, much more comprehensive relationship to the cosmos, to the great world, to the macrocosm than our limited faculties of perception and cognition? What, after all, do we actually perceive? We actually perceive a very small part of the world, a small portion of the world enters through our eyes and our ears into our bodily existence between birth and death. Even if we are people with many enjoyments who maintain a broad awareness of everything that we perceive with our senses and develop in our ideas and imaginations, it is a small part of the world that enters in this way into our existence.

How is it if we turn from the nervous system to which the life of ideas belongs to the breathing life to which the feeling nature belongs? We can acquire a concept of this which is at the same time suitable for elevating our feelings if we consider the following. You all know that the Sun rises in a certain point in spring. At the beginning of spring, on 21 March, the Sun rises in the morning in a particular point. But this point is not the same for all times, as you know. In olden times the Sun rose at the beginning of spring in the constellation of the Bull, then in the constellation of the Ram; so the vernal point moves constantly and has now entered the constellation of the Fishes. If one takes what I am saying into account, one will therefore be contemplating the progress of the vernal point through the zodiac. The vernal point itself moves further in the zodiac. When a point moves further in a circle, it must of course arrive again at the same place after a certain time. This advance of the vernal point and the return to the same place of the zodiac are known to ordinary astronomy. Thus it is known that if in a particular year of the past the vernal point lay in the Ram, in the following year a tiny bit further and so on, and then entered the realm of the Fishes and so forth, it will after a certain time again be in the Ram. The time that the vernal point therefore needs to move through the entire zodiac is approximately 25,900 years, thus roughly 26,000 years. In this number of 26,000 years a measure of the outer cosmos is therefore expressed: the measure in which the vernal point advances. In this number we have, as it were, that with which the course of the Sun in the cosmos is measured. We could make an approximate statement of this nature. If we bear this number in mind, we can link it with something else that we now want to consider.

A human individual breathes in and out, taking a certain number of breaths in a minute. We do not take a similar number of breaths at every age between birth and death, but there is a certain average number of breaths that a person of medium age and strength exhibits in one minute, namely eighteen breaths a minute. Now we calculate how many breaths a person takes in the course of twenty-four hours. So first we must multiply the breaths that he takes in one minute by sixty, which makes one thousand and eighty, and then again by twenty-four, and we then obtain the number of breaths that a person takes in one day, thus a day and a night, i.e. 25,920 breaths. Remarkably, when we calculate the breaths that a person takes in the course of twenty-four hours, we arrive at the same number that we came up with when reckoning the number of years resulting from the advancing movement of the Sun in the great cosmos. This vernal point moves—always in a retrograde direction—for so many years; and a person breaths in one day for the same number of times. The same number! Just think how wonderfully this validates that Biblical saying, that the wisdom of the world has ordered everything according to measure and number.[121] A number that is inscribed in the cosmos confronts us in the breaths that we take in twenty-four hours. One can therefore also take this number into consideration, and one will find that human breathing has a relationship with the great world of the kind that was derived yesterday from spiritual science.

But now we are again confronting something that is also a kind of breathing, for breathing is none other than a special case of the general world rhythm. The essence of what was meant yesterday by breathing is rhythmical movement, rhythm. Let us consider something that is very similar to breathing, a quite different rhythmical movement that we know from our spiritual-scientific studies. When we go to sleep, our ego and our astral body leave our physical and etheric bodies; when we awake, our ego and our astral body enter into our physical and etheric bodies. I have often compared this departing and re-entering process with exhalation and inhalation. Just as we breathe air in and out in an eighteenth part of a minute, so in the course of twenty-four hours do we as physical human beings breathe in our ego and our astral body when we awake and out when we go to sleep; when we wake up again we breathe them in again and when we go to sleep again we breathe them out. In the course of the twenty-four hours of an ordinary astronomical day there is merely a more extensive outbreathing and inbreathing of our ego and astral body. Very remarkably, therefore something is breathing! We may to begin with disregard what is breathing, but there is definitely a rhythm that, as it were, represents a slow breathing, whereby a breath lasts for twenty-four hours. Now as you know, in the Bible there is the notion of the patriarchal age,[122] of seventy or seventy-one years. This does not of course mean that this is something other than the average age. Many people die very early, many become a hundred or over a hundred years old, but something of an average is denoted by the patriarchal age. Thus if one has in mind something of an average with respect to a human life, one can speak of between seventy and seventy-one years. Let us work out how many days this is. If we calculate this, we would arrive at the number of great breaths that we take in an earthly life, when we exhale and inhale the ego and astral body in the course of twenty-four hours. Let us work this out: in one year we take approximately three hundred and sixty-five of such breaths, as many as the year has days. In seventy years, therefore, this would be seventy times as much: this would make 25,550. If we suppose that we reckon with seventy-one years, we come somewhat closer since this makes 25,915. Thus a person needs only to live a little beyond the age of seventy-one and he will have taken 25,920 such breaths. This means that when someone is a little over the age of seventy-one, he will have exhaled and inhaled his ego and astral body 25,920 times; thus as often as a person exhales and inhales his ordinary breath in one day. Just think: again the same number!

You see, therefore, that we can view human life as one day, and the particular day that we are living through as one breath; and then our life of seventy-one to seventy-two years is denoted by that number which is also the number of the advance of the vernal point, which is the number of breaths in one day. Our life is one great day, and the great being in whose midst one can imagine the Earth to be exhales and inhales the ego and astral body as often as we leave and enter with our individual breath. Thus our individual earthly life would be one day, a day of some kind. Of what is this day a part? Multiply seventy-one by three hundred and sixty-five, and you will of course arrive at the year for the day of seventy-one years. If you reckon seventy-one years as one day and ask: What is a year of this day, thus three hundred and sixty-five times as many? This is again 25,920 years. That is, if we reckon our individual earthly life with its 25,920 breaths, representing our waking up and going to sleep, as one day, reckon a human life as one day, and see what year corresponds to this one human life with its 25,920 breaths, it is the circulation of the vernal point, 25,920 years! We arrive at a wonderful numerical rhythm.

I therefore said that we arrive at an idea that must be elevating for our feelings, for through measure and number we are enabled to feel that we are part of the macrocosm. Numbers tell us what knowledge demonstrates to us, that what belongs to breathing and, hence, to the feeling life is the world of Inspiration, the great world to which we belong not only between birth and death but also in the time between death and a new birth and in repeated earthly lives. In a certain sense we lie in the womb of the rhythm of our whole solar system; in the individual movements of our breathing we follow the great macrocosmic rhythm of the entire solar system. This is a thought that places us with certainty within the whole, great life of our Sun-oriented universe. In the course of time human beings will have to make many similar observations, and they will then be convinced that on this path they can come to spirit-filled experiences for our age and for the ages that follow in the sense that was spoken of here the day before yesterday, as stimulations of the inner life. In olden times it was the case that inspirations came to man, as it were, from without. This has today been lost through the nature of the retrogressive phase of human evolution. We are now in a period in which mankind must—if it is not to fall wholly into decadence—energetically begin a development of the human soul from within. And only someone who understands it to be a need of earthly evolution that, from the fifth post-Atlantean period in which we are living on into the time towards which we are moving, spiritual life must take hold of the innermost human soul, really understands the needs of our time. What spiritual science says about this is not said out of some arbitrary idea or for purposes of agitation but it is said out of a knowledge of the need of human evolution.

Let us now consider this evolution of humanity from a somewhat different point of view. We shall return once more to the first post-Atlantean period, thus to the age directly after the great Atlantean catastrophe. As we have frequently done so far from a different viewpoint, we emphasized the day before yesterday how in this first post-Atlantean period man still had a relationship with that series of hierarchic beings whom we call the Archai or Spirits of Personality. The spiritual life still manifested itself in these primal times of humanity, because the life-age was regressing at that time in such a way that we can compare it with the present life-age between fifty-six and forty-eight, as I explained the day before yesterday. Man was, as it were, under the guidance of spiritual beings. How did these spiritual beings approach him? At that time human beings did not see nature as they do today. Nature is today viewed as a kind of mechanistic order. People regard abstract, almost mathematical laws of nature as their ideal. Take the images of what you see spread out around you when you go out into nature. Compare what is out there with what is said in botanical and zoological text-books about plants and animals. What is in these books of botany and zoology is what is manifested today to the human mind. Such a botany, such a zoology of which humanity today is so inordinately proud did not exist in that period. If one compares what modern botany, modern zoology and modern biology have to say about nature with what sprang forth within it for that old knowledge, one arrives at quite a different perspective. At that time there was no botany or zoology, but there was instead something else, something that is very little understood by present-day humanity. It came from nature itself, and I should like to call what came forth from nature the light-filled, formed word. Just as we today see nature through our senses and our intellectual powers, these people did not see this but nature transmitted to them forms of light; and these forms of light at the same time resounded, said something, spoke of what they are. And every human being could in certain conditions of his consciousness experience this atavistic clairvoyance, as a result of which the light-filled, formed word approached him from the natural world; one could also say 'words', for a fullness of such forms came that spoke forth from nature. The human individual knew: You too belong to this world whence these light-filled words derive. You are also fully part of it. But now you are here in nature, where minerals, plants and animals surround you. You are in nature by virtue of the fact that you are the bearer of an outward physical body; through this you belong to this nature. But nature lets the light-filled word spring forth; you belong to it in your soul-nature in the same way that your body formed of flesh belongs to the outward mineral, plant and animal world. You resided within this world of the light-filled, light-formed word before your birth or conception, and you will be in it after your death. You will again live within it.

In the first post-Atlantean period one heard at least an echo and saw an after-image of the world in which one lives between death and a new birth as in certain states of consciousness one beheld nature. In the second post-Atlantean period it was already somewhat different; for the word was lost to these atavistic states of consciousness. The forms no longer spoke, but they were still there, light-filled forms were still there; it was only that they had become silent. That which lay outwardly before the senses was experienced inwardly as darkness in this light-filled formative web, and one's own body was experienced as a part of the darkness. Thus one could say: light and darkness! One's own body is governed by darkness. In that it comes from the light and goes into the darkness, it enters through birth or conception into earthly life; in that it goes through the gate of death, it returns through the dark world into the light. There is in the world a battle between light and dark, between Ormuzd and Ahriman.

Thus did Zarathustra, who was the leader of the second post-Atlantean cultural epoch, speak to his pupils. One does not understand what Zarathustrianism means by its teaching of Ormuzd and Ahriman unless one relates it to the manner of perception of the people at that time.

Things were different again in the third post-Atlantean period. When people beheld the outer world, the light-filled forms had gradually been lost to this outward perception in the third post-Atlantean period. But they still had the power to place themselves in an intermediate state between sleeping and waking, in the way that we are today able to enter the state of sleep. They only had to exert themselves somewhat. In the case of sleep one does not need to exert oneself, but a certain effort was necessary in this other kind of state. If one made such an effort, one could conjure up around one a world of light that now came from nature, from without. So what was the nature of the progression from the second post-Atlantean cultural period to the third, the Egypto-Chaldaean-Babylonian age? What was this transition like? In the second, in the Persian cultural period people still saw the forms of light when they extended their gaze outwards and could say: My soul belonged to this light-filled world before it passed through conception. This light-filled world no longer shone forth from without in the third cultural period, but people were able, as it were, to squeeze it out from themselves; they then conjured forth from their souls what was present in the spiritual world before their birth or conception and what will be in the spiritual world after their death. Thus we can say: the third post-Atlantean age had the world of light as a soul-experience. Human beings had the world of light as a soul-experience; man was therefore in a certain sense directed by the outer world more towards his inner being. It was no longer within his nature to look at the outer world and to see the world of light, that is, the spiritual world, in his surroundings. It had therefore become necessary at this time always to initiate a small circle of people, so that they were enabled again to see the outer world of light, and so that they could bear witness that what was drawn forth from the inner regions of the soul was indeed the same as what lived in the spiritual surroundings.

There now came the fourth post-Atlantean period, the Graeco-Latin epoch. In this fourth period light no longer came forth when a person entered a particular state, as in the third period. Light no longer came; no longer did there come from the depths of man's being that which had been an echo of the life of the soul before conception and the life of the soul after death. But there emerged a certainty that the inner nature of man's being is filled with soul. This certainty was present. One still felt something of what had formerly been beheld when the soul had been brought inwardly to perception. People no longer beheld the light, but they still felt the warmth of the light. This is how it was in the Graeco-Latin age. So we must say: No longer was the world of light known inwardly as a soul-experience, but the soul itself was known as a soul-experience.

But it was inevitable that this became ever weaker and weaker in the course of time. And how do all the associated circumstances come to expression? They expressed themselves in the following way. We shall have to devote our attention especially to the Greeks if we want to understand the situation. As an average person has today, the Greeks had an awareness of their body. But through what I have described, they also had the consciousness that the soul ensouls the body. They felt the soul as enlivening, imbuing the body with life. This feeling that the Greeks still had has been lost. That history has nothing to say about this, that this feeling has been lost today, is only because we are living today in the age of materialism. No one really understands Homer, no one understands Sophocles or Aeschylus, if he does not read them with the feeling that the Greeks still had a different soul-experience from someone today. If one were to read Aeschylus with this feeling, one would make translations that are different from those supplied today and which are much admired, and which truly do not resemble Aeschylus in their most intimate aspects.[123] But the fact that this was so had a quite particular consequence for the Greeks, namely that during the time between birth and death they felt the enlivening soul-element in their bodies, and they therefore also still came to have a different feeling, the feeling that the body and the soul belong wholly intimately together. Never in human evolution has this feeling been so active as in the age of

Greece. For in earlier epochs that preceded the age of Greece, human beings actually always had the feeling that what pertains to the soul belongs to the world of light, the world of the word, the world of the Logos, in which a person lives before birth and after death. Now, in the materialistic age, it is the case that people no longer have a sense of the soul. In Greek times, and to a somewhat diminished degree and translated into dry, intellectual content in the Latin age of Rome, there was an experience of the inner affinity of body and soul. The growth and decline of the body appeared to the Greeks as an expression of the growth and decline of the life of the soul. The Greek loved the body, just as he loved the soul. This feeling, in the way that it was present to the Greek, did not exist previously in the same way (as I have just explained), and it does not exist today either. But the consequence of this was that feeling which is so profoundly expressed in the words that are spoken by Achilles: 'Better a beggar in the upper world than a king in the realm of the shades'.[124] The Greek had to pay for the beautiful harmony that he experienced between body and soul with the idea that—unless he was affiliated to the mysteries—in view of what happens to the soul after death in the spiritual world he vanished without trace.

Now what is remarkable is that the great Greek philosopher Aristotle,[125] who was a great thinker but not initiated into the mysteries, spoke in graphic terms about the soul's experience after death in the way that one could speak about it at that time, when it was possible to conceive of the inner harmony between body and soul after the manner of the age of Greece. And when in the Middle Ages Aristotle was rediscovered in so-called Scholastic philosophy, the Scholastics said: In philosophy one must think about the soul in the way that Aristotle did. If one wants to know more about it, this can only come from faith. In purely human research, one cannot penetrate any further than Aristotle.

How far did Aristotle come in his capacity as someone who is so rightly regarded as the philosophical expression of the Greek way of perceiving the body and soul? His insight extended to what one can express in the words of the recently deceased masterly specialist on Aristotle, Franz Brentano,[126] who says: If someone has lost a limb, he cannot any longer use this limb; he is in a certain sense no longer a whole human being. If he has lost two limbs, he is even less a whole human being; while if he has lost his whole body [says Aristotle and with him Franz Brentano] and is after his death still a soul, which Aristotle does not deny, he is in a state of incompleteness with respect to the state in which he is between birth and death. He is not a complete human being. And this is indeed the true teaching that Aristotle, the greatest thinker of the Greek world, gives about immortality, that a person is a complete human being only here between birth and death. Once he passes through the portal of death, he is only part of a human being; he is, it is true, immortal, but at the cost of no longer being a full human being. This is indeed that with which the Greek had to pay for his beauty, his harmony, that that age of humanity had arrived—in contrast, as you know, with the human life-age—when one could indeed sense the soul inwardly but when one could not as yet behold the life of the soul in the spiritual world, when one had to say of the soul: it is after death no longer a complete human being. Only to those who were initiated into the mysteries, thus in whom cognitive forces were incorporated that went beyond the normal, was that which the soul experiences between death and a new birth revealed. That is the great difference between Plato and Aristotle, that Plato was initiated in the mysteries and Aristotle wasn't. Thus Plato has to be understood in quite another sense than Aristotle, who came to the 'Chimborazo of thinking'* but could not penetrate to the mysteries of the spiritual world.

It therefore happened that those who had power in this age aspired to something different from what one can develop in normal human life. Who were the people who had power, who were in a position to develop this power? To be sure, there was a great, meaningful world of initiation which was disseminated here and there and filled the cultural world of that time, but these mysteries gave people that of which Plato said that it should lift them above the mud of the past.[127] Those who had power in this fourth post-Atlantean period sought above all for such a quality in their souls whereby they could

---

* Chimborazo is a mountain in Ecuador.—Translator

participate in the spiritual world. According to the general karma of humanity, one normally had to wait in the sense of the initiation-principle of that time until one was brought into the mysteries. In Greece this was the general custom. The Roman Caesars could do without this. The Roman Caesars, who gradually set themselves up as the rulers of the then world, were able to use their power for being initiated in the mysteries. And so we see that already before Augustus the Roman Caesars strove for initiation simply through their absolute power. They compelled one or another priest to initiate them in the mysteries. Thus in this fourth period a strange phenomenon can be observed: on the one hand we have the principle of the mysteries, the essential nature of the mysteries which still existed but were gradually disappearing and were in gradual decline (I have often explained why this had to happen in this way, because the Mystery of Golgotha came in their stead), on the other hand the priests were compelled to reveal their secrets to the Roman Caesars. Augustus was the first Caesar to be initiated in the fourth post-Atlantean period; but his successors were also initiates of this kind. They were distinguished in their nature from other initiates, who were initiated in the mysteries on account of moral qualities and especially moral development. The Roman Caesars were initiated on account of their absolute power, in that they could compel the priesthoods to reveal their secrets to them.

And so we see that even such a successor of Augustus as Caligula[128] was an initiate. Because of this, such a person as Caligula was familiar with the mysteries of the spiritual universe. He was aware that the impulses of this spiritual universe are coming to life again in the soul, that the human ego is a divine element in the world of the divine. What for the initiated priests was a holy truth of humility became for the Caesars a symbol of outward worldly power. For what did someone like Caligula know? The others devoted their attention to what had come down from ancient times in mythological figures of the Gods; it was to this that they prayed. An initiate like Caligula knew what these Gods had to signify. He knew above all things that man belongs in his innermost being to the same world. Caligula knew from experience that he belonged to the same world as those beings who have their reflections in these Gods: Bacchus, Hercules, Mercury, Apollo and Zeus. Caligula knew the secret that he could associate with the Gods of the Moon world in a sleep-like condition. And it is no mere myth but an absolute truth when it is revealed of Caligula that he cultivated an association with Luna, the Moon Goddess, as it was said in sleep (by which is meant, in a different state of consciousness), and from this derived nourishment for the consciousness of his power. In me lives the world—he said to himself—for I am within it. In that he looked upon the Gods, he perceived himself as a God among Gods. And this was quite seriously meant by the initiated Roman Caesars when they said this. The initiated priest knew how he entered into the dwelling-place of the Gods, and the Roman Caesar forcibly established community with the Gods. 'My brother Jupiter', 'my brother Zeus': these were designations that Caligula was forever using. And it was Caligula who directed the question to a tragedian as to who was greater, Jupiter or he, Caligula. And when the tragedian did not want to answer that Caligula was greater than Jupiter, he had him scourged. These are not myths, they are historical realities. Hence also the parades in which Caligula appeared before the people as Bacchus with the thyrsus and ivy wreath, because he had the awareness that he might transform himself into those figures whom he knew as images of the Gods. He appeared as Hercules with the club and lion's skin, as Mercury with the staff of Hermes, as Apollo with the radiant crown and surrounded by choirs. He appeared thus in order to bring to his people the awareness that he belonged to the Gods and not to human beings. This is how it was at that time in which, one could say, the less good picture of what was great in the world of Greece was manifested in that of Rome. Of course, no one saw this better than such a one as Caligula or other initiated emperors like Commodus and others. Caligula once heard that a court action had taken place in which a judge condemned a defendant to death; and since it was a special case, he said when the affair was reported to him that it would have been equally good if the judge had been condemned to death, for he was worth no more than the other. This is how he viewed the moral condition of his time. In the world of Rome there indeed appears the opposite of the world of Greece. People no longer have any conception of the inner condition of Rome under the Caesars; but it is necessary to form some idea of it, for this is one of the roots from which our new, fifth cultural epoch has developed as a further continuation.

Nero, too, was such an initiate, an initiated emperor. Because of this, Nero was able to perceive something quite particular. Those who were initiated in the mysteries at that time knew that evolution has descended down to a certain point and that it must again ascend, but it must also become more spiritual. This is what is meant by the 'Parousia',[129] the new age of which Christ Jesus also speaks.

If you compare what is living in all these ancient cultural epochs until the age of Greece with the later time, you find that in these ancient cultural epochs the soul and spiritual aspects are in a certain sense still manifested through the bodily nature. Then this ceases; they are no longer made manifest and must now be sought in other ways. If a person wants to seek the soul and spirit through what he can see with his eyes and hear with his ears, he can no longer find them. The heavenly kingdoms were formerly manifested through bodies, now they must draw nigh in the spirit. The heavenly kingdoms must draw nigh. This is the prophecy of John the Baptist. It is also what Christ Jesus meant by the Parousia. However, theologians have hitherto dwelt on the strange standpoint of believing that Christ meant by the Parousia that the Earth would have to be physically transformed. Blavatsky likewise finds fault with Christ Jesus's statement about the Parousia, the coming of the Kingdom of Heaven, when she says: It was predicted that the heavenly kingdoms are coming to the Earth, but the grain has not improved, the grapes are no more plentiful than before; no heavens have come to the Earth.[130] All those who speak in this way do not understand what is meant. What Christ Jesus meant, what John meant, had already come: the heavenly kingdoms had already come when Christ Himself had incarnated in Jesus of Nazareth. The process is to be understood wholly in spiritual terms.

But an initiate like Nero knew this also from the mysteries; and he rebelled against the idea. He came instead to the crazy notion that he expressed by saying: Well yes, the world is in decline, so let it also come to an end! And this is the psychological reason why Nero set fire to Rome (which he did indeed do), because he wanted to have at least the spectacle that from there the fire-brand would come that would reduce the whole world to ashes. For he no longer thought anything of this world. He did not want to accept the renewal which came through the Mystery of Golgotha. But while he was mad, he was nevertheless also a genius. Through his absolute power he had forcibly brought about his initiation, and all the ideas that he had were bigger than the ideas of those who had not had this preparation. Nero is therefore also in a certain sense the first psychoanalyst, but a psychoanalyst on a large scale and not one like Freud and others refer to; for Nero deified the body, in that—like a psychoanalyst—he wanted to draw forth the soul and spirit from the subconscious. The modern psychoanalyst says: What is down there in the soul? Disappointments, every kind of extinguished life, and so on—and then he says: The general animalic mud of the soul is down there; there is not much beauty about it. If one listens to a psychoanalyst today, it is rather as if someone is describing a field that has just been manured and has then been sown with seeds for the next season, but he sees only the manure, the dung. So the psychoanalyst sees only that part of the soul which is, of course, comparatively speaking, indeed dung. He does not see the eternal in the soul, what goes from life to life. This is why psychoanalysis is so dangerous, because it does indeed penetrate into the subconscious but instead of the soul-spiritual kernel it sees the animal-like mud; as if one sees not the sprouting seeds but only the manure. Nero was a great psychoanalyst in that he said: In man there is nothing other than general animalic mud, everything else is simply illusion; formerly it was different, when human beings were still close to the divine, but now man consists only of this animal-like mud; there is not even the smallest part that is chaste, everything in man has gone to the dogs— this was what Nero said. One sees from this that in those who had in this way been forcibly initiated there was the feeling that the world had become materialistic. In these circles the old, spiritual principle of initiation had been wholly translated into material terms. When Commodus, who not only made himself one of the initiated but also an initiator, wanted to give the symbolic blow to someone whom he had himself to initiate, he immediately struck him dead. Instead of bestowing upon him spiritual death, that is, rebirth, he struck him dead! Thus Commodus the initiator. This is a historical fact.

The event that occurred in this fourth period was the Mystery of Golgotha. And since the spirit can no longer come from the outward material world, it must be regained in a new way. The ascent within has received an impulse through the Mystery of Golgotha. But we are living in the fifth period, when this regaining of the spirit has not yet progressed very far, when those forces which were displayed so grotesquely in Roman times are still strong within people and battle against the impulse of ascent that was brought through the Mystery of Golgotha. And so it is understandable that in the fifth post-Atlantean period it is mainly the age of materialism that has come to be dominant in the way that people think and feel.

The Mystery of Golgotha has already brought a fresh impetus, so that the great inheritance of the Romans has disappeared to some extent; but it has not as yet been possible for people to rekindle the soul-spiritual dimension also in a more natural way; there is a need for a more intensive, more thorough familiarity with the Christ impulse. This must become ever more and more established. And so in the fifth cultural period normal people do not confront the soul itself when they experience themselves. The feeling, the inner experience of the soul has disappeared for normal people. A person feels himself in the experience of the body; he feels himself as a body, as a body deriving from the natural world.

Self-experience of the body! And so it is especially from science that the soul has disappeared and is disappearing from it ever more and more. The soul must be regained from within. The fifth post-Atlantean cultural period, which began in approximately 1413 or 1415, is only in its early stages. Humanity will have to evolve further within it in such a way that the spirit increasingly becomes inwardly sovereign. But it initially makes itself felt in the realm of the soul through a particular phenomenon, through the phenomenon that in man himself something material manifests itself which was formerly not so material: thinking itself. Such a thinking as we have it in the fifth period would have been impossible for the Greeks, and certainly for the Egyptians, Chaldaeans or ancient Persians. Behind the Greeks there still were to a certain extent imaginative conceptions, and in more ancient times even more; and anyone who can actually read Aristotle is aware of imaginations that are still active even in dry Aristotle, because thinking still occurred more consciously in the etheric body. Now thinking has been drawn completely into the physical body, and there it takes on an abstract character, of which our time is so proud. Thinking that becomes totally abstract is thinking which is indeed bound to matter, to the matter of the brain. And this thinking manifests itself in the most epoch-making impulses which must again be deepened, otherwise thinking will be ever more and more materialistic. And as thinking becomes increasingly materialistic, life must also become more and more so. It is characteristic of our present fifth epoch that there are fundamental ideas which are to work as impulses; but they work only as abstract ideas.

There was a time when abstraction as a principle of life reached its highest point. Everything is necessary—please understand me rightly, I do not want to make outright criticisms, I am not speaking from a standpoint of sympathy and antipathy but I am characterizing in the way that one does scientifically. I do not therefore want to cast aspersions—no one should think such a thing—if I say that there was a period when abstract ideas about the world celebrated their greatest triumph: freedom, equality and brotherhood. They were pronounced in a highly abstract way. This is not said out of a conservative or reactionary standpoint but in order to characterize human evolution at that time. Everything calls for freedom, equality and brotherhood at the end of the eighteenth century, not from the soul but from the thinking brain. And this continued into the nineteenth century in such a way that we feel it still echoing on everywhere today from force of habit. In the course of the ninteenth century people became thoroughly accustomed to the abstraction of thinking and were content with this way of thinking, because it makes them feel so clever. They believe that they have the truth in thinking and feel no need to immerse themselves in reality with their thinking. Immersing oneself in reality is something that must again be learnt;

otherwise everything continues to be a mere declamation of abstract ideas that have no value for life.

This is the great sickness of our time—the declamation of abstract ideas that have no value for life. When people say today that there must now come a time when an unimpeded course is demanded for ability or competence in the world, when ability is allotted its rightful place, what could be more laudable than this idea? What a wonderful ideal: let ability win through! There are times when people in the present materialistic age believe that they are bearing the whole future in their hands when they express such an ideal. But what is the use of such an abstract ideal if it continues to be the case that one's son-in-law or nephew is considered to be the most capable? What matters is not that one acknowledges, expresses and declaims an abstract ideal but that one is able to dive down with one's soul into reality, and understands how to comprehend, come to know, penetrate, experience and develop reality in its essence. To express beautiful ideas and make oneself feel good in the pronouncement of beautiful ideas will increasingly prove to be harmful. Love for reality, knowledge of and adjustment to reality are qualities that must be embraced by our soul. But this can only happen if people again learn to acquire knowledge of the whole of reality; for sense-perceptible reality is only the outer shell of reality. If someone who sees a magnet in the form of a horseshoe says that one can best shoe the horse with this, does he have the full reality of the situation? No, only when he recognizes that there is magnetism in the iron does he have the full reality. But the way that someone behaves who does not know what to do with a magnet except shoe a horse is equivalent to someone who wants to found a branch of natural science or political science under the assumption that the visible world is everything and that everything can be understood with concepts that have been derived from the visible world. This is an utter abstraction and represents the damaging effect of abstract ideals. People do not recognize this harmfulness because the ideals are true, because they are also good; but they are ineffective. They serve only the egoism of a human knowledge that takes delight in living in such ideals. But no world is governed by this. The best that it can achieve is a world governed in the way that it has come to be in the first half of the twentieth century.

One must take full note of such feelings if one wants to understand our time more deeply. The soul-life, which has—as I have described—so gradually ceased to be part of our surroundings, from the world that we perceive around us, must be enlivened within us. Ideas must become realistic again; they must again become alive. Brotherliness is a beautiful idea, but expressed as an abstraction it means absolutely nothing. If one knows, firstly, that the human soul-essence is living on the physical plane in and through the body, thus a soul clothed with the body and a body imbued with soul, if one knows, secondly, that man is not merely a body imbued with soul but actually a soul, and, thirdly, if one knows that the soul is filled with spirit, one therefore knows the soul to be threefold and man as threefold, one knows man in his composition of body, soul and spirit; and one has then made a beginning with making the abstract three ideas of brotherhood, freedom and equality into actual realities. To say of man in general, of this human abstraction, that he should live in brotherhood, freedom and equality is nothing but a torrent of words. It is necessary to acquire a living knowledge that man, in so far as he lives in a body in the physical world, needs a social order which is based on the foundation of true brotherhood, but that brotherhood can be understood only if one considers human beings in bodily terms. This is the beginning of the right idea of brotherhood. Brotherhood has a significance only if one knows that man is of a threefold nature and brotherhood is applicable to the bodily aspect. Freedom: for this one must know that man has a soul, for bodies can never become free. There are no possibilities for bodies to become free; human evolution can consist only in that souls become free. Freedom, expressed as a general idea of humanity, is an abstraction. Free souls for bodies living in a brotherly way is a concrete idea. Human beings are equal in the spirit. An old folk saying conveyed an awareness of this: after death all are equal. People then looked upon the spirit. In that human beings live as spirits, they are equal here as regards the Earth; but to speak of equality has a significance only if one speaks of this third member of man's being.

It must become alive, my dear friends, so that one says: That which goes about in some kind of order here on the Earth lives in body, soul and spirit. Evolution must advance in such a way that bodies live in brotherliness, souls in freedom and spirits in equality. There is not enough time today to explain this further, but you will already notice today the quite enormous difference between abstract ideas of equality, freedom and brotherhood and concrete ideas imbued with knowledge which are then applied to what is right.

But what is the basis of all this abstraction? After all, what was relatively recently still a truth of the mysteries has become wholly lost to mankind, namely that man consists of body, soul and spirit. For the Greeks it was still a universal truth to view man in terms of body, soul and spirit. This was still taken for granted by the first Church Fathers. That which lay in the declining phase of human evolution (which needs the ascending impulse of the Christ principle) was dogmatically prescribed through the Council of Constantinople in 869, when the spirit was abolished.[131] Forgive me for expressing this so drastically. It was only an outward statement of what was manifested in the consciousness of humanity through the circumstances that I have described. Since that time it was no longer possible to teach in theology that man consists of body, soul and spirit; one had to teach that man consists only of body and soul, as professors of philosophy continue to teach today. And if the good Wundt[132] or another philosophy professor of our present time really has no idea that man is of a threefold nature but always speaks of body and soul, he certainly does not know that he is merely following the ordinances of the Council of Constantinople of 869 AD. He is totally unaware that his teaching merely replicates the decision of this Council. Yes, this 'objective' knowledge sometimes—if one has more precise knowledge of its antecedents—has quite remarkable presuppositions. The 'objective' knowledge of our present age in philosophy cannot be conceived of without the Council of Constantinople; but the gentlemen concerned are not aware of this.

What has been obscured in this way—that man consists of body, soul and spirit—must be rediscovered through spiritual science.

That is why it was with full consciousness that the first thing that I tried symptomatically to emphasize in our Central European, anthroposophically oriented spiritual science had to be structurally pervaded (in the book *Theosophy*) by the division of man's being into body, soul and spirit. The entire book is structurally based on this. It had in a radical way to be placed again and again before humanity; thus it was presented with threefold man in the context of evolution.

You can see how, when one stands on the ground of spiritual science, everything is justified down to the very details, and also how spiritual science is abundantly capable of giving us such ideas, such impulses of feeling and will that can enable us to become true collaborators in the right progress of human evolution in our time. And I would always wish that I could call forth a feeling that spiritual science should not remain a teaching, that it should not remain something that people are accordingly accustomed a science to be but something that can foster a soul-life that is inwardly alive. This seems to me to be far more important than mere enrichment with concepts, which are of course also necessary; for if something is to be enlivened it must first be understood. We must have the concepts within us, but they should not remain dead and must become alive. Spiritual science then has the effect out of itself that when it is grasped in a real way it stimulates the whole human being. But it is also then necessary that the whole human being tries to understand it with feeling and with will, for he can then accordingly live within it. He should then never run out of love for true knowledge and for the further evolution of humanity. Especially this love is still a tender, delicate plant in our time. And it is understandable, even if also infinitely sad, if—in the realm of the spiritual-scientific movement as we understand it—the distorting effect of personal interests of sometimes an unpleasant kind upon the delicate plant of love for the knowledge demanded by our time leads to hatred celebrating its orgies in those who approach spiritual science not out of a pure longing for knowledge, and who do so in such a way that if their vanity is not satisfied their self-love is transformed into hatred. For only real love can become the victor over hatred, whereas self-love is even a generator of hatred.

If we have a right feeling for this, we shall also manage to cope with the phenomena to which I have twice referred, with those phenomena that so sadly gather their forces over the Anthroposophical Society, in which we see that people with powerfully hateful impulses emerge from its circles. We shall not conquer these things until we also address a principle of our materialistic age, as we are so gladly doing today—the principle that 'I want to have my peace!': when one closes one's eyes to certain things or does not want to call them by their right name. When numerous defamatory pamphlets[133] appear now, nothing is achieved if one takes them so seriously that one refutes particular sentences or phrases; for it does not matter to the sort of gentlemen who write them whether they end up with this or that sentence. For example, one has to say to a person who had to be refused when he submitted a book that could not be published by our press, who—because he felt offended in his arrogance— became an enemy of the Anthroposophical Society despite having hitherto fully ascribed to it: What you write is sheer nonsense, you know this perfectly well; you are writing all this because your book was rejected. That is the truth. When one understands how to serve spiritual science, it does not matter that one refutes particular details of these writings as invention and fabrication; rather does one show in his true light someone who has belonged to the anthroposophical movement in all its glory and then afterwards does such things as many have begun to do and will do so increasingly.

Or there is—as I related a few days ago—the person who wanted to be a great painter but in the course of trying begged to be allowed to learn; and when considerable efforts were made to enable him to improve his skills he knew everything better. He asserted that he wouldn't become a great painter by learning but it should be explained that he was a genius! If he then has the misfortune not to become one and, despite people providing him with teachers, is unable to learn to paint but only daubs, and if others are not able to recognize his daubing as great paintings, one comes and says: It's all a question of practice. One treats such a person in the right way by telling him the truth. It should not look as though spiritual science were thus jeopardized and matters such as this are not put in their rightful place.

Things already have a karmic fulfilment. The right thing should also happen in many other areas in our circles, as has occurred in an important point of principle. Just reflect on the fact that since 1911 all threads with the Theosophical Society of Mrs Besant have been severed,[134] and that England's war against Germany began only in 1914. This is an area where it may be said: The Anthroposophical Society acted prophetically.

Much in general is being reviled—this is of course not a criticism directed against the English people but against those who disseminate invective and who in this way abuse the principle of nationality; but despite the way that, contrary to all better knowledge, Mrs Besant reviles our Anthroposophical Society and me, such reviling is nevertheless a rarity. And after we first made the book *The Great Initiates* popular in Germany, we performed Schuré's plays; and we also had to experience that we were attacked by Schuré[135] in the most impossible manner. These are things that, as it were, occur more in wider circles. But also in more restricted areas enemies are gradually building up their power.

Anthroposophists must acquire a little foresight and a little will in order to see what is going on and what will come. One acquires this foresight if one takes seriously what has also rightly been placed as a motto at the head of our Anthroposophical Society: 'Wisdom lives in the light'.[136] Whoever is able to understand the words 'Wisdom lives in the light' with sufficient depth will adopt the right attitude.

This is what I must recommend to you on this occasion, my dear friends. I hope that our time together can be the starting-point of a good collaboration in the spirit, even if we are unable to be together physically. Let us try to think, to feel and to will in the spirit of our anthroposophically oriented spiritual science, and we shall then work together in the right way.

LECTURE 12

STUTTGART, 23 FEBRUARY 1918

THERE has hardly been a time in the evolution of mankind when it has been so necessary as it is now to enter deeply into the riddles of supersensible life, even though there is probably been no time when people have had such an aversion to penetrating into problems of a supersensible nature, and it is especially questions that seem to be furthest removed which have a quite particular concern for the modern human soul. Let us therefore today consider to begin with things that the materialistic mentality of the present would wish to thrust as far away as possible from human consciousness, although they are an intricate part of human life; and indeed, to know that what I intend to speak about is intimately related to human life is one of the particular challenges of our time. We shall begin with a few observations about a theme with which we are well familiar in order to approach something that, from one or another standpoint, we have often considered from a different point of view.

We all know that from a spiritual-scientific perspective it is of particular significance to view human life in terms of two great contrasts which feature in everyday life, namely the alternating states of sleeping and waking; and we have through our spiritual-scientific research again and again explored these polar-opposite states of sleeping and waking from all manner of different aspects.

Now from a whole variety of descriptions you know that this distinction that one generally makes between sleeping and waking, whereby human life is divided in such a way that one spends roughly two-thirds or more of the day in a state of waking consciousness (or sometimes less) and one third in sleep, is essentially only an external, superficial observation. Even if one explores the matter that has been thus stated in its immediate aspect more fully in order to penetrate behind the character of sleeping and waking, it remains somewhat superficial when compared to the depths that can be arrived at in this regard for a perception based on spiritual science; for we need to realize that the state of sleep is not only present in our soul-life when we are asleep in the superficial sense, thus not only during the time that elapses between going to sleep and waking up, but that our soul also to a certain extent brings this condition of sleep into the so-called waking state. Even when we are awake in the sense of ordinary consciousness, we are actually only partially awake. In this ordinary condition of consciousness we are never fully awake. And if from a spiritual-scientific standpoint we ask ourselves in what way are we fully awake, we would have to answer: We are awake with respect to all that we call perception of the outer, sensory world and the assimilation of these perceptions through ideas. In our life of perception and ideas, and hence in our life of thought, we are indubitably awake. We would not in any way be able to speak of our waking state if we were not inclined to refer to a certain inner state of soul which exists when we perceive the outer world in a fully awake condition and think and form ideas about it as such a waking state.

But we cannot say that we are awake as regards our feeling life in the same sense as we are in our faculties of perception and conception. It is an illusion if someone believes that from waking up to going to sleep he is as awake in his life of feeling and emotions as he is in his perceptions and thoughts or ideas. When someone is deceived by this illusion, this is because we always accompany our feelings with mental pictures. We not only visualize outer things, we not only form pictures of tables and chairs, of trees and clouds, but we also conceptualize our feelings; and in that we do this we are awake in the conceptions of our feelings. But feelings themselves surge forth from unconscious depths of the soul. For someone who can observe inner soul-processes, feelings, emotions and also passions surge forth in a manner that is no more inwardly awake than the impressions of dreams. Dream-impressions have the character of pictures. We know that for ordinary consciousness we must distinguish them very precisely from outer perceptions. Our consciousness is no more wakeful with respect to real feelings than it is to dreams. If immediately after waking up every dream were to be accompanied by a thought or mental picture (in the way that we always add a thought or mental picture to our feelings), so that we were unable to distinguish the dream from the thought, we would also consider our dreams to be the content of a waking experience. In themselves, our feelings are experienced in no more wakeful a state than our dreams.

And our will-impulses are to still less a degree experienced in a waking state of consciousness. With respect to the will, a person is in a perpetual state of sleep. He visualizes something when he wants it; he has a mental picture when—to take a simple example— he stretches out his hand to take hold of something. But what goes on in our soul-life and our bodily life when we stretch out a hand to reach something remains as deeply in the unconscious as dreamless sleep. Whereas we dream away our feelings, we are actually asleep in our will-impulses. As a person of feeling we dream, as a person of will we are asleep in the so-called waking state, so that even when we are in the waking state—hence from waking up to going to sleep— we are awake only with half of our being, whereas with the other half of our being we continue to sleep. We are awake with respect to our perceptions and our life of thought, we are asleep and in a world of dreams when it comes to our life of will and our feeling life. Such things cannot be verified more clearly than through the explanations that have just been given; for one's capacity to recognize such things depends on whether one can rightly observe the life of the soul. Anyone who is able rightly to observe this life of the soul will inevitably discover the inner similarity between feelings and emotions, on the one hand, and dreams. There is a very beautiful treatise by Friedrich Theodor Vischer[137]—that 'V-Vischer' who is particularly well-known in this city—about *Dream Fantasy*, where he has in a very fine way emphasized this right observation concerning the relationship between the life of feelings and the world of dreams.

Even when we are awake, we therefore go through life surrounded not only by the world that we perceive through our senses, by the world that we think, but by a world of which we can really only dream in our feelings, a world in which we dwell with our will-impulses but of which we experience no more than we experience of our surroundings in sleep, in other words nothing at all. But a world of which someone who is asleep experiences nothing is nevertheless around us. Just as the tables and chairs and the other objects are in the room in which the sleeping person is while he is asleep, so does man know nothing of that world whence his impulses of feeling and will derive because he is in a perpetual state of sleep with regard to this world. But it is this world with respect to which we are continually asleep that we share with human souls that are no longer incarnated in a physical body.

We have tried from many different viewpoints spiritual-scientifically to build a bridge between the so-called living and the so-called dead. We can also build this bridge in imaginative terms by becoming conscious that in our ordinary waking state we are connected with human beings incarnated in physical bodies, because they are accessible to our faculties of perception and to our life of thought. We are not connected with the so-called dead in our ordinary waking state, because we are constantly asleep to a part of the world that surrounds us. Were we to penetrate into this world that we sleep through in this way, we would no longer be separated from the world in which human beings dwell between death and a new birth. Just as we are surrounded by the air, so are we surrounded by the world in which human beings exist between death and a new birth; but we know nothing of this world for the reason that we sleep through it. Clairvoyant consciousness of the kind that we have often characterized leads to a perception of this world to which we are otherwise asleep, this world in which a person lives between death and a new birth. If one carefully takes account of what is contained in *Knowledge of the Higher Worlds* or in similar books, it is not so difficult to enter this world in such a way that one acquires a degree of certainty that one's soul passes through the gate of death as a living soul, that it enters another world and returns to Earth in a new life.

It is far more difficult to penetrate into this world that a person lives through between death and a new birth so that clear, definite connections can be established between a human individual here in a physical body and departed souls. These connections are always present in a certain way, at any rate between certain living people and certain deceased people. But in what I have already said today one can see the reasons why a person is not aware that relationships always exist between him and certain so-called dead people; and it is what clairvoyant consciousness experiences when it is able to form a connection with individual people who have died that can enable us to understand why in ordinary waking consciousness a person does not come to know anything of his relationships to the dead, which, as said, always exist as real relationships. If such conscious relationships are to be established between an awakening clairvoyant consciousness and certain dead people, one has to have certain soul-experiences which are totally different from the soul-experiences that we are accustomed to have in waking consciousness. It becomes very clear in this realm that one has to set aside all that one has cultivated for the knowledge of one's physical surroundings and replace it by something else if one wants to penetrate into the spiritual world with a clairvoyant consciousness. When the clairvoyant encounters a quite specific so-called dead person, he is able to enter into an appropriate form of communication with him; but he has to lay aside certain habits of soul. The soul-experiences that one has in such a case naturally appear somewhat surprising to people to whom such conceptions are wholly unfamiliar.

When we encounter another person here in the physical world and confer with him, we know that when we say something to the other person what we say comes from our own vocal organs, it as it were radiates from us and passes over to the other person. And when he answers us or communicates something to us this radiates from his vocal organs over to us. It is quite different when there is a relationship between a clairvoyant consciousness and a quite specific dead person. The situation then is that one has to completely change one's habitual behaviour. When we communicate something to a deceased person, when we ask him a question or say something to him, we must—however strange it may sound—have acquired the capacity whereby what we ourselves say comes towards us from him, so that it originates from him and radiates forth to us. In order to be able to communicate with someone who has died, we must be capable of so excluding ourselves and living in him that it is he who speaks when we ask him something or tell him something. And again, when he answers us, when he wants to tell us something, this comes forth from our own soul; it is produced in such a way that we know that it, as it were, radiates forth from us. Thus we have to achieve a kind of inner inversion if we want to arrive at a real relationship with a dead person; and although this is simple enough to characterize, it is very difficult as a soul-experience. Relating to one's surroundings in an opposite way to what is customary in the physical world is a very difficult attitude to adopt. And yet a genuine relationship with the so-called dead is only possible under these conditions.

If, on the other hand, you reflect on the inner transformation that is necessary, you will understand that there can always be relationships between the so-called living and the so-called dead but that the so-called living show little inclination to acknowledge them; for the so-called living are accustomed—and such a habit has a greater significance than one thinks—to perceiving something that they themselves say as streaming forth from them, and when the other person says something they perceive it as coming from this other person. People who are deeply rooted in the prejudices of the physical world must inevitably find something of the kind that I have just expressed to be very foolish. But it is a fact that one cannot gain insight into the spiritual world unless one gets used to the idea that much—I am not saying all, but most things—in the spiritual world is opposite in nature to what we are accustomed to here in the physical world; and one of these complete contrasts is the one that I have just explained. Only by entering through a very inwardly focussed exertion into such unfamiliar territory can one form a judgement as to the connections that ordinarily exist between any particular person and certain people who have crossed the threshold of death and to how these relationships are formed.

As already stated, these connections always exist. But if we want to envisage them we should not fail to add to the ordinary polar-opposite experiences of waking and sleeping two others which are of particular importance for the relationships of the so-called living to the so-called dead. However, to experience these consciously is again contrary to our familiar habits of perception. That is to say, we need to take account not only of ordinary waking and sleeping but also of going to sleep and waking up. These fleeting states of going to sleep and waking up are just as important for the life of the human soul as the more enduring periods of sleeping and being awake, but they pass fleetingly by. A person does not experience the moment of waking up because it is directly followed by the state of being fully awake, and he is not inclined to observe sufficiently quickly what he would have to observe in order to be able to take hold of the fleeting moment of waking up; this is drowned and overwhelmed by the waking life which immediately follows. In more primitive and naive conditions of human life, when much was known about such things, there was also an indication of what this meant for the human soul. But the more that materialism progressed, these things were gradually forgotten. One can often hear it said by country folk that when one awakes one should not look immediately at the light shining in from the window, that one should not immediately open one's eyes. Such advice derives from a very deep instinct, namely that in order to retain something of what is present at the moment of waking up one should not immediately drown the moment of awakening by the waking life of the day.

Just as important is the moment of going to sleep, although people mostly go to sleep straightaway and consciousness then ceases. Hence the moment of going to sleep is not sufficiently attended to in our ordinary state of consciousness.

What can be experienced and also is experienced at the moment of falling asleep and of waking up is highly important for the relationships that someone who is incarnated here in the physical world has to the dead. Such things can of course be observed only with a clairvoyant consciousness. But when a clairvoyant consciousness has managed to establish such connections with certain deceased people—connections which can only be established through the kind of total transformation of the soul's inner attitude that has been referred to—it can also form a judgement as to the nature of the real but unconscious relationships of the so-called living with the so-called dead. And the most favourable moment to bring everything that we have developed by way of relationships with specific dead people to those who have died is that of going to sleep; while the most favourable moment for bringing answers or communications from the dead into physical earthly life is that of waking up.

You should not object if what I have been saying now means that the time for posing a question or imparting information to a dead person is the moment of falling asleep, and that only at the moment of waking up does one receive an answer or a return communication. Temporal circumstances are completely different when it comes to the supersensible world. What is separated by an interval of several hours here for the physical world does not need to be thus separated in real supersensible life. One can truly say that, whereas when one asks someone something here in physical life one expects an immediate answer, the relation between question and answer that pertains in the supersensible world is such that one directs questions to the dead when going to sleep and one receives the answer on waking up. This relationship between the living and the dead is one that is constant.

Anyone who has lost other people who were close to him on the physical plane through their having passed through the gate of death indeed has such relationships, which have their fullest expression when going to sleep and waking up. The only reason that they are not brought to consciousness is that these favourable moments flash rapidly by, and most people are not accustomed to grasp with their consciousness what approaches their souls in these fleeting moments. In order to retain what comes to us in such fleeting moments, nothing is more suitable than studying the subtler, more refined thoughts of spiritual science. Anyone who so concerns himself with spiritual science that it is not merely cerebral knowledge but an inner substance of the soul, which is understood not with cleverness but with love so that it enters fully into the soul, anyone who relates to the thoughts of spiritual science not only with curiosity or with a thirst for knowledge but pursues them with love, will find that this love endows the soul with such strength that with a little attentiveness he gradually becomes aware of the great significance of the moments of falling asleep and waking up. And the more that spiritual science penetrates into human souls, so much the more will human individuals receive into their actual lives not only what they experience when they are awake but also that which comes to them from a supersensible world when going to sleep and especially when waking up. But we must be clear that we can actually form such real relationships of the kind I am referring to only with those dead people with whom we are in some way karmically connected; and we are karmically connected with far more souls than we might think. The karmic connection is just as necessary for there to be a conscious link between the living and the dead as it is necessary to direct one's eye upon a sensory object in order to perceive it. Even as in the latter context the sensory connection must be established, so is it a precondition for there to be a connection between the living and the dead that certain karmic relationships exist or at least are established between them.

If we now first consider the moment of going to sleep, this is the moment that is particularly favourable for bringing to someone who has departed, who was loved and revered by us and was karmically connected with us, experiences developed through our connection with him. The moment of going to sleep is particularly suitable for this. We do, of course, develop our relationships with those who have died with whom we are karmically connected in the waking life of the day, from waking up until falling asleep. We commemorate the dead. All that we think in relation to the dead, that we would gladly bring to them and gladly tell them, is concentrated at the moment of going to sleep and—even if this remains unconscious for ordinary consciousness—reaches the dead. But a certain soul-attitude is particularly favourable for these communications, and another one is unfavourable.

You see, thinking merely in a dry, cold way of the dead is little suited to really reaching them or to conveying a message to them. If it is our wish that the moment of going to sleep really becomes a portal through which our own soul-experiences that have connections with the dead reach them, we must concern ourselves with the dead while we are awake differently than through dry, cold thoughts. We must try to bring life to thoughts which have connected us with the dead person in question while he was still dwelling here among the so-called living. But we must especially impart to the thoughts what can establish a feeling connection. To think indifferently about a dead person is of little help. But it is good to recall what leads one to have a feeling connection with him, how it was to be with him, how one conversed with him, how one developed an active interest in something that particularly interested him; or to call to mind a situation where one was together here in life with the one who has died and there was something that particularly affected him and also oneself, where one tried to share something that one had experienced with the other out of fondness for him in order to have a common experience of it. Not dry thoughts but thoughts infused with live and warm feelings! These thoughts then remain within us until the moment of falling asleep. And then the gateway through which they may surely come to the dead person can be found.

We should not deceive ourselves about these things. We dream of someone who has died. When we dream of a dead person this is in very many cases—naturally not in all cases—due to a real connection with this person. But what we dream—in so far as it follows the moment of going to sleep—is really only a dream-like, pictorial transformation of what we communicate to the dead. We do not experience the moment of going to sleep, when such thoughts as have just been characterized are transmitted to the dead, because this moment of going to sleep flashes by so quickly. But this moment of falling asleep re-echoes in the following sleep, in the dream. If we understand all this rightly, we will not interpret dreams of dead people as messages from the dead. They might be messages, but not as a general rule. They are semi-conscious impulses that tell us the following. If we dream of a dead person, this means that on a preceding day we knowingly or unknowingly sent such a thought to the dead person as I have described. This thought found its way to the dead person, and the dream shows us that we have indeed spoken to him. What the dead person then answers, what the dead person communicates to us, these messages from the dead come to us particularly easily at the moment of waking up. And they would reach the so-called living far more readily if they had but the time and inclination in our present time to pay a little attention to what rises up from the depths of consciousness between the lines of the book of life.

Yes, people today are vain and self-seeking, and when anything arises in their souls they mostly have not the slightest doubt that this is due to their own genius. To be modest is something that life instils into us; but it is not so easy to be modest in one's innermost being. To be modest also means that one really learns to distinguish between what arises from the forces of one's own soul and what derives from supersensible impulses originating from elsewhere. Just as someone with a clairvoyant consciousness senses and perceives the answer of the dead person rising up from his own soul, so do these answers, these messages from the dead emerge from the depths of the soul during the time from the moment of waking until falling asleep. But just as people are unable to see the stars during the day (although they are constantly in the sky) because the sunlight obscures them, so in their ordinary consciousness do they not perceive what is continually emerging from the depths of their soul because outer life, called into being by the impressions of the senses, overwhelms it. If we have an intimate knowledge of our own soul, we learn to distinguish between what we ourselves originate and what sounds forth from our own soul as something from elsewhere; and then we gradually learn to recognize the messages of the dead also in the waking life of day. But then something of the greatest importance is connected with this knowledge; for we say to ourselves that we are in reality not separated from the dead, the dead are living among us. They do not proclaim themselves like other sensory beings that send us their impulses from without; they proclaim themselves from within; they speak to us through our own inner being; they bear us along with them.

It is true that in the present time and in the immediate future, people will—however necessary this is—find it difficult not to think that the impulses out of which they act derive only from the outer world of the senses, to recognize that in what we call our social life or our life in general not only are the so-called living active but also the so-called dead, that the dead are always present working in us and with us. In former times people had knowledge of this in the form of myths. When in these ancient times people revered worthy departed souls as tribal lords or ancestral divinities, this was due to the fact that through their atavistic consciousness they knew that the dead are always there, that they constantly work with the living. This consciousness had for good reasons to be lost to mankind, but it must be regained! People will again need to know that the dead are around us, that they speak to us through our souls, that we have communion with the dead. They will need to recognize that spiritual science must be asked how life actually functions, and that ordinary science inevitably leads one astray because it is unable to distinguish between what comes from the sensory world and what comes from the supersensible world. Our writing of history has indeed gradually become the most abject nonsense. There is talk of ideas that are supposed to live in history as if ideas flew like humming-birds or birds of other kinds, whereas in truth the impulses that mainly predominate in history are those of the dead.

This awareness of the life that we share in common with the dead must develop further. And as this awareness develops, as the soul-life of human beings is refined through the concepts of spiritual science (which will not happen if it is understood theoretically and not lovingly), the dead will also become present for humanity. Then that great part of reality which remains unconscious and unnoticed in our time will be taken into consideration. Only then will one be living with and in the whole of reality. This is a task for humanity from this time onwards; for at the present time we are living in the midst of a great catastrophe. The deeper reason why this catastrophe has arisen is that human beings have lost the capacity to live within reality. They have become separated from it by their materialistic consciousness. They believe themselves to be close to reality because they recognize only one part of reality, namely its sense-perceptible aspect, whereas they look upon the other part as an object of mere fantasy; and through failing to recognize the one half of reality they are separated from reality as a whole. They therefore do not arrive at a coherent concept of reality. If people could only realize that what I have just said has a great deal of practical bearing on the present!

Our children and young people learn history today. In our modern age and already for a long time before it people have been accustomed to learning history, that is to say, what they regard as history. But how much have they learnt of history? After all, because of the events—events of an elemental nature—which are constantly taking place, people are very often called upon to ask: What does history teach us about this? Again and again one can read statements to the effect that history can teach us this or that. But people learn nothing whatever from reality; and never could one have learnt as much from reality as in the last three and a half years. However, countless people are sleeping through this infinitely significant reality.

When these catastrophic events began, some very clever people who thought that they had learnt a lot from history expressed their views as to how long this period of war, as they call it, was likely to last. Giving good reasons for confirming what they were able to state, they said that this catastrophe of the war cannot, according to all the knowledge that is available, last longer than four to six months. And these were experts in their field who said this. Well, the facts turned out differently. And one does not need to be an unthinking person to be so misled by what is called history in modern times as to make such a judgement. Someone who certainly did not lack the ability to think took up his professorial chair in history at the university in 1789, and gave an inaugural address[138] in which this truly not insignificant person then said that history teaches that it is very probable that in future the nations of Europe will have all kinds of disputes with one another, but that they will no longer be able to tear one another apart; mankind has progressed too far for this to happen. This was the claim made by a not insignificant person called Friedrich Schiller in 1789 when he took up his chair at the university, basing it on historical research which even Schiller was understandably able to adopt. But what ensued after Schiller said this? The French Revolution; the great wars at the beginning of the nineteenth century. And if it really was a teaching of history that the peoples of Europe would, as members of one great family, never again be able to shed one another's blood, all the events of the present would be completely impossible.

However strange it may sound, it is necessary to re-learn such things. What is generally called history is not really history at all. In the historical life of human beings, forces of a supersensible nature are involved. The dead have an influence upon historical life, and a judgement from history can only arise if this judgement has a spiritual-scientific foundation. So long as this does not happen, history can never teach one anything; it will never be a practical science, it will never be in a position to provide maxims for what has to happen. Hence people today are so helpless in the face of events, because it is necessary in our time that spiritual-scientific maxims become practical foundations for life. So long as this does not happen, the present catastrophic events will in truth not be overcome.

I said that in order to approach the dead it is particularly favourable to cherish the thoughts that derive from a feeling relationship with someone who has died and which are remembered in such a way that one recalls this feeling relationship. In order to receive an answer from a dead person it is particularly favourable if we really know him, if we have the possibility of penetrating into his being, so that he engages with our life. Spiritual science is able to give us impulses for penetrating into the nature of others; for through the materialistic soul-constitution of today there is little possibility for people to know one another in life. They think they know one another, but they pass each other by, they talk past each other. One can today be married to someone for thirty or more years and have little knowledge of the other. A certain sensitivity of the soul is necessary in order to know someone else. If one is able to know another person's being as one knows oneself, the precondition is given for calling his true being before one's soul. If we summon before our minds the being of a deceased person to whom we want to ask questions by recalling something that connects us in a feeling way with him and vividly evoking his being, we shall surely also receive an answer; but it will be up to us to develop the necessary attentiveness for the interplay of what we direct to the dead person with what will surely return from him if the feeling relationships referred to are recalled. It is then possible that what we bring to the dead person will find its answer if we are able livingly to place before our soul what we have received from his being with real understanding.

Clairvoyant consciousness can provide information about many other specific connections with the dead. I shall speak today about one of these. You see, those who as relatives or friends or as people karmically connected with us in some way pass through the gate of death either as children or else as older people. If one observes with a clairvoyant consciousness something of the nature of the connections with these various dead souls, one can say the following about what it means to die at these different ages. When children or young people pass through the gate of death, one can characterize the relationship that they have to those who are left behind as follows. Children or young people have not lost those with whom they were closely connected, they remain in their immediate surroundings. It is through this that what we feel as grief, as sorrow, acquires its character. When a person endowed with clairvoyant consciousness observes the grief that a mother or a father has over a child whom they have lost, this grief is quite different from the pain that one feels as a young person when one loses an older relative or friend. It is true that in a superficial, outward respect these soul-experiences are more or less similar, but if one understands them more intimately they are fundamentally different. Those who die younger do not go away, they actually stay where they are (one can describe the relationship in this way); and they live on with our souls, they continue to live in our souls. And it is the grief, the sorrow that we feel that those dying at a younger age themselves experience within us. This is translated into our grief, our sorrow. They remain with us. It is a transformation of their own grief, which does not have to be grief but then becomes grief in us when it is transformed within our souls.

The sorrow that one feels for an older person is a grief that is felt personally. I might say that it is not so much a grief evoked by sympathy as an egotistical grief, a grief arising from one's own egotism; for if one wants to characterize the relationship of younger people remaining here on Earth to older people who have died from the standpoint of a clairvoyant consciousness, one can say that the older person does not lose us. We do not lose those who die young; those who die in old age do not lose us who are left behind; they in a certain sense take our souls with them, they take their forces along on their further path. They do not lose those who remain on this side of the threshold. Thus the relationship to such an older departed soul is quite different to that with one who is younger. The older soul does not have the tendency to live in the soul of one who has remained here, because it takes along with it the inner being, the imprint of the other's inner being.

It is not without significance to be aware of what I have just said; for it sheds light on what we call the remembrance of the dead. In the case of younger people it is good to form, to inspire this act of remembrance—or I might say the cult of the dead—in such a way that we remain in a more general, universal sphere, that we so arrange the thoughts, cultic actions or other things that are to accompany the memorial that we do not so much enter into the individual, personal nature of the one who has died as have great world-feelings and world-thoughts that have a connection with him. A person who has died young will then have a good feeling. In the case of an older person it is especially good if one can focus upon his individual nature, if the thoughts that one directs to him are formed in such a way that they have something to do with his personality and are shaped around his particular being. Where someone younger is concerned, it is particularly beneficial if the memorial service is arranged so that there is a kind of cultus, a cultus fixed for general purposes that has a symbolic significance. For younger departed souls the Catholic memorial service is particularly suitable; in most countries it enters less or even not at all into individual aspects but is a general, symbolical service having validity for everyone. For the young departed souls who do after all remain, it is best to mark their death with rites that are equally valid for all, to develop universal cosmic symbols, universal feelings in connection with them. For older departed souls the Protestant memorial service, which enters more into the course of the individual life and relates more to the personal nature of the one who has died, is better. Also in the individual remembrance that one devotes to such an older person who has died, it is preferable to emphasize what is connected with him personally, thus what is applicable not just to any dead person but only to him or her.

If one knows these things, our life of feeling with respect to those who have died becomes differentiated. We can then distinguish how to relate to a younger or an older departed soul. Life is enriched in its most intimate aspects if one derives the thought from spiritual science that not only do souls living in physical bodies form part of one's life but also disembodied souls. Only then does one enter into the full reality.

It must again and again be said that it does not lead very far to speak in general terms of the spirit. To speak of spiritual life in general as certain philosophers do, or as people also do who think that by speaking in general of spirit and spirit and spirit they are overcoming materialism, does not lead us very far at all. It is necessary to summon up the courage—and it does take a certain courage to do this now—to reach right down into present-day cultural life. We must summon up the courage unreservedly to profess such matters as we have also spoken of today before our contemporaries, however great the scorn of materialistically minded people may be. It is scarcely conceivable today how utterly fatal it would be for mankind, how totally catastrophic it would be, if people in the most important parts of the world know nothing of these things and therefore do not think about them, so that they are so far removed from the reality which must then overwhelm them so devastatingly. The present world-catastrophe will be ascribed to all sorts of impulses, but not to those from which it has its deepest origins.

This is the place to reflect upon the whole significance that an anthroposophically oriented, spiritual-scientific world-conception of the kind that we have in mind here must have for the cultural and spiritual life of Europe. In a future time that is not so far distant, it will have a great significance how people relate to the spirit and to spiritual insights; for important, significant things are undergoing preparation in the life of earthly humanity. If one emerges only a little from the sleepy state in which so many people are engulfed, one cannot fail to think more deeply about certain things than have been pondered for several centuries in Europe. The times are pressing for a change in the way people think. One can indeed see that people are beginning to think differently; but the question is whether or not this revising of their thinking is something that they undertake with sufficient depth, or whether they approach it in the way that very many people do at present. One sees that there is a tendency to think differently, but it sometimes manifests itself in a very curious way. Hundreds if not thousands of examples could be given to illustrate this.

You see, one of those people who have changed their thinking in the course of the last three and a half years is the French former socialist and journalist Gustave Hervé.[139] He publishes a journal which he calls *Gloire*, which has also been renamed from a name that is less provocative. This Hervé is one of those who presently write in the sense of a raging French chauvinist. Even when compared to a tigerish, bull-like chauvinist like Clemenceau,[140] one could say that Hervé is actually even more of a French chauvinist—and he has changed the way he thinks. Four years ago he was still thoroughly cosmopolitan; he still at that time poured scorn upon anyone who was not even a French chauvinist but was in some way inclined towards French nationalism. He was really cosmopolitan, this Hervé. Now what he writes is so poisonous that from every line that he writes one can read that what he would most like is that the French Tricolour would be an instrument with which to defeat everything opposed to the French. Nevertheless, Hervé made a significant remark before the war started. What he said was: The Tricolour belongs on the dung heaps! So little was this man who is now one of the most chauvinistic of Frenchmen oriented towards French nationalism that he brought himself to say that the Tricolour—he means the French flag—belongs on the dung heaps. To such an extent did he despise everything of a nationalistic kind. He has now done some relearning and rethinking, although of course in a way that is not very profound. What is to happen in a particular time indeed happens—it is important that one takes it into account; but it may be asked *how* it transpires in the case of one or another person, how one or another person really takes account of his task for humanity. In the course of this relearning, it is above all necessary that Europeans do not sleep through matters of significance which are presently being prepared for earthly humanity as a whole.

In Asia and in the Orient in general, many judgements are being developed about Europe, particularly about Central Europe (at present this is the main focus of our interest), judgements which will gradually become linked to historical impulses. The Oriental, the Japanese, the Indian, the Chinese all gradually feel called upon to develop certain impulses. To a great extent, they have already developed such impulses; and among leading Orientals there are certain judgements, especially regarding the nature of Central Europe and specifically Germany, which should be noted, for what lives in these impulses will become history in a not too distant future. It may seem strange to say this, but one should at the present time develop a keen discernment for such things; one should know that, in order to be abreast with reality, it is necessary today to foresee to a certain extent what must come about. The Orientals who are preparing themselves to enter into a relationship with Europe, and are forming their judgements which will one day become world-political realities, have their ancient conceptions of spiritual or cultural life. They see what has been taking place in Europe during the last few centuries, but they view it in a one-sided way; because Europe, and especially Central Europe, is manifesting its own being in a one-sided fashion.

What, for example, do leading Orientals believe concerning the nature of Central Europe? They believe what they have to believe in accordance with what they mainly see. They believe that Central Europe is particularly gifted in organizing political, commercial and other concerns; that it is particularly adept in ensuring that the way that science is taught in European schools is in accordance with the authority of this science. Yet these Orientals do not especially value what derives either from this organizing facility or from science, for they are aware that, in contrast to this, they have an ancient spirituality originating from impulses that are entirely different from those that we have in Europe. A leading Oriental will never be impressed by what arises, for example, from European natural science; he will never be impressed by the achievements of European industry, even if in an outward way, as do the Japanese, he accepts them; he will never be impressed by what European organization is able to bring about. To his mind, all this has no relationship to the true nature of things. He feels instead a real relationship between his soul and the soul of the universe; he feels spiritually related to the soul of the universe. Of this we may be quite clear.

On the other hand, the Oriental would have a quite different relationship to the way of looking at things that we have cultivated here today or elsewhere than he has to European machine culture, European organization and to the intellectual science of Europeans. Moreover, however strange it may seem it may be meaningful to dwell upon the following question: What would an Oriental say if he could know that from what cultural life in Europe has brought forth through Herder, Schiller, Goethe, through the Romantics, a true, concrete spiritual contemplation of the world can emerge which contributes something special to the spiritual contemplation of the Orient that the Oriental cannot find through his own attributes but which he could value and with which he could ally himself? Of course, you can say that Goethe is sufficiently well-known to the whole world, and the leaders of Oriental cultural life can also come to know Goethe; for Goethe is a source, an inexhaustible source for the cultural life of Central Europe. All this is perfectly true. But has Central Europe even now really managed to recognize Goethe as such a source? One could say much about this. The Oriental looks at what Central Europe has been able to make of Goethe. Much could be said by way of elaboration; but I shall add this as an example. Although Central Europe has passed Goethe's most important impulses by in silence, it nevertheless has a Goethe Society. This Goethe Society was founded at a highly favourable moment. Indeed, it can be said that few constellations were as favourable for such things as they were at the end of the 1880s. When Goethe's last descendant left his unpublished works to a princess, everything could have been started and well taken hold of, there was an initial impulse that could lead one to believe that now the spiritual sources of Goethe's inspiration will be revealed! Much happened, and it was at that time that the Goethe Society was founded.

But let us return to the Oriental who says: In the Orient we have a life which connects the soul directly with the world-soul. In Europe they have organizations of a political and social character, they have machines and industrial development, they have a science that is taught in schools and imposes its great authority upon human souls; but they have no notion of a relationship between the human soul and the soul of the universe.

If he knew what connections are latent there, he would know the potential of what might arise in accordance with what could be experienced through Goethe; he would speak and think and feel differently. But what does he see? Well, he may perhaps acknowledge the fact that Central Europe managed to establish a Goethe Society in order to honour one of its greatest men. But it also appointed a former Finance Minister[141] as the chairman of this Goethe Society. This one fact symbolizes many things. One might say, nevertheless, that it should be our impulse to let the world know that from the source of the German spirit there can arise what can be seen as the impulses of spiritual science. These impulses will not be overlooked over there in the Orient. If they are ignored, the judgement that will inevitably form in the Orient as a historical impulse would be that this European culture is essentially harmful to mankind. And this judgement has become deeply rooted. It would quite certainly be corrected if it were known that the cultural and spiritual life of Central Europe can itself transform even the most mechanical aspect of mechanisms into beauty within human souls through those impulses that it has within it, and which it can develop into a true knowledge and a real further unfolding of the supersensible. This is how it could work from the one side.

Let us now cast our eye in the other direction. In the West, in America, people look not only upon Central European life but European life as a whole in the way that it can be known only from without, because of course they see not only the Goethe Society with the former Finance Minister at its head but also other things in a similarly superficial way, but not what can live within human souls as has been pervading our souls today. Whereas in the East they say that this Europe is harmful, over there in America they find it superfluous. For Americans, too, can build machines, run industrial organizations and found Goethe Societies with people who understand as much about Goethean Science as is necessary to set up financial budgets; but out of themselves Americans do not have what flows as a deep wellspring of spiritual life from Goethe, and they can only have this if they take it from Central Europeans.

This is no mere eccentricity, my dear friends; it is a question that is deeply connected with the practical, urgent needs of the present that we should consider how to relate to the impulse to do whatever we can to let the world know and feel what potential for spiritual development lives within European culture and what paths to the supersensible currently reside within it. Today it is more than ever necessary to be aware that spiritual science is not only something that can nourish our own soul but that spiritual science must become something through which we, as people of Central Europe, can fulfil our task in the evolution of mankind.

Lecture 13

STUTTGART, 24 FEBRUARY 1918

YESTERDAY we tried to gain a more precise knowledge of the world which surrounds us in such a way that we share it with those who have passed through the gate of death and also with those beings of soul and spirit whom we regard as beings of the higher hierarchies. This has enabled us to have some insight into a part of that reality which influences human life, even though with our faculties of sense-perception and our associated intellectual capacities we have no knowledge of it in our ordinary waking consciousness. Since this world is a reality, one that contributes to the shaping of human life, it makes a great deal of sense that in the time that now confronts us, when—as I have often said—human beings are increasingly required to take the overall course of human evolution in hand out of their own free initiative, a knowledge also of supersensible realities penetrates into the human soul. Yesterday's lecture, whose theme of the life of the so-called dead is one that should make a deep impression upon every human soul, concluded with the indication that such a knowledge of the supersensible is quite particularly necessary in our time. On the other hand, there is a very real need to form precise thoughts about such things as we were considering yesterday; for in our time even half-awake, dreaming individuals should be dimly aware that decisions of the greatest importance are having to be made.

In the course of our deliberations I have in one place or another repeatedly given indications regarding what can be said out of the sources of spiritual research about the character of the modern age, of the age itself and of the near future. Such things could of course be presented to humanity in our time only with caution and circumspection, and this is more or less the case also with those who think along anthroposophical lines. Just consider how much by way of an understanding of this difficult, catastrophic time of ours can be found in the lectures about the Folk-souls given in Christiana several years before these catastrophic events.[142] And perhaps you may also recall that at a time when it was indeed necessary to point out the seriousness of what was happening, I spoke of the social life, of the life that people share in common with one another in our time, in such a way that I expressed myself quite strongly and even starkly. In these lectures, which also had to do with the life of human beings between death and a new birth,[143] I said that the moral, social life of the present has engendered something that one can describe as a social carcinoma, as a terrible social illness of a cancerous nature. Perhaps at the time this was felt to be a strong expression; but there may perhaps have been a growing conviction that the facts now justify the choice of such a forceful expression.

In any case, what I already indicated yesterday is true and should stimulate reflections on a deeper level; namely, that while it is easy enough to be dimly aware of the weighty impulses residing in our times, mankind is little inclined today really to grasp the present phenomena in their full seriousness. People today are far too lazy, they surrender far too willingly to those comfortable thoughts that one can find at present in the world-conception of natural science; for these concepts can be acquired on the leading-strings of outward experience, they do not demand much inner spiritual exertion and nevertheless greatly flatter people's vanity. Whereas what is necessary is that humanity should awaken, really awaken to much that our present time has to teach us and not continue to be asleep to it. Waking up will, however, only be possible if certain fundamental matters are considered no longer as fantastical dreams but as a reality that directly influences the events of our time. In the course of our studies[144] I have therefore frequently indicated that in the last third of the nineteenth century a significant change took place in relation to humanity. I have also referred to these things here in Stuttgart. We shall call these to mind again today from a particular point of view.

I have indicated that the autumn of 1879 was a turning point for human evolution in modern times. If one wants to understand this present phase of human evolution more precisely, one would have to say that what occurred in the last third of the nineteenth century is only the result of something that took place previously in the spiritual world. It began in the spiritual world in the 1840s; and the time from the 1840s until the end of the 1870s is an important period, one that is full of significance. What happened at that time did not occur on the physical plane; but in the year 1879 the after-effects began to be manifested on the physical plane, and since that time these after-effects have been enacted there. They are a kind of reflection of what had previously happened in the spiritual world. If one were to characterize what lay at the foundation of this, one could say that it was the manifestation in a particular region and in a particular sphere of something that frequently occurs in the evolution of humanity, and which has always been referred to by those who have been able to observe such things as a battle of Michael with the dragon. Such battles of normally progressing beings of the higher hierarchies against spirits of hindrance or obstruction have taken place in the most diverse realms. Such a battle took place in the context of the cultural evolution of mankind in spiritual heights, in those spiritual heights directly bordering upon the Earth, in the decades from the 1840s to the end of the 1870s. It was then in 1879 that this battle ended with a victory (if one would so describe it) of the good powers against certain spirits of hindrance, who were at that time—and it can indeed be expressed as such—cast down from the spiritual worlds to earthly circumstances, so that they have ever since been working and weaving amidst the conditions of earthly life. Thus as an integral part of what is developing in the spiritual evolution of mankind, spirits of hindrance who were vanquished as regards the higher world only at the end of the 1870s have been cast down into the lower world and have henceforth held sway in human beings.

If one turns one's attention to these spirits of hindrance, these spirits of an ahrimanic nature, with whom those spirits whom one can call Michaelic spirits have waged a mighty battle, one must state that in former times these ahrimanic spirits had their positive significance, they had their tasks in previous ages of spiritual evolution. These tasks were accomplished in such a way that they were guided by good higher spirits. We should not conceive of the so-called evil spirits in a manner that we think that we must flee from them and if possible get rid of them. Egotistically ridding oneself of them is actually the best means of ensuring that they remain. Rather should we bear in mind that these so-called evil spirits are also in the service of the wise ordering of the world. One can therefore say: These spirits of an ahrimanic nature have for centuries and even millennia had the task of grouping human beings in those communities and associations that have to do with the blood. In their earthly connections, human beings relate in such a way that blood-ties also give rise to and bring about bonds of affection and love. They are grouped together in families, tribes, nations and races. All these things have at their foundation certain laws of the times. These are governed by beings of the higher worlds. What has given humanity its specialized character, what has divided it in such a way that blood lies at the foundation of these divisions, was guided by these ahrimanic spirits but under the direction of good spirits.

But now a different period was to be inaugurated. For as long as human beings are, as it were, led through the blood, the human individual could not take his destiny in hand himself in the way that we have often indicated. It was therefore necessary that the service of these ahrimanic spirits as it has been rendered was eliminated from the spiritual world. These spirits wanted to continue their activity of grouping human beings in accordance with blood-ties; but humanity was to be led towards a more universal conception of its collective spirit. What is frequently spoken of in our circles, that mankind has to be understood as a totality throughout the Earth, is indeed no mere slogan but a present necessity. This is based on the fact that a fierce and intense battle has taken place between the Michaelic spirits and the spirits of an ahrimanic nature who formerly differentiated human beings in accordance with blood-ties.

This battle ended with the casting down of the ahrimanic spirits, so that they now hold sway among human beings where they create confusion; for since their conquest their intention has been to cause confusion with regard to everything that can be derived from concepts and ideas associated with blood-ties and blood-relationships. It is especially important to bear in mind that these impulses are actively involved in everything that people can bring about here on the physical plane through thoughts and feelings, and that one cannot understand things as they really are if one does not take them into account. The way in which people speak today about the relationships between peoples and similar matters is confused by these ahrimanic spirits who have been vanquished by the spirit of Michael.

I have often mentioned the idea that we should be saying that since the end of the 1870s the so-called Michael age has dawned. We should look upon Michael as the Time-spirit in place of Gabriel. This means a great deal: Michael as Time-spirit! The Time-spirits who were active in previous centuries worked differently from this Time-spirit. The other Time-spirits who exerted an influence upon human evolution in previous centuries have worked by influencing the subconscious. The task of the Time-spirit, Michael, who has been active in human destinies since the last third of the ninteenth century is this: increasingly to bring what is to take place in earthly evolution to consciousness within human beings. This Michaelic Time-spirit has indeed descended and is working on the physical, earthly plane.

With all this, something is connected for our time which can easily be misunderstood. Our time is one that has many different contradictory elements. If one characterizes it superficially, one could easily regard it as purely materialistic. But it is not only that; the reality is far more complicated. All in all one can say that this modern age is in its fundamental character remarkably spiritual, quite extraordinarily spiritual; and in human evolution as a whole there have never been concepts and ideas that are more spiritual than those that have been brought to the surface by modern natural science. But these concepts are, if I may use such epithets, nebulous and abstract. In themselves and as regards their substance they are thoroughly spiritual; but if they are not rightly applied they are incapable of expressing anything of a spiritual nature. These natural-scientific concepts which are injected into every branch of culture are a sharply two-edged sword, if I may employ this paradoxical expression. If they are used as they are today by academic science, they are indeed spiritual; but when applied only to the outward material world their spirituality is negated. One can, however, also use these natural-scientific concepts in such a way that they can serve as material for meditation: one can meditate upon them. They will then lead most surely into the spiritual world. If those who profess an allegiance to a natural-scientific world-view were not too lazy to apply their ideas in a meditative way, these people would very soon venture into spiritual science. The issue lies not with the content of natural-scientific ideas but with the way in which they are applied. The concepts are exact, they have depth; but their application is kept within materialistic bounds. This cannot so readily be clarified in every detail, but we must come to an understanding; and so we have to let many such truths approach us only, as it were, through a kind of reflection.

Thus people live in concepts, thoughts and ideas which are nebulous and, I could say, highly distilled in their nature, so that only a considerable force can lead from them to spiritual science; and these are the thoughts that are to impress themselves upon human evolution through the Michael age. But they are also those thoughts which are most subject to confusion through the ahrimanic spirits of hindrance who, as indicated, were vanquished by Michael in heaven and cast down from heaven to the Earth. Their influence is evident in so many spheres where people believe that they are thinking rightly but where they are to a high degree exposed to the confusion emanating from these spirits.

Considerations of this nature make it apparent how evolution— and we shall to begin with focus on human evolution—is actually proceeding. Here we need to call attention to a significant law of evolution which we also need to study from different viewpoints. It is a highly superficial way of looking at things if one supposes that the events in history simply arise from what went before, that what happens in the year 1918 is a consequence of 1917, 1916 and so on. That is a superficial observation. Things actually take a very different course; for the way that they take place is that what has occurred in the spiritual domain continues to work further in the ensuing periods but in a particular way. One can single out any year, but let us take the year 1879 as an example. In such a case something happens in 1880 which is influenced by the fact that what happens in 1878 is retrospectively repeated; 1881, as it were, retrospectively repeats what happened in 1877 and so on. One can, however contradictory it may seem, proceed from any point of human evolution and one will always find that the events of earlier years appear later on in the form of important impulses. One can therefore expect that in an important period of time this law will also manifest itself in human evolution with particular clarity and importance.

I have often already indicated, and have indeed spoken of this before these catastrophic events, that the important moment marked by the year 1879 is merely the result of what had taken place in the spiritual world since the 1840s. If we now apply the law of which I have just spoken, we can say the following. 1879 is an important year; certain spirits who had formerly been working as spirits of hindrance in the spiritual world were cast down and have since then been active as forces of impediment and confusion among human beings on the physical plane. What happened in 1879 is, so to speak, the conclusion of a previous event which began between 1841 and 1844 and then continued through the decades that followed. If we take the year 1841, we have the period of battle in the spiritual world from 1841 until 1879. Those beings who are ruled by that spirit whom one calls Michael—he could also be called by other names—therefore embarked in 1841 upon the fierce, intense battle in the spiritual world that arrived at its conclusion (as far as the spiritual world was concerned) in 1879. Thus it lasted thirty-eight years. Now I said that what happens at an earlier time works back upon the time that follows. If one adds a further thirty-eight years to 1879 one arrives at 1917. So just as 1880 repeats what happens in 1878 and 1881 the events of 1877, so in a certain way is what was in 1841 taken up in the spiritual world as one of the most important battles repeated in 1917. It is indeed the case that this year of 1879 is an incisive moment which opens up a vista of energetic impulses working forwards and backwards. And in a certain sense those events that had to take their course in the 1840s, and which one can characterize as a battle of normal, forward-looking spirits against certain spirits of hindrance, are being repeated now on the physical plane from 1917 and 1918 onwards. This is a calculation that I am not making only today; for many of you know that I have often spoken about these events, and that from the standpoint of these events the year 1917 must be viewed as being an important point of departure for future happenings.

These things should not, of course, be viewed in such a way that one says: Well, we lived through the year 1917! Indeed, we did; but only few people experienced the events taking place in this year as they really were, few people had the inclination to evaluate them in waking consciousness. This is the essential point.

With all these thoughts I wanted only to indicate that we are indeed living at an important moment of human evolution, and that it is necessary to take many things more seriously at the present moment than they are by and large taken by present-day humanity. I have indicated how particularly necessary it is that one does not fail to take note of the normal spiritual impulses in our time. What, then, is of foremost importance in our present time, what is its keynote? What has really gained influence in this age? What has streamed forth into the whole of wider culture? Actually only that which has grown on the roughest terrain of the natural-scientific world-conception. This rough terrain of the natural-scientific world-conception, however, only has the power to understand what is dead and lifeless and never the living, which is so infinitely necessary in this age of natural science. People have as yet no wish to see the connection of such things with the general events in the world. They do not want to see that the more that humanity endeavours to form concepts that relate to what is dead, the more is social life, any kind of community life, destroyed by what they do. It is necessary that the ideas of natural science become mobile, that they are so enlivened that they can indeed be applied to the life that people share in common and that they can also explain it.

The course of evolution in this modern age has been as follows. In what has been recognized as real science, only those concepts with which one can comprehend lifeless nature have been engendered. These thoughts have been totally unsuitable for under-standing human life. There has, nevertheless, been a wish to use them for this purpose. Thus official scientists have applied these ideas to history, to social science, social policy and so on. But since these concepts are useless for this, there are no ideas that can be applied to social life; and the social life of the Earth has now gone beyond human control; it has become what it has now been for well-nigh four years. People will have to learn to bring focus to their thoughts and also to imbue them with life.

What natural scientists themselves formulate is certainly intel-lectually stimulating, has certain applications and is conscientiously methodical, but only for outer nature. Today every scientist works in his field and has no intention of extending the concepts that have been developed in any particular domain to a world-conception that embraces the whole of human experience. If you take one such con-cept you will at once see what I mean. The ordinary physics teacher today who studies a compass needle with one end pointing to the north and the other to the south explains to his pupils that this con-stancy of the direction in which the needle points derives from the magnetism of the Earth, that the Earth is also a great magnet; and it would be ridiculous if this teacher were to seek the forces that cause the needle to point in these directions in the compass needle itself. He seeks to explain this from qualities of the Earth; he seeks the cause in the cosmos. In this purely lifeless region, natural-scientific concepts do indeed have some value; for these it is possible to arrive at some kind of result. Hence it would not occur to anyone to say of a compass needle that the force that causes it always to point in a certain direction lies within the needle itself; for it is accepted that these forces derive from the magnetic North and South Poles of the Earth. The biologist does not do this. He sees a hen preparing to lay an egg. It would not occur to him to pose the same question as does the physicist with the compass needle. The biologist simply says that if an egg is developing in the hen, the cause of this process lies within the hen. Were he to think in the same way as does the physicist with the compass needle, he would say that, whereas the hen is indeed the place where the egg is developing, cosmic forces are involved when the egg is being formed in the same way that the cosmos exerts its influence upon the compass needle. I must go beyond the narrow limits of nature and enlist the help of what is outside it. The place where the egg-cell is forming is indeed in the hen, but forces are working in from the cosmos in the same way as they give direction from the cosmos to the compass needle.

There is an urgent need to develop such a concept and to work it through systematically. But according to the official science of biology this is ridiculous, sheer fantasy and the height of folly, because it has completely lost its way in the blind alley of the lifeless. This official science cannot even arrive at comprehensive ideas of such things as this, and it is far less able to say anything about how human beings might manage rightly to live together socially or politically. How can one cherish any hope that from this unadulterated natural-scientific conception of the world there might emerge something that humanity so badly needs, namely an enlivening, a rejuvenating of these conceptions? Not least in the important sphere of human life, there is no question of this. We shall clarify this by means of a thought that we shall endeavour to grasp in a spiritual-scientific way.

Merely contemplating the human skeleton shows us something of extraordinary importance, something truly sublime. If you look at the human skeleton, you see that the head is actually merely positioned on the trunk portion of the skeleton, it is a world in itself. The rest of the skeleton is differently formed. If one applies Goethe's idea of metamorphosis, one can indeed perceive the transformation of the trunk into the head portion of the skeleton; but this latter part is spherically formed; the head is a reflection of the whole cosmic sphere. The other part is formed in a more moon-like way. This is something of immense significance, and it shows us that if we want to acquire fruitful thoughts about man by contemplating the human form we need to consider what this form can reveal to us. Our natural science is truly amazing, but it is illiterate where knowledge of the world is concerned. It proceeds like someone who does not read the pages of a book but describes first A and then B, thus does not read but merely describes the letters. It is, however, necessary to progress to the stage of reading; one must understand the forms of nature in such a way as not only to describe them as natural science does but to explain them in their relationships and transitions. One then takes the step from reading the forms and phenomena of nature to deciphering the meaning of the world. It is true that people who hear what is being said but in their illiterate state are obtusely governed by their thick heads will protest that statements of this kind are quite repugnant. Good examples could be presented of such reactions to what can be deduced from the skeleton and can be extended to the whole human organism. Man is of a twofold nature, and this duality in his nature comes to expression in the marked contrast between the head and the rest of the organism.

If one studies these two parts of man's dual nature in the light of spiritual science (it would be possible to include other parts, but this is not essential today), one can deduce something of enormous significance from the mere form of man's being if one really focusses one's attention on it. In spiritual-scientific terms one can see that the human head undergoes a development from birth through earthly life which can be distinguished from the development of the rest of the organism, just as with respect to its form the head can likewise be distinguished from the rest of the organism. It is very interesting to discover that the head develops three or four times as fast as the other parts of the organism. If one contemplates the rest of the organism, one can ascribe to it a general name in so far as it is mainly organized by the heart; so that one then has a contrast between the head organism and the heart organism. This heart organism develops three or four times more slowly than the head organism. If we were only head, we would at roughly the age of twenty-seven or twenty-eight already be old people who are ready to die; because the head develops so quickly. The rest of the organism develops four times as slowly, and so we live into our seventies or eighties. But this does not alter the fact that we indeed have a development of the head and a development of the heart, that we bear these two natures within us. The development of our head is also, as a rule, complete by the age of twenty-eight; the head does not develop further. What does continue developing is the rest of the organism; and it transmits its developmental forces to the head. Anyone who is able to contemplate the human form and characteristic aspects of its development may not arrive at such a fact but can nevertheless find something to confirm it (discerning it as a fact is possible only through spiritual science). Thus who has not observed a little child, and on seeing it again a few years later may have said that only when it was older had it developed a striking likeness to someone or other. This is connected with the fact that the hereditary forces are actually hidden in the rest of the organism. The head is formed wholly out of the cosmos; and only when the hereditary forces work from out of the rest of the organism (and this is a slower process) does the physiognomy of the head begin to resemble the rest of the organism. This is only an example of how the findings of spiritual science can be confirmed by outward facts. It is important to bear in mind that the head undergoes a much faster path of development than the rest of the organism.

You see, in former times when people were less free and guided to a greater extent, it was not as significant to know such things as it is now. Good spiritual powers then exercised their governance; they, as it were, established harmony between the speed of the head's development and the speed of development of the rest of the organism, they brought these into balance. But now the time has begun when human beings must themselves ensure that such things as this are harmonized. To this end they must be able rightly to understand them, they must be able to penetrate them; and they will be trespassing against the course of evolution if they fail to do so. And there is an important area of human life where we sin greatly against these things. This sin already comes to expression sporadically today because we have passed the last third of the ninteenth century; but it will become massively evident if people are unable to take hold of spiritual impulses. The way that this is apparent at present is as follows. There is no awareness of the fact that normal development renders it necessary that what a person is given takes into account that his head development is three or four times faster than that of the rest of his organism; and an area where this comes to expression in a particularly harmful way is that of education and for the following reasons. Under the influence of the natural-scientific view of the world, thoughts have been developed which have gradually become mere ideas for the development of the head and give nothing for the development of anything else; they are thoughts which are acquired at the speed that the head develops and the development of the rest of the organism cannot keep pace with it.

These are observations of the greatest significance. Ideas have gradually been developed which occupy only the head and leave the heart cold and empty. As I say, they are at present sporadic in nature; but they will take hold to an ever greater extent. If you are able to observe life, you can test this for yourself. Because of the dual nature of his head and heart development, it is necessary that a person in his youth should not receive an education only for his head. In youth the head must primarily be considered, because the rest develops more slowly. (If one wanted to educate the rest of a person's organism in the same way that he is educated with respect to his head, he would spend his whole life at school.) In school education one can only address the head. But today the head is addressed in such a way that it cannot give anything of a soul and spiritual nature to the rest of the organism. Throughout life the rest of the organism endows the head with its inherited impulses. We would otherwise die at the age of twenty-seven, for the head has this predisposition. But in the same way the head should pass on to the rest of the organism what it has received through education. You can test for yourselves that modern education does not manage this properly by asking: Is it not so that those who have received a school education only remember the feeling element of their education in later life? They mostly do not even remember that, but they are pleased if they can quickly forget everything. This only goes to show that the rest of the organism contemplates what the head has received by way of education. If the rest of the organism were to receive from the head the living essence that it needs, one would not only recall one's memories but would look back at what the teacher has given one as a kind of paradise to which one looks back every hour in later life with inner satisfaction and devotion, immersing oneself in it ever and again as a source of rejuvenation. It would be a source of rejuvenation if it were to comprise an education for the heart and not merely for the head.

A person would then for the duration of his life have something from his childhood years, from school, for the rest of his organism, which develops four times more slowly; and this would also work back upon his organism.

All this is at present only in its beginnings and it will become ever worse as time goes on. People will become senile at an early age, because they will at best remember in a cerebral way what they have taken in through their head and has significance only until the twenty-seventh year. After that, what one remembers comes to a standstill, it becomes unusable; and the person ages. He becomes in an inner soul-spiritual sense prematurely old, because the education that the head has received is not capable of flowing over into the development of the heart, which is four times slower.

These things must be taken into account. But if they are to be properly considered, our school education must become totally different; and instead of the dead thoughts that prevail everywhere today, there must be living thoughts. Something like the Kant-Laplace theory leads people to remember in such a way that they grow old. But the true reality of the soul-spiritual beginnings of our universe from which its physical aspect has evolved will, if it is included in the right way in the curriculum, be a life-long source of rejuvenation. It is possible to form the curriculum not only by making methodical changes but through a complete transformation of the subject-matter in an anthroposophical sense such that a person has something throughout his life that he not only recollects in thoughts but which is a life-long source of perpetual rejuvenation. There must be a conscious aim to achieve a situation where people who are barely fifty years old are not old but that they can inwardly still sustain themselves on what they received in youth; that what they received as children can be a source of refreshment, a refreshing draught. But then it must be given in such a way that it is not merely suited to the development of the head but that it is fitting for the development of the whole human organism, which proceeds three or four times more slowly than the development of the head.

A comprehension of such things means to imbue the dead thoughts of natural scientists and, hence, also of our general education with life. Do not underestimate the great social significance of what is being said here. You might well think that this was of significance only in the strict domain of natural science itself. This is not so. Natural science exerts an influence upon the whole of modern education, on the full extent of the present phase of human evolution. These natural-scientific ideas extend right into Sunday newspapers and magazines; and even someone who only takes from his Sunday newspaper everything that constitutes his beliefs, the true and real beliefs that he feigns to uphold in his church or position of authority, is today infected by natural science, which can only impregnate everything with death, even if this death-like quality is evoked in the most spiritual of ways. These things must be perceived with absolute clarity.

So you see that anthroposophically oriented spiritual science is indeed concerned not merely with something that can satisfy a subjective curiosity but with something that has to make a deep impact upon the whole development of our time. And to repeat, for our consciousness that can be schooled by anthroposophy this influence upon the development of our time is connected with the knowledge of what took place between 1841 and 1879 and until 1917 in the evolution of humanity both supersensibly and in the sensory world, above and on the physical plane. These things cannot be taken sufficiently seriously; and indeed, there is a great deal that is not taken seriously enough at present. But the healing process of mankind will depend on people adapting to the importance of focussing upon feelings and thoughts about world evolution. We shall now devote attention to this.

If you look back at the last few decades, you may ask what—with the exception of certain individuals—has been the prevailing attitude towards questions with a wider perspective, towards the great questions confronting the world. There has throughout been the tendency to popularize the thoughts of modern science, to popularize these thoughts with the illustrative means available in modern times. When there are announcements that some aspect of modern science is to be presented with lantern slides, this creates a quite particular sensation and is especially encouraged. What has been the attitude of the social classes or groups with the greatest say towards the great questions of the world in modern times? There was considerable interest when someone was able to relate what he experienced on an expedition to the North Pole or when exploring Brazil. No reproach is intended in relation to such interests. When someone speaks of how he has managed to understand the mysteries of the cockchafer's eggs, one feels that it is necessary that—as a good member of the educated middle-class—one should listen to such lectures, even if after five minutes (unless roused by a lantern slide) one has fallen asleep. But where is the real will to elevate an idea that people have to a world-conception? It is thoroughly characteristic where such a will can be found, and everyone today is obliged to ponder about this. Where have the liveliest debates, the liveliest interests in questions relating to world-views, been for the last few decades? Where Social Democrats have been meeting. This is where world-views are promulgated. But in other strata of society there is no knowledge of this, because wherever possible good care is taken to avoid really knowing anything of human life.

But what kind of a world-view do Social Democrats form for themselves? One that works only with the same thoughts that are incorporated in machines; a view of the world that develops its conceptions only in the mechanical sphere: historical materialism, a materialistic conception of history, materialistic conception of social life. You can read about these ideas in every socialist newspaper. Most people do not do this, but it would be very useful to be informed. Those people who have been forced to attend to machines, who have nothing else to do from morning to evening and who—when they come away from the machines in the evening—again have to deal with a social organization that is actually a reflection of the machine, have a world-conception which regards the world as if it were a machine. They have developed a world-conception which does not reckon with anything individual. There is a true and thoroughly valid saying that 'death makes everything the same'; but one could also say that a world-conception which is concerned with the mechanical, with what is dead, also makes everything the same, extinguishes all individual existence, everything living. Thus all individual existence, everything living, would be extinguished by that world-conception that would derive its ideal from the machine. So long as these dire consequences were not apparent, people allowed themselves to dream or sleep through these things; they adopted the attitude of rejecting all questions related to wider world-perspectives and gradually lost the connection with all the impulses that are able to imbue human social and educational life with understanding. And the fact is that in more recent times the only people working with such questions of wider world-perspectives have been those with mechanistic thoughts. Even science itself has been dominated by mechanistic thoughts. If you read the book by Theodor Ziehen,[145] which is a model work for modern science, and read the final chapter, you will see that he belongs to those who say that natural science cannot attain to thoughts that engender ethics, morality and aesthetics; but then he goes on to say that everything that is not scientific is merely the stuff of fantasy. Between the lines, everything that is not scientific is subjected to slander. It is true that at the end of his book Theodor Ziehen says graciously: concepts such as freedom, ethics, morality and so on must be approached from other sides; any true science must reject the idea of responsibility. A human being can no more be responsible than a flower can be responsible for its ugliness.

From the standpoint of natural science, this is perfectly correct—if one's standpoint is one-sided, if the thoughts that one applies are purely those of the lifeless. But one is then applying thoughts that cannot reach the living, and certainly not the ego.

It is interesting how Theodor Ziehen speaks about the ego. In these lectures, which were transcribed and then printed so that they retain the style of lectures, he says the following: Gentlemen, the ego is a complicated concept; if you reflect on what the word 'ego' or 'I' leads you to think, what results from this? Firstly, you will think of your bodily nature, then of family connections, then your property and assets; and then you think of your name and titles (he omits orders and insignia) and then... well, he mentions other such things. What he is saying is that all that psychologists have elaborated is merely a fiction. Well, such a modern scientist, when he speaks about the ego, arrives at things that would never occur to anyone who seriously reflects on this matter, who considers what he means by the ego. But it is a serious matter that concepts based on lifeless things necessarily lead to the destruction, annihilation and devastation of life. A theory deriving from a lifeless machine which has been formulated as a social world-conception works not constructively when applied to a life-situation but destructively. Humanity has not resolved to understand this; and so it will have to experience things in their most extreme form. For what has happened? In that region where wellsprings of immense impulses for the future are to arise, in the East, the theory of the lifeless, the continuation of the mechanistic world-view in a social setting, is working destructively in the form of Leninism and Trotskyism.

Consider the situation with the seriousness it requires. Someone who values only the lifeless, and values only the lifeless also in man—even if he is so great a scholar as Theodor Ziehen—is not himself his own true social interpreter (and he would not have the courage for this) but Lenin[146] and Trotsky[147] are the ones who draw the right conclusions for human society. What Lenin and Trotsky implement are the consequences of thoughts fostered by a purely natural-scientific conception of the world. It is only because this natural-scientific world-conception makes compromises and does not draw the necessary conclusions from its ideas that it is not Leninism and Trotskyism.

It is also important that things are looked upon in terms of their actual reality. What is not true has an objective influence. Thoughts are realities; they are not mere concepts. It is not sufficient to say that even if no one knows anything about a lie it nevertheless exercises an influence. This is true; but it is also true to say that if a lie exists that is not recognized as a lie this does not change its influence; it works in the real world as a lie. An untruth may not be intentional, but it nevertheless works as a lie.

I may perhaps have already mentioned here that there are some books today which address the question of Christ Jesus from the standpoint of modern science. These books are most interesting, because they are uncompromisingly written. A Danish book comes first to mind.[148] There are also others which truly express what present-day psychologists and psychiatrists whose thinking is imbued with natural science are bound to think about Christ Jesus. What does Christ Jesus become in such books? He becomes an epileptic, a pathological case, someone predisposed to illness. And the Gospels are interpreted such that every chapter is full of stories about illnesses. This is of course all nonsense; but only someone who has spiritual insight is entitled to say that it is nonsense. From the standpoint of someone who accepts the validity of natural-scientific psychology and psychiatry this notion of Christ is perfectly correct, because it draws the right conclusions. And someone who as a modern psychiatrist speaks in this way is a better person, a more honest and truthful person, than someone who accepts modern psychiatry and nevertheless thinks differently about Christ, as do those pastors or priests who wholly accept the validity of natural science and yet make compromises.

A lie has an influence even if it is draped in piety, for it is a real power. It is above all necessary today that one does not bury life in compromises but that one always bears in mind what needs to be considered from particular aspects. If a modern psychiatrist does not want to regard Christ as an epileptic or madman (as present-day psychiatry would conceive of Him), he must abandon psychiatry as it is currently practised and stand firmly on the ground of spiritual science. If people were only capable of standing with absolute clarity on the foundations of what they are able to recognize, we would—in addition to what can be recognized—have the right impulses for what must continue to work further.

In recent days a note was handed to me about a book with which I was already familiar but which had certainly horrified the lady (for it was probably a lady who had written the note). The note informed me of what Alexander Moszkowski[149] has written. I do not have the book here, but from the note you will get some idea of the contents: "'Anyone who has ever burdened the desks of a grammar school will never forget the hours spent 'enjoying' Plato's account of the conversations between Socrates and his friends, unforgettable because of the infinite tedium that streams from these discourses. And one may perhaps recall that one actually found the discourses incredibly stupid; but of course one did not dare to express this view, for the man in question was, after all, Socrates, the 'Greek philosopher'." Alexander Moszkowski's book *Socrates—the Idiot* (Verlag Dr Eysler & Co., Berlin) settles everything thoroughly with this wholly unwarranted estimation of the good Athenian. In this short, entertainingly written book the historian Moszkowski undertakes nothing less than wholly to strip Socrates of his dignity as a philosopher. The title *Socrates—the Idiot* is meant literally. It may well be supposed that the book will stimulate learned discussions.'

Someone who likes making compromises will of course say that we have been made thoroughly aware that Socrates was a great man and not an idiot, and now along comes Moszkowski and says what he does! But today it is necessary to think quite differently about something of this kind. Anyone who knows Moszkowski is aware that he stands firmly upon the ground of the natural-scientific world-conception to the point of embracing the Quantum Theory, that he may therefore be classed as one of the most extreme representatives of the modern stance of natural science. And it must be said that Moszkowski is far more honest than those others who also think that they adhere to the standpoint of natural science but do not think that they should regard Socrates as a fool who has contributed nothing to the ideas that have formed our intellectual world. Instead they make the compromise of setting Socrates up as a great man.

The point is that things do not right themselves today for the simple reason that people lack that sense for truth whereby they uncompromisingly draw the necessary conclusions. Thus someone who wants to value Socrates today should not be attributing validity to Moszkowski's presuppositions.

However, this is difficult today and has been so for three or four centuries. Things have been left to follow their own course until they have developed into what they have become in the last three to four years. They must be understood in their fundamental soul-spiritual character, which is where their deeper impulses reside. It is particularly necessary to bear in mind today that truth and a sense of truth must penetrate into human souls! Then the things that are viewed in the light of this sense of truth and are illumined by it will be able to manifest their true aspect; and simply because one sees things in their true aspect, one will necessarily turn to spiritual science. For there is much urgency in the way that the present speaks, and matters such as educational questions, questions related to teaching, can be studied today from a spiritual-scientific standpoint. Just as the question regarding the different speeds of the development of the head and the heart is important for education, so are there many questions that are fundamental, important and significant for social life, historical life and legal affairs. We must extract ourselves from the terrible belief—in which we are trapped—in the authority of what natural science asserts. This is sorely necessary at present. What the scientific world-conception designates as 'real' consists of ideas that can never extend to the realm of human social life. Humanity is presently living today under the influence of this shortcoming. If one considers things at a deeper level, this is what one sees.

This is what I wanted to say to you today. May each one of you now come to the conclusion that it is essential to open our eyes and view things in the light that we can derive through spiritual science.

I spoke yesterday of how Orientals regard our development. In many respects Orientals, with their naive and intuitive spiritual capacities, perceive our inconsistencies and our tendency to compromise; and there are now critical perceptions from leading Orientals which are significant and interesting to pursue. There is in the Asiatic East increasingly the view that the Orient must take the further evolution of humanity in hand. If there were more understanding for what is proclaimed from here as spiritual science, these views could well be dispelled! But this understanding must also be something living; one must not only want to receive something interesting through spiritual science that gives one an inner sense of pleasure, but one must want to have something that pervades one's whole life. And one must be able to have the view that it is only through the insights of spiritual science that there can be a real understanding of social, moral and legal questions. What people have thought for several decades under the influence of the world-view of natural science is not equal to the demands that present realities place before us. No, it is at best able to reflect those views that people now develop, views which would kill the whole world spiritually because they are derived from the world of the lifeless. In future times, when people will again think more objectively about these things, when the passions that so greatly influence judgements will have abated (and I am fully convinced that this is possible), it will be said: One of the most important characteristics of the period around 1917 was that the world-conception which was conceived only for the head and makes everyone senile had come to be adopted. It will eventually (and perhaps in the not too distant future) be called Wilsonism, in reference to the great schoolmaster from whom a large portion of humanity is imbibing a so-called social and political world-view. Not for nothing is a mere school-wisdom that has absolutely no notion of anything spiritual one of the most important political forces in the form of Wilsonism. This is important, it is a hugely significant symptom of our time. And yet it is not possible today to speak really penetratingly and comprehensively about these things. But from the indications that I have given today you will have realized how important it is to try to understand them, how infinitely important it is to grasp them not only through emotions and feelings but through knowledge.

I have perhaps also already mentioned something here that I shall say again, because it is important. It is not difficult now to express views about Wilson here in Central Europe; but I can refer to the fact that in a cycle that was held long before these events, when the whole world including Central Europe still admired Wilson, I characterized him exactly as I am doing now.[150] It is a case of approaching the impulses governing the present time—and do so erroneously—from far deeper sources. In the context of our anthroposophical work our friends had the opportunity to see how, long before there was an outward need to see things in their true light, attention was drawn to the right way of viewing them. Let us hope that they will be understood better in the future than people were willing to understand them in the past! And one thing that I shall especially lay upon your hearts is that much that is presented in the realm of our anthroposophical knowledge can be understood infinitely better than there has hitherto been the will to understand it. It can penetrate even deeper into people's hearts and souls and awakened to a more intense life than has previously been the case. May this happen! For what happens in this respect has a connection with much that can potentially bring not disaster but salvation to human beings, and be a remedy for many past failures and for further missed opportunities should people be only willing to listen to what can be achieved outside spiritual science. Even among our friends there are many who have a double entry in their book of life. The one entry has to do with their anthroposophical studies and books in order to gain something for the private use of their hearts and souls. The other entry relates to outer life, where they give something solely on the basis of natural-scientific authority. They often do not notice that this is so; but it is good if they were conscientiously to examine their souls in this respect so that there can be a harmonious interplay between these two entries.

Human life can after all only be conducted in a uniform way. The spirit must also pervade the world-conception of natural science; and the religious life must likewise be penetrated by that light which can be gained through spiritual science. Take hold of these things that I have said to you in the way they are intended, and they will lead these studies of the times up into supersensible heights in such a way that they can become alive in your imaginations. You will then see that an anthroposophical education offers not only a training for the head but that it is also able to give humanity an education for the heart. It is indeed a heart education; it serves the whole of humanity, not only a humanity that would otherwise die at the age of twenty-seven. It enables people to live courageously and capably for the whole of their lives; whereas an education that does not consider the different speeds of head and heart development will make them senile, nervous, lacking in harmony and at odds with themselves. Observe life itself and you will find this confirmed, for life can be a great teacher with respect to what anthroposophically oriented spiritual science draws down from spiritual heights. Take everything that I have said in all the different aspects that I have spoken of today as addressed to your hearts, my dear friends, for the education of our heart through the spirit of the world; and maintain the bond that links us together as members of our movement. Let us work together in this way, let us resolve to continue our work as well as we can wherever we happen to be.

Lecture 14

I HAVE already drawn attention here to the fact that one can again and again hear an objection that is directed against concerning oneself with spiritual-scientific truths, an objection which, moreover, clearly betokens that it derives from a marked laziness of the human soul. It is the objection of those who say: I do not have a problem with the idea that when someone passes through the gate of death he enters another world of a spiritual nature; but as to how this world is formed and what is its nature I shall wait to see! Here on this Earth one has to devote oneself to one's material obligations, and one will surely see what another world is like when one finds oneself in this other world. It cannot be denied that this objection has something very convenient about it. Only someone with an interest in spiritual-scientific truths is in a position to examine this objection carefully, for through such an examination he can be strengthened in his view of the necessity to devote attention to the truths of spiritual science. In order to give you some kind of a notion of such an examination, we shall from a particular point of view call to mind the relationship that exists between human life here and that human life which takes its course between death and a new birth.

Let us be clear that, in the course of his life here in the physical body, a person receives only a part of what is connected with his life into his ordinary consciousness, for events constantly take place which are connected with our life but pass fleetingly by it in such a way that we do not bring them clearly before our ordinary consciousness. We sometimes bring facts to a degree of semi-consciousness but not the full consequences that these facts of everyday life have for us. If you think back in the evening over the events of your day, you will think above all of the places you have been to (we could also choose something else, but this will suffice) and the people you encountered. All this has a great significance for you, for your immediate surroundings are reflected in your soul. And of the many things that are thus reflected in your soul, there is something that comes only to the smallest degree to consciousness in daily life. There is, nevertheless, a great difference between whether you were, say, at nine o'clock this morning near Stuttgart railway station or out in the forest, for in each case something totally different will have been living in your soul. We do not normally appreciate that this has a deep significance. It is only from what I might describe as less obvious indications that it is often possible to derive the significance of such matters. Take the following situation. You can confirm it—naturally not in this case but in other cases—if you pay some attention to life. Thus you came here this evening. Someone sitting in the first row had, shall we say, some reason to leave the room before I finished speaking; he stands up, walks along the aisle and goes out. A person sitting in the third row saw him, but (so at least I suppose) this person in the third row has been listening attentively—which does after all happen—and in his ordinary consciousness he was only half or fleetingly aware of this individual who went out. He will be able to observe that he may perhaps dream remarkably little of what I have said here; for if one could produce some statistics about this it would probably be the case that the number of venerated listeners who do much dreaming about what I say here would not be so very great. But you will easily be able to see—not through this example but through a similar one—that you dream of the person who got up and went out. That is to say: you will in numerous instances of life be able to observe that in sleep consciousness you fall back on those things that pass fleetingly by your consciousness during the day.

This is why people know so little of what they have been dreaming; for much of what is dreamed is of such a kind that it passes somewhat imperceptibly by during the day. That which is clearly grasped in consciousness is for the most part very little dreamed about. Something becomes the subject of dreams only if it is linked with certain feelings or sensations that one does not bring clearly to consciousness. And when someone wakes up, he recalls so little of his dreams because he paid little attention in his previous period of life to what he dreamt about. This also plays its part in the limited capacity to remember dreams. In short, what I want to say is that countless events pass rapidly by in human life which only very fleetingly enter our consciousness but which have a great significance for the life of the human soul, even though they remain within the depths of the unconscious or subconscious. Everything that, if I may so express it, takes its course between the lines of life initially has great significance when a person has passed through the gate of death.

We have frequently described this time that a human individual spends between death and a new birth from many different points of view. Thus one thing constantly mingles with another, and only by choosing a variety of viewpoints does one arrive at a certain understanding of this realm. Everything that passes imperceptibly by ordinary consciousness is then unfolded when someone has passed through the gate of death; and I should like to call what he initially experiences over a lengthy period as the unfolding of pictures. Essentially it is a process of passing through experiences of imaginative consciousness that a person then undergoes. A considerable number of pictures are unfolded of scenes of life that we have to a very limited degree brought to consciousness; and of what we have brought to consciousness here, the things that are unfolded are those by which we were likewise little affected here. The other things that came clearly to our consciousness appear after death more as a recollection, as memory-pictures; but what was little attended to here is unfolded as though in pictures of present realities.

Today it is for me especially important to point out that the first third of life between death and a new birth essentially has to do with the unfolding of pictures, it is essentially concerned with a life in imaginations. These imaginations can help us to establish a connection between those of us who have remained here and those who, as people karmically connected with us, have passed through the gate of death. Then comes the second third, when this soul-spiritual human life is to a greater extent filled with inspirations. It then becomes clear to a person what significance the pictures that he initially experienced have in the whole context of the world, how he is incorporated in the world context. For everything that a person experiences has a significance for the world as a whole. One should not think that it is a matter of indifference that one once met someone to whom one perhaps paid little attention when one was in his vicinity. This is unfolded in pictures, and that which is of significance for world evolution as a whole comes to revelation in inspirations in the second third of life between death and a new birth.

In the last third, a similar aspect of life is enacted in intuitions. A person has then to place himself in what constitutes his soul-spiritual surroundings; he lives as though submerged with his consciousness in his soul-spiritual surroundings. And in this last third, he prepares through being thus immersed for becoming incorporated in the physical body after birth or conception. The intuitions in the last third of life between death and a new birth are the introduction to that intuition—which is of course then subconscious or unconscious—which consists in that the individual in question dives down into the body that has been bequeathed to him in the hereditary stream of parents, grandparents and so on. And something is left to the person when he now makes the transition from the world of soul and spirit to the physical world. As you consider this, reflect on the fact that a person actually lives for a long time in soul-spiritual intuitions and is accustomed to living in them; and so he will want to retain some aspect of what has become customary when he has entered into the physical body. This he indeed does. For what is the main soul-aspiration in the first seven years until the change of teeth (you can read about this in the booklet *The Education of the Child from the Standpoint of Spiritual Science*)? As I have previously said, a craving for imitation. The child always tries to do what is done in its surroundings; it does not proceed from its own intentions; it transplants itself into the actions of those who live in its surroundings and imitates them. This is an echo of the intuitions in the last third of life between death and a new birth. Thus we are born as imitative beings, because we translate into physical life what we have for a long time been doing yonder in another world in a soul-spiritual manner. One understands how a person grows into this physical life by turning one's gaze back to what he became used to doing in the spiritual world.

Here you see yourself confronted by a thought from spiritual science which is of a kind with many that must arise during the coming centuries and millennia of spiritual life. These thoughts will change much with respect to what people have hitherto concerned themselves with. Just consider that it has for the last few centuries been normal that, when the question of immortality is the subject of reflection, there is a focus on thinking about what is after death. People always think: Can a person retain what he develops in physical life beyond death? This is what is of primal importance to them. This question of immortality is certainly important, but it will acquire a different aspect if one considers what I could refer to as the other half of the question of immortality, when one is not interested in what follows on after death and what emerges in consequence of life here on the Earth but, rather, when one will ask how what we experience here in the physical body has a connection with what we experienced previously. For the life that we have previously experienced, our life here is the beyond. It is primarily in this sense that thoughts in this regard are being considered. People will see that they can only understand life here on the Earth if they understand it as a continuation of the spiritual life from whence they have come. They will begin to take an interest again in that life which precedes this earthly life. One can indeed say that, with the exception of the last third of the ninteenth century, people still had a certain interest in the question of immortality, but only in so far as the spiritual life in immortality is a continuation of earthly life. Philosophical scholars have had such an interest, but—despite asserting that the science or scholarship which they cultivate is without prejudice—such scholars are in many respects miserable wretches who, while believing that their science is without prejudice, have nevertheless done none other than perpetuate the prejudices that have come from certain streams. Consider that the Church at the time of Origen[151] condemned the idea of the pre-existence of the soul, that it therefore condemned Origen because he taught this idea of pre-existence, so that the Church was in a certain predicament. There was Origen, the Church's greatest teacher, and it could not be denied that Origen taught this doctrine. But this was forbidden by the Church. Thus there was indeed a predicament. It had become customary throughout the Middle Ages to teach nothing about pre-existence. The professors of philosophy skilfully continued this, and those who wrote about philosophy likewise, even though they believed that they were unprejudiced in their thinking. They did the same also with regard to other questions, of which I have already presented examples here. Now it is above all necessary to make it clear that the direction of thoughts, the way people view reality, will have to experience a radical change through spiritual science. This earthly life will only appear with its true value when there is a conscious perception that it is a continuation of a spiritual life. And it can only be understood when it is conceived of as such. But then if one regards the matter in this way, one will also gain a more healthy judgement for the other side of the question. When one becomes clearer that this earthly life has a significance for the life in yonder world, that a person in that world aspires to come here to the Earth in order to have this earthly life because he needs it, one will ask far more about the value of this earthly life out of such presuppositions than people have done hitherto.

But there is one matter that can especially indicate how significant it is to ask about the value of this earthly life. Two things are often not greatly distinguished from one another. A person thinks—and: a person has thoughts. But the two things are actually very different. Thinking is a power that someone has, an activity; and this only leads to thoughts. Now, we bring the activity of thinking, this power that lives in thinking from the life between death and a new birth, into this earthly life. We apply this power of thinking to outward sense-perceptions through the senses and form for ourselves thoughts about the surroundings that we have around us here. But these things in our surroundings have no significance for the life between death and a new birth, for there they are nothing. They have an existence only here for the senses. Hence the thoughts that we form for ourselves about those things that are spread out before our senses likewise have no significance for the life after death; but it is of significance for the life after death that we bring something to the power of thinking, for this power of thinking remains with us throughout the life between death and a new birth. The thoughts that we take from our sense-perceptions cannot yield us any fruit after death. They merely serve there as points of reference for recalling the ego during the life between birth and death.

Think of two human individuals. The one has no interest in what one can learn about life in the spiritual worlds through something such as spiritual science. He merely forms thoughts about what the senses offer and what ordinary science teaches; and this, too, is none other than what is offered by the senses. And he says: I want to wait until I enter the spiritual world before finding out anything about it. These people, I would say, are from a certain standpoint not in such a bad way as those who appeared in the nineteenth century and believed with all their scientific convictions that they had to deny the very existence of a spiritual world, in accordance with the statement that the playwright makes through one such person: If it is true that there is a God in heaven, I am an atheist![152] The atheism of the nineteenth century was born from convictions of this nature, from such 'thoughtful soul-searchings'. But let us take a person who simply does not want anything to do with forming thoughts about the spiritual world. This would be the one person. The other lets himself form thoughts about the spiritual world. These thoughts are different from those that one receives through the senses. It cannot, after all, be denied that the thoughts are different. For this is already apparent in that the thoughts through which a spiritual world is not apprehended are—in the view of most people living today—the clever thoughts, the real thoughts; whereas the thoughts that spiritual science describes are crazy, fantastic or just plain daft (and so on).

But let us take these two people. In what situation are these people when they have passed through the portal of death? The one who has received no thoughts about the spiritual worlds and who therefore has nothing by way of thoughts about the spiritual worlds to pass through his soul is, as a soul-being after death, in the same position as someone who has a physical organization but has nothing to eat and has to go hungry. For the thoughts that we form here about the spiritual worlds are the nourishment for one of the principal forces that remain to us after death: for the power of thinking. We have the capacity to think, just as we have here the capacity to be hungry, but this capacity of hunger cannot be nourished between death and a new birth. We can have Imagination, Inspiration and Intuition between death and a new birth, but we cannot have thoughts as such. We must acquire these here. We must enter into life between birth and death in order to acquire thoughts here. We are nourished by these thoughts that we have acquired here throughout the time between death and a new birth, and we hunger for these thoughts if we do not have them. That is the difference. Someone who does not want to have any thoughts here about the spiritual worlds is condemned to spiritual starvation; and someone who is able to nourish himself and, hence, to live between death and a new birth is of the nature of the second person to whom I referred, who has the kind of thoughts that we cultivate here. Thus if materialism alone were to become the prevailing view of human beings, they would—if I may put it thus—in future increasingly succumb to a typhus of hunger between death and a new birth. The consequence of this would be that in their following incarnation they would enter the physical world in a stunted form. The spiritual world would go into decline, and the physical world would—in the future that humanity still has to pass through during this earthly age—go into decline together with the spiritual world. The notion of 'après nous le déluge' has already been brought to a certain awareness for an unsuspecting humanity, which does not know what this is really about.[153] This remark, après nous le déluge, even if it was not actually made, lies at the very foundation of the soul in a materialistic time. It has absolutely no significance for anyone who has knowledge of reality; for what humanity does in the present, whether or not it wants to immerse souls in the spiritual worlds, is what also lays the foundation for the future of evolution. The salvation of the Earth itself depends upon humanity not ceasing to form thoughts about the spiritual worlds. Those who live in the present would have increasingly to comprehend this; for immeasurably much depends on the course of human evolution being understood in a spiritual way.

We have tried to develop important thoughts about the spiritual worlds, for eventually the spiritual worlds do after all reach right into our physical world even if one does not understand them. And we have developed thoughts of the most diverse kind. Now, someone who can really think will have the capacity to comprehend the significant factor of this spiritual-scientific thinking for reality. One simply cannot understand reality as a whole if one only wants to think in accordance with natural science, just as one also cannot understand material existence if one only thinks as a natural scientist and not along the lines of spiritual science. I should like to relate to you a very strange and paradoxical example.

I believe that I have already emphasized here some time ago that a highly significant, substantial book appeared a year and a half ago by an outstanding naturalist of the present, Oscar Hertwig, a pupil of Haeckel, entitled *The Evolution of Organisms; a Refutation of Darwin's Theory of Chance.*[154] This is an excellent book which occupies a place of great eminence in the scientific research of the present. I have availed myself of many opportunities to emphasize its essential and predominant aspects. For it is a remarkable book also from the point of view of cultural history. You know that in 1869 Eduard von Hartmann appeared with his *Philosophy of the Unconscious,*[155] in the heyday of Darwinism which was celebrating its materialistic interpretation at that time. Eduard von Hartmann expressed his opposition to it. Naturalists then cried out: Well, he is a mere dilettante of a philosopher who speaks about spirit and understands nothing about natural science! I have often described what happened next. One day a book appeared[156] of which even the Haeckel pupil Oskar Schmidt[157] wrote: Someone has appeared who understands something of natural science. He has furnished Hartmann with this! We could not say it better; he identifies with us, and we shall greet him as one of ours! There was a great deal of publicity on the naturalists' part, and a second edition became necessary. Then the author made himself known: it was Eduard von Hartmann! They stopped all the publicity. Such a rebuff had to happen in order to show people that those who speak of the spirit are just as clever as those who deny the spirit. Eduard von Hartmann continued to write much to indicate how one-sided the thinking of Darwinism is. He did not find much approval. But one can say that after calm, well-schooled research a man like Oscar Hertwig has arrived at the point of thinking in such a way that Eduard von Hartmann had already expressed himself in 1869. He even often quotes him in his book. And everything is built up in an exemplary way in this book *The Evolution of Organisms*. One can see in it a model example of what could grow, and has grown, out of the natural-scientific method of the present.

Now you see, a few weeks ago a kind of continuation of this book appeared by the same man: *Resisting Social, Ethical and Political Darwinism*.[158] One can scarcely conceive of a more stupid book than this one, with which Oscar Hertwig has followed his first, groundbreaking work. It could not be more unsatisfactory, more tinny. So you see that on the ground of our spiritual science it is necessary to cultivate a certain lack of trust in authority, for if our dear friends—on the basis of the praise that I have lavished on a truly remarkable book (and I shall continue to do so)—now buy the second book on this authority in the expectation of finding something great, they will be very disappointed. Spiritual science seeks to encourage us to acquire a truly free faculty of judgement; to be prepared at every moment and in every direction freely to confront the phenomena that come towards us. A belief in authority cannot be cultivated in such circumstances within spiritual-scientific endeavours, since otherwise we get not spiritual science but a caricature of it. So what is the source of what I have described? It comes down to the fact that one can today be a great, epoch-making naturalist, that is, one can be capable of developing everything relating to material events and their manifestations in accordance with the methods of the nineteenth and twentieth centuries; but as soon as one then begins to reflect about that which lies in the human sphere, about what lives in someone when human beings are socially engaged with one another, when they live together ethically and morally, when they want to develop political structures, in the moment when one begins to reflect upon those things where the spiritual element is involved, one can—despite being a naturalist of genius—be an absolute dimwit, for natural science is of absolutely no avail here. And such a literary example has appeared in our time in order really to substantiate what one can thus discern from spiritual science and place it fully within reality. For one may read this second book by Oscar Hertwig and one will observe that one does not actually find a single thought about what relates to social, ethical and political life; and such thoughts indeed have their place in the present, in that it is not exactly rich in fruitful social, ethical and—especially—political ideas. But this, too, is because purely natural-scientific thinking is hugely over-valued. Oscar Hertwig does his level best in this respect; he would like to divert this natural-scientific thinking away from social, ethical and political thinking. But since he lacks any insight into this latter sphere, it is of no avail if he dismisses the former. There are in this book the most curious spiritual gymnastics. I shall draw attention to one of these, always with the proviso that the first book which I have cited is excellent.

People do not notice that Oscar Hertwig is an authority; our time is not one to believe in authority, but it seizes hold of every authority that has an official stamp. People allow themselves to be instructed; there is much that they do not even notice. But in his second book Oscar Hertwig wants to make it clear what one must do in order to think in a properly scientific way. He can do this, but he does not understand what is involved. It can also be done instinctively. The methods are splendid; one needs only to be trained for this, one does not need to have to develop thoughts about what one does. Oscar Hertwig therefore comes to the following strange sequence of thoughts. He speaks of how one should undertake scientific research in order to come to know things in one's surroundings. Then he says: Astronomers have given us the great model for physical, chemical and biological thinking, and it would be a question of people learning to think about physical, chemical and living phenomena in the way that astronomers think about the phenomena of the heavens. It is very suggestive if one then says: One must imitate the greatness of the thinking of Kepler, Copernicus and Newton in order to understand the phenomena that are around one! But just think what is hidden behind this! The phenomena of life are around us; the facts are very close to us, and we are constantly coming up against them. And now we are to be the recipients of a science whereby we are oriented towards realities that lie as far from us as possible; and it is therefore because we are as far removed as possible from the realities of the phenomena of the heavens that we are to develop from this the knowledge of what actually surround us. One cannot form a thought that is dafter than this. But thousands and thousands of people may read about such a crazy idea and have no suspicion that such stupidities are corrupting the whole of modern thinking, that when they are gobbled up they inevitably have the effect of increasingly estranging people from reality. One cannot then even look into questions concerning social, ethical or political structures if one proceeds from such a thinking and such statements. It is one of the tasks of spiritual science to survey with absolute clarity what resides within the so-called cultural life of the present.

I said that it had to be our concern to give some indications of the spiritual forces that extend their influence into the ordinary physical world. We have again and again spoken of how in his life man is, as it were, involved with three cultural streams; in the luciferic, the ahrimanic and in one that is actually in accordance with human evolution. I have often indicated that one should not say: I shall avoid the luciferic influence, I shall avoid the ahrimanic influence—if one avoids these, one will surely become immersed in them; but one must develop some clarity about this, one must really study and come to understand the way that man is placed within these three streams. One must make knowledge of Lucifer and Ahriman a part of one's life.

There is much in the social and historical structure of mankind in recent centuries or millennia that has been very strongly under the sway of luciferic impulses which have emanated from human beings. I could say much about what has thus been influenced by Lucifer, but I should like to mention just one aspect where each person will immediately be able to perceive this luciferic influence.

It is, is it not, true that a large part is played in the way in which people relate to the various aspects of their life, the various standpoints that they adopt, by ambition or vanity. There would surely never be any aspiration for this or that post if the social structure had not represented an opportunity for this vanity to be spurred in one or another direction. Everything to do with titles, ranks and Orders rests ultimately on this luciferic element. And now just try in an unprejudiced way to form thoughts with respect to the extent to which the way that people's attitude to life is purely influenced by the fishing-rods of ambition and the bait associated with them. Just try to consider how people are placed with one above the others and someone else below the others; how social organizations reckon with this ambition. Try to form a clear idea of how this has built up the social structure. Lucifer has played a very significant part in all of this.

Let us consider another phenomenon which is now beginning to be practised and admired; and the place to contemplate such things in a proper, down-to-earth way is here within the arts or humanities. Among the various things that are now coming to be favoured by many at present, you will if you pay sufficient attention find what are now called 'ability tests'. Ability tests serve to separate the gifted from the ordinary ranks of children and young people. A real idol-worship is threatening to be developed with these ability tests. How is this done? Trained psychologists are enlisted who understand nothing about the soul but understand psychology all the better for it; psychologists who are educated in accordance with the methods of the present and who are thereby capable of seeking out the most talented from a group of young people or children in order that the right person can later be in the right place as a matter of course. The belief is that fewer will in future be enticed by ambition or vanity, and instead there are these ability tests. These tests are related to speed of comprehension and to memory. Meaningless words are written down, and the one who can retain them more quickly has a better memory than the one whose capacity to retain them is less speedy. Then there are intelligence tests. One word, a second word, a third word with no connection with the others, is given, and then one lets the pupils find a connection. Thus one writes, for example, the words 'robber' and 'mirror'. One person thinks: the robber sees himself in a mirror. Another thinks: I have a mirror in my room, a robber creeps in and I see him in the mirror. The latter has thought in a more complicated way, he is therefore more gifted. Then some statistics are added, and those who are the most intelligent are fished out; they are then selected as those who are the right people to put in the appropriate place.

You see, anyone who, from such presuppositions as have now been established here, makes an objection to these wonderful achievements of the present is considered to be a right and proper fool who knows nothing of what it is all about.

Now let us translate all this into our spiritual-scientific perspective. What is one testing when one tests someone in this way? One is not testing anything that has to do with his soul. It is only necessary to consider one thing: that probably the most significant people of the past, those who reached the highest level of achievement, would according to such tests have been considered to be less gifted. Consider even someone like Helmholtz,[159] who is regarded by people today as a celebrity; if he had been subjected to such an ability test, he would certainly not have been appointed to the post that he subsequently attained. These ability tests have absolutely nothing to do with the development of the soul-capacities of the human individuality but rather with the sum of ahrimanic forces that reside within man. It is not the person who is being tested but the ahrimanic powers engendered within him through undertaking this test. And just as one has hitherto been reckoning with luciferic powers, so does one now begin to count on ahrimanic powers and establish a social structure which is built up purely on the ahrimanic element. To be sure, such things can only be perceived by those who really take spiritual-scientific insights into account, who want to perceive the world spiritually. For what I have now related to you about ability tests is regarded as one of the most significant achievements of the present, namely that the social structure of the future can be built up on the foundation of this test. And the poor general public, which is after all not prone to believe in authority, does not even have the possibility of reflecting upon what is entailed with such a matter. It does not have the possibility of forming clear thoughts about all this. However, it is this that matters.

If you form thoughts today from much of what we have been considering regarding what initially has to happen for mankind, what has to happen in the sense of the stream of spiritual evolution, you will ask the right questions. You will then try to understand human individualities in order to bring to them what cannot but be interesting. You will then not set out to test ahrimanic capacities, for these ahrimanic capacities will lead to humanity being treated purely as a collection of machines. Only the mind in the outward bodily nature is being tested. A person is tested only in so far as he is a machine when one subjects him to this ability test; and one brings about a social selection that makes only the best kinds of physical machine into leaders of humanity. There is never any reflection about what lies at the foundation of the soul, which cannot come to the surface through such tests. But I shall not reproach anyone for pursuing such things in an idolatrous way, for someone who does not concern himself with spiritual science can do no other than adhere to the judgement that this is the most intelligent thing that one can do in the present. But this gradually leads very far from real human life, from human realities. It leads into abstract areas, into what is dead in human life and governed only by the spirituality of Ahriman. One must see the full seriousness of such matters, how people are drawn away from reality. And this is something that comes towards one with particular intensity at present: that people are drawn away from reality. Anyone who has no sense for spiritual reality gradually loses the sense for the ordinary outward reality that surrounds him every day, unless he is compelled through his profession or some other factor to pay attention to reality.

I shall give you an example of this. Something very endearing happened in recent days. An article appeared in a widely-read newspaper by Fritz Mauthner, the linguistics specialist.[160] In this article Fritz Mauthner, who is a remarkably clever man, makes mockery of a little book which appeared in the collection *From Nature and the Spirit-World*[161] and which presents astrological ideas in the way they have developed wholly in the sense of modern materialistic science (and in the way that a present-day university professor would do so). At the end the author describes Goethe's horoscope and argues that one could show through this how things happened in the course of Goethe's life. But actually the good professor is merely having fun at the expense of those who appreciate horoscopes. He wants to classify them as something that can be interpreted in a particular way. Fritz Mauthner carries on mocking through three pages of the *Berliner Tageblatt*. People were unable to understand why he did all this mocking. There was actually not the slightest reason to mock. Indeed, he has the same opinion as the one who wrote the little book; both regard astrology from the same standpoint. And very soon the *Tageblatt* conveyed a correction by the author, where he said that he did not understand Mauthner, that he had not expressly said in every other line that he was mocking astrology but he actually had no more interest in it than Fritz Mauthner; he was fully in agreement with him. The *Berliner Tageblatt*—newspapers are very clever—adds that there was no reason to take the author's part and to reproach Fritz Mauthner for his misunderstandings. Fritz Mauthner had, after all, been for many years the drama critic of the *Berliner Tageblatt* and is now writing letters about drama for this newspaper.

For his part, Fritz Mauthner says that he has nothing to say about this counter-criticism from the author. Thus there was the strange fact that two people were wholly in agreement with one another but the one is having a go at the other. Thus Fritz Mauthner becomes furious if he merely hears something about astrology, or if someone writes something about horoscopes. It would otherwise not be conceivable that he should have written this article. He writes as if the other were the most passionate of astrologers who wanted to impose on people the validity of his interpretation of Goethe's horoscope. Here you have an example of how two people are quarrelling with one another, the one—Fritz Mauthner—on his own account and the other who is compelled to do so because Fritz Mauthner started attacking him; two people between whom there is not the slightest difference in their opinions. How can this be? Something of the kind can only occur when two people have absolutely nothing to do with the narrowly limited reality in question, when both are living out of something other than reality. It is a most glorious example, for Fritz Mauthner is a very clever man, but behind all the talk there is nothing whatsoever. There is not the slightest reason for someone to behave in this way.

Here you have an example of a wholly logical building up of thoughts that have absolutely nothing to do with reality. Thoughts enter in which cease to have anything to do with spiritual reality, for what is thought then completely loses its connection to reality. It is important to understand something of this kind. This is also the terrible seriousness of the situation. For ultimately, it does not especially matter whether Fritz Mauthner and the Heidelberg professor hack away at one another and their worlds have absolutely no meaning because no reality lies behind them, or whether there were two politicians, one of whom is speaking in America and the other in Europe, and who may likewise perhaps be in agreement despite their total differences. If all people who speak in this way have nothing to do with what lives in a real sense in things, there arises this estrangement from reality which then extends further. It has indeed extended further. This is merely a grotesque example that I have given, this example of Fritz Mauthner and Professor Boll. But you see this everywhere, for this is how people carry on today. And where does it lead? To quarrels. It is relatively easy to be united when one is dealing with reality; but if one relates to reality in this sort of way, it leads to arguments. People will gradually see how much of our catastrophic events is connected with this fundamental mood of the present, and how serious this is. Then you go out—and the newspaper concerned is one of the most read in Germany—and ask the many readers whether they see the grotesque and paradoxical aspect of what is coming to light here! All this passes them by. But the events do not simply pass by, they have their furious effects and influences. For what is happening in such a situation is none other than the misuse of human spiritual forces. Just think if these spiritual forces that are being used for nothing—because they are estranged from reality—were applied in the right sense, this would contribute to a greater awareness of reality and would lie within the normal stream of development; but as it is, Ahriman reaps the benefits. It is an estrangement from reality for the middle stream*, but when it happens it slips into a sphere where it begins to matter. This is where the matter becomes serious. Something passes everyone by, but then it slips into another sphere and brings about real events. It brings about events that do not correspond to the true circumstances; for the way that this brings events about is described purely superficially, purely rationally, purely intellectually.

Everyone thinks that our present age does not trust authority. People test everything and what is best they keep! Nevertheless, it does of course happen that they do trust authority. Someone like Fritz Mauthner has countless followers who believe everything he says. They will naturally be impressed by such an article. Think how many thoughts are prompted by such an article. They are all drawn into the ahrimanic sphere in which the article flows. The whole thing is unreal, and events are thereby thrust into unreality. This is what matters.

What one should do with these things, my dear friends, is this: ever and again to indicate the immense seriousness that lies behind such observations. For what I have characterized in individual cases can be met with absolutely everywhere. We are at a time when we achieve something right only if we resolve to see things absolutely clearly, to view them without prejudice, to relate in an unprejudiced way to life. This is our task. And spiritual science can guide us towards it by rightly building the bridge between the inner human life and reality; for in this respect people live today in the most terrible hazy mist. It has to be so, for people must learn to rely on themselves. They must learn to create clarity for themselves and not to receive clarity through authority. This must become one of the important achievements of spiritual-scientific endeavours for the individual human soul, namely to gain a free, clear, unprejudiced judgement concerning what life surrounds one with; and to desist from the prevailing tendency of the whole of humanity today to sleep through

---

* It is not entirely clear what Rudolf Steiner means by 'the middle stream'. From the context it may be supposed that he is referring to the social realm of human engagement.—Translator

events. People sleep through what is in front of their eyes. And covering them up in a hazy mist is the endeavour of those who come one-sidedly with all kinds of monistic or 'scientifically underpinned' (as they say) ideas but who are to all intents and purposes materialists. For they claim, even assert, that they are building the bridge to reality. They lead away from reality. Tell Oscar Hertwig that he was observing things in an unreal way and he will laugh at you; he cannot see that this is what he is doing. But as spiritual scientists you will inevitably receive something like a sting when you read that the immediate facts of life are to be considered in accordance with the model of celestial phenomena, where the facts lie as far away as possible. Thus to go through life paying attention not to what we see in books but to what we experience before our very eyes from morning to evening—not, of course, when we are among anthroposophists— offers such things that we must attend to in an unprejudiced way. For mankind is standing at a significant turning point. And what I said is not a criticism of the time but merely an expression of what is necessary in that people say: This is so. It is good that it has come to this point, for people are thereby called upon to stand on their own feet, to become independent. The Gods have not set themselves the task of guiding human beings through evolution as soul-spiritual automata lacking in independence, and they must therefore also enter into situations such as the present. It is wise and good, but it must be recognized and thereafter dealt with in the right way.

One of the fruits of our spiritual-scientific studies must be to enable these convictions to emerge from the deepest impulses of our being as the innermost spur of our energy for life. Then we shall perhaps establish not a pleasurable, comfortable revelling in ideas that are remote from reality, which is good if the aim is to make people sleep through life; the endeavour will, rather, be to establish that true divine service of life which leads the divine-spiritual powers who are the foundation of all reality to making this divine-spiritual power a reality in this earthly life through the most significant instrument for this Earth.

Lecture 15

STUTTGART, 26 APRIL 1918

One fundamental characteristic of the spiritual-scientific studies that we have been pursuing is not appreciated in its full significance even in our own circles. If one refers to this fundamental characteristic of our spiritual-scientific endeavours in an abstract way, many of us might perhaps even think: Of course this is properly understood, how should this not be the case! Nevertheless, it is not so. The fundamental characteristic that I have in mind is that it is an aim of our spiritual science not only to indicate in general terms that the spiritual world is a reality, that in the spiritual world individual cosmic beings live as realities, but to show ever and again in the individual situation that what occurs around and within us in our ordinary life between birth and death is a creation of the spiritual world. I should emphasize that the opinion might exist that, when one directs one's spiritual gaze in seriousness to the spiritual world, it is already naturally implied that what is around us will be viewed as a creation of the spiritual world. But it is a far cry from these general, wholly abstract, empty, meaningless thoughts to those spiritual places where it can be grasped in specific detail that the sensory world is a creation of the spirit. I shall illustrate this today by means of a particular example, which can at the same time demonstrate how far present-day humanity is from having some inkling of what it means to say that the sense-perceptible created world around us as we experience it between birth and death is a creation of a spiritual reality.

In order to explain in detail the particular example that we want to consider today, I should like to remind you of what I felt obliged to say yesterday in the public lecture.[162] We shall approach this matter today more closely and in greater detail with reference to certain practical applications.

I spoke yesterday and also previously here in this branch about what I might refer to as a process whereby humanity becomes ever younger in the course of its evolution. Briefly to recapitulate what this is about: if we go back in human evolution to that catastrophe in earthly development that we call the Atlantean catastrophe, when the continent which at that time lay between present-day Europe and America was submerged, giving rise to America in the West and Europe in the East, we find that—beginning from our own epoch—there are five epochs of human evolution. The first post-Atlantean epoch, which followed as a cultural epoch immediately after the Atlantean catastrophe, is the ancient Indian culture. It goes far back beyond what can be found through outer historical documents. You will find it described to the extent that is necessary in my book *An Outline of Occult Science*. However, what is important for us today is that we are fully aware that in that cultural epoch human beings participated with their soul and spirit in their bodily development until their fifties. The nature of this participation should be understood differently from what one experiences today. When we feel tired or old, we do not participate in our bodily development in the way that a child does in its first seven years. No, what we experience today in a bodily sense in later years does not come directly to the awareness of our soul and spirit. We do not take part in the declining aspect of our development. If we were able to participate in a bodily sense in the decline of our development, we would—by undergoing a process of regression or atrophy—learn an enormous amount about the spiritual world together with a shrivelling, a mineralization of the brain and a scleroticizing of the body. We would experience through our body what we must learn today through spiritual science if we are inherently willing to approach such experiences. In the ancient Indian culture, people accompanied this descending line of development into their fifties; they were children right into their fifties, but children who were growing old.

Then came the second post-Atlantean culture, that of ancient Persia, which again belongs to prehistory. During this epoch, human beings participated in what they underwent in a soul-spiritual sense in conjunction with their body until the end of their forties. Then in the third cultural period, humanity as a whole again became younger. In the Egypto-Chaldaean age, souls became emancipated from the body approximately between the thirty-fifth and forty-second year of life. Then came the age of Graeco-Latin culture, when the Mystery of Golgotha took place. People then underwent the kind of development in conjunction with the body that only a child has today until the age of thirty-five. And today we are in the fifth post-Atlantean cultural epoch (where we have been since the fifteenth century), when we participate until the end of our twenties in what the body experiences; we no longer have any experience of the descending line of development. Thus through his natural disposition a person today is so little inclined to receive spiritual impulses as such into his soul.

In ancient times, the physical, bodily nature itself gave access to the spirit; today it does not do so. The spirit therefore has to be embraced by the soul itself; but the soul refuses to do this. In ancient times it was an absurdity not to believe in the spirit. A person would have had to die before the age of thirty-five were he not to believe in the spirit. In experiencing the time after the age of thirty-five, he experienced through what was taking place in a descending line of development in his body something that was directly revealed as spirit. It was not conceivable for people in ancient times not to believe in the spirit. But because things have developed in the way they have, a moral impulse, a wonderful moral impulse of humanity (in so far as its natural course of development is concerned) was lost. I ask you not to underestimate this wonderful moral impulse which has been lost in the course of this natural process and which must be found anew in a spiritual, ethical way. In those ancient times children knew from their elders that when one has gone beyond one's thirty-fifth year one experiences something as a human being that one cannot experience when one is younger. Make yourself livingly aware of this feeling that children and young people grew up under the impression: I have something to expect when I enter the descending line of development; I shall then have something to experience that I cannot know now, something that my physical, bodily nature does not now give me. Imagine what it must have felt like when—in strong contrast to today—one awaited the process of ageing under such circumstances. It is something so different from today if one awaits the ageing process knowing that something is coming that cannot come before.

This is now different, but not in so drastic a way as one might perhaps think. For after all, if one expresses a truth such as has just been indicated, the present-day bad habits of thinking have the immediate need to translate this into an 'either-or' situation. But matters are never really such that one has to do with an either-or alternative but by and large it is a case of one as well as the other. When one now again reaches old age, the spiritual dimension does not emerge of its own accord. But when the spark of the spirit is kindled in the soul in the manner intended by spiritual science, it stands one in good stead that one becomes old; for something rises up from the declining body that enters in a particular way into what one has come to know on a spiritual-scientific path. If you remain without a scientific contact with the spirit (this scientific contact is not meant in a specialized sense but as something that can be accessible to anyone, even to the simplest soul, for spiritual science can become available to everyone if mankind so wishes), you will not experience anything special when you become old; you will not be able to appreciate the ageing process. You will also not have any particular expectation in childhood and youth for becoming old. It is different if the spark of spiritual knowledge is kindled in the soul not through a natural course of development but through one that is educational, through a development where human souls are engaged in a community setting. If it is rightly understood what spiritual science can livingly impart to the soul, a mood will consciously be engendered by this spiritual science whereby one can say: There is something that awaits me when I grow old. It means something to become old. When I am thirty-five years old, what lives within me will be different from what it is now when I am a young fellow of twenty. This mood is something immense for the human soul; it is a mood that I should like to refer to as the mood of expectant life which simply knows: the creation which you experience through your own being is something that you must in all seriousness regard as a creation out of the spirit.

But at the present time, when people do not want to have anything to do with knowledge of the spirit, is it seriously considered—beyond the uttering of mere platitudes—that man is created out of the spirit? No, in actual practice this does not happen at all. For were this to happen, people would say to themselves that there is a spiritual creation; we do not grow old in vain, the spirit manifests itself within us in ever new ways. What arises within us and comes to expression from within our own being will constantly reveal itself in its different aspects. To live in expectation, to expect something from old age and from the ageing process with every year that passes is a consequence resulting from taking seriously the proposition that what is around us and within us is a creation of the spirit. This is a mood of expectancy which must find its place in all educational endeavours, which must flow into the whole conception of education. Thus from an early age children, and also later when they are young men and women, will acquire the feeling: for as long as we are young, the spirit does not give us everything; but when we become old it will reveal to us ever new things which will arise in our souls. One needs only the stimulus of knowledge of the spirit in order not to fail to see or disregard what seeks to rise up from the depths of one's being; for it is not without significance and is indeed deeply meaningful that we become old. Young people today are annoyed if one still expects them to have such a feeling; for people of the youngest generation already of course feel themselves mature enough to be elected to Parliament and chosen to represent the government, even though that is not their place; for judgements about the structure of human social circumstances should only be made out of a mature perspective of life. If one has this expectant mood of life, one knows that one cannot have a living knowledge, a knowledge based on experience, of such notions as one may have about outward organizations unless one has reached a certain age.

It should not be said that, when it is rightly understood, spiritual science is an abstraction that does not enter into practical life. Spiritual science, if it is increasingly and rightly understood, indeed has its place in practical life, for it can penetrate right into one's actual feelings; it will enable a person to anticipate and await what each new year of his life can bring him in a different way. Spiritual science contains the most active seeds for educational development, the most vigorous educational impulses. It contains moral impulses that have a completely different influence upon the human soul from those moral impulses on which people pride themselves today; for it has impulses which stream towards the human soul from life in its full significance, for the universal sense of life. I do not of course thereby mean to say that everyone who has knowledge of spiritual science is bound to bring all ideals to fulfilment. But it is altogether the case with the moral element that it initially hangs over a person as an ideal, and that it needs to be incorporated within him in accordance with the free impulse of his will. Spiritual science indeed has within it these significant moral impulses. It is not only a nurturer of earthly morality, it is a nurturer of a universal morality. These things need to be perceived with the requisite insight. But it is highly necessary that the kind of conviction associated with what I have explained gains access through spiritual science to human souls; for the dire catastrophe that our present age has inaugurated is that we live in a time of transition when something new wants to come to in-dwell the human soul, but people have not lost their attachment to the old; they do not want to embrace new feelings and are especially reluctant to do so where educational principles are concerned. In the outer life emanating from materialistic culture, one largely finds that precisely the opposite is promoted from what the future so strongly demands of humanity. It is above all necessary that this perception of the significance of life in the becoming is an integral part of growing up. And in our time everyone is in this sense still growing up, for spiritual science has been embraced to so small a degree that each person must first be imbued with what spiritual science has to give the human soul through education. Humanity must be freed from the belief that at the age of twenty or twenty-five one has reached full maturity, that one has completed one's education and needs merely to live out one's life in such a way that its significance resides at best in applying what one has learnt or in enjoying life and in other such ways.

If one looks more deeply into the circumstances of life, what I have been saying becomes deeply relevant to our inner experience. This is something that in ancient times developed within man of its own accord and which now needs to develop within the feeling life of human beings through education: a life filled with expectation. How meaningful it is when a person of thirty says: Secrets will be revealed to me in future as a result of this aging process simply because I have become five or ten years older; I have something to look forward to. Just reflect on what this is and what it means to introduce such an idea into education! But it is also something real. It is a flowing essence that asserts itself within a person, which in former times asserted itself of its own accord and needs to be nurtured in the modern age. For what thus arises within man is indeed *there*; because we are not aware of it, because we do not pay attention to it, this does not mean that it is not there. Do not think that you can escape from growing wiser, from apprehending secrets, when becoming older if you are not aware of these secrets. The spirit is active within you. You will all become rich in spiritual attributes! The difference is merely that the one willingly receives them, while the other—if he has resolved to become a clever man already in his twenties (today this is particularly the case among the so-called intelligentsia)—refuses to receive anything later for his development. The youngest people today write articles and poems and they do all kinds of other things. But what feelings do they have for all these things? How little feeling they have for the meaning of life, consisting as it does in the emergence of human development as a creation out of the spirit! But the spirit cannot be dislodged, even if the youngest people today compose plays or write reviews and the like. It may nevertheless be possible that they have the spirit, even though they know nothing of the spirit that is developing within them.

What happens with this spirit, with the real spirit that in ancient times developed out of itself? Yes, my dear friends, this spirit is inevitably reduced to dust. Truly, it becomes dispersed. It spreads out in the spiritual atmosphere, it spreads out in the aura of humanity. And this is something that must again and again be said to our modern age, although people will not of course believe it for the simple reason that they view it as pure fantasy if someone says to them: Here is a young writer of reviews who considers himself to be very clever. He knows nothing of the spirit, but the spirit is passing over into the aura of humanity, it becomes dispersed. But his spirit is nevertheless there.

The aura of humanity is today completely impregnated with this rarefied spirit. This spirit must be brought into a state of coherence again by human beings, and specifically through the mood of which I have spoken; for we are today very close to the point where a terrible evil would inevitably arise if this rarefied spirit were to continue ever further in its development. It is a significant law of spiritual life that a spirit becomes something entirely different from what it was originally if it abandons its bearer. Please grasp this carefully: a spirit that abandons its bearer becomes dispersed, it becomes something entirely different from when it is held together by its bearer. It deteriorates and becomes degraded to a significant extent; it is ahrimanically transformed. And the inevitable result of this—which is something that is not yet clearly apparent, because we are still in its early stages—is that if this is not attended to there will be a terrible spiritual desolation. People will search for something that keeps them occupied, because they have allowed the spirit that should be concerning them to lose its coherence. A search for something without knowing what one is searching for is a phenomenon that will inevitably become increasingly widespread if the evil is not checked. Today we are seeing the early stages of these symptoms in much of what I have already mentioned.

What does someone who has omitted to be attentive to his spirit do today? He searches for something or other, but this quest manifests itself in a curious fashion in all sorts of different areas. One very common way is that associations are founded, associations with good programmes. All sorts of demands are placed before people. These may be very clever, but they are generally things arising from the fact that one has remained at the level of childhood, and an idea from childhood becomes ossified to the point where it is let loose upon the world at a later age of life in the form of programmes for associations. In areas such as this there seems to be an incredible amount to do; but there is little knowledge of being really active in the spirit, of setting out from a small seed of spiritual activity enabling people to join it of their own accord, and livingly and actively to maintain something of the nature of a human community.

You see, this is the cause of so many conflicts that arise in our Society, conflicts which remain latent for certain reasons and which I do not want to discuss here. Where I can myself exercise some kind of influence, I should like to keep as far away as possible from all statutes, all rules, all laws. For ultimately, why does one need statutes when a number of people unite for the cultivation of spiritual life? One can draw up statutes to show them to the authorities; that is a different matter, it has nothing to do with the thing itself; what actually matters is what such statutes mean to us. The essential point is that such a community should live, that every new person can contribute something *new*. Such a community should be alive, it cannot become fixed by statutes of some kind; when it has existed for five years it must be no less different than a child who is now twelve is from when he was seven. But this is not the way that people think at present. The way of thinking of the present time is to live as far as possible in abstractions, to entangle everything in abstractions. That is one thing. One could give many examples of this, all of which emanate from the fact that there is no awareness of the disintegrating life of the spirit. People seek, they seek in every possible way. Just think how many women's and other associations there are today in any town of a certain size! People search and search, because they do not know that what they should be retaining is being dispersed. Thus they search because they do not have that to which they pay no heed. This search signifies a desolation of life. This desolation would take on terrible dimensions if humanity fails to understand that the mood of life of which I have just spoken to you must be engendered.

For what people do not want to understand today is life in all its directness! The principle that what exists is a creation of the living spirit undoubtedly calls for a mobility of experience. It is in a certain sense uncomfortable to say that one can never see oneself as something complete or finished; but it is a necessity if the spiritual evolution of humanity is to advance further. Thus to understand spiritual science in such a way that it stimulates life, that it really penetrates into what is required at the present point in human evolution, is the task of those who really want to dedicate themselves to it; hence to share in the life of humanity and to recognize what it has to undergo in the present phase of evolution, what is its destiny to undergo.

Try to acquire an unprejudiced view of the events that are taking place around you. Most people actually sleep through what is going on around us today. They think only that the kind of situation that existed before 1914 must come again, and they wait for the arrival of such a state of affairs. They do not understand at all how necessary it is that humanity works its way through to wholly new ideas that did not exist before. It is a primal task of spiritual-scientific thinking to understand life also in its historical context.

That is the one aspect: that the spirit becomes atomized, dispersed, if people do not take notice of it, as generally happens today. But only one part dissipates, the other remains behind; it becomes stuck in the human organism but does not come to consciousness. It unconsciously impregnates the organism. It works into the blood, the flesh; it is active in the unconscious. Thus one part of what a person should be conscious of in the course of his life becomes dispersed, while the other part is driven down into unconscious depths. What does it do in this realm of the unconscious?

Let us examine somewhat more closely the particular reason why the spirit is partly driven down in to the unconscious. This is brought about mostly by those erroneous educational principles which seek to make children and young people clever beyond their years, so that children remain children as little as possible. How greatly people pride themselves today on awakening an independent power of judgement in the child as early as possible, on educating children from the earliest possible age differently from the way described in my little book *The Education of the Child from the Standpoint of Spiritual Science*. It is necessary that the child lives above all in pictorial representations, that the intellectual element is introduced to the child as late as possible. There is very little understanding of this. Moreover, our present culture itself has little understanding of this issue. We should not, however, seek to impede the course of this modern culture; spiritual science will never adopt a reactionary stance. It will of course take account of the outward, material advance of culture; but this outward, material advance of culture requires us to create a counter-balance. It was different in the times when people did not learn to read and write at an early age. I do not want to promote illiteracy, please do not misunderstand me; but today it is considered a misfortune if people are illiterate, for a person's worth is seen not in what lives vitally within him but in what is brought to him, which ultimately has incredibly little to do with the human soul as it actually is. In those ancient times when writing was still of a pictorial nature, when every letter revealed a verbal mystery, writing was something very different. But today, what relation do those little sprites that appear on white paper before the eyes of very young children and have to be deciphered, those little sprites that the children them-selves conjure forth on the paper, have to the soul? They are merely signs, arbitrary signs. One might well think that everything to do with writing could be arranged completely differently. Many people today have already attempted different methods. Shorthand has also been introduced. There is no inevitability about the way this is introduced at present; it could also be done quite differently. Nevertheless, this is a necessary requirement of earthly culture; a reactionary may oppose it, but not the spiritual scientist. It had, of course, to be like this. But a counter-balance will come. It will not be an ideal of spiritual science to abolish school; but a counter-balance will be that children receive a pictorial form of instruction, where through all that they learn their souls are brought into connection with these mysteries. Every animal, every plant expresses in its forms something that is mysteriously connected with the whole of creation. Only at a certain age does one possess a real freshness of soul (if one can sense what is meant by such an expression). It is at a particular age of life that one must grow together with the created world.

Let us take an example. I have already reminded you of a remark that my old friend Vincenz Knauer,[163] the historian of philosophy, often reiterated. Out of his thoroughly medieval scholastic con-sciousness, he said in reply to those who maintain that everything consists of the same kind of material substance: Well, you should look at the way that this same substance manifests itself in a wolf and in a lamb if you lock up a wolf so that it cannot get food of any other kind and feed it exclusively on lambs. If the substance of lambs is the same as that of wolves, the wolf would gradually have to change into a lamb, or at least it would become as meek as a lamb. This clearly indicates that in what forms the wolf (which we call the group-soul), in that living essence that determines its structure, there is something quite different from the structure of the lamb. To observe merely substance as such and not substance in its various forms or spiritualized substance leads not to the mysteries of creation but away from them. The animals around us have a great variety of forms. Just see how, in this respect, man is different from animals and give some serious thought to what this really means. Apart from small differences due to varying racial characteristics that can be significant but do not extend to the differences between animal species, human beings have a similar form all over the Earth. Why? Because the conditions of equilibrium in them are different than in animals. Animals are the result of conditions of equilibrium which develop in relation to the Earth. You can see this in apes, which have a well-nigh upright form. The form of animals is such that their spinal column is parallel to the surface of the Earth, so that the rear part of their bodies is the same height as the front part. The most significant aspect is that man is organized in such a way that what in the animal is beside the rear part of the body is above it, that it covers the rear part. In man the line that passes through the head to the Earth coincides with the line of gravity, which is not the case with animals. Through the fact that man is called upon to establish his own position of equilibrium to the Earth, which becomes a caricature in the ape but is a natural state of being for man, he raises himself out of the particular form that every animal species has. Man therefore does not have so defined a configuration as do the species of animals, because he raises himself above the animal form; he raises his form into an erect position with his head resting above the rear part of his body. This is something of immense significance. Darwinists have not even begun to consider it. Nevertheless, this is the essential point.

Today I can only give indications; if I were to explain it further I should need to give several lectures, and this would serve to shed light upon the deeply significant question of the difference between man and animals. But what is of interest to us today is not so much this but, rather, that man overcomes the animal form in himself by adopting his upright position, by taking up a different position of equilibrium on the Earth. He thereby makes himself independent from the Earth. But if we turn to the etheric body, there is a difference. The etheric body is mobile; at every moment it takes on a different shape in every human being. If someone looks at a lion, you will clairvoyantly see the form of the lion in such a person. If you look at a hyena, you will supersensibly resemble a hyena. As human beings we overcome outer forms in their physical aspect, but in the etheric body we adapt to what is around us. This is again what so significantly distinguishes man from animals. An animal has its particular form. A lion when encountering a dog cannot imitate the form of the dog in its etheric body; it remains also inwardly a lion, in reality it recognizes only another lion. Man, however, is versatile; he is many-sided, he adapts to his surroundings with respect to his etheric body. But what matters is whether this adaptation is regular or irregular, whether it influences life in a meaningful or meaningless way. The fact that animals are formed in so diverse a way, that they rigidly maintain that in their physical form which man, through constantly transforming himself, can become, means that the entire animal kingdom is not only what the modern zoologist sees but that every animal form has a particular significance. One can in a certain way discern this meaning of the entire animal kingdom. And if we begin to grasp the meaning of what lives around us in rigid forms, and of which we then have a meaningful experience through ourselves taking on those forms, we build a bridge between ourselves and the spiritual world.

In ancient times human beings tried instinctively to feel the meaning of their surroundings. The various symbolical stories about animals—animal fairy tales, legends, fables and the like—are an indication of what extends into historical times from this period. We cannot return to this ancient time. But something different must be developed instead so that people do not merely learn what is now abstractly crammed into them about the forms of animals. How such animals are described in present-day school text-books! The descriptions are so boring to children because they are totally superficial. But let the descriptions be meaningful, let the lion once more become something that is fashioned in the created world differently from the hyena, the kangaroo. It will then be possible for people meaningfully to find their place in creation; they will embrace the created world in a living way.

This will have a definite consequence, for the spirit becomes mobile and full of content if it immerses itself in this way in creation. It will then not be satisfied with what official science generally imparts today. Many things can then be experienced today. If you study the evolution of animal species as put forward by today's official science, even where it is relatively unprejudiced, you can experience some strange things. One does not even need to go as far as Darwinism, one can remain with Lamarck,[164] whose ideas are much cleverer than what has developed materialistically out of Darwinism. Here you can also find described how the various animal forms have developed by adapting to the conditions of life. Certain animals have developed webbed feet, because their life-circumstances led to their living in water. Other animals have acquired prehensile organs, because they had to find their nourishment high up on trees and so forth. Indeed, if organs have developed through such habits of life, they must previously have been different. Animals that have acquired webbed feet must previously have had other kinds of feet; the webbed feet then developed through their conditions of life. One gradually comes to see that those animals that have webbed feet developed these from other feet, and those that do not have webbed feet evolved their feet out of earlier and different forms. That is indeed the case, but people do not notice; they learn very dutifully, but they do not take proper note. If a giraffe has a long neck, their explanation is that it developed from a short one because the giraffe had to reach the top of trees. But if the giraffe had a short neck, it would have developed it from a long neck because of different life-circumstances. People do not notice how they play about with these things as if they were throwing balls around. They have absolutely no idea today of the chaos and chaotic way of thinking of a world-conception that does not build a meaningful bridge to what lives around them as human beings.

But having a meaningful experience of one's surroundings is one thing that should be an integral part of education; and they need to be experienced not merely in an intellectual way but meaningfully, so that with one's whole soul one takes in the forms of the animal kingdom, the plant kingdom and the mineral kingdom. How much it would mean to a boy or girl of fourteen or fifteen if one were to say to them during a walk: Just look at those cloud formations! And then again on a further walk: Now look at those clouds. Impress them on your mind, so that you have a picture of these forms! After the child or young person has been enabled to gain an impression of the broader context, one goes to one's bookshelf and takes down Goethe's scientific writings,[165] where he describes in a meaningful way the various cloud forms, how one emerges into and arises out of another. The child will immediately understand this; it will immediately gain insight into this living, pictorial way of seeing the forms of clouds and will experience something wonderful.

Or one may let a child observe a plant in the garden, how it is in the spring, in the summer and in the autumn, and then read to the child from Goethe's poems on the metamorphosis of plants. One then has something that leads to a meaningful relationship with nature.

Such things are needed in order to engender the mood of a life filled with expectancy; they are needed in order to prevent the spirit from becoming stuck and entering into the blood, into the flesh, so that it may accordingly be grasped inwardly by the soul. Certain things should not in the course of evolution enter into the flesh but must remain within the soul.

What happens when they enter into the flesh, into the blood? They then give rise in the subconscious to emotions, passions to which names are given, to which masks are ascribed, and which are sometimes quite different from the masks with which they are endowed. So much exists today—and comes to expression in human evolution—which has come about because what should have remained in the soul has passed over into the blood, into the flesh. And what arises as a result? Conflicts, discord and disharmony are disseminated throughout the Earth. This is veiled in every possible form, in the way that an Italian cannot tolerate a German or an Englishman a German, or a German a speaker of Romance languages; it is veiled in these passions that rage over the Earth. One must, however, be aware of the deeper reasons for these phenomena, and it is necessary to understand the nature of humanity's task in order to achieve what must be achieved.

As regards the present, there are clear signs which show us what we need to learn in order to guide humanity towards a flourishing future. It is important not to remain on the surface of things as people tend to do today but to look into the depths of human souls. That the nineteenth century—because it was a time of transition, because it allowed what should have remained in the realm of the soul to pass over into the flesh, into the blood—went astray in the realm of education, is a reality that is being fought over on the battlefields of today. The blood, which has received what should have passed into human souls, is currently holding sway in the passions wreaking havoc over the Earth. The effect of this is that people are unable to understand one another; it means that they are at cross-purposes with one another; it means that they have so little sense of one another's feelings and life-experiences.

The signs of the time are serious, very serious, but they represent a challenge to look into the depths of what is going on in the world in order from these depths to recognize the nature of our task. As I already said last time, this is not an objection directed to the wisdom of the world, to the divine wisdom. The divine wisdom has to show humanity these signs because humanity is not an automaton but must become independent. The question to be asked is not why mankind met with all these things but what can be done for mankind's salvation. What matters is what we do and the universal nature of our ethical impulses. This is what we are asked to do from week to week, from hour to hour, from minute to minute: to become involved in what has to happen. And those who, in the way that has been indicated today, live in the expectancy that every new year of life brings something that was previously a mystery to them kindle in their souls what mankind will also need in the future: a sense of immortality that is not dead but living. Those who know that each new year brings them new mysteries also know that life after death also brings them new mysteries; for them, the doubt in the continuing existence of that which brings something new in contrast to the development of the body is meaningless. To such people, this life after death is also real, thoroughly real; to them it will not only be a matter of that egoistic principle that is met with so frequently today but a principle of humanity.

In our time we cross the threshold of death and bring with us much in the way of observations of life that we have not taken further here on Earth. But this still has a significance for the Earth. The wisdom that we have acquired here is still of benefit to the Earth when we have crossed the threshold of death. But here on the Earth there must be people who want to use this wisdom. Those who have experiences know how to speak of them. In order not to appear ridiculous, one must in public circles speak of these things as, for example, I did yesterday, that Planck[166] would think quite differently today from the way he thought in the 1880s. As spiritual scientists, we actually mean something different when we say this. We know that this man's soul has brought so much through the portal of death which is richly available, which can still be of use to the Earth. Indeed, someone who knows that his living feeling for living souls is not diminished by the portal of death also knows that the so-called dead are constantly connected with us, that we only have to be open to receive the influences that emanate from them. Anyone who has experience of this may perhaps also modestly speak of these things from personal knowledge. I know that I did not only form a connection with Goethe's world-conception; I wrote what I did in various ways about Goethe's world-conception only because I knew that it derived from the inspiration emanating from the soul of Goethe itself, naturally in so far as one can be receptive to this as a feeble inheritor of his legacy.

But this is associated with being able to form a living relationship with the soul while it is still alive, not merely an abstract veneration for the dead but receiving the living being of the dead into our souls incarnated here in the physical body. How many fruitful, meaningful and living impulses will flow into earthly evolution if the dead can become the counsellors of the living. I know how far away we are at present from such a view. I know that the present tendency is to ask the opinion of someone of the age of twenty-two or twenty-three (or perhaps twenty-four, depending on the age-limit for the respective parliaments) regarding a law that is to be enacted. But people do not ask what Goethe would have to say about what should become law. However, they will one day. The dead will be our fellow citizens.

If we adopt the mood of soul whereby each year can reveal a new mystery for us, we will also take a further step; we shall also know what it means to make the great transition through the portal of death together with the collective fruits of earthly evolution. The dead will then be the counsellors of the living; for what matters is not simply to believe in immortality but that what is immortal can become fruitful in all the fields where it has the potential to be so. A person needs strength in order to break through the mantle that separates him today from what the spiritual world still conceals from him.

You see, the modern way of thinking exists more or less so that we can develop the strong power that we need to break through to the spirit. But the time has already come today when people must clearly perceive many things because they need to understand them. Thus the signs are displayed before the human soul because people must learn that this should absolutely not be there; it must be completely overcome. And because they are themselves to overcome it, it had to appear among them.

There are two extremes in outer life (although there are many such extremes) in opposition to one another: Wilsonism and Trotskyism or Leninism, you can call them whatever you want. The two phenomena are there, born out of an unspiritual world-conception, the most unspiritual world-conception imaginable. It is humanity's task to see that everything that ultimately leads to Leninism or to Wilsonism is obliterated. But lots of Wilsonism and Leninism can be found everywhere; they are very, very widespread, but people are not aware of this. Such things must be seen for what they are. And someone who studies spiritual science to some extent knows that it gives him the insight to perceive things clearly also in this realm. It is today a life's necessity to perceive the world clearly, to have insight into events and not sleep through them; for people are only too ready to mask the truth. Moreover, they are all too credulous; they therefore believe in the masks and do not see what lies hidden behind them. One cannot develop that way of thinking which makes possible the intellectual mobility that is necessary for spiritual science unless in conjunction with such intellectual mobility one acquires a clear, calm perspective regarding what is going on in the world. One should not sleep through events; one must wake up through spiritual science unless one prefers to be lulled by a certain love of ease. There is a great need for letting such a spiritual attitude flow into the soul, but the will—especially of many who feel themselves to be the leaders of humanity—to take this need into account is lacking. The will for the spirit is evident today in the simplest natures; yet they are deficient in self-knowledge, because they are led astray by what is generally regarded today as 'public opinion'. (Schopenhauer called it 'private stupidity'.[167]) Those in leading positions are mostly inclined to speak of the limitations of human nature where they are unwilling to lead people beyond these limits. You find this today in every area. How good it would be for people—to mention just one example—if something can happen of the kind that now happens to the French theologian Loisy,[168] who has also adopted such an uncertain position between modernism and non-modernism, although he had apparently stood for a time on his own feet. But now, in the face of the present catastrophic events, he has asked himself: What has become of Christianity in the events of the present world-situation? Has Christianity perhaps failed? Loisy does not mean Christ as such, but he asks himself whether Christianity has not neglected many things. Several people have written something about this question of conscience raised by Loisy. One writer said that one must reckon with man's imperfections; Christianity certainly wants something different from what is happening on the Earth, but what is taking place must happen because of human imperfections. It is not so important to reflect about this, but what does matter is to ponder and reflect and understand how man can become more perfect, how man can become nobler, how man can rise in his moral standing by becoming more and more integrated in the universal essence of the world. Questions must by and large be asked quite differently from the way that people are inclined to ask them today.

These are the feelings that I wanted to present to you during this time that we have spent together. Even more than before, I am concerned that my words will be understood not only intellectually but in the way they are intended to be grasped, so that they kindle something in our hearts that can become seeds for gaining insight into what has to happen in the course of human evolution. For in perhaps not too long a time each person will in accordance with his particular nature and karma find himself faced with important questions of life which he will not be equipped to deal with if he remains content with old familiar ideas. We must learn to acquire new ideas. Spiritual science will be able to be for us a guide towards such new ideas. The aim of my words has been to stir your souls to wakefulness. Even if they appeared to be based on factual concerns, these facts were chosen in such a way that they touched the very things that are at present of the greatest importance for people in their life of feelings and in what they relate to with their hearts.

Lecture 16

STUTTGART, 21 MARCH 1921

THAT I am speaking to you today has been made necessary because of a question posed at the last historical seminar.[169] This question concerns the matter of blame for the last catastrophic war, and it is one that is so important and—one can say today—has such important historical dimensions that the answering of this question, in so far as is possible in so short a time frame, is a matter that demands to be shared also with you.

I should like to preface what I shall say with a few observations in order that you may have some idea of the sense in which I want to speak about this question. In lectures that I have given at the Goetheanum in Dornach I have never hidden the views that I have been obliged to form about the theme of this present debate and conflict, and I have never made a secret of the fact that these views appear to me to be ones that should come primarily to expression before the whole world. I am not of the view that in this important question the facts today are such that there is justification for constantly saying that one should submit the objective judgement solely to history, that one will be able to form an objective judgement of this whole affair only at a future time. Especially because of constantly growing prejudices, the possibilities of arriving at a healthy judgement of this question will in course of time become considerably fewer, although it may be possible by some means or other. I expressly say 'perhaps'; for I do not myself believe that one will be able to arrive at a better judgement of this question in the future than already in the present.

That is the first thing that I should like to say. I have to say it for the following reason. As you well know, those attacks—there are no words with which I would wish to characterize them now—which relate to the culturally political aspect of my activities[170] proceed mainly from that quarter which one can call the 'all-German', and I must of course expect that people of this persuasion will interpret whatever I affirm in the most unbridled fashion. But on the other hand I do not believe it to have been necessary to say anything particular by way of defence in this particular direction, for the foolish accusations that something is being directed against Germany have their origin in the fact that already during the war the Goetheanum was erected in the north-western corner of Switzerland, thus a symbol for what is to be accomplished not merely within Germany but through German spiritual and cultural life before the whole world. When one has in such a way borne witness to what the German spirit represents, I do not think that one needs many words in whatever way to refute ill-intentioned accusations.

What I have further to say is this, that I have always tried not to influence in any way the judgements of those who hear what I say in this direction, and I should like to observe this today as far as possible (and it is possible only to a limited extent if one bears in mind the need for brevity). In everything that I have said I have, through the specifying of these or those facts, these or those moments, had my eye on giving in each case foundations for the forming of my own judgement. And just as I do in the whole context of spiritual science, namely that I never anticipate a judgement but only try to bring forth the materials for the forming of a judgement, so is it also my intention to do so in these matters relating to the outer world of history.

Now to come to the matter at hand, it seems to me that the discussions that are undertaken today about the question of blame all more or less rest upon impossible presuppositions. For my part I think that with these same presuppositions, in whatever way one may apply them, one can calmly prove that the somewhat remarkable Nikita,[171] the King of Montenegro, bears the complete blame for the war. I believe that with these arguments one can also even make the case that Helferich[172] is an extraordinarily wise man, or that the formerly fat Herr Erzberger[173] did *not* during the war in a remarkably active way thread his way through all possible subterranean depths and cellars of European will. In short, it is my contention that with these arguments there is incredibly little that can be achieved. On the other hand, I believe that it is absolutely correct what the present German Foreign Minister Simons[174] has recently said in his speech in Stuttgart; that it is necessary to deal seriously with the question of blame or guilt. To this I would, however, add that this should indeed also happen; for if one says that something is necessary one has not carried out what needs to happen, and it is absolutely necessary that it happens. That it is necessary to address the question of blame follows from the fact that at the head of these last unfortunate negotiations in London Lloyd George,[175] the most crafty statesman of the present time, has placed a sentence regarding the present implications of which one is in a state of embarrassment to find even remotely appropriate words: Everything that we are negotiating has its foundation in that the powers united by the Entente have resolved the question of blame.

Now if everything that we can negotiate happens under the aspect that the question of blame has been resolved, then if it has not been resolved it is really a matter of starting the negotiations from the beginning by seriously raising the question of blame. It must emphatically be stated that nothing has really happened of a fundamental nature hitherto with respect to the question of blame other than a very strange decision of the victorious powers. This decision is based wholly upon the rules of present world-events, not upon an objective judgement of the facts but simply upon a diktat of the victors. In order to profit accordingly from their victory, it is necessary for the victors to dictate to the world that the other side bears the blame for the war. It is not possible to profit from the victory as those on the side of the Entente would like, as they even must—it can be granted—profit from it from this standpoint, if the other side is not saddled with the full blame. You will easily see that they would not be able to act as they do if they were to say: Yes, these people are actually not to be judged, shall we say, for the way things turned out during the catastrophe of the war.

Thus the important thing—for everything else is mere words or has not even become published words—is that for the time being nothing has been done other than that a diktat has been issued by the victors; and that what should actually never have been allowed to happen has happened in an incomprehensible fashion, that this diktat of the victors has been signed, constitutes a fact that one cannot sufficiently lament. For one cannot say that this signature had to be given in order not to make the misfortune even greater. Someone who has insight into the real events knows that one will only come through the present world-situation with the truth and with the will for total truth. It may even perhaps be that a way through will be found today. The times are too serious, they call for too great decisions for a solution to be found other than with the full will for truth.

I should like to emphasize that since in the brief time that is available to me I am not in a position to present the situation so that from the content of my statements what I say could also appear conclusive, I shall in the way that I portray things in nuanced form at any rate try to give you a foundation for forming a judgement in this realm. Now I have through many years' experiences, through a careful observation of what is taking place in world-historical evolution, come to understand that above all in the case of the Anglo-Saxon people, and especially of certain groups of human beings within this Anglo-Saxon people, a certain thoroughly world-historical, grandiosely held political view exists. In certain people working behind the scenes of Anglo-Saxon political life (if I may describe them as such), there exists a political viewpoint which I should like to summarize in two main categories. Firstly, the view exists—and a considerable number of individuals who stand behind the actual political figures, who are sometimes only front men, are imbued with this point of view—that through certain world-evolutionary forces the mission must fall to the Anglo-Saxon race to exercise a world-domination, a real world-domination for the present and the future over many centuries. This is firmly rooted in these individuals, even though I would say it is firmly rooted by world-influences in materialistic ideas and in a materialistic way; but it is so firmly rooted in those who are the true leaders of the Anglo-Saxon race that one can compare it with the inner impulses which the ancient Jewish people had of its world mission. To be sure, the ancient Jewish people understood this in a more moral, more theological way; but the intensity of the conception is no different in those who really lead the Anglo-Saxon race from how it was manifested in the ancient Jewish people. Thus we have primarily to do with this principle, which you can follow also outwardly, and with the particular nature of the conception of life that is present in the Anglo-Saxon people and especially in its leading representatives. The view prevails that, on this basis, everything must be done in accordance with such a world-impulse, that one should not shrink from anything that accords with such a world-impulse. This impulse is brought in a manner that is, it has to be said, in an intellectual sense utterly grandiose to the hearts and minds of those who then in the more subordinate positions—among whom those belonging to the state secretariat may also be included—lead political life. It is my belief that anyone who is not aware of this situation cannot possibly understand the course of world-evolution at this present time.

The second of these two categories, which underlies the global policy that is so sad and pernicious for Central Europe, is the following. People are far-seeing. From the standpoint of the Anglo-Saxon world this policy is admirable; it is underpinned by the belief that world-impulses rule the world and not the little practical impulses by which politicians of various hues often arrogantly let themselves be guided. This policy of the Anglo-Saxons is in this sense admirable; it reckons with the impulse of world history also in particular practical measures. The second category is this. There is an awareness that the social question is a world-historical impulse which must necessarily be resolved. There are none of the leading figures among the Anglo-Saxon individuals under consideration who would not say to themselves with what I might describe as a remarkably cold, matter-of-fact countenance: The social question must be resolved. But such people would add that it should not be resolved in such a way that the Anglo-Saxon mission might suffer any damage as a result. Words of this kind are often spoken: It is not appropriate for the Western world to be ruined by socialist experiments. And these people are then inwardly engaged with the intention of making the Eastern world, and specifically the world of Russia, the field for socialist experiments.

What I am now expressing to you is a view that I could trace back to the 1880s, and as far as I know it may go even further back. It was known quite coldly among the Anglo-Saxon people that the social question must be resolved, that there was a wish that the Anglo-Saxon world should not be ruined through this and that therefore Russia must become the country for experiments in the social domain. Thus a tendency in this direction was developed in politics, a tendency that was developed with all clarity. Especially all questions relating to the Balkans, including those through which the unsuspecting Central Europeans of Bosnia and Herzegovina were inveigled into the Berlin agreement,[176] all these questions were dealt with under this point of view. The whole way that the Turkish problem was dealt with on the part of the Anglo-Saxon world can be understood from this same viewpoint; and there was the hope that, through the way that the socialistic experiments took the course that they would have to take if the world of the proletariat went astray in the pursuance of Marxist or similar principles, these socialistic experiments would also become for the world of the workers a clear teaching, through their outcome of utter destruction, in what does not work, that things cannot be done in this way. Thus the idea was that the Western world would be protected by being shown in the East what socialism brings about, if it can be disseminated in such a way that the Western world does not want it.

You see, these phenomena, which it will also be possible to confirm historically, constitute that which has for several decades been at the foundation of the situation in Europe, of the world situation; and from these same phenomena there emerges what, I might say, indicates a plane for world-historical events that lies in juxtaposition to the physical world. We need only to read with due attentiveness what the starry-eyed idealist Woodrow Wilson, who is nevertheless a good historian by present-day standards, lets shine through his words in his various speeches.[177] But we need this only in order to have a symptom for what I want to say. Through the whole of recent history it has been the case that the Orient, even if one does not notice this, has been a kind of discussion problem for the whole of European civilization. To the objective observer there remains nothing other than to say: through the world-historical events of the modern era England has been favoured with a certain inauguration of the mission that I have characterized to you. This goes far back to the discovery of the possibility of reaching India by sea. The whole configuration of modern English politics has, by way of a circuitous route, its origin in this event, and you have what I should like to call the whole trend of the global stream carried by the mission of England: it goes from England through the ocean around Africa to India. (I can indicate this only in a brief, schematic way; what I am saying would, of course, require many hours of explanation, but in the present context an indication will have to suffice.) Immeasurably much can be learnt from this line.[178] This line is the one for which the Anglo-Saxon world-mission veritably battles and will battle to the bitter end; it will if necessary even to battle to the bitter end against America. The other line which is equally important is the one that represents the path over land, which played a great role in the Middle Ages but became an impossibility for modern economic and commercial developments through the discovery of America and through the Turkish invasion of Europe. But between these two lines lie the Balkans; and it became Anglo-Saxon policy to deal with the Balkan problem in such a way that this line was totally eliminated as regards economic development, that the sea route alone could develop. Anyone who wants to see can see what I have just now been indicating in all that took place from 1900 and already earlier to the Balkan wars which immediately preceded the so-called world war and to the year 1914.

A further matter is England's relationship to Russia. This line does not of course interest Russia in the least; but Russia is of interest to its own attitude to this line.* As you have already seen, England has a particular intention regarding Russia, the socialist experiment, and it therefore has to implement its whole policy towards on the one hand enabling this economic and commercial line to come into being, and

---

* Rudolf Steiner is presumably referring here to the line representing the land-route to India; and it would therefore make sense that the word 'its' in the second part of this sentence refers to England.—Translator

on the other hand confining and enclosing Russia in such a way that it could provide the ground for socialist experiments. This was nevertheless essentially the world situation. All that was done until 1914 in the realm of world politics was under the influence of this tendency. As said, it would take many hours to explain this in detail; but I wanted here to give some brief initial indications.

The counterpart to this, to which I drew attention when I wrote my 'Appeal to the German Nation and to the Civilized World' in 1919,[179] is the other fact that in Central Europe people have unfortunately always been closed to the idea that a political position has to be sought under the aegis of such visionary historical impulses. Within the continent of Europe it could unfortunately not come to the point where someone became involved in observing the measures that were adopted from the particular standpoint that it was a question of developing such visionary tendencies. You see, people come and say: You must be practical in your politics! A politician must be a practical person! Now let me clarify by means of an example what the practicality of such people signifies. There are numerous people who say that what the Stuttgartians are doing with their threefolding and their 'Kommenden Tag' and so on is all humbug. All this is unpractical; they are unpractical idealists! Well, call these people to mind and think how it will, with any luck, be that the years will have arrived when—if I may put it thus—we have been blessed with good fortune, when we have achieved, have accomplished something that has found its place in the world. Then you will see that the same people who now say that all this is mere unpractical nonsense now come and want to set about making use of their practical knowledge in order to disseminate with all their eloquence and industry what they previously decried as unpractical nonsense. Everything is then suddenly seen as practical. This is the only point of view that these people have for their way of doing things. What is always of importance is this, that one needs to see that everything must be considered in terms of its origin, and that what 'practical' unpractical people call 'unpractical' is something that is often sought as the foundation of their practice. It is only that they do not want to enter into any kind of position, and they are as a result initially useless for what happens in reality.

Such a practice was approximately also the one that has been followed by the politicians of Europe. There is no other way of putting it. And what really matters is to see that the sense of futility, the arrival at a point of nullity as regards politics was a tragic situation for Central Europe when things were thrusting towards a decision. Thus what is of essential importance is that it must be perceived how absolutely necessary it is that we in Central Europe are able to raise ourselves to the heights of a visionary political viewpoint that is borne by the spirit. Without this we simply cannot emerge from the confusion of the present. If we do not make such a resolve, what we see happening around us will continue to come about. I am of the view that the political problems, which are today still constantly being dealt with under the influence of old maxims, are so entangled and confused that they cannot be solved even initially out of these old impulses. And let us suppose that the Entente statesmen had assembled—I am saying this as something that I have formed as an honest view—and had, for my sake even under the leadership of Lloyd George, hatched up those same peace demands that they presented to the world before the conference in London; but let us suppose that through some kind of event they had lost the details of these peace demands and had even forgotten what they were (of course this is an impossible hypothesis, but I am wanting to make a point), and now suppose that Simons had had this pathetic concoction delivered to him and had from his side presented these same demands, even quite literally, I am convinced that they would have been rejected with the same indignation with which the offer made by Simons at the London Conference was rejected. For one is dealing not with solvable problems but with the fact that people talk around problems, which cannot be solved on this basis. That is what has to be said for anyone who seeks the truth in this realm.

Now let us go a stage deeper into the purely physical events. You know that the catastrophe of the war had its outward beginning with the Serbian ultimatum. I have spoken so often about the cause of this, about everything that preceded this ultimatum, and it will be possible for you to inform yourselves about these things; so I may speak today in a more cursory way. The whole circle of entanglements had their origin in the Austrian ultimatum to Serbia. Now anyone who has knowledge of Austrian politics, and especially the historical development of Austrian politics in the second half of the nineteenth century, knows that this Austrian ultimatum to Serbia was to be sure a dangerous game in the military sense but that once one had formed the policy that was being pursued it was a historical necessity. One cannot say anything different from this: Austrian politics were being enacted on a territory where from the 1870s onwards it had been impossible to muddle along with the old governing principles, and the notion of muddling along is not an expression that I have coined but is a phrase uttered in Parliament by Count Taaffe, whose name was frequently written in Austria as 'Ta-affe' ['Affe' means 'ape']. He said: All we can do is continue muddling along.

Now because of the complexity of the circumstances in Austria there was a need to arrive at a clear insight into the question: How should an association of different national groups study the nature of cultural affairs? After all, in an association-state such as Austria was, there was in the questions of nationality something of the outward expression of cultural or spiritual life. Austrian politics have not even begun to look at this question properly, let alone actually studied it. And if with a certain will I devote time to weighing up things, not merely to grouping them according to particular inclinations or in terms of outward history, there appear to me to be more decisive elements in the prehistory of the Serbian ultimatum than that in which the events culminated, namely the assassination of the heir to the Austrian throne, Franz Ferdinand. I look for example at the fact that from the autumn of 1911 until early 1912 economic debates took place in the Austrian Parliament which even became a significant element in the street, and which always linked up with the circumstances existing in Austria at that time. On the one hand, a whole number of businesses were shut down because the whole political system of Austria was driven into a corner to such an extent that it did not know what's what and tried fruitlessly to find new markets but was unable to find any. This led in 1912 to the closure of numerous businesses and to prices rising enormously. Unrest because of rising prices, which included the involvement of revolutionaries, then arose in Vienna and in other regions of Austria, and the debates about price rises, in which the deceased Member of Parliament Adler[180] took so great a part, led to five shots being fired at the Minister of Justice from the gallery. These were the signals; thus business life in Austria could no longer function, economic life could not sustain itself. What did the Interim Minister Gautsch[181] find to say as the main content of his speech at that time? He said that one must with all energy, that is, with the old administrative measures of Austria, see to it that the agitation against the price rises disappears. This indicates to you what the mood from the other side was like.

The cultural life featured in national battles. Economic life had been driven into an impasse (you can study this in every detail), but no one had the heart and mind to see that it was necessary to study the conditions for the further development of the cultural life and the economic life separated from the old views of the state, which especially in Austria were manifested in their utter emptiness. In Austria one could see the necessity of so setting about the study of world-historical affairs that everything worked towards a threefolding of the social organism. This simply follows from such facts as I have now been describing. No one wanted to think about it, and because no one wanted to think about it things therefore took the course they did. You see, one needs only to illumine with a few strokes what was taking place in Austria under the influence of the effects of the Berlin Congress at the beginning of the 1880s and one will see what forces were at work there. In Austria the circumstances were already so far advanced at the beginning of the 1880s and even earlier that the Polish Member of Parliament Otto Hausner[182] said in an open session of parliament: If people continue working like this in Austrian politics, we shall in three years no longer have a parliament but something quite different. He had in mind the governmental chaos. Now of course, people exaggerate in such debates and use hyperboles. What he had prophesied for the future in three years' time came not already in three years, but it came about within a few decades.

I could cite countless extracts from the Austrian parliamentary debates around the turn of the 1870s and 1880s, from which it would become evident to you how it was seen in Austria that the agricultural problem was also rearing its head in a most terrible way. For example, I remember very well that at that time in connection with the justifying of the building of the Arlberg railway it was said by certain politicians of all sorts of different shades that it is essential to construct this railway because this shows that it simply no longer works to carry on working rightly with agrarian methods if in the same way as formerly the immense influence from the West with agricultural production continues to hold sway. Of course, the problem was not understood in the right way, but the prophecy that was expressed was correct. And all these things—one could mention hundreds—would show that Austria in July 1914 had arrived at the point where it had to be said: Either we can go no further, we must abdicate as a state, we must say we are helpless!—or we must somehow extricate ourselves through playing a dangerous game, through something that creates prestige for an upper class. Anyone who adopted the standpoint that Austria must find a way forward—and I should like to know how an Austrian statesman could have remained a statesman if he had not had this standpoint; even such a twit as Count Berchtold[183] could not say otherwise than that something of this sort must happen—had no choice but to play a dangerous game. However strange it may be from certain points of view, one must understand this in its historical impulses.

Now we have, so to speak, the starting-point at *one* place. Consider this starting-point at a different place, namely in Berlin. I should like to tell you wholly objectively about something purely factual so as to give you an idea of what was going on there. You see— please do not take it amiss if I give an objective characterization also here—it was in the year 1905 that the man on whose shoulders the decision regarding war and peace rested in Berlin in 1914, the then General and later Colonel-General von Moltke, was appointed chief of the General Staff. When he was appointed the following scene was enacted—I shall describe it as briefly as possible. General von Moltke[184] was convinced that he could not take over the responsible position of chief of the General Staff without first discussing the conditions of accepting this office with the commander-in-chief, the Kaiser. The point at issue was that through the attitude of the generals to the commander-in-chief the situation had hitherto been that he—you have probably already read about this somewhere or other—often gave the supreme command in manoeuvres on the one or the other side, and you well know that this commander-in-chief had also regularly prevailed in this respect. Now the man who was to be summoned in 1905 to take over the responsible position of chief of the General Staff said: Of course, it is not possible to take this on under such conditions; for things can also become serious, and one may then see how one can conduct war under the preconditions of having to organize manoeuvres with the commander-in-chief as an ultimate authority who must prevail. General von Moltke now decided to present this openly to the Kaiser in a completely transparent way. The Kaiser was utterly astonished that his chief of the General Staff-to-be should tell him that this would not do, for the Kaiser did not seriously understand how to conduct a war. Thus one had to prepare things in such a way that they could also function when the real thing happened, and he could only take over the office of chief of the General Staff if the Kaiser refrained from ultimate leadership. The Kaiser said: Yes, but what is now the situation? Have I not really won? Is this the way it has turned out? He had no idea what his retinue had done, and only when his eyes were opened did it become clear to him that things could not continue as they were, and one must even say that he accepted the conditions with a fair degree of willingness; this should be stated quite openly.

Therefore, my very dear listeners, now that I have presented this fact to you for the forming of a judgement of your own, I ask you—and I may add here in parenthesis that there is abundant reason today that in such matters I am not biased, for I can at any moment be examined by someone who is sitting here[185]—also to consider where there are any errors, whether it was not also highly characteristic that around the commander-in-chief there were certain individuals (who also had their followers) who may not have spoken as did the later Colonel-General in 1905 but who also acted differently after taking on an office. It is not necessary today that one constantly tries to prove something to the world; one should wait until the objective facts can be ascertained; but the point is merely that one should have the earnest will to make reference to these objective facts.

And now one does not need to speculate about a Privy Council of 1914, of which it is certain that Colonel-General von Moltke had no idea that it had taken place, for in July he had been absent in Karlsbad for a course of treatment until shortly before the outbreak of the war. This is important to emphasize, because when there is talk about Germany's warmongers one must say the following: to be sure, there were such warmongers, and if one were to tackle the special problem of warmongers it would be inadequate to suggest that the personalities whom I have also mentioned previously were whiter than white. And finally, what I have said regarding ascribing to Nikita of Montenegro—I do not know whether he is white or black—a heavy burden of blame for the war may derive from the fact that already on 22 July 1914 the two daughters, these—please forgive the expression— demonic women in Petersburg,[186] said in the presence of Poincaré[187] at a particularly splendid court festivity for the French ambassador,[188] who achieved the remarkable feat that in his memoirs he related the affair in minute detail: We are living at a historical time; a letter has just come from our father indicating that in the coming days we shall have war. It will be quite wonderful. Germany and Austria will disappear; we shall be able to shake hands in Berlin.

This is what the daughters of King Nikita, Anatasia and Militza, said to the French ambassador in Petersburg on 22 July (I beg you to note the date). This is also a fact that can be indicated.

Now I would say, one does not need to concern oneself with all the less important details. On the other hand, a significant role is played by the fact that things had so come to a head in Berlin by 31 July 1914 that all decisions about war and peace in Berlin had come to rest on the shoulders of General von Moltke, and he of course could form a judgement about the situation out of none other than purely military foundations. This is what one has to take into account; for in order to assess the situation in Berlin at that time it was really necessary that one knew exactly, I would even say, from hour to hour what was taking place in Berlin on Saturdays from around four o'clock in the afternoon until eleven o'clock at night. These were the decisive hours in Berlin in which an immense world-historical tragedy was being enacted. This world-historical tragedy unfolded in such a way that the chief of the General Staff at the time could do none other from what had happened, or at least from all that it was possible to know in Berlin about recent events, than to carry out the General Staff plan, to carry out what had for years been prepared for the eventuality that occurred which it had in the end been possible to foresee only as something that was in the process of occurring.

The various alliances were so constituted that there was no other way of thinking about the European situation than this: if the turmoil in the Balkans extended to Austria, Russia would definitely participate. Russia had France and England as its allies. They had to take part in some way. But then the scenario would automatically unfold—there is really no question about this—that Germany and Austria had to unite in a common cause, and from Italy one had the most definite assurance, even stipulated in detail through an agreement reached shortly beforehand defined even to the number of divisions, how it would participate in an eventual war. These were the things that could be known in Berlin; these were the things that a man who was really aware of only two things as points of departure with regard to the world-situation had before him. These were the two maxims that General von Moltke had: firstly, if it came to a war, this war would be terrible; it would be an event of terrible proportions. And anyone who knew the deeply sensitive soul of General von Moltke knew that such a soul would not be able to rush into what it saw as something very terrible with a truly light heart. The other maxim was, however, a boundless devotion to duty and a feeling of responsibility, and this could not have any other effect than the one that it had.

If what happened at that time was to have been prevented, it would have to have been prevented from the side of German politics; that would have to have been prevented which you perhaps itself judge as something to prevent if I draw your attention to the following facts. It was on Saturday afternoon; what was to lead to a decision was approaching, and after four o'clock the chief of the General Staff von Moltke met the Kaiser, Bethman-Hollweg and a number of other men in a mood that actually seemed to be fairly rosy. A message from England had just come—I do believe that this message can hardly have been read properly, since otherwise it could not have been construed as it was construed; in the view of the German politicians this message stated that England could still be accommodated. No one had a real notion of the Anglo-Saxon world's belief in its mission; on the contrary, it was always the Vogel-Strauß policy that was pursued; this was tragic. When this telegram was read out it was now believed with a light heart that things could turn out differently, and what happened was that the Kaiser did not sign the mobilization document. Thus I expressly note that on the evening of 31 July the order to mobilize had not been signed by the Kaiser, although the chief of the General Staff's military judgement was that one should give no weight to such a telegram but that the war plan must unconditionally be implemented. Instead of this, the assignment was given to the officer on day duty to telephone in von Moltke's presence that the troops in the West were not to go beyond the enemy frontier, and that the Kaiser had said: Now we certainly do not need to march into Belgium.

Now what I am saying to you is stated in notes that General von Moltke wrote[189] after the very remarkable occurrence of his departure from office, notes which were to be published by agreement with Frau von Moltke in May 1919, at that decisive moment when Germany had the opportunity to tell the world the truth immediately before the signing of the Versailles diktat. And since what he wrote was so pervaded with the expression of inner honesty, anyone who reads what was to be published then and what had flowed from the pen of Herr von Moltke himself will not for one moment be able to arrive at the judgement that it would not have made a significant impression on the world before the Versailles diktat was issued. Well, it was printed on a Tuesday afternoon and it was to appear on Wednesday. I do not want to enter into the description of further details. A German general came to me who from a thick convolution of files wanted to make it clear to me that three points in these notes were incorrect. I had to tell the general that I have worked philologically for a long time. Bundles of files do not impress me before they have been assessed in a philological sense, for anyone making a historical investigation examines not only what is included in it but also what is absent. But I had to say the following: You have made your contribution; the world does of course recognize that you have precise knowledge of the events. If I let the pamphlet appear with von Moltke's memoirs, will you swear an oath that these three points are incorrect? He said: Yes!

I am fully convinced that these three points are correct, for they are also psychologically right in the way they are stated. But it would of course have been to no avail if the pamphlet had been enabled to appear (and all sorts of other chicanery were also a contributory factor); it would simply have been confiscated, that was very obvious. I could not let a pamphlet appear which would have elicited an oath sworn before all the world that the three points are incorrect. For we live in a world where what matters is not what is correct or incorrect but where power is the decisive factor.

I know that what I have written on page five of this pamphlet, and which I considered to be necessary in order to shed light on the situation in the right way, has been taken particularly amiss. I wrote: The calamitous invasion of Belgium, which was a military necessity and a political impossibility, shows how everything in Germany was placed at the highest level of military judgement in the times that preceded the war. The writer of these lines put the following question to Herr von Moltke, with whom he had had many years of friendship, in November 1914: What did the Kaiser think about the invasion? The reply was: Until a few days before the outbreak of the war he knew nothing about it, for being the kind of person he was there would have been the fear that he would have blurted it out to the whole world. That could not be allowed to happen, for the invasion could be successful only if the opponents were unprepared. I then asked: Did the Chancellor know about it? The answer was: Yes, he knew about it.

Thus politics have to be pursued in Central Europe in such a way that one takes chattering into account, and I ask you: Is it not a terrible tragedy if politics have to be conducted like this? The full proof can therefore be derived from these foundations that it is correct what Tirpitz[190] (for whom I otherwise have no particular liking) says about Bethmann-Hollweg,[191] that the latter had sunk metaphorically into a kneeling position and also outwardly brought the nullity of his politics to expression in his physiognomy. This nullity also came to expression later in that he emphasized to the English ambassador that if England were to launch an attack his whole political fabric would be like a house of cards. This did indeed occur, and this house of cards collapsed, and the chief of the General Staff had to write in his memoirs about the situation in which he was at that time on Saturday evening: The mood became ever more lively, and I stood completely alone.

The military judgement was therefore left to stand on its own; politics had completely broken down. This came about for the Germans that they no longer wanted to soar up to the great ideals which belong quite especially to their nature, ideals that are manifested in the great, significant epochs of German cultural development but to which there was no wish to aspire at the end of the nineteenth and the beginning of the twentieth century. That such a situation could only yield a disastrous outcome weighed like a heavy burden on the soul of the chief of the General Staff; and when an officer came to him in order that he might sign the instruction to telephone the troops not to go beyond the Belgian-French border, the chief of the General Staff threw down his pen onto the table so that it broke in pieces and said he would never sign such an order; the troops would become uncertain if such an order were to come from the chief of the General Staff. And then the chief of the General Staff was delivered from a mood of the most intense grief and despair. It was meanwhile long after ten o'clock. Another telegram had arrived from England, and—I would prefer not to specify the details—the commander-in-chief now pronounced the following words: Now you can do as you wish!

You see, one has to enter into the details, and I have given only a few main features of what happened on the continent. I should also like to mention the reciprocal gesture that happened on the other side. It will one day be authenticated—again, I can say that I do not relate this lightly—that at the same time that what I have narrated was happening in Berlin, Asquith and Grey[192] were saying: So what's really going on? Have we hitherto been conducting our English politics with a blindfold over our eyes? (They meant that English politics is determined from somewhere else; their eyes have been blindfolded.) And they said: Now the blindfold has been removed (this was Saturday evening); now that we can really see, we are standing before the abyss; only now can we launch into war.

This is the reflection beyond the Channel, and I beg you to take all this in such a way that it could be considerably extended, for in the time allotted to me I cannot do other than to present to you as a kind of mood what casts at least some light on the things that have happened.

And then, when you hear all this, I would ask you to read with this premiss what I have written in my 'Thoughts during the time of war', which I subtitled as being directed 'To the Germans and those who do not believe they have to hate them'.[193] All these details are considered there. I beg you to reflect upon what I have written there from this point of view, that it is not a question of what in the ordinary sense one calls moral guilt or moral innocence but that things must be elevated to the height of historical processes, in that something of tragic proportions has taken place where one can begin to speak of historical necessities which should not be subjected to the idle chatter of such judgements as I referred to at the beginning. Things are far more serious than the world on both sides supposes; nevertheless, the situation is such that it must be made known to the world, that steps can indeed be taken towards bringing order to the confusion. But there is at present no possibility that what one undertakes in this direction is presented to the world without its being distorted and slandered.

What I have said to you today about Colonel-General von Moltke gives a possibility of judging this man at this utterly critical hour; but there are, as you know, people of whom it is said that they were active in the General Staff who cause slanderous things to be said about Colonel-General von Moltke, including also the fanciful absurdity that he had been in touch with anthroposophical organizations before the Battle of the Marne and had as a result not done his duty. When these things are said from such a point of view one sees what moral state we have entered into today, and it is difficult to open up a right path for the truth within this moral attitude. To this end we need many, many active people; and only now that I have given you the basic premises of which I have spoken, I should like to read to you a passage from Moltke's memoirs which will show you what lived in this man's soul, firstly with regard to his opinion about the necessity for war and, secondly, with regard to his feeling of responsibility. For it is not a question of constructing a brutal concept of guilt but of entering into what lived in people's souls at that time. These are very simple words that Moltke has written, words which have often been expressed; but there is a difference whether they were written by any old person or by the one on whose soul the decision concerning the war lay. He wrote: 'Germany has not brought about this war, and it has not entered into it out of a lust for conquest or with aggressive intentions towards its neighbours. The war was forced upon it by its opponents, and we are fighting for our national existence, for the continuing existence of our people, for our national life.'[194]

If one is investigating actual realities, one does not arrive at a true picture by beginning somewhere at random; one must begin from where the realities, the actual events are at work. And if one can demonstrate that an essential aspect of the events themselves is being enacted in a man's soul, this is part of the facts that have created the situation if such a consciousness was dwelling in this soul. It is also part of the essential picture—if one is seeking to judge the situation—to look at what was taking place in between forty and fifty individuals who played a part in the outbreak of this terrible catastrophe; and anyone who acquires a judgement about these things not from prejudices but from actual information knows that all other than these forty to fifty individuals who brought about the war, who initiated activities amidst the constellation of circumstances in Europe, were taken largely unawares.

In the course of the war I have truly had the opportunity to speak about the matters in question with many people who were already able to judge something of the situation, and I have never minced my words. For example, I said to someone close to the leadership of a neutral state that it can be regarded as worthy of note that in our time which calls itself democratic some forty to fifty people were directly involved in bringing about this catastrophe in the international world. It would be necessary that one would first to some extent raise oneself up to the vantage-point from which alone one might judge this situation properly. Instead, an enormous amount is spoken about these serious, epoch-making events from the superficialities of White Papers and the like, and it has always been very difficult for someone who would not speak if he did not know things differently from many others to show what needs to be said to its best advantage wherever the situation that has arisen since 1914 is to be judged. This began for me already in the time when the 'J'accuse' books[195] were thrust at me in Switzerland, and I could say nothing other to people—you know how dangerous situations sometimes were—than what was true, although this would often be least understood. I said that they should read in such a book not the legal hair-splitting stuff that it contains but, rather, what lies in the style; they should take into account the whole structure, the whole presentation of the book; and if they have any taste they would have to say that it is political trash! I have had to say this again and again to people who belong to neutral and non-neutral regions. Of course, I am not therefore saying that in this 'J'accuse' book there are not many things that are correct; but it derives from a viewpoint that is to the very least degree suitable for addressing the world-historical tragedy of the situation in which the world came to be in 1914. And one must consider the underlying depths even if one is required only in some degree to speak about the question of blame.

Yet this question of blame also has something further to teach. You see, after the ill-starred declaration of a desire for peace[196] had been issued by Germany in the autumn or winter of 1916 and the whole fantasy of Woodrow Wilson's Fourteen Points had run its course, I had at that time—I was never with any degree of urgency met far beyond half-way because of people's resistance to me— approached those who had responsibility with the request, which to be sure seemed paradoxical to many, that there might be some valid- ity in presenting the idea of the threefolding of the social organism before the world in contrast to these unrealistic Fourteen Points of Wilson's, which in spite of their unworldliness were able to bring ships, cannons and human beings abundantly into the arena. And I have been obliged to experience that many have very well perceived that something of this kind should happen but that no one had the courage to do something in this direction, absolutely no one. For the conversation that I had with Kühlmann,[197] the witness who was present is there again today. So in these matters I cannot engage in any kind of untruthfulness. But I nevertheless have this to explain, and also in this respect I would certainly not tell you anything that is incorrect, since it is known precisely how things have turned out.

I must also add the following by way of an example. You see, already in January 1918 I considered the spring offensive of 1918 to be an absolute impossibility, and in the course of a journey that I had to make from Dornach to Berlin I came into conversation with a certain person—it was known that when the decisive moment would arrive this person would be called to the leadership of affairs—about the situation that really only emerged in November 1918, and when I had also here found a certain understanding for the threefolding of the social organism I arrived in Berlin. There I had to speak with someone. Those who were able to inform themselves about the way that the wind blows already knew about the offensive in January 1918, although one could not speak about it; and I had to speak with someone from the military who was very close to General Ludendorff.[198] The conversation had come roughly to the point when I said: I do not want to expose myself to the danger that I shall be reproached for wanting to interfere with matters of military strategy, but I want to speak from a certain starting-point which has nothing to do with a military dilettantism which I could well have. I said that Ludendorff might possibly achieve everything in a spring offensive that he could only dream of; but I nevertheless consider this offensive to be preposterous—and I gave three reasons that I had for saying so. The man to whom I was speaking became visibly stirred and he said: What do you want? Kühlmann has your pathetic concoction in his pocket, and he has gone with it to Brest-Litovsk. This is how we are served by politics. Politics mean nothing to us. We militarists can do nothing other than fight, fight, fight.

In 1914 the chief of the General Staff was in a situation that he had to describe in the evening hour: 'The mood became more and more lively, and I stood completely alone'.[199] With respect to the mood between ten and eleven o'clock he had to write: The Kaiser told me: 'Now you can do as you wish!' And in 1918 someone could say to me: Politics mean nothing to us; they are in a state of total collapse; we can do nothing other than fight, fight, fight.

My dear listeners, things have not changed, even today they have not changed, and I should like to give you a negative, to be sure only subjective, proof that they are no different.

Further things have been said emanating from the same unreality, the same abstract quality with which Woodrow Wilson has spoken, a quality that showed its true colours through the way that Woodrow Wilson conducted himself in Versailles. Harding[200] has continued to speak in the same vein; and I see in Harding's speech, which is as confused as it can possibly be, which is devoid of any sense of reality and again brings only the old slogans to a situation where we are now faced with economic as well as the political decisions of that time, nothing of the concerns that people have with what is approaching. Whether we have the first Wilson who demonstrates his confusion in Versailles, or whether we hear something later from the same quarter, is of no particular significance. What matters is that one has a watchful eye and a clear sense of reality.

One would then also perceive such things as the fact which is well-nigh incredible for anyone who has a feeling for the assessment of political situations, that this statesman who is characteristic of the modern trend, Lloyd George, said recently: One cannot allot to Germany moral guilt for the war in the old sense; people slipped into it in their stupidity.

He spoke in this way a few weeks ago, and you know how he spoke in London with regard to Simons. You can gauge from this what degree of truth there is in speeches which people give, and there is generally no impetus among people as a whole to look at these things; but this must be acquired, it must be acquired by gaining a broad sense of vision. This breadth of vision has figured in this catastrophe, and our misfortune is that no one had any notion of what it was. The possibility must be given that this broader understanding on which everything depends will become part of any decision also in Central Europe.

However, for as long as what is true is subjected to slander on the part of those who think they have got a monopoly on Germany in a particular kind of way, for as long as one is called a traitor to Germany by such people,[201] in spite of what has been said (although not really understood) regarding what would alone be suitable for creating the position that is fitting for the true German spirit, things cannot become any better. People who are of a quite different will, who have above all else the will to recognize the truth, must get together.

To be sure, there have also been warmongers in Germany; but everything that has originated from them has not been of significance at the crucial moment. But there is significance in what I have explained in the last chapter of my book *Towards Social Renewal*, namely, that it has been through losing a sense of vision that political life has arrived at a state of nullity. We shall only raise ourselves aloft in German life if we rise to a broad sense of vision; for someone who stands with a warm heart and not merely with his gob (please forgive the coarse expression) in German life knows that a true German quality means to grow together with a broad visionary outlook. But we must find our way back to the visionary, idealistic side of the German people; and it is out of what I have learnt that I am saying these things to you today. Despite the question being posed I might perhaps not have needed to answer; but I wanted to answer this particular question, and something that leads to the answering of such questions will become apparent to you if I present to you the concluding passage that the person who posed the question passed on to me in an appendix. He writes: I considered it to be very valuable to publish and widely disseminate the correct, clear view of this whole question of blame for the war.

Well, in May 1919 this was to have happened. The memorandum had also been printed. The world within Germany prevented this memorandum from appearing. Let us not remain content with merely forming the judgement that something of this kind needed to happen; one should support those who are not satisfied with making this judgement but have long tried to carry out at the crucial moment what is being proposed here. We shall then be able to progress further.

My dear listeners, it is because I nevertheless believe that there are among the German youth individuals who will again find the path to the true German spirit, who have the mind and heart and receptive souls for the receiving of the truth, it is because I was able to speak here out of a certain perspective to younger people, perhaps to the best part of our younger generation, that I decided to address these indications to you today.

NOTES

Text sources: It has not been possible in every case to establish who compiled the notes or shorthand reports on which the texts of the lectures are based. The first lecture is a report which Adolf Arenson wrote from memory and in accordance with notes taken by various participants. Lectures 9–15 were recorded in shorthand by Hedda Hummel (Cologne). It is not known who took the other lectures down in shorthand.

Only one of the lectures has been published in book form in English—that of 23 November 1915, as part of a volume entitled *Life beyond Death* (Rudolf Steiner Press, 1995). The following lectures are available in typescript form from the Library, Rudolf Steiner House, London: 13 and 14 February 1915 in Typescript Z 270, 22 November 1915 in Typescript Z 367, 24 November 1915 in Typescript NSL 187, 23 February 1918 in NSL 298, 24 February 1918 in NSL 241 and 26 April 1918 in Typescript NSL 245. The other eight lectures have not previously been translated.

1   The notes of this lecture cannot be regarded as wholly reliable. There is much that is suggestive of omissions and even of erroneous recording of the spoken words. The reader should take account of the notes to the text at the end of the volume. The present text is based upon typed notes. It was not possible to check these with the original sources. The lecture of 13 September 1914 in Munich (GA 174a) is similar as regards its content.

2   'All those can work together in a brotherly way in the Society who consider a common spirituality in all human souls, whatever their differences as regards beliefs, nation, class or sex, to be the foundation of a loving interaction with one another.'

3   In the Gesamtausgabe (Collected Works), *Die Rätsel der Philosophie* has meanwhile appeared in a single volume (GA 18). The passage to which Rudolf Steiner is referring, which is concerned with the transition from the French philosophers Boutroux (1845–1921) and Bergson (1859–1890) to the German philosopher Wilhelm Heinrich Preuß (1843–1909), can be found on page 564 of the German edition and on page 423 of the English edition, *Riddles of Philosophy*, Anthroposophic Press, New York 1973.

4   Maurice Maeterlinck (1862–1949), Belgian writer and poet. His first philosophical work *Le trésor des humbles* appeared in 1896 and in German translation in 1898 under the title *Der Schatz der Armen*. In this book there is a chapter about Novalis which begins with the words: 'Human beings go different ways, says our author; anyone who follows them and compares them will see strange constructs arising. I have chosen three such individuals whose paths lead us to different summits.' Whereupon he specifies the Flemish mystic Ruysbroeck, Emerson and Novalis. In 1895 he had rendered Novalis's unfinished novel *Die Lehrlinge zu Sais* and his *Fragmente* into French and went on to publish them.

5   The battle at Mylae referred to took place during the First Punic War, which lasted from 264–241 BC, under the Roman general C. Duilius.

6   This refers to the conquest of Lüttich during the night of 5/6 August by the 14th Infantry Brigade under Ludendorff. Through this the highly endangered execution of the German military campaign was made possible.

7   Eleven lectures given at Christiania (Oslo) in June 1910 (GA 121).

8   Annie Besant (1847–1933) was from 1907 onwards the president of the Theosophical Society. When she declared that the Indian boy Krishnamurti was the bearer of an expected earthly reincarnation of Christ, Rudolf Steiner had to oppose this notion. This led to the exclusion of the German Section under his leadership from the Theosophical Society and to the founding of the Anthroposophical Society (1912/13).

9   The first of the four Mystery Plays which were written in the years 1910–1913 (GA 14). The three figures referred to are Philia, Astrid and Luna, who in the dramatis personae are called 'friends of Maria', 'whose archetypes are revealed in the course of the play as Maria's soul-forces'.

10   Rudolf Steiner writes as follows about Herman Grimm in his autobiography, *The Course of My Life* (Chapter 14): 'It was as an art historian that Herman

Grimm had become concerned with Goethe; in this capacity he gave lectures about Goethe at the University of Berlin which he then published as a book. But he could well be looked upon as a kind of cultural descendant of Goethe. He originated from those circles of German cultural life that had always retained a living tradition of Goethe and which could in a sense think of themselves as having a personal connection with him. Herman Grimm's wife was Gisela von Arnim, the daughter of Bettina, the author of the book *Goethes Briefwechsel mit einem Kinde* (Goethe's Correspondence with a Child).' Herman Grimm lived from 1828 until 1901. The three quoted passages derive from his book *Homers Ilias* (Homer's Iliad), two vols., 1890–95. See p. 214 of the 1907 German edition.

11 Four lectures between 12 and 16 July 1914, published under the title *Christ and the Human Soul* (GA 155). The things said in relation to 'surprises' that had occurred 'recently' probably relates to an address that Rudolf Steiner gave during that cycle, of which only inadequate notes exist (an address of 16 July 1914 about the Johannesbau (St John's Building or Goetheanum)).

12 Between 1909 and 1913 there were annual gatherings of the Theosophical (in 1913 the Anthroposophical) Society in Munich in the second half of August. On each occasion Rudolf Steiner gave a lecture-cycle in connection with a dramatic performance. An event of this kind was envisaged and announced for August 1914. It could not take place because of the outbreak of the war.

13 The assassination was on 28 June. Probably an inaccuracy in the notes of the lecture.

14 On 1 September Rudolf Steiner gave a lecture for members there entitled 'The Destinies of Individuals and of Nations' (the first lecture in GA 157).

15 In September 1914 Rudolf Steiner stopped briefly in Vienna on his way back from Berlin to Switzerland. The quotation is from an article by Robert Michael in *Österreichische Rundschau*, 40th year, vol. 5, 1.9.1914, p. 302–306.

16 In the lecture 'The Creative World of Colour' (GA 286), included in *Architecture as a Synthesis of the Arts*, Rudolf Steiner Press, London 1999.

17 Gottlieb von Jagow (1863–1935) was the state secretary of the German Foreign Office during the years 1913–1916.

18   It has not been possible to identify the source.

19   This maxim (in its original form: 'Wisdom is only in truth') derives from Goethe and can be found in *Goethe's Natural-Scientific Writings*, edited by Rudolf Steiner with introductions, footnotes and elucidations in the text published in Kürschner's *Deutsche National-Literatur* 1884–1897, 5 volumes, Dornach 1975, GA 1 a–e, vol. 4, part 2, 'Sprüche in Prosa', section 1, 'Das Erkennen'. Rudolf Steiner chose the maxim as a motto for the principles that he gave to the newly founded Anthroposophical Society in 1913. See lecture 2 in *The Anthroposophic Movement* (GA 258), Rudolf Steiner Press, Forest Row 2022.

20   Rudolf Steiner subsequently changed the word in the penultimate line rendered by George and Mary Adams in this translation as 'glory' (the original German word was '*Lob*', literally meaning 'praise') to 'light' ('*Licht*'). It is the earlier German word that is used in the bilingual text of *Verses and Meditations* (Rudolf Steiner Press, 1961/1993).

21   In addition to the lecture on 30 September 1914 (see the first lecture in this volume), Rudolf Steiner also gave a lecture for members on 6 December 1914 in Stuttgart of which no notes are extant.

22   In the shorthand report and in the previous German edition this sentence runs as follows: '*Und es wäre das größte Unglück,—und wird von keiner Notwendigkeit jemals herbeigeführt werden können, wenn jemals das slawische Element das germanische besiegen würde*'. (The words between the two commas may roughly be translated by the phrase 'and can never happen'.) These latter words are omitted in the edition from which the present translation has been made, since in the editor's view they do not fit either linguistically or semantically into the rest of the sentence.

23   David Friedrich Strauß (1808–1874), *Krieg und Friede, zwei Briefe an Ernest Renan nebst dessen Antwort auf den ersten* (War and Peace, two letters to Ernest Renan together with his answer to the first), Leipzig 1870. Renan's letter is dated 13 September 1870.

24   The publication *Über die ästhetische Erziehung des Menschen, in einer Reihe von Briefen* by Friedrich Schiller (1759–1805) appeared in 1795.

25   Johann Gottlieb Fichte (1762–1814) gave his *Reden an die deutsche Nation* in the winter of 1807–08 in Berlin. This was immediately after Prussia's defeat by Napoleon. The town of Prussian Eylau was still occupied by French troops.

26 A few years before the First World War, the Indian boy Krishnamurti—who later became known as a philosopher—was within the theosophical movement made out to be the bearer of an anticipated reincarnation of Christ in the earthly sphere. Rudolf Steiner's opposition to this notion led to the exclusion from the Theosophical Society of the German Section under his leadership and to the founding of an Anthroposophical Society. Krishnamurti subsequently out of himself rejected the role that had been intended for him.

27 Johannes Tauler, c. 1300–1361.

28 Meister Eckhardt, 1260–1327.

29 Angelus Silesius, 1624–1677.

30 Robert Hamerling, 1830–1889. The first collected edition of his works (in four volumes) appeared only in 1900. Ten years later an edition of the *Sämtliche Werke* edited by Michael Maria Rebenlechner appeared in 16 volumes. The first volume of this edition contains a detailed description of Hamerling's life and work.

31 Raskolnikov is the name of the hero of the famous novel *Crime and Punishment* (1867) by Dostoyevsky (1818–1881).

32 The source of this idea has not been identified.

33 The person in question was the naturalist Carl Vogt (1817–1895), and the source was *Politische Briefe an Friedrich Kolb* (Political Letters to Friedrich Kolb), reprinted from the Schweizer Handels-Courier, Biel 1870.

34 '*Warum nennen "sie" das Volk Fichtes und Schillers ein Barbarenvolk?*' (Why do 'they' call the nation of Fichte and Schiller a nation of barbarians?), Stuttgart, 15 February 1915. In the Collected Works the parallel lecture given in Berlin on 15 November 1914 is printed in GA 64.

35 GA 121.

36 See the first lecture in this volume.

37 The first of Rudolf Steiner's four Mystery Plays, written in 1910. The passage referred to can be found in the first scene. The four plays appear in the Collected Works in a single volume, GA 14.

38 See above all the volume entitled *The Event of Christ's Appearance in the Etheric World* (GA 118). Several of these lectures are included in the volume *The Reappearance of Christ in the Etheric,* SteinerBooks 2022.

39 For example, in the lecture of 1 January 1914, the fourth lecture in the cycle *Christ and the Spiritual World* (GA149); in that of 17 January 1915,

the fourth lecture in *The Destinies of Individuals and of Nations* (GA 157); and in several lectures in *The Mystery of Death* (GA 159).

40   Constantine, who ruled in Rome from 313 until 337 (and who was the sole ruler from 323), was favourable to and acknowledged Christianity, whereas his predecessors had had the Christians persecuted.

41   Jeanne d'Arc, 1412–1431.

42   This is known as 'The Dream Song of Olaf Åsteson'. Rudolf Steiner made a version of it in German and spoke several times about it, above all during the Christmas and New Year periods of the years 1912 to 1915. The lectures relating to it are published in the volume *Our Connection with the Elemental World* (GA 158). The text of the Dream Song is included there on pages 140–147.

43   Ernst Mach (1838–1916), *Beiträge zur Analyse der Empfindungen*, first published in Jena in 1886, with several editions since. The quotation is not verbatim.

44   *The Inner Nature of Man and the Life between Death and a New Birth*, eight lectures given in Vienna in April 1914 (GA 153).

45   This was Sybil Colazza, who died in January 1915. The funeral ceremony took place on 31 January 1915. See *Our Dead, Memorial, Funeral and Cremation Addresses* (GA 261), English edition SteinerBooks 2011, p. 104–110.

46   See ibid., p. 90–92.

47   Sophie Stinde, 1853–1915. From 1902 onwards she had been a member of the Executive Council of the Munich branch, then a Council member of the German Section of the Theosophical Society. She also helped in the production of Rudolf Steiner's Mystery Plays in Munich and in bringing the conception of the building to realization.

48   The memorial words were spoken in Munich on 30 November 1915. See *Our Dead*, p. 151–162.

49   This probably refers to the lecture of 26 November 1914, included in GA 64.

50   In *Faust* Part 2, Act 2, 'Laboratory', Homunculus says to Mephistopheles: 'You from the north,/And in the age of mist brought forth [literally, "became young"]'.

51   The relevant sections can be found, respectively, in the chapter entitled 'Sleep and Death' (GA 13) and in the chapter 'The Soul in the Soul-World after Death' (GA 9).

[52] In the fourth and especially the fifth lectures in this volume.

[53] *The Soul's Probation*, Scene 1 (GA 14).

[54] Moritz Benedikt (1835–1920), professor in Vienna. He was with Lombroso the founder of criminal anthropology. Published his *Anatomische Studien an Verbrechergehirnen* (Anatomical Studies of Brains of Criminals) in 1878.

[55] See note 8.

[56] Cf. lectures 2 and 3 in this volume.

[57] Cf., for example, *The Mission of Individual Folk Souls* (GA 121) and *The Destiny of Individuals and of Nations* (GA 157).

[58] Johann Gottlieb Herder, 1744–1803. Especially in the chapter on the Slavic peoples in the sixteenth volume of his *Ideen zur Philosophie der Geschichte der Menschheit* (Ideas relating to a philosophy of the history of humanity).

[59] No record of the lecture given on 13 March 1916 in Stuttgart entitled '*Ein vergessenes Streben nach Geisteswissenschaft innerhalb der deutschen Gedankenentwickelung*' (A forgotten aspiration for spiritual science within the development of German thought) has survived. The parallel lecture given in Berlin is, however, published in GA 65.

[60] Elizabeth I reigned from 1558 to 1603. Under her rulership the mighty fleet of Spain was conquered by the English and the foundation laid for the supremacy of Great Britain in Western Europe.

[61] Georg Wilhelm Friedrich Hegel (1770–1831), Friedrich Wilhelm Joseph Schelling (1775–1854), Johann Gottlieb Fichte (1762–1814).

[62] In the public lecture of 25 November 1915, published in the journal *Anthroposophie* 1931/32, vol. 1–2, under the title '*Das Weltbild des deutschen Idealismus. Eine Betrachtung im Hinblick auf unsere schicksaltragender Zeit*' (The world picture of German idealism. A study concerning our destiny-laden time). Cf. also the parallel lecture in GA 64.

[63] Rudolf Steiner edited Goethe's scientific writings in Kürschner's *Deutsche National-Literatur* and provided them with introductions and notes (1884–1897). The introductions appeared as a separate publication under the title *Einleitungen zu Goethes Naturwissenschaftlichen Schriften. Zugleich eine Grundlegung der Geisteswissenschaft (Anthroposophie)* (Introductions to Goethe's Scientific Writings. At the same time a foundation of Spiritual

Science (Anthroposophy)), GA 1. Compare also the book *Goethes Welt-anschauung* (Goethe's World-Conception), 1897, GA 6.

[64]   See note 26.

[65]   Helena Petrovna Blavatsky (1831–1891). Founded the Theosophical Society together with H.S. Olcott. Cf. Rudolf Steiner, *The Occult Movement in the Nineteenth Century* (GA 254). For further insight into these complex issues, see Sergei O. Prokofieff, *The East in the Light of the West*, Temple Lodge, Forest Row 2009.

[66]   Annie Besant came in the autumn of 1904 to Germany at Rudolf Steiner's invitation and gave lectures in Hamburg and in a number of other German cities. See the volume of articles from *Lucifer-Gnosis*, GA 34, 1960, p. 553 f.

[67]   See the reference to note 65.

[68]   In the lecture of 18 March 1916 Rudolf Steiner says: '...everything associated with medical advice must be kept away from my person...' (GA 174a, *Central Europe between East and West*).

[69]   A lecture given in London in 1902.

[70]   'Madame de Thèbes', the pseudonym of, allegedly, Anne Victorine de Savigny, who published an occult almanac every year in Paris. Cf. the following note.

[71]   *Almanach de Mme de Thèbes. Conseils pour être heureux*, Paris 1912. Cf. also the lecture of 24 March 1916 in GA 65.

[72]   *Paris midi*, cf. GA 65 and also the following note.

[73]   Jean Jaurès, 1859–1914, leader of the French Socialists. Opposed the entry of France into the war in 1914 and was murdered in the first days of the war. *Paris midi* (Maurice de Wallef) and a whole number of other Parisian newspapers had made 'advance announcements' and threats (cf. Jaurès's speech in the chamber of 4 July 1913: '*...dans vos journaux, vos articles, chez ceux qui vous soutiennent, il y a contre nous, vous m'entendez, un perpetual appel à l'assasinat! ... et M. Paul Adam ajoutait pour vous que tous ces hommes tomberaient frappés au premier jour de la declaration de guerre*') ('...in your journals, your articles, among those who support you, there is—believe me—a constant appeal for assassination directed against us! ...and M. Paul Adam added in this same sense that all these men [those such as Jaurès who, as opponents of the three-year period of service, were in the view of the right-wing French press 'in a pact with the devil'] will

be the first to be killed when war is declared'). Cf. *La voix d'outre tombe Discours de Jean Jaurès. Recueillis et commentés par Victor Schiff*, Berlin 1919, p. 18: *Discours à la chambre le 4 juillet 1913*. Jaurès advocated a two-year period of military service. (Notes 70–73 are derived from the research of C.S. Picht published in his edition of the lecture of 24 March 1916 in the journal *Anthroposophie*, 16th year 1933/4 book 2.)

[74] Catherine A. Tingley founded a splinter group of the Theosophical Society called 'Universal Brotherhood' in Point Loma, California.

[75] Mabel Collins, *Light on the Path. A treatise written for the personal use of those who are ignorant of the Eastern wisdom, and who desire to enter within its influence.* Shortly after its publication by the Theosophical Society, it was translated from the English into German; and a second edition was published in Leipzig in 1888. See Rudolf Steiner's 'exegesis' in *Guidance in Esoteric Training* (part of GA 245), Rudolf Steiner Press 1972.

[76] See lectures 4–6 in this volume.

[77] See note 59.

[78] Meister Bertram, c. 1345–1415. Panel of the Grabow altar-piece from 1379, Kunsthalle, Hamburg. Cf. also *The Human Spirit, Past and Present* (GA 167), Rudolf Steiner Press, Forest Row 2015.

[79] 21 February 1916: '*Ein vergessenes Streben nach Geisteswissenschaft innerhalb der deutschen Gedankenentwickelung*' (see note 59), hitherto unpublished. Cf. the parallel lecture in Berlin on 25 February 1916 in GA 65 (not currently available in English).

[80] Bertha von Suttner, 1843–1914, pacifist writer, author of *Die Waffen nieder* ('Put down your weapons'), led an International Peace Bureau and received the Nobel Peace Prize in 1905.

[81] This was Tsar Nicholas II, who in 1908 had suggested the idea of a general Peace Conference in The Hague where there were discussions about the limitation of armaments and the maintaining of the status quo.

[82] In the lecture '*Unsere Weltlage. Krieg, Frieden und die Wissenschaft des Geistes*' (Our world situation. War, peace and the science of the spirit) given on 12 October 1905 (GA 54). This lecture was most recently published in English translation in *Anthroposophical Review*, no. 7:3.

[83] This was during the public lecture given in Stuttgart on 13 March 1916 (see note 59). Rudolf Seiner mentioned Karl Christian Planck (1819–1880) especially often in 1916. Cf. GA 65. It is, for example, clear from Rudolf

Steiner's comments in his book *The Riddles of Philosophy* that, while he would not have agreed with all of Planck's philosophical views, he greatly valued him as a thinker and—what is more to the point in the present context—considered that he was not sufficiently appreciated or widely known.

84 Ernst Haeckel, 1834–1919.

85 Karl Ernst von Baer, 1792–1876. The quotation on p. 124 comes from *Reden und kleinere Aufsätze vermischten Inhalts* (Addresses and shorter essays on various themes), St Petersburg 1864–76, vol. I, p. 71 f.

86 Tertullian (160–220), Christian theological writer; Gregory of Nazianzus (329–390), Church Father.

87 Hermann von Helmholtz, 1821–1894.

88 *Gedanken während der Zeit des Krieges* (1915). Printed in *Aufsätze über die Dreigliederung des sozialen Organismus und zur Zeitlage 1915–1921* (GA 24). Not available in English.

89 Julian Offray de Lamettrie, 1709–1751. The quotation is from *L'homme machine*.

90 The lecture was preceded by commemorative words for the deceased members Barth, Rettich and Dieterle. See *Our Dead. Memorial, Funeral and Cremation Addresses 1906–1924*, GA 261, English edition Steinerbooks 2011, p. 215 f.

91 As is evident from Rudolf Steiner's letter of 20 November 1905 to Marie von Sivers, this relates to the lecture given on 19 November 1905 in Colmar. Cf. *Correspondence and Documents, 1901–1925* (GA 262), p. 67.

92 This is a paraphrase of a sentence from the chapter entitled 'Conditions' in *Knowledge of the Higher Worlds*, where it is qualified by the accompanying passage. Cf. also the Preface to the fifth edition of 1914 and the Appendix to the eighth edition of 1918, where further qualifications are added.

93 Karl V, 1500–1558; François I, 1494–1547.

94 Leo Königsberger, 1837–1921.

95 Woodrow Wilson: see note 113.

96 This probably refers to the dissertation of F. Stepun, *Wladimir Solewjew*, Heidelberg 1910. Solovyov's book *God, Man and Church: the Spiritual Foundations of Life* (to give the title of the 1938 English translation) was published in a German translation by Nina Hoffmann in 1907. Further volumes of his works appeared in 1911 and 1912, and in 1914 and 1916

there appeared the first two volumes of his complete works in German. This edition was extended in 1921/22 with two further volumes; and Rudolf Steiner wrote an introduction to the third volume. Vladimir Solovyov lived from 1853 to 1900.

[97] See note 90.

[98] Marie Steiner-von Sivers, 1867–1948.

[99] Cf. the lectures of 29 May 1917 in GA 176 (*Aspects of Human Evolution*) and 10 June 1917, intended for GA 255 (an English translation is available in Typescript Z 184, *Characteristics of the Present Time*).

[100] Max Seiling, 1852–1928.

[101] *Theosophie und Christentum*, Berlin 1910.

[102] *Wer war Christus?*, Munich 1917.

[103] The newspaper article by Seiling is not available.

[104] Max Heindel, who also called himself Graßhoff. Concerning the plagiarist Heindel, who dashed off books from writings and lectures by Rudolf Steiner which he published under his own name and who founded an occult society in California, cf. Rudolf Steiner in *Mitteilungen der Anthroposophischen Gesellschaft (Theosophischen Gesellschaft)*, no. 1, Part 1, Cologne, March 1913, p. 23.

[105] This was issued by The Rosicrucian Fellowship, first edition, Chicago 1909. A German translation was published in Leipzig shortly afterwards.

[106] Dr Hugo Vollrath, at the time proprietor of the *Theosophisches Verlagshaus* (Theosophical Publishing House).

[107] Arthur Schopenhauer, 1788–1860. *Die beiden Grundprobleme der Ethik*, I, 'Über die Freiheit des menschlichen Willens', Frankfurt 1841. 'Alles, was geschieht, vom Größten bis zum Kleinsten, geschieht notwendig' (p. 93).

[108] Ernest Renan, 1823–1892. His book *La vie Jésu* was published in German translation in 1863.

[109] From a letter dated 6 September 1845 to Abbé Cognat. It was published in German translation in *Errinerungen an meiner Kindheit und Jugendzeit*, Basel 1883. The quotation does not reproduce Renan's exact words.

[110] This is likewise not a literal quotation, and the reference can be found in German translation in Renan's book *Jugenderrinerungen* (Youthful Memories), Frankfurt am Main 1925, p. 318.

[111] Richard Wahle, 1857–1935. *Die Tragikomödie der Weisheit*, Vienna and Leipzig 1915. The actual wording is as follows: 'We have no more philosophy than an animal, and only the frantic attempts to arrive at a philosophy and the final resignation in not knowing distinguish us from the animals', p. 132.

[112] Maurice Barrès, 1862–1923. The quotations are taken from an article by André Germain published in German in the *Internationale Rundschau*, 1st year, vol. 3, Zurich, 20 July 1915, '*Abschied vom Führer der Jugend*' (Farewell from the Leader of Youth).

[113] Woodrow Wilson, 1856–1924, President of the United States from 1913 until 1921. Wilson's speeches: *The New Freedom* (1913, German translation, Munich 1914, Wilson's notes in *The War, the Peace* (German translation, Zurich 1918).

[114] In the dialogue *Phaedo*, Chapters 25–29.

[115] In the third Mystery Play *The Guardian of the Threshold*, Scene one (words of Hilarius). See *Four Mystery Plays*, 1910–1913 (GA 14).

[116] Rudolf Kjellén, 1864–1922. *Der Staat als Lebensform*, Leipzig 1916.

[117] Numa Denis, Fustel de Coulanges, 1830–1889, *La cité antique*.

[118] Alexander von Bernus, 1880–1965. Publisher of the journal *Das Reich*, Munich 1916–1920.

[119] It has not been possible to establish to whom this refers.

[120] This was entitled '*Menschenseele und Menschenleib in Natur- und Geist-Erkenntnis*' (Human Soul and Human Body in the Knowledge of Nature and the Spirit), 14 May 1917, hitherto unpublished in the *Gesamtausgabe* (Collected Works).

[121] Genesis 15:5 and 22:17. See Rudolf Steiner, *Deeper Secrets of Human Evolution in the Light of the Gospels* (GA 117), Rudolf Steiner Press, Forest Row 2021, p. 44.

[122] Psalm 90 verse 10.

[123] In other lectures Rudolf Steiner mentions in this connection the—at that time—very celebrated philological historian Ulrich von Wilamowitz-Moellendorf (1848–1931); thus, for example, in the volume translated as *Materialism and the Task of Anthroposophy* (GA 204), Anthroposophic Press, New York 1987, where on p. 113 he says: '...the leading cultural moron of modern civilisation, Wilamowitz,... who clothed the Greek tragedians in modern, trivial garments that won the undying

admiration of all those who penetrate as deeply into the Greek word as they are distant from the Greek spirit'.

[124] *Odyssey*, 11th song, line 488 f.

[125] In his book *Aristoteles und seine Weltanschuung* (Aristotle and his World-Conception) and in the chapter '*Das Diesseits als Vorbereitung auf ein allbeseligendes und jedem gerecht vergeltendes Jenseits*' (This Side of the Threshold as a Preparation for a Yonder Side that is most Blissful and rightly Valid for Everyone), Franz Brentano gives a comprehensive summary of Aristotle's remarks about the soul's experience after death, which are scattered throughout his various writings.

[126] Franz Brentano (1838–1917). *Die Psychologie des Aristoteles*, Mainz 1867. Rudolf Steiner gives a free rendition of what Brentano says on p. 196 of this book.

[127] In the 13th chapter of the dialogue *Phaedo*. The passage concerned runs as follows: 'And so may also those who have arranged initiations for us not be bad people but indicate to us in good time if someone reaches the lower world uninitiated and unconsecrated that he comes to lie in the mud, but when the purified and initiated arrive there they dwell with the Gods'.

[128] Gaius Julius Caligula (12–41 AD), Roman Caesar 37–41 AD.

[129] The Second Coming of Christ.

[130] Helena Petrovna Blavatsky, 1831–1891. In *The Secret Doctrine* vol. III, Ch. 39, 'Cycles and Avatars'.

[131] Since this Council, the so-called trichotomy—whereby man consists of body, soul and spirit—has been rejected as a heresy.

[132] Wilhelm Wundt, 1832–1920, medical doctor, philosopher and psychologist, founded in Leipzig the first institute for experimental psychology; wrote among other things *Grundzüge der physiologischen Psychologie* (Principles of Physiological Psychology) and *Völkerpsychologie* (Psychology of Nations).

[133] See notes 99–102.

[134] In 1911 the decisive disputes between the leadership of the Theosophical Society in Adyar and the German Section under Rudolf Steiner took place—this was in connection with the founding of the so-called 'Order of the Star of the East' by Annie Besant. The formal separation ensued only at the end of 1912.

135 Édouard Schuré, 1841–1929. Schuré, who had been connected with Rudolf Steiner and Marie von Sivers since 1906, had published a hate-filled article against Steiner in France during the First World War. After the war he regretted his behaviour—which was dictated by chauvinistic passion—and asked verbally and by letter for forgiveness. In August 1922 Schuré participated in the so-called 'French Course' (*Cosmology, Religion and Philosophy*, GA 25).

136 See note 19.

137 Friedrich Theodor Vischer, 1801–1887: '*Der Traum. Eine Studie zu der Schrift* Die Traumphantasie *von Dr. Johannes Volkelt*' in *Altes und Neues*, Stuttgart 1881.

138 On 25 May 1789 for a teaching position at the University of Jena: '*Was heißt and zu welchem Ende studiert man Universalgeschichte?*' (What means, and to what end does one study, world history?).

139 Gustave Hervé, 1871–1944. Journalist and author.

140 Georges Clemenceau, 1841–1929, French statesman known as 'the tiger'. He was Prime Minister from 1906 to 1909 and from 1917 until 1920, and was chairman of the Versailles Peace Conference.

141 In 1918 the chairman of the Goethe Society was the retired Prussian Minister of State and Finance, the president of the Rhine Province Georg Kreuzwendedich Freiherr von Rheinbaben.

142 *The Mission of Individual Folk-Souls* (1910), GA 121.

143 *The Inner Nature of Man and the Life between Death and a New Birth*, GA 153.

144 Cf. among other lectures *The Fall of the Spirits of Darkness*, GA 177.

145 *Leitfaden der physiologischen Psychologie in 15 Vorlesungen* (Basic Textbook of Physiological Psychology in 15 Lectures), 5th edition Jena 1900, p. 161 and 205 (the quotations are not word for word).

146 Vladimir Ilyich Lenin, 1870–1924.

147 Lev (Leon) Davidovich Trotsky, 1879–1940.

148 This is probably the book by E. Rasmussen, *Jesus, eine vergleichende psychopathologisiche Studie* (Jesus, a comparative psycho-pathological study), Leipzig 1905.

149 Alexander Moszkowski was a journalist in Berlin and the publisher of a journal called *Lustige Blätter* (literally, cheerful pages).

150 In *The Occult Foundations of the Bhagavad Gita* (GA 146), lecture 5.

151 Origen, 182–253.

[152] The quotation derives from Ludwig Anzengruber (1839–1889), *Ein Faustschlag*, a play in three acts, Act 3, Scene 6, Kammauf: '...Keep me from all antiquated traditions of the body, they do not concern me in the least, for—even if it is true there is a God!—I am an atheist'.

[153] '*Après nous le déluge*' (after us the flood) is a remark attributed to the French king, Louis XV (1710–74).

[154] Oscar Hertwig, 1849–1922, *Das Werden der Organismen*, Jena 1916.

[155] Eduard von Hartmann, 1842–1906, *Philosophie des Unbewußten. Versuch einer Weltanschauung*, Berlin 1869.

[156] *Das Unbewußte vom Standpunkt der Physiologie und Deszendenztheorie: eine kritische Beleuchtung des naturphilosophischen Teils der 'Philosophie des Unbewußten' aus naturwissenschaftlichen Gesichtspunkten* (The Unconscious from the Standpoint of Physiology and the Theory of Evolution: a critical study of the part of the *Philosophy of the Unconscious* relating to the philosophy of nature), Berlin 1872; 2nd edition under the name of Hartmann including 'general preliminary observations' and additions, 1877.

[157] Oskar Schmidt, 1823–1886, zoologist. *Die naturwissenschaftlichen Grundlagen der 'Philosophie des Unbewußten'* (The Scientific Foundations of the *Philosophy of the Unconscious*), Leipzig 1877. Regarding the anonymous book (by Eduard von Hartmann) he writes that it 'has fully confirmed all who have not sworn allegiance to the unconscious in their conviction that Darwinism is in the right', p. 3.

[158] Oscar Hertwig, *Zur Abwehr des sozialen, des ethischen und des politischen Darwinismus*, Jena 1918.

[159] Hermann Ludwig Ferdinand Helmholtz (1821–94) was a German physicist and physiologist. He was the inventor of the opthalmoscope.

[160] Fritz Mauthner, 1849–1923. Author of *Wörterbuch der Philosophie* (Dictionary of Philosophy). The article '*Goethes Horoscop*' appeared in the *Berliner Tageblatt*, 47th year 1918, no. 161 (evening edition of 28 March).

[161] '*Sternglaube und Sterndeutung. Die Geschichte und das Wesen der Astrologie*' (Astrology and its Interpretation. The History and Nature of Astrology). Presented by Prof. Dr Franz Boll with the collaboration of Prof. Carl Bezold, Leipzig and Berlin 1918. (*Aus Natur und Geisteswelt* vol. 638.)

[162] '*Die Rätsel des geschichtlichen Lebens der Menschheit nach Ergebnissen der Geisteswissenschaft*' (The Riddles of the Historical Life of Mankind according to the Results of Spiritual Science), 25 April 1918. Published in *Die*

Menschenschule, 1961, 35th year vol. 10. An English translation exists of this and a lecture given on the previous day under the title *Reincarnation and Immortality*. Rudolf Steiner also spoke about the same subject in the lecture of 14 March 1918 in Berlin (GA 67). This has not been translated.

[163] Vincenz Knauer, 1828–1894, Professor of Philosophy in Vienna whom Rudolf Steiner frequently encountered in delle Grazie's house in Vienna. Cf. Rudolf Steiner, *The Course of My Life*, Ch. 7. The passage referred to can be found in Knauer's book *Hauptprobleme der Philosophie*, Vienna and Leipzig 1892, 21st lecture, I Die Erkenntnisquellen, p. 136 f.

[164] Jean-Baptiste Lamarck, 1744–1829, French botanist and zoologist.

[165] Goethe's descriptions of cloud formations are in volume 2, 'Meteorology'. See note 19. In his book *Man or Matter* (Faber and Faber 1958), Ernst Lehrs refers at some length to two British pioneers in the field of meteorology, John Ruskin (1819–1900) and Luke Howard (1772–1864).

[166] Karl Christian Planck, 1819–1889. Cf. Rudolf Steiner, *The Riddles of Philosophy*, GA 18, and *The Riddle of Man*, GA 20.

[167] Cf. *Die beiden Grundprobleme der Ethik* (The two basic Problems of Ethics), preface to the first edition, and Friedrich Nietzsche, *Menschliches— Allzumenschliches* (Human, All Too Human), 8th section 482.

[168] Alfred Loisy, 1857–1940, historian of religion. Excommunicated on account of his books of Biblical criticism.

[169] From 12 to 23 March 1921 a seminar entitled '*Weltgeschichte im Sinne der Anthroposophie*' (World History in the Light of Anthroposophy) took place in Stuttgart within the context of the '*Freien anthroposophischen Hochschulkurse*' (Courses arranged by the Free Anthroposophical University) under the leadership of Dr W.J. Stein, Dr Karl Heyer and Dr Eugen Kolisko.

[170] It is not entirely clear what this refers to.

[171] Nikola or Nikita, Prince and King of Montenegro, 1860–1918.

[172] Karl Helferich, 1872–1924, General Secretary of State and leader of the German National Party, opponent of Erzberger.

[173] Matthias Erzberger 1875–1921, leader of the German Centre Party, opponent of Helferich. Was murdered by predecessors of National Socialism.

174 Walter Simons, 1861–1937, from 1920 to 1921 Foreign Minister of the German Reich and afterwards president of the imperial court in Leipzig.

175 David Lloyd George, 1863–1945. From 1902–1922 the dominating figure in British politics.

176 This was the result of the Berlin Congress of 1878 about the Balkans. Austria was entrusted with the occupation of Bosnia and Herzegovina (hitherto Turkish).

177 Cf. note 120.

178 The drawing to which this explanation relates has not been preserved.

179 '*An das deutsche Volk und die Kulturwelt*', printed in *Die Kernpunkte der sozialen Frage* (1919), GA 23. An English translation was published in 1985 as an appendix to *The Renewal of the Social Organism* (GA 24). See also the most recent English edition of GA 23, *Towards Social Renewal*.

180 Victor Adler, 1852–1918, at the time the undisputed leader of the socialists in Austria. Cf. Rudolf Steiner, *The Course of My Life*, Ch. 8.

181 Paul Freiherr Gautsch von Frankenthurn, 1851–1918; 1897–98 Austrian Minister-President.

182 Otto Hausner, 1827–1890. Cf. *The Course of My Life*, Ch. 4, also *Karmic Relationships* vol. 2, GA 236.

183 Leopold Anton Graf Berchtold, 1863–1942, Austrian diplomat, Foreign Minister from 1912 to 1915.

184 Helmuth von Moltke, 1877–1916, the younger: nephew of the 'older' Field Marshall-General of the same name (1800–1891).

185 This can only have been Gräfin (Countess) Eliza Moltke-Huitfeld.

186 Two daughters, Anatasia and Miltza, of the Montenegran king Nikita were married at the tsar's court.

187 Raymond Poincaré, 1860–1934, one of the most important French politicians before, during and after the First World War. Visited Russia 21–23 July 1914.

188 Maurice Paléologue, 1859–1944, ambassador in Petersburg 1913–1917. Wrote *Am Zarenhof während des Weltkriegs* (At the Tsar's Court during the World War), published in three volumes in German, 1925.

189 Helmuth von Moltke, *Erinnerungen, Briefe, Dokumente 1877–1916*, Stuttgart 1922. The planned publication in 1916 did not occur for the reasons given by Steiner; the already printed pamphlet was withdrawn. Rudolf Steiner's Foreword is printed in *The Renewal of the Social Organism*, GA 24.

[190] Alfred von Tirpitz, 1849–1930. German Grand Admiral and Secretary of State for the navy, creator of the German military fleet before World War I. Wrote *Erinnerungen* (Memoirs), Leipzig 1919.

[191] Theobald von Bethmann-Hollweg, 1856–1921. German Chancellor 1909–1917. For Tirpitz about Bethmann, cf. his *Erinnerungen*, Ch. 16, '*Der Ausbruch des Krieges*' (The Outbreak of the War).

[192] Herbert Henry Asquith (1852–1928) and Sir Edward Grey were English ministers (Asquith was Prime Minister 1908–16 and Grey was Foreign Secretary 1905–16).

[193] Cf. note 88. It was written in 1915.

[194] See note 189. These words are included in *Light for the New Millennium*, ed. T.H. Meyer, Rudolf Steiner Press, London 1997, p. 105.

[195] *J'accuse, von einem Deutschen* (J'accuse, by a German), 2nd edition Lausanne 1915. Under this title, a certain person by name of Grelling, who concealed his authorship through anonymity, circulated pamphlets hostile to Germany during the First World War. Rudolf Steiner has more to say about his less than complimentary view of these pamphlets in, for example, the lecture of 17 June 1915, *The Mystery of Death* (GA 159).

[196] In December 1916 from the side of the German Government.

[197] Richard von Kühlmann, 1873–1948, German diplomat, 1917–18 State Secretary of the Foreign Ministry.

[198] Erich Ludendorff, 1865–1937. German army leader in World War I.

[199] See op. cit. in note 194, p. 108.

[200] Warren Gamaliel Harding, 1865–1923, in 1920 Wilson's successor as President of the United States.

[201] It should be pointed out that shortly before Rudolf Steiner gave this lecture, an article had appeared in the National Socialist newspaper *Völkische Beobachter* on 15 March 1921 attacking him in the strongest possible terms as the sinister power behind the scenes of Germany's unwillingness to stand up for itself in post-war negotiations. The author was none other than Adolf Hitler.

Rudolf Steiner's Collected Works

The German Edition of Rudolf Steiner's Collected Works (the *Gesamtausgabe* [GA], published by Rudolf Steiner Verlag, Dornach, Switzerland) will be completed in the year 2025. The works are organized either by type of work (written, spoken, artistic creations), chronology, audience (public or other), or subject (education, art, etc.). For ease of comparison, the Collected Works in English (CW), listed below, follows the German organization and numbering.

The volumes that have so far been published in the English Collected Works edition appear *in italics with their published titles*; all other volumes, including those that have appeared in editions other than the CW, are set in Roman type with *literal translations* of the German titles. Published English titles are not necessarily the same as the German.

This list is current as of the date of this volume's publication.

A. Written Works

I. Writings 1884–1925

CW 1	Introductions and Selected Commentary on Goethe's Natural-scientific Writings
CW 1a–e	Goethe's Natural-scientific Writings
CW 1f	Editorial Afterwords to Goethe's Natural-scientific Writings in the Weimar Edition (1891–1896)
CW 2	*Goethe's Theory of Knowledge: An Outline of the Epistemology of His Worldview*
CW 3	Truth and Science
CW 4	The Philosophy of Freedom
CW 4a	Documents to 'The Philosophy of Freedom'
CW 5	Friedrich Nietzsche, A Fighter against His Own Time
CW 6	Goethe's Worldview
CW 7	Mysticism at the Dawn of Modern Spiritual Life and Its Relationship with Modern Worldviews
CW 8	*Christianity as Mystical Fact and the Mysteries of Antiquity*

II. Collected Essays

CW 37	Writings on the History of the Anthroposophical Movement and Society 1902–1925

III. Publications from the Literary Estate

CW 38/1	Complete Letters, Vol. 1: Weimar Period 1879–1890
CW 38/2	Complete Letters, Vol. 2: Weimar Period 1890–1897
CW 38/3	Complete Letters, Vol. 3: Early Berlin Period 1897–1905 [forthcoming]
CW 38/4	Complete Letters, Vol. 4: Activity within the Theosophical Society 1905–1912 [forthcoming]
CW 38/5	Complete Letters, Vol. 5: From the Founding of the Anthroposophical Society to the Opening of the Goetheanum 1913–1920 [forthcoming]
CW 38/6	Compelte Letters, Vol. 6: The Last Years 1920–1925 [forthcoming]
CW 40	Truth-Wrought Words
CW 40a	Sayings, Poems and Mantras; Supplementary Volume
CW 41a	Translations and Free Renderings from the Old and New Testaments
CW 41b	Translations and Free Renderings of Various Works
CW 42	Stage Adaptations I: Dramas by Edouard Schuré
CW 43	Stage Adaptations II: The Oberufer Christmas Plays
CW 44	Sketches, Fragments and Paralipomena on the Four Mystery Dramas
CW 45	Anthroposophy: A Fragment from the Year 1910
CW 46	Posthumous Essays and Fragments 1879–1924
CW 47/48	Notebooks and Notepads (digital edition)
CW 49	Notes for and about Helmuth and Eliza von Moltke and Relatives, 1904–1924 [forthcoming]
CW 50	[Blank number]

B. Lectures

I. Public Lectures

CW 51	*On Philosophy, History, and Literature: Lectures at the Worker Education School and the Independent College, Berlin, 1901–1905*
CW 52	Spiritual Teachings Concerning the Soul and Observation of the World
CW 53	The Origin and Goal of the Human Being
CW 54	The Riddles of the World and Anthroposophy
CW 55	Knowledge of the Supersensible in Our Times and Its Meaning for Life Today
CW 56	Knowledge of the Soul and of the Spirit
CW 57	Where and How Does One Find the Spirit?
CW 58	The Metamorphoses of the Soul Life. Paths of Soul Experiences: Part One
CW 59	The Metamorphoses of the Soul Life. Paths of Soul Experiences: Part Two

CW 60 The Answers of Spiritual Science to the Biggest Questions of Existence
CW 61 Human History in the Light of Spiritual Research
CW 62 *Results of Spiritual Research*
CW 63 Spiritual Science as a Treasure for Life
CW 64 Out of Destiny-Burdened Times
CW 65 Out of Central European Spiritual Life
CW 66 Spirit and Matter, Life and Death
CW 67 The Eternal in the Human Soul. Immortality and Freedom
CW 68a On the Being of Christianity
CW 68b The Cycle of the Human Being within the Sense-, Soul-, and Spirit-World
CW 68c Goethe and the Present
CW 68d The Being of Man in the Light of Spiritual Science
CW 69a Truths and Errors of Spiritual Research. Spiritual Science and the Future of Mankind
CW 69b Knowledge and Immortality
CW 69c New Christ-Experience
CW 69d Death and Immortality in the Light of Spiritual Science
CW 69e Spiritual Science and the Spiritual Goals of Our Time
CW 70a Human Soul, Destiny and Death
CW 70b Paths to the Knowledge of the Eternal Powers of the Human Soul
CW 71a Soul Immortality [forthcoming]
CW 71b The Human Being as a Soul and Spirit Being
CW 72 Freedom – Immortality – Social Life
CW 73 The Supplementing of the Modern Sciences through Anthroposophy
CW 73a Specialized Fields of Knowledge and Anthroposophy
CW 74 The Philosophy of Thomas Aquinas
CW 75 *Anthroposophy and the Natural Sciences: Foundations and Methods*
CW 76 The Fructifying Effect of Anthroposophy on Specialized Fields
CW 77a The Task of Anthroposophy in Relation to Science and Life: The Darmstadt College Course
CW 77b Art and Anthroposophy. The Goetheanum-Impulse
CW 78 Anthroposophy, Its Roots of Knowledge and Fruits for Life
CW 79 The Reality of the Higher Worlds
CW 80a The Being of Anthroposophy
CW 80b The Inner Realm of Nature and the Being of the Human Soul
CW 80c Anthroposophical Spiritual Science and the Great Civilizational Questions of the Present
CW 81 *Reimagining Academic Studies: Science, Philosophy, Education, Social Science, Theology, Theory of Language*
CW 82 *Becoming Fully Human: The Significance of Anthroposophy in Contemporary Spiritual Life*
CW 83 *The Tension between East and West*

CW 108   Answering the Questions of Life and the World through Anthroposophy

CW 109   The Principle of Spiritual Economy in Connection with the Question of Reincarnation. An Aspect of the Spiritual Guidance of Humanity

CW 110   *The Spiritual Hierarchies and the Physical World: Zodiac, Planets, and Cosmos*

CW 111   Introduction to the Foundations of Theosophy

CW 112   The Gospel of John in Relation to the Three Other Gospels, Especially the Gospel of Luke

CW 113   The Orient in the Light of the Occident. The Children of Lucifer and the Brothers of Christ

CW 114   The Gospel of Luke

CW 115   Anthroposophy – Psychosophy – Pneumatosophy

CW 116   *The Christ-Impulse and the Development of Ego-Consciousness*

CW 117   *Deeper Secrets of Human Evolution in Light of the Gospels*

CW 117a   The Gospel of John and the Three Other Gospels

CW 118   The Event of the Christ-Appearance in the Etheric World

CW 119   *Macrocosm and Microcosm: The Greater and the Lesser World: Questions Concerning the Soul, Life and the Spirit*

CW 120   The Revelations of Karma

CW 121   *The Mission of Folk Souls*

CW 122   The Secrets of the Biblical Creation-Story. The Six-Day Work in the First Book of Moses

CW 123   The Gospel of Matthew

CW 124   *Background to the Gospel of St Mark*

CW 125   *Paths and Goals of the Spiritual Human Being: Life Questions in the Light of Spiritual Science*

CW 126   Occult History. Esoteric Observations of the Karmic Relationships of Personalities and Events of World History

CW 127   *The Mission of the New Spiritual Revelation: The Pivotal Nature of the Christ Event in Earth Evolution*

CW 128   An Occult Physiology

CW 129   *Wonders of the World: Trials of the Soul, Revelations of the Spirit*

CW 130   Esoteric Christianity and the Spiritual Guidance of Humanity

CW 131   From Jesus to Christ

CW 132   *Inner Experiences of Evolution*

CW 133   The Earthly and the Cosmic Human Being

CW 134   *The World of the Senses and the World of the Spirit*

CW 135   Reincarnation and Karma and Their Meaning for the Culture of the Present

CW 136   *Spiritual Beings in the Heavenly Bodies and in the Kingdoms of Nature*

CW 137   The Human Being in the Light of Occultism, Theosophy and Philosophy

CW 138   On Initiation. On Eternity and the Passing Moment. On the Light of the Spirit and the Darkness of Life

CW 251   On the History of the Anthroposophical Society 1913–1922

CW 252   On the History of the Building Association and the Goetheanum Association 1911–1924

CW 253   *Sexuality, Inner Development, and Community Life: Ethical and Spiritual Dimensions of the Crisis in the Anthroposophical Society in Dornach, 1915*

CW 254   The Occult Movement in the 19th Century and Its Relationship to World Culture. Significant Points from the Exoteric Cultural Life around the Middle of the 19th Century

CW 255b   Anthroposophy and Its Opponents

CW 256   [Blank number]

CW 257   Anthroposophical Community-Building

CW 258   *The Anthroposophic Movement: The History and Conditions of the Anthroposophical Movement in Relation to the Anthroposophical Society: An Encouragement for Self-Examination*

CW 259   The Year of Destiny 1923 in the History of the Anthroposophical Society. From the Burning of the Goetheanum to the Christmas Conference

CW 260   The Christmas Conference for the Founding of the General Anthroposophical Society 1923/24

CW 260a   The Constitution of the General Anthroposophical Society and the School for Spiritual Science. The Rebuilding of the Goetheanum

CW 261   *Our Dead: Memorial, Funeral, and Cremation Addresses 1906–1924*

CW 262   Rudolf Steiner and Marie Steiner-von Sivers: Correspondence and Documents, 1901–1925

CW 263/1 Rudolf Steiner and Edith Maryon: Correspondence: Letters, Verses, Sketches, 1912–1924

CW 264   *From the History and Contents of the First Section of the Esoteric School: Letters, Documents, and Lectures: 1904–1914*

CW 265   *Freemasonry and Ritual Work: The Misraim Service*

CW 265a   Teaching and Instruction Lessons for Members of the Knowledge-Cultic Section of the Esoteric School 1904–1914 [forthcoming]

CW 266/1 *From the Esoteric School: Esoteric Lessons 1904–1909*

CW 266/2 *From the Esoteric School: Esoteric Lessons 1910–1912*

CW 266/3 *From the Esoteric School: Esoteric Lessons 1913–1923*

CW 267   *Soul Exercises: Word and Symbol Meditations*

CW 268   *Mantric Sayings: Meditations 1903–1925*

CW 269   Ritual Texts for the Celebration of the Free Christian Religious Instruction. The Collected Verses for Teachers and Students of the Waldorf School

CW 270   Esoteric Instructions for the First Class of the School for Spiritual Science at the Goetheanum 1924, 4 Volumes

III. Lectures and Courses on Specific Realms of Life
Lectures on Art

CW 271   *Art and Theory of Art: Foundations of a New Aesthetics*
CW 272   *Anthroposophy in the Light of Goethe's* Faust: *Volume One of Spiritual-Scientific Commentaries on Goethe's* Faust
CW 273   *Goethe's* Faust *in the Light of Anthroposophy: Volume Two of Spiritual-Scientific Commentaries on Goethe's* Faust
CW 274   Addresses for the Christmas Plays from the Old Folk Traditions
CW 275   Art in the Light of Mystery Wisdom
CW 276   *The Arts and Their Mission*
CW 277a   The Origin and Development of Eurythmy 1912–1918
CW 277b   The Origin and Development of Eurythmy 1918–1920
CW 277c   The Origin and Development of Eurythmy 1920–1922 [forthcoming]
CW 277d   The Origin and Development of Eurythmy 1923–1924 [forthcoming]
CW 278   Eurythmy as Visible Song
CW 279   *Eurythmy as Speech Made Visible: Speech Eurythmy Course*
CW 280   The Method and Nature of Speech Formation
CW 281   The Art of Recitation and Declamation
CW 282   Speech Formation and Dramatic Art
CW 283   The Nature of the Musical Element and the Experience of Tone in the Human Being
CW 284   *Rosicrucianism Renewed: The Unity of Art, Science & Religion: The Theosophical Congress of Whitsun 1907*
CW 285   [Blank number]
CW 286   Paths to a New Style of Architecture. 'And the Building Becomes Man'
CW 287   *Architecture as Peacework: The First Goetheanum, Dornach, 1914*
CW 288   *Architecture, Sculpture, and Painting of the First Goetheanum*
CW 289   The Building-Idea of the Goetheanum: Lectures with Slides from the Years 1920–1921
CW 290   *Toward a New Theory of Architecture: The First Goetheanum in Pictures* [no longer in the German GA]
CW 291   The Being of Colours
CW 291a   Knowledge of Colours. Supplementary Volume to 'The Being of Colours'
CW 292   *Art History as a Reflection of Inner Spiritual Impulses*

Lectures on Education

CW 293   General Knowledge of the Human Being as the Foundation of Pedagogy
CW 294   The Art of Education: Methodology and Didactics

Lectures on Medicine

Lectures on Natural Science

Lectures on Social Life and the Threefold Arrangement of the Social Organism

Lectures and Courses on Christian Religious Work

CW 342   *First Steps in Christian Religious Renewal: Preparing the Ground for The Christian Community*

CW 343   Lectures and Courses on Christian Religious Work, Vol. 2: Spiritual Knowledge – Religious Feeling – Cultic Doing

CW 344   Lectures and Courses on Christian Religious Work, Vol. 3: Lectures at the Founding of The Christian Community

CW 345   Lectures and Courses on Christian Religious Work, Vol. 4: Concerning the Nature of the Working Word

CW 346   Lectures and Courses on Christian Religious Work, Vol. 5: The Apocalypse and the Work of the Priest

Lectures for Workers at the Goetheanum

CW 347   The Knowledge of the Nature of the Human Being According to Body, Soul and Spirit. On Earlier Conditions of the Earth

CW 348   On Health and Illness. Foundations of a Spiritual-Scientific Doctrine of the Senses

CW 349   On the Life of the Human Being and of the Earth. On the Nature of Christianity

CW 350   Rhythms in the Cosmos and in the Human Being. How Does One Come To See the Spiritual World?

CW 351   The Human Being and the World. The Influence of the Spirit in Nature. On the Nature of Bees

CW 352   Nature and the Human Being Observed Spiritual-Scientifically

CW 353   The History of Humanity and the World-Views of the Folk Cultures

CW 354   The Creation of the World and the Human Being. Life on Earth and the Influence of the Stars

C. Artistic Works

CW A 1–10;
57   The Architectural Work I: The Goetheanum and Its Predecessors

CW A 11   The Sculptural Work

CW A 12   The Goetheanum Windows. The Speech of Light. Sketches and Studies

CW A 13–16;
52–56   Painting Work

CW A 14   Sketches for the Painting of the Small Dome of the First Goetheanum

CW A 27–43 The Architectural Work II: Commercial and Residential Buildings in Dornach and Other Places [forthcoming]

CW A 45   The Graphic Work

CW A 48   The Drawing Work

CW A 51   The Art of Jewellery as a Goethean Language of Form

CW A 54.0   A Path of Training in Painting. Pastel Sketches and Watercolours
CW A 54.1   Nature Moods. Nine Training Sketches for Painters

Eurythmy Figures

CW A 26   Skectches of the Eurythmy Figures
CW A 26a   The Eurythmy Figures of Rudolf Steiner, Artistically Executed by
           Annemarie Bäschlin
CW A 26b   Eurythmy Figures from the Time When They Were Created

Eurythmy Forms

CW A 23/1   Volume I: Eurythmy Forms for Poems by Rudolf Steiner
CW A 23/2   Volume II: Eurythmy Forms for the Calendar of the Soul by
            Rudolf Steiner
CW A 23/3   Volume III: Euythmy Forms for Poems by J. W. von Goethe
CW A 23/4   Volume IV: Eurythmy Forms for Poems by Christian Morgen-
            stern
CW A 23/5   Volume V: Eurythmy Forms for Poems by Albert Steffen
CW A 23/6   Volume VI: Eurythmy Forms for German Poems by Fercher von
            Steinwand, Hamerling, Hebbel, C. F. Meyer, Nietzsche, among others
CW A 23/7   Volume VII: Eurythmy Forms for English Poems
CW A 23/8   Volume VIII: Eurythmy Forms for French and Russian Poems
CW A 24   Volume IX: Eurythmy Forms for Tone Eurythmy

Blackboard Drawings from Lectures

CW A 58/1   Volume I: 20 Plates from Public Lectures 1920–1924 in CWs 73a,
             74, 76, and 84
CW A 58/2   Volume II: 38 Plates from Lectures in 1919 in CWs 191 and 194
CW A 58/3   Volume III: 34 Plates from Lectures in 1920 in CWs 196 and 198
CW A 58/4   Volume IV: 33 Plates from Lectures in 1920 in CWs 199 and 200
CW A 58/5   Volume V: 31 Plates from Lectures in 1920 in CW 201
CW A 58/6   Volume VI: 46 Plates from Lectures 1920–1921 in CWs 202–204
CW A 58/7   Volume VII: 38 Plates from Lectures in 1921 in CWs 205 and 206
CW A 58/8   Volume VIII: 42 Plates from Lectures in 1921 in CWs 207–209
CW A 58/9   Volume IX: 40 Plates from Lectures in 1922 in CWs 210–212
CW A 58/10   Volume X: 35 Plates from Lectures in 1922 in CWs 213–215
CW A 58/11   Volume XI: 41 Plates from Lectures 1922–1923 in CWs 216,
             218–220
CW A 58/12   Volume XII: 37 Plates from Lectures in 1923 in CWs 221–225
CW A 58/13   Volume XIII: 38 Plates from Lectures in 1923 in CWs 227–230
CW A 58/14   Volume XIV: 36 Plates from Lectures in 1923 in CWs 232 and 233
CW A 58/15   Volume XV: 37 Plates from Lectures in 1924 in CWs 233a, 234,
             and 243
CW A 58/16   Volume XVI: 56 Plates from the 'Karma Lectures' in CWs
             235–238 and 240

SIGNIFICANT EVENTS IN THE LIFE OF
RUDOLF STEINER

1829:	June 23: birth of Johann Steiner (1829–1910)—Rudolf Steiner's father—in Geras, Lower Austria.
1834:	May 8: birth of Franciska Blie (1834–1918)—Rudolf Steiner's mother—in Horn, Lower Austria. 'My father and mother were both children of the glorious Lower Austrian forest district north of the Danube.'
1860:	May 16: marriage of Johann Steiner and Franciska Blie.
1861:	February 25: birth of *Rudolf Joseph Lorenz Steiner* in Kraljevec, Croatia, near the border with Hungary, where Johann Steiner works as a telegrapher for the South Austria Railroad. Rudolf Steiner is baptized two days later, February 27, the date usually given as his birthday.
1862:	Summer: the family moves to Modling, Lower Austria.
1863:	The family moves to Pottschach, Lower Austria, near the Styrian border, where Johann Steiner becomes stationmaster. 'The view stretched to the mountains . . . majestic peaks in the distance and the sweet charm of nature in the immediate surroundings.'
1864:	November 15: birth of Rudolf Steiner's sister, Leopoldine (d. November 1, 1927). She will become a seamstress and live with her parents for the rest of her life.
1866:	July 28: birth of Rudolf Steiner's deaf-mute brother, Gustav (d. May 1, 1941).
1867:	Rudolf Steiner enters the village school. Following a disagreement between his father and the schoolmaster, whose wife falsely accused the boy of causing a commotion, Rudolf Steiner is taken out of school and taught at home.
1868:	A critical experience. Unknown to the family, an aunt dies in a distant town. Sitting in the station waiting room, Rudolf Steiner sees her 'form', which speaks to him, asking for help. 'Beginning with this experience, a new soul life began in the boy, one in which not only

the outer trees and mountains spoke to him, but also the worlds that lay behind them. From this moment on, the boy began to live with the spirits of nature . . .'

1869: The family moves to the peaceful, rural village of Neudorfl, near Wiener Neustadt in present-day Austria. Rudolf Steiner attends the village school. Because of the 'unorthodoxy' of his writing and spelling, he has to do 'extra lessons'.

1870: Through a book lent to him by his tutor, he discovers geometry: 'To grasp something purely in the spirit brought me inner happiness. I know that I first learned happiness through geometry.' The same tutor allows him to draw, while other students still struggle with their reading and writing. 'An artistic element' thus enters his education.

1871: Though his parents are not religious, Rudolf Steiner becomes a 'church child', a favourite of the priest, who was 'an exceptional character'. 'Up to the age of ten or eleven, among those I came to know, he was far and away the most significant.' Among other things, he introduces Steiner to Copernican, heliocentric cosmology. As an altar boy, Rudolf Steiner serves at Masses, funerals, and Corpus Christi processions. At year's end, after an incident in which he escapes a thrashing, his father forbids him to go to church.

1872: Rudolf Steiner transfers to grammar school in Wiener-Neustadt, a five-mile walk from home, which must be done in all weathers.

1873–75: Through his teachers and on his own, Rudolf Steiner has many wonderful experiences with science and mathematics. Outside school, he teaches himself analytic geometry, trigonometry, differential equations, and calculus.

1876: Rudolf Steiner begins tutoring other students. He learns bookbinding from his father. He also teaches himself stenography.

1877: Rudolf Steiner discovers Kant's *Critique of Pure Reason*, which he reads and rereads. He also discovers and reads von Rotteck's *World History*.

1878: He studies extensively in contemporary psychology and philosophy.

1879: Rudolf Steiner graduates from high school with honours. His father is transferred to Inzersdorf, near Vienna. He uses his first visit to Vienna 'to purchase a great number of philosophy books'—Kant, Fichte, Schelling, and Hegel, as well as numerous histories of philosophy. His aim: to find a path from the 'I' to nature.

October
1879–1883: Rudolf Steiner attends the Technical College in Vienna—to study mathematics, chemistry, physics, mineralogy, botany, zoology, biology, geology, and mechanics—with a scholarship. He also attends lectures in history and literature, while avidly reading philosophy on his own. His two favourite professors are Karl Julius Schröer (German language and literature) and Edmund Reitlinger

(physics). He also audits lectures by Robert Zimmermann on aesthetics and Franz Brentano on philosophy. During this year he begins his friendship with Moritz Zitter (1861–1921), who will help support him financially when he is in Berlin.

1880: Rudolf Steiner attends lectures on Schiller and Goethe by Karl Julius Schröer, who becomes his mentor. Also 'through a remarkable combination of circumstances', he meets Felix Koguzki, a 'herb gatherer' and healer, who could 'see deeply into the secrets of nature'. Rudolf Steiner will meet and study with this 'emissary of the Master' throughout his time in Vienna.

1881: January: '... I didn't sleep a wink. I was busy with philosophical problems until about 12:30 a.m. Then, finally, I threw myself down on my couch. All my striving during the previous year had been to research whether the following statement by Schelling was true or not: *Within everyone dwells a secret, marvellous capacity to draw back from the stream of time—out of the self clothed in all that comes to us from outside—into our innermost being and there, in the immutable form of the Eternal, to look into ourselves.* I believe, and I am still quite certain of it, that I discovered this capacity in myself; I had long had an inkling of it. Now the whole of idealist philosophy stood before me in modified form. What's a sleepless night compared to that!'
Rudolf Steiner begins communicating with leading thinkers of the day, who send him books in return, which he reads eagerly.

July: 'I am not one of those who dives into the day like an animal in human form. I pursue a quite specific goal, an idealistic aim—knowledge of the truth! This cannot be done offhandedly. It requires the greatest striving in the world, free of all egotism, and equally of all resignation.'

August: Steiner puts down on paper for the first time thoughts for a 'Philosophy of Freedom'. 'The striving for the absolute: this human yearning is freedom.' He also seeks to outline a 'peasant philosophy', describing what the worldview of a 'peasant'—one who lives close to the earth and the old ways—really is.

1881–1882: Felix Koguzki, the herb gatherer, reveals himself to be the envoy of another, higher initiatory personality, who instructs Rudolf Steiner to penetrate Fichte's philosophy and to master modern scientific thinking as a preparation for right entry into the spirit. This 'Master' also teaches him the double (evolutionary and involutionary) nature of time.

1882: Through the offices of Karl Julius Schröer, Rudolf Steiner is asked by Joseph Kürschner to edit Goethe's scientific works for the *Deutschen National-Literatur* edition. He writes 'A Possible Critique of Atomistic Concepts' and sends it to Friedrich Theodor Vischer.

1883: Rudolf Steiner completes his college studies and begins work on the Goethe project.

1884:   First volume of Goethe's *Scientific Writings* (CW 1) appears (March). He lectures on Goethe and Lessing, and Goethe's approach to science. In July, he enters the household of Ladislaus and Pauline Specht as tutor to the four Specht boys. He will live there until 1890. At this time, he meets Josef Breuer (1842–1925), the co-author with Sigmund Freud of *Studies in Hysteria,* who is the Specht family doctor.

1885:   While continuing to edit Goethe's writings, Rudolf Steiner reads deeply in contemporary philosophy (Eduard von Hartmann, Johannes Volkelt, and Richard Wahle, among others).

1886:   May: Rudolf Steiner sends Kürschner the manuscript of *Outlines of Goethe's Theory of Knowledge* (CW 2), which appears in October, and which he sends out widely. He also meets the poet Marie Eugenie Delle Grazie and writes 'Nature and Our Ideals' for her. He attends her salon, where he meets many priests, theologians, and philosophers, who will become his friends. Meanwhile, the director of the Goethe Archive in Weimar requests his collaboration with the *Sophien* edition of Goethe's works, particularly the writings on colour.

1887:   At the beginning of the year, Rudolf Steiner is very sick. As the year progresses and his health improves, he becomes increasingly 'a man of letters', lecturing, writing essays, and taking part in Austrian cultural life. In August–September, the second volume of Goethe's *Scientific Writings* appears.

1888:   January–July: Rudolf Steiner assumes editorship of the 'German Weekly' *(Deutsche Wochenschrift).* He begins lecturing more intensively, giving, for example, a lecture titled 'Goethe as Father of a New Aesthetics'. He meets and becomes soul friends with Friedrich Eckstein (1861–1939), a vegetarian, philosopher of symbolism, alchemist, and musician, who will introduce him to various spiritual currents (including Theosophy) and with whom he will meditate and interpret esoteric and alchemical texts.

1889:   Rudolf Steiner first reads Nietzsche *(Beyond Good and Evil).* He encounters Theosophy again and learns of Madame Blavatsky in the theosophical circle around Marie Lang (1858–1934). Here he also meets well-known figures of Austrian life, as well as esoteric figures like the occultist Franz Hartmann and Karl Leinigen-Billigen (translator of C.G. Harrison's *The Transcendental Universe).* During this period, Steiner first reads A.P. Sinnett's *Esoteric Buddhism* and Mabel Collins's *Light on the Path.* He also begins travelling, visiting Budapest, Weimar, and Berlin (where he meets philosopher Eduard von Hartmann).

1890:   Rudolf Steiner finishes Volume 3 of Goethe's scientific writings. He begins his doctoral dissertation, which will become *Truth and Science* (CW 3). He also meets the poet and feminist Rosa Mayreder

(1858–1938), with whom he can exchange his most intimate thoughts. In September, Rudolf Steiner moves to Weimar to work in the Goethe-Schiller Archive.

1891:   Volume 3 of the Kürschner edition of Goethe appears. Meanwhile, Rudolf Steiner edits Goethe's studies in mineralogy and scientific writings for the *Sophien* edition. He meets Ludwig Laistner of the Cotta Publishing Company, who asks for a book on the basic question of metaphysics. From this will result, ultimately, *The Philosophy of Freedom* (CW 4), which will be published not by Cotta but by Emil Felber. In October, Rudolf Steiner takes the oral exam for a doctorate in philosophy, mathematics, and mechanics at Rostock University, receiving his doctorate on the twenty-sixth. In November, he gives his first lecture on Goethe's 'Fairy Tale' in Vienna.

1892:   Rudolf Steiner continues work at the Goethe-Schiller Archive and on his *Philosophy of Freedom. Truth and Science,* his doctoral dissertation, is published. Steiner undertakes to write Introductions to books on Schopenhauer and Jean Paul for Cotta. At year's end, he finds lodging with Anna Eunike, née Schulz (1853–1911), a widow with four daughters and a son. He also develops a friendship with Otto Erich Hartleben (1864–1905) with whom he shares literary interests.

1893:   Rudolf Steiner begins his habit of producing many reviews and articles. In March, he gives a lecture titled 'Hypnotism, with Reference to Spiritism'. In September, volume 4 of the Kürschner edition is completed. In November, *The Philosophy of Freedom* appears. This year, too, he meets John Henry Mackay (1864–1933), the anarchist, and Max Stirner, a scholar and biographer.

1894:   Rudolf Steiner meets Elisabeth Fürster Nietzsche, the philosopher's sister, and begins to read Nietzsche in earnest, beginning with the as yet unpublished *Antichrist.* He also meets Ernst Haeckel (1834–1919). In the fall, he begins to write *Nietzsche, A Fighter against His Time* (CW 5).

1895:   May, *Nietzsche, A Fighter against His Time* appears.

1896:   January 22: Rudolf Steiner sees Friedrich Nietzsche for the first and only time. Moves between the Nietzsche and the Goethe-Schiller Archives, where he completes his work before year's end. He falls out with Elisabeth Förster Nietzsche, thus ending his association with the Nietzsche Archive.

1897:   Rudolf Steiner finishes the manuscript of *Goethe's Worldview* (CW 6). He moves to Berlin with Anna Eunike and begins editorship of the *Magazin für Literatur.* From now on, Steiner will write countless reviews, literary and philosophical articles, and so on. He begins lecturing at the 'Free Literary Society'. In September, he attends the Zionist Congress in Basel. He sides with Dreyfus in the Dreyfus affair.

1898:   Rudolf Steiner is very active as an editor in the political, artistic, and theatrical life of Berlin. He becomes friendly with John Henry Mackay and poet Ludwig Jacobowski (1868–1900). He joins Jacobowski's circle of writers, artists, and scientists—'The Coming Ones' (*Die Kommenden*)—and contributes lectures to the group until 1903. He also lectures at the 'League for College Pedagogy'. He writes an article for Goethe's sesquicentennial, 'Goethe's Secret Revelation', on the 'Fairy Tale of the Green Snake and the Beautiful Lily'.

1898–99:   'This was a trying time for my soul as I looked at Christianity. . . . I was able to progress only by contemplating, by means of spiritual perception, the evolution of Christianity. . . . Conscious knowledge of real Christianity began to dawn in me around the turn of the century. This seed continued to develop. My soul trial occurred shortly before the beginning of the twentieth century. It was decisive for my soul's development that I stood spiritually before the Mystery of Golgotha in a deep and solemn celebration of knowledge.'

1899:   Rudolf Steiner begins teaching and giving lectures and lecture cycles at the Workers' College, founded by Wilhelm Liebknecht (1826–1900). He will continue to do so until 1904. Writes: *Literature and Spiritual Life in the Nineteenth Century; Individualism in Philosophy; Haeckel and His Opponents; Poetry in the Present;* and begins what will become (fifteen years later) *The Riddles of Philosophy* (CW 18). He also meets many artists and writers, including Käthe Kollwitz, Stefan Zweig, and Rainer Maria Rilke. On October 31, he marries Anna Eunike.

1900:   'I thought that the turn of the century must bring humanity a new light. It seemed to me that the separation of human thinking and willing from the spirit had peaked. A turn or reversal of direction in human evolution seemed to me a necessity.' Rudolf Steiner finishes *World and Life Views in the Nineteenth Century* (the second part of what will become *The Riddles of Philosophy*) and dedicates it to Ernst Haeckel. It is published in March. He continues lecturing at *Die Kommenden*, whose leadership he assumes after the death of Jacobowski. Also, he gives the Gutenberg Jubilee lecture before 7,000 typesetters and printers. In September, Rudolf Steiner is invited by Count and Countess Brockdorff to lecture in the Theosophical Library. His first lecture is on Nietzsche. His second lecture is titled 'Goethe's Secret Revelation.' October 6, he begins a lecture cycle on the mystics that will become *Mystics after Modernism* (CW 7). November–December: 'Marie von Sivers appears in the audience. . . .' Also in November, Steiner gives his first lecture at the Giordano Bruno Bund (where he will continue to lecture until May, 1905). He speaks on Bruno and modern Rome, focusing on the importance of the philosophy of Thomas Aquinas as monism.

1901:   In continual financial straits, Rudolf Steiner's early friends Moritz Zitter and Rosa Mayreder help support him. In October, he begins the lecture cycle *Christianity as Mystical Fact* (CW 8) at the Theosophical Library. In November, he gives his first 'theosophical lecture' on Goethe's 'Fairy Tale' in Hamburg at the invitation of Wilhelm Hubbe-Schleiden. He also attends a gathering to celebrate the founding of the Theosophical Society at Count and Countess Brockdorff's. He gives a lecture cycle, 'From Buddha to Christ,' for the circle of the *Kommenden*. November 17, Marie von Sivers asks Rudolf Steiner if Theosophy needs a Western–Christian spiritual movement (to complement Theosophy's Eastern emphasis). 'The question was posed. Now, following spiritual laws, I could begin to give an answer. . . .' In December, Rudolf Steiner writes his first article for a theosophical publication. At year's end, the Brockdorffs and possibly Wilhelm Hubbe-Schleiden ask Rudolf Steiner to join the Theosophical Society and undertake the leadership of the German section. Rudolf Steiner agrees, on the condition that Marie von Sivers (then in Italy) work with him.

1902:   Beginning in January, Rudolf Steiner attends the opening of the Workers' School in Spandau with Rosa Luxemberg (1870–1919). January 17, Rudolf Steiner joins the Theosophical Society. In April, he is asked to become general secretary of the German Section of the Theosophical Society, and works on preparations for its founding. In July, he visits London for a theosophical congress. He meets Bertram Keightly, G.R.S. Mead, A.P. Sinnett, and Annie Besant, among others. In September, *Christianity as Mystical Fact* appears. In October, Rudolf Steiner gives his first public lecture on Theosophy ('Monism and Theosophy') to about three hundred people at the Giordano Bruno Bund. On October 19–21, the German Section of the Theosophical Society has its first meeting; Rudolf Steiner is the general secretary, and Annie Besant attends. Steiner lectures on practical karma studies. On October 23, Annie Besant inducts Rudolf Steiner into the Esoteric School of the Theosophical Society. On October 25, Steiner begins a weekly series of lectures: 'The Field of Theosophy'. During this year, Rudolf Steiner also first meets Ita Wegman (1876–1943), who will become his close collaborator in his final years.

1903:   Rudolf Steiner holds about 300 lectures and seminars. In May, the first issue of the periodical *Luzifer* appears. In June, Rudolf Steiner visits London for the first meeting of the Federation of the European Sections of the Theosophical Society, where he meets Colonel Olcott. He begins to write *Theosophy* (CW 9).

1904: Rudolf Steiner continues lecturing at the Workers' College and elsewhere (about 90 lectures), while lecturing intensively all over Germany among theosophists (about 140 lectures). In February, he meets Carl Unger (1878–1929), who will become a member of the board of the Anthroposophical Society (1913). In March, he meets Michael Bauer (1871–1929), a Christian mystic, who will also be on the board. In May, *Theosophy* appears, with the dedication: 'To the spirit of Giordano Bruno'. Rudolf Steiner and Marie von Sivers visit London for meetings with Annie Besant. June: Rudolf Steiner and Marie von Sivers attend the meeting of the Federation of European Sections of the Theosophical Society in Amsterdam. In July, Steiner begins the articles in *Luzifer-Gnosis* that will become *How to Know Higher Worlds* (CW 10) and *Cosmic Memory* (CW 11). In September, Annie Besant visits Germany. In December, Steiner lectures on Freemasonry. He mentions the High Grade Masonry derived from John Yarker and represented by Theodore Reuss and Karl Kellner as a blank slate 'into which a good image could be placed'.

1905: This year, Steiner ends his non-theosophical lecturing activity. Supported by Marie von Sivers, his theosophical lecturing—both in public and in the Theosophical Society—increases significantly: 'The German Theosophical Movement is of exceptional importance.' Steiner recommends reading, among others, Fichte, Jacob Boehme, and Angelus Silesius. He begins to introduce Christian themes into Theosophy. He also begins to work with doctors (Felix Peipers and Ludwig Noll). In July, he is in London for the Federation of European Sections, where he attends a lecture by Annie Besant: 'I have seldom seen Mrs Besant speak in so inward and heartfelt a manner... Through Mrs Besant I have found the way to H.P. Blavatsky.' September to October, he gives a course of 31 lectures for a small group of esoteric students. In October, the annual meeting of the German Section of the Theosophical Society, which still remains very small, takes place. Rudolf Steiner reports membership has risen from 121 to 377 members. In November, seeking to establish esoteric 'continuity', Rudolf Steiner and Marie von Sivers participate in a 'Memphis-Misraim' Masonic ceremony. They pay 45 marks for membership. 'Yesterday, you saw how little remains of former esoteric institutions.' 'We are dealing only with a "framework" ... for the present, nothing lies behind it. The occult powers have completely withdrawn.'

1906: Expansion of theosophical work. Rudolf Steiner gives about 245 lectures, only 44 of which take place in Berlin. Cycles are given in Paris, Leipzig, Stuttgart, and Munich. Esoteric work also intensifies. Rudolf Steiner begins writing *An Outline of Esoteric Science* (CW 13).

In January, Rudolf Steiner receives permission (a patent) from the Great Orient of the Scottish A & A Thirty-Three Degree Rite of the Order of the Ancient Freemasons of the Memphis-Misraim Rite to direct a chapter under the name 'Mystica Aeterna.' This will become the 'Cognitive-Ritual Section' (also called 'Misraim Service') of the Esoteric School. (See: *Freemasonry and Ritual Work: The Misraim Service,* CW 265.) During this time, Steiner also meets Albert Schweitzer. In May, he is in Paris, where he visits Édouard Schuré. Many Russians attend his lectures (including Konstantin Balmont, Dimitri Mereszkovski, Zinaida Hippius, and Maximilian Woloshin). He attends the General Meeting of the European Federation of the Theosophical Society, at which Col Olcott is present for the last time. He spends the year's end in Venice and Rome, where he writes and works on his translation of H.P. Blavatsky's *Key to Theosophy.*

1907: Further expansion of the German Theosophical Movement according to the Rosicrucian directive to 'introduce spirit into the world'—in education, in social questions, in art, and in science. In February, Col Olcott dies in Adyar. Before he dies, Olcott indicates that 'the Masters' wish Annie Besant to succeed him: much politicking ensues. Rudolf Steiner supports Besant's candidacy. April–May: preparations for the Congress of the Federation of European Sections of the Theosophical Society—the great, watershed Whitsun 'Munich Congress,' attended by Annie Besant and others. Steiner decides to separate Eastern and Western (Christian–Rosicrucian) esoteric schools. He takes his esoteric school out of the Theosophical Society (Besant and Rudolf Steiner are 'in harmony' on this). Steiner makes his first lecture tours to Austria and Hungary. That summer, he is in Italy. In September, he visits Édouard Schuré, who will write the Introduction to the French edition of *Christianity as Mystical Fact* in Barr, Alsace. Rudolf Steiner writes the autobiographical statement known as the 'Barr Document.' In *Luzifer-Gnosis,* 'The Education of the Child' appears.

1908: The movement grows (membership: 1,150). Lecturing expands. Steiner makes his first extended lecture tour to Holland and Scandinavia, as well as visits to Naples and Sicily. Themes: St John's Gospel, the Apocalypse, Egypt, science, philosophy, and logic. *Luzifer-Gnosis* ceases publication. In Berlin, Marie von Sivers (with Johanna Mücke (1864–1949) forms the *Philosophisch-Theosophisch* (after 1915 *Philosophisch-Anthroposophisch) Verlag* to publish Steiner's work. Steiner gives lecture cycles titled *The Gospel of St John* (CW 103) and *The Apocalypse* (104).

1909: *An Outline of Esoteric Science* appears. Lecturing and travel continues. Rudolf Steiner's spiritual research expands to include the polarity of Lucifer and Ahriman; the work of great individualities in history; the Maitreya Buddha and the Bodhisattvas; spiritual economy (CW 109); the work of the spiritual hierarchies in heaven and on earth (CW 110). He also deepens and intensifies his research into the Gospels, giving lectures on the Gospel of St Luke (CW 114) with the first mention of two Jesus children. Meets and becomes friends with Christian Morgenstern (1871–1914). In April, he lays the foundation stone for the Malsch model—the building that will lead to the first Goetheanum. In May, the International Congress of the Federation of European Sections of the Theosophical Society takes place in Budapest. Rudolf Steiner receives the Subba Row medal for *How to Know Higher Worlds*. During this time, Charles W. Leadbeater discovers Jiddu Krishnamurti (1895–1986) and proclaims him the future 'world teacher,' the bearer of the Maitreya Buddha and the 'reappearing Christ.' In October, Steiner delivers seminal lectures on 'anthroposophy,' which he will try, unsuccessfully, to rework over the next years into the unfinished work, *Anthroposophy (A Fragment)* (CW 45).

1910:   New themes: *The Reappearance of Christ in the Etheric* (CW 118); *The Fifth Gospel; The Mission of Folk Souls* (CW 121); *Occult History* (CW 126); the evolving development of etheric cognitive capacities. Rudolf Steiner continues his Gospel research with *The Gospel of St Matthew* (CW 123). In January, his father dies. In April, he takes a month-long trip to Italy, including Rome, Monte Cassino, and Sicily. He also visits Scandinavia again. July–August, he writes the first Mystery Drama, *The Portal of Initiation* (CW 14). In November, he gives 'psychosophy' lectures. In December, he submits 'On the Psychological Foundations and Epistemological Framework of Theosophy' to the International Philosophical Congress in Bologna.

1911:   The crisis in the Theosophical Society deepens. In January, 'The Order of the Rising Sun,' which will soon become 'The Order of the Star in the East,' is founded for the coming world teacher, Krishnamurti. At the same time, Marie von Sivers, Rudolf Steiner's co-worker, falls ill. Fewer lectures are given, but important new ground is broken. In Prague, in March, Steiner meets Franz Kafka (1883–1924) and Hugo Bergmann (1883–1975). In April, he delivers his paper to the Philosophical Congress. He writes the second Mystery Drama, *The Soul's Probation* (CW 14). Also, while Marie von Sivers is convalescing, Rudolf Steiner begins work on *Calendar 1912/1913*, which will contain the 'Calendar of the Soul' meditations. On March 19, Anna (Eunike) Steiner dies. In September, Rudolf Steiner visits Einsiedeln, birthplace of Paracelsus. In December, Friedrich Rittelmeyer, future founder of The Christian Community, meets Rudolf Steiner. The *Johannes-Bauverein*, the 'building committee,' which would lead to the first Goetheanum (first planned for Munich), is also founded, and a preliminary committee for the founding of an independent association is created that, in the following year, will become the Anthroposophical Society. Important lecture cycles include *Occult Physiology* (CW 128); *Wonders of the World* (CW 129); *From Jesus to Christ* (CW 131). Other themes: esoteric Christianity; Christian Rosenkreutz; the spiritual guidance of humanity; the sense world and the world of the spirit.

1912: Despite the ongoing, now increasing crisis in the Theosophical Society, much is accomplished: *Calendar 1912/1913* is published; eurythmy is created; both the third Mystery Drama, *The Guardian of the Threshold* (CW 14) and *A Way of Self-Knowledge* (CW 16) are written. New (or renewed) themes included life between death and rebirth and karma and reincarnation. Other lecture cycles: *Spiritual Beings in the Heavenly Bodies and in the Kingdoms of Nature* (CW 136); *The Human Being in the Light of Occultism, Theosophy, and Philosophy* (CW 137); *The Gospel of St Mark* (CW 139); and *The Bhagavad Gita and the Epistles of Paul* (CW 142). On May 8, Rudolf Steiner celebrates White Lotus Day, H.P. Blavatsky's death day, which he had faithfully observed for the past decade, for the last time. In August, Rudolf Steiner suggests the 'independent association' be called the 'Anthroposophical Society.' In September, the first eurythmy course takes place. In October, Rudolf Steiner declines recognition of a Theosophical Society lodge dedicated to the Star of the East and decides to expel all Theosophical Society members belonging to the order. Also, with Marie von Sivers, he first visits Dornach, near Basel, Switzerland, and they stand on the hill where the Goetheanum will be built. In November, a Theosophical Society lodge is opened by direct mandate from Adyar (Annie Besant). In December, a meeting of the German section occurs at which it is decided that belonging to the Order of the Star of the East is incompatible with membership in the Theosophical Society. December 28: informal founding of the Anthroposophical Society in Berlin.

1913: Expulsion of the German section from the Theosophical Society. February 2–3: Foundation meeting of the Anthroposophical Society. Board members include: Marie von Sivers, Michael Bauer, and Carl Unger. September 20: Laying of the foundation stone for the *Johannes Bau* (Goetheanum) in Dornach. Building begins immediately. The fourth Mystery Drama, *The Soul's Awakening* (CW 14), is completed. Also: *The Threshold of the Spiritual World* (CW 147). Lecture cycles include: *The Bhagavad Gita and the Epistles of Paul* and *The Esoteric Meaning of the Bhagavad Gita* (CW 146), which the Russian philosopher Nikolai Berdyaev attends; *The Mysteries of the East and of Christianity* (CW 144); *The Effects of Esoteric Development* (CW 145); and *The Fifth Gospel* (CW 148). In May, Rudolf Steiner is in London and Paris, where anthroposophical work continues.

1914:	Building continues on the *Johannes Bau* (Goetheanum) in Dornach, with artists and co-workers from seventeen nations. The general assembly of the Anthroposophical Society takes place. In May, Rudolf Steiner visits Paris, as well as Chartres Cathedral. June 28: assassination in Sarajevo ('Now the catastrophe has happened!'). August 1: War is declared. Rudolf Steiner returns to Germany from Dornach—he will travel back and forth. He writes the last chapter of *The Riddles of Philosophy.* Lecture cycles include: *Human and Cosmic Thought* (CW 151); *Inner Being of Humanity between Death and a New Birth* (CW 153); *Occult Reading and Occult Hearing* (CW 156). December 24: marriage of Rudolf Steiner and Marie von Sivers.
1915:	Building continues. Life after death becomes a major theme, also art. Writes: *Thoughts during a Time of War* (CW 24). Lectures include: *The Secret of Death* (CW 159); *The Uniting of Humanity through the Christ Impulse* (CW 165).
1916:	Rudolf Steiner begins work with Edith Maryon (1872–1924) on the sculpture 'The Representative of Humanity' ('The Group'— Christ, Lucifer, and Ahriman). He also works with the alchemist Alexander von Bernus on the quarterly *Das Reich.* He writes *The Riddle of Humanity* (CW 20). Lectures include: *Necessity and Freedom in World History and Human Action* (CW 166); *Past and Present in the Human Spirit* (CW 167); *The Karma of Vocation* (CW 172); *The Karma of Untruthfulness* (CW 173).
1917:	Russian Revolution. The U.S. enters the war. Building continues. Rudolf Steiner delineates the idea of the 'threefold nature of the human being' (in a public lecture March 15) and the 'threefold nature of the social organism' (hammered out in May–June with the help of Otto von Lerchenfeld and Ludwig Polzer-Hoditz in the form of two documents titled *Memoranda,* which were distributed in high places). August–September: Rudolf Steiner writes *The Riddles of the Soul* (CW 20). Also: commentary on 'The Chymical Wedding of Christian Rosenkreutz' for Alexander Bernus (Das Reich). Lectures include: *The Karma of Materialism* (CW 176); *The Spiritual Background of the Outer World: The Fall of the Spirits of Darkness* (CW 177).
1918:	March 18: peace treaty of Brest-Litovsk—'Now everything will truly enter chaos! What is needed is cultural renewal.' June: Rudolf Steiner visits Karlstein (Grail) Castle outside Prague. Lecture cycle: *From Symptom to Reality in Modern History* (CW 185). In mid-November, Emil Molt, of the Waldorf-Astoria Cigarette Company, has the idea of founding a school for his workers' children.
1919:	Focus on the threefold social organism: tireless travel, countless lectures, meetings, and publications. At the same time, a new public stage of Anthroposophy emerges as cultural renewal begins.

The coming years will see initiatives in pedagogy, medicine, pharmacology, and agriculture. January 27: threefold meeting: 'We must first of all, with the money we have, found free schools that can bring people what they need.' February: first public eurythmy performance in Zurich. Also: 'Appeal to the German People' (CW 24), circulated March 6 as a newspaper insert. In April, *Towards Social Renewal* (CW 23) appears—'perhaps the most widely read of all books on politics appearing since the war'. Rudolf Steiner is asked to undertake the 'direction and leadership' of the school founded by the Waldorf-Astoria Company. Rudolf Steiner begins to talk about the 'renewal' of education. May 30: a building is selected and purchased for the future Waldorf School. August–September, Rudolf Steiner gives a lecture course for Waldorf teachers, *The Foundations of Human Experience (Study of Man)* (CW 293). September 7: Opening of the first Waldorf School. December (into January): first science course, the *Light Course* (CW 320).

1920:   The Waldorf School flourishes. New threefold initiatives. Founding of limited companies *Der Kommende Tag* and *Futurum A.G.* to infuse spiritual values into the economic realm. Rudolf Steiner also focuses on the sciences. Lectures: *Introducing Anthroposophical Medicine* (CW 312); *The Warmth Course* (CW 321); *The Boundaries of Natural Science* (CW 322); *The Redemption of Thinking* (CW 74). February: Johannes Werner Klein—later a co-founder of The Christian Community—asks Rudolf Steiner about the possibility of a 'religious renewal,' a 'Johannine church.' In March, Rudolf Steiner gives the first course for doctors and medical students. In April, a divinity student asks Rudolf Steiner a second time about the possibility of religious renewal. September 27–October 16: anthroposophical 'university course.' December: lectures titled *The Search for the New Isis* (CW 202).

1921:   Rudolf Steiner continues his intensive work on cultural renewal, including the uphill battle for the threefold social order. 'University' arts, scientific, theological, and medical courses include: *The Astronomy Course* (CW 323); *Observation, Mathematics, and Scientific Experiment* (CW 324); the *Second Medical Course* (CW 313); *Colour.* In June and September–October, Rudolf Steiner also gives the first two 'priests' courses' (CW 342 and 343). The 'youth movement' gains momentum. Magazines are founded: *Die Drei* (January), and—under the editorship of Albert Steffen (1884–1963)—the weekly, *Das Goetheanum* (August). In February–March, Rudolf Steiner takes his first trip outside Germany since the war (Holland). On April 7, Steiner receives a letter regarding 'religious renewal,' and May 22–23, he agrees to address the question in a practical way. In June, the Klinical-Therapeutic Institute opens in Arlesheim under the direction of Dr Ita Wegman. In August, the

Chemical-Pharmaceutical Laboratory opens in Arlesheim (Oskar Schmiedel and Ita Wegman are directors). The Clinical Therapeutic Institute is inaugurated in Stuttgart (Dr Ludwig Noll is director); also the Research Laboratory in Dornach (Ehrenfried Pfeiffer and Gunther Wachsmuth are directors). In November–December, Rudolf Steiner visits Norway.

1922:   The first half of the year involves very active public lecturing (thousands attend); in the second half, Rudolf Steiner begins to withdraw and turn toward the Society—'The Society is asleep.' It is 'too weak' to do what is asked of it. The businesses—*Der Kommende Tag* and *Futurum A.G.*—fail. In January, with the help of an agent, Steiner undertakes a twelve-city German lecture tour, accompanied by eurythmy performances. In two weeks he speaks to more than 2,000 people. In April, he gives a 'university course' in The Hague. He also visits England. In June, he is in Vienna for the East–West Congress. In August–September, he is back in England for the Oxford Conference on Education. Returning to Dornach, he gives the lectures *Philosophy, Cosmology, and Religion* (CW 215), and gives the third priests' course (CW 344). On September 16, The Christian Community is founded. In October–November, Steiner is in Holland and England. He also speaks to the youth: *The Youth Course* (CW 217). In December, Steiner gives lectures titled *The Origins of Natural Science* (CW 326), and *Humanity and the World of Stars: The Spiritual Communion of Humanity* (CW 219). December 31: Fire at the Goetheanum, which is destroyed.

1923:   Despite the fire, Rudolf Steiner continues his work unabated. A very hard year. Internal dispersion, dissension, and apathy abound. There is conflict—between old and new visions—within the Society. A wake-up call is needed, and Rudolf Steiner responds with renewed lecturing vitality. His focus: the spiritual context of human life; initiation science; the course of the year; and community building. As a foundation for an artistic school, he creates a series of pastel sketches. Lecture cycles: *The Anthroposophical Movement; Initiation Science* (CW 227) (in Wales at the Penmaenmawr Summer School); *The Four Seasons and the Archangels* (CW 229); *Harmony of the Creative Word* (CW 230); *The Supersensible Human* (CW 231), given in Holland for the founding of the Dutch Society. On November 10, in response to the failed Hitler-Ludendorff putsch in Munich, Steiner closes his Berlin residence and moves the *Philosophisch-Anthroposophisch Verlag* (Press) to Dornach. On December 9, Steiner begins the serialization of his *Autobiography: The Course of My Life* (CW 28) in *Das Goetheanum*. It will continue to appear weekly, without a break, until his death. Late December–early January: Rudolf Steiner re-founds the Anthroposophical Society (about 12,000 members internationally) and takes over its leadership. The new board members are: Marie Steiner, Ita Wegman, Albert Steffen, Elisabeth Vreede, and Gunther Wachsmuth. (See *The Christmas Meeting for the Founding of the General Anthroposophical Society*, CW 260.) Accompanying lectures: *Mystery Knowledge and Mystery Centres* (CW 232); *World History in the Light of Anthroposophy* (CW 233). December 25: the Foundation Stone is laid (in the hearts of members) in the form of the 'Foundation Stone Meditation.'

1924: January 1: having founded the Anthroposophical Society and taken over its leadership, Rudolf Steiner has the task of 'reforming' it. The process begins with a weekly newssheet ('What's Happening in the Anthroposophical Society') in which Rudolf Steiner's 'Letters to Members' and 'Anthroposophical Leading Thoughts' appear (CW 26). The next step is the creation of a new esoteric class, the 'first class' of the 'University of Spiritual Science' (which was to have been followed, had Rudolf Steiner lived longer, by two more advanced classes). Then comes a new language for Anthroposophy—practical, phenomenological, and direct; and Rudolf Steiner creates the model for the second Goetheanum. He begins the series of extensive 'karma' lectures (CW 235–40); and finally, responding to needs, he creates two new initiatives: biodynamic agriculture and curative education. After the middle of the year, rumours begin to circulate regarding Steiner's health. Lectures: January–February, *Anthroposophy* (CW 234); February: *Tone Eurythmy* (CW 278); June: *The Agriculture Course* (CW 327); June–July: *Speech Eurythmy* (CW 279); *Curative Education* (CW 317); August: (England, 'Second International Summer School'), *Initiation Consciousness: True and False Paths in Spiritual Investigation* (CW 243); September: *Pastoral Medicine* (CW 318). On September 26, for the first time, Rudolf Steiner cancels a lecture. On September 28, he gives his last lecture. On September 29, he withdraws to his studio in the carpenter's shop; now he is definitively ill. Cared for by Ita Wegman, he continues working, however, and writing the weekly instalments of his *Autobiography* and *Letters to the Members/ Leading Thoughts* (CW 26).

1925: Rudolf Steiner, while continuing to work, continues to weaken. He finishes *Extending Practical Medicine* (CW 27) with Ita Wegman. On March 30, around ten in the morning, Rudolf Steiner dies.

Index